Table of Contents

MW01049209

TDC 56, chairwoma
TDC 56 judges
TDC 56 judges' choi
TDC 56 entries selec
TDC² 2010, chairman's statement 253
TDC² 2010 judges 254
TDC² 2010 judges' choices and designers' statements 256
TDC² 2010 entries selected for typographic excellence 264
TDC Intro 010, chairman's statement 276
TDC Intro 010 judges 277
TDC Intro 010 entries selected for typographic excellence 280
TDC 7 reprint 295
TDC officers 344
TDC members 345
Type Index 348
General Index 351

Chairwoman's Statement

As a chairperson of anything, there are a lot of things that one could worry about. So naturally, as the chairperson of TDC 56, the first thing I did was worry. I worried we wouldn't have enough entries because of the economic climate in 2009. I worried there might be a blizzard and hoped the judges wouldn't have more exciting plans for that third week in January.

When I didn't worry, it was fun. My most exciting duty was putting together a panel of judges. This is akin to putting together your dream dinner party of some of your favorite designers. You mix it up with designers from different areas, and with different expertise and different regional and foreign accents. When everyone accepted my invitation, my only worry was that the panel was too good to be true.

Fortunately, the number of entries was only slightly down from the previous year; a decline of any kind was to be expected in such a tough economy. Still, the quality of the work was impressive. With 242 winners, it is our most robust book in years. The book is proof that great design and typography are alive and well. More impressive: This year's competition speaks to designers doing their best and most creative work with smaller budgets.

We saw traditional print formats like magazines, books, book jackets, posters, menus, brochures, catalogs, calendars, packaging, and annual reports, as well as fresh type design in new iPhone apps. New digital reading devices such as the iPad—now available in color—have shifted our eyes more and more to the electronic screen. Still, as evidenced by the competition, we designers have an ongoing love affair with the printed page, and fortunately, the clients to support it.

The Type Directors Club clearly has a passion for print also. Unlike many design organizations today, TDC is still publishing its annual book of TDC competition winners. I am thrilled that Paul Sahre accepted the task of designing this book containing the best type and typography from 2009.

So after all the worry, I can only be grateful.

Thank you judges, TDC board members, and TDC Director Carol Wahler. And congratulations to all the TDC 56 winners.

—Anne Twomey

TDC 56 Judges

Anne Twomey

Francesco Cavalli

Brian Collins

Kristina DiMatteo

Joe Duffy

Abbott Miller

Michael Riley

Henry Sene Yee

Anne Twomey, Chairwoman, TDC 56

Anne Twomey is a graphic designer specializing in book jacket design. Currently, she is vice president, creative director of Grand Central Publishing, where she oversees the design of more than 300 covers a year.

Originally trained as a painter, practical fiscal considerations and a love of all communication arts led her to a career in graphic design. Twomey's love of letterforms began with her first fountain pen, but was solidified with a felt-tip pilot pen in Ed Benguit's lettering class at the School of Visual Arts in New York City. Classes with Milton Glaser, among others, and working with early mentors George Abrams and Milton Charles sharpened her eye. Photo-Lettering's *One Line Manual of Style* was her early textbook, and the latest TDC Annual each year became her bible.

As an art director at several major New York book publishers, Anne has had the opportunity to design covers for many best-selling and celebrity authors. She relishes working with journalists and first-time novelists, as well as with brand-name authors. She's had the opportunity to collaborate with some of the most talented photographers, illustrators, and designers on earth. She has won awards from the Type Directors Club, the AIGA 50 Books/50 Covers competition, *Communication Arts* magazine, the Art Directors Club, *Print,* the New York Book Show, the Society of Illustrators, *Photo District News, Creativity,* and *HOW* magazine. She has also juried shows for the TDC, the New York Book Show, the Art Directors Club, the Society of Illustrators, and Communication Arts.

Twomey has served on the TDC board for the past four years.

Francesco Cavalli, Judge

Francesco Cavalli is a founder and creative director of Leftloft, a graphic design studio established in Milan in 1997. The studio started up as a design collective, the result of a friendship among the founding partners, who met at university—the Politecnico di Milano—while studying urban planning. Francesco lives in Milan and in New York City, where he runs the U.S. office.

Engaged as a teacher in the Milan Polytechnic's faculty of design, Cavalli is also president of the Ministero della Grafica, (the Graphic Ministry), a cultural association promoting Italian design culture through events such as the Italian Biennale of Graphic Design and the Spaghetti Grafica annual report and exhibitions.

Brian Collins, Judge

Brian Collins is chief creative officer of COLLINS:, a design company dedicated to inventing brand experiences and communications that shape companies and people for the better. Prior to embarking on this enterprise, Collins was chairman and chief creative officer of the Brand Integration Group (BIG) at Ogilvy & Mather.

Collins's clients have included Coca-Cola, CNN, Levi Strauss & Co., American Express, Motorola, Mattel, IBM, Amazon.com, MTV, Hershey's, and the Alliance for Climate Protection. His work has been featured in the *Wall Street Journal,* the *New York Times, BusinessWeek,* ABC News, and *Fast Company,* which named him one of five American Masters of Design. Collins is the founder of Designism, an annual symposium in New York City focusing on the role of social activism in design and advertising. In 2009, COLLINS:, was awarded a Gold Pencil from the One Show, a Clio gold for design, the 4A gold for Strategic Excellence, and a Cannes Silver Lion. Brian Collins is a distinguished alumnus of the Massachusetts College of Art. He is vice president of the Art Directors Club and is on the faculty of the School of Visual Arts in New York. In 2008, he received an honorary doctorate from the Art Center College of Design in Pasadena, California. He speaks globally on design and innovation at venues including the World Economic Forum in Davos, Switzerland, and is a member of the forum's Global Agenda Council.

Kristina DiMatteo, Judge

Kristina DiMatteo is a designer and art director based in New York City. After graduating from the School of Visual Arts (SVA) in New York, DiMatteo worked at Red Herring Design and Time Inc. Custom Publishing. She then joined the design team at *The New York Times Magazine,* where she art-directed special issues and features.

DiMatteo's next position was art director of *Print* magazine, where she led the team to two consecutive National Magazine Award wins in the General Excellence category and garnered other honors, including the Society of Publication Designers' silver medal for Magazine of the Year.

While at *Print,* DiMatteo served on the executive board of the New York chapter of the American Institute of Graphic Arts and returned to SVA to teach. DiMatteo's work has been recognized by AIGA, the American Society of Magazine Editors, the Art Directors Club, the Society of Publication Designers, and the Type Directors Club. She currently does independent work and freelances in New York.

Joe Duffy, Judge

Joe Duffy, principal and chairman of Duffy & Partners, is one of the most respected and sought-after creative directors and thought leaders on branding and design in the world. Joe's work includes brand and corporate identity development for some of the world's most admired brands, from Aveda to Coca-Cola and Sony, and from Jack in the Box to Susan G. Komen for the Cure. Duffy's work is regularly featured in leading marketing and design publications and exhibited around the globe.

In 2004, he founded Duffy & Partners as a new kind of branding and creativity company, partnering with clients and other firms in all communication disciplines. Also in 2004, he received the Legacy Medal from AIGA for a lifetime of achievement in the field of visual communications. Duffy's first book—*Brand Apart*—was released in July 2005, and in 2006 *Fast Company* magazine recognized him as one of the Fast 50 most influential people in the future of business. In March 2010, Duffy was honored with the AIGA Fellow Award for his many years of leadership in the design and business community.

Abbott Miller, Judge

Abbott Miller is a partner in the international design consultancy Pentagram, where he has created identities, exhibitions, environments, books, and websites for a broad range of clients. As an author and curator, he has explored design through exhibitions and books. Over the course of his career he has worked with some of the most important curators and thinkers in art, fashion, design, and architecture.

Miller is the designer and editor of *2wice,* a magazine that explores the visual and performing arts. Recent projects include the design of the permanent exhibitions for the new Harley-Davidson Museum in Milwaukee, and "Design for a Living World," a landmark exhibition produced for The Nature Conservancy. He has also created patterns for Knoll wall covering and a textile for Maharam. Miller's work is represented in numerous museum collections, including the San Francisco Museum of Modern Art and the Art Institute of Chicago.

Michael Riley, Judge

Michael Riley was born in Palo Alto, California, and studied graphic design at the Rhode Island School of Design. Riley has been directing and designing film and television main title sequences, theatrical trailers, television commercials, and corporate identity packages since 1991.

His first experience with a company that experimented with film title design was during an internship under Tibor Kalman, at M&Co in New York. When he saw Kalman use typography as a thoughtful, conceptual, and expressive element in a Talking Heads music video, he realized the possibilities of mixing design with film.

In 1991, Riley began working at R/Greenberg Associates in New York designing for film and television. He became creative director and partner in 1997 at Imaginary Forces in Hollywood. In 2005, he opened Shine, where he leads a team designing film and television main-title sequences, theatrical trailers, television commercials, content for film, and branding identity packages. Riley has received numerous design honors, including a Gold Medal from the D&AD, the British Design and Art Directors Association; three Emmy nominations; and an Art Directors Club Silver Medal for the design of the Marvel Pictures theatrical logo. Riley is a member of the Directors Guild of America in the commercial director category, and at the Television Academy, he is a member of the executive committee under the title design peer group. Riley is also an adjunct faculty member at Art Center College of Design, in Pasadena, California.

Henry Sene Yee, Judge

Henry Sene Yee is the creative director of Picador. A Bachelor of Fine Arts graduate of the School of Visual Arts in New York City, he started his career in editorial design, freelancing at Condé Nast and *Rolling Stone* magazine. Yee got his first job in book publishing working for Louise Fili, then the art director at Pantheon Books/Random House. He left to work at St. Martin's Press as a senior designer and was eventually promoted to senior art director and then to his current position at Picador, a leading literary trade paperback imprint launched in 1995.

Yee has won numerous awards from leading graphic design organizations, including the American Institute of Graphic Arts (50 Books/50 Covers), the Art Directors Club (Gold Cube), the Type Directors Club, the New York Book Show, the Society of Illustrators, *Print* magazine (Regional Design Annual), *Communication Arts*, *Graphic Design USA*, and *Graphis* magazine. He can always be seen with a camera in one hand, a martini in the other.

TDC 56 Judge's Choice

Judge's Choice, Francesco Cavalli

The *XX-* project is a sort of book/object, at the same time simple and ever changing. It's a surprising archive containing a mix of images, typography, and colors. While at first glance it looks like an object from the past, a closer look reveals its soul and the beautifully designed grid that allows different layout designs. Definitely contemporary.

Judge's Choice, Abbott Miller

Some books exude a sense of thought and energy that is almost palpable, as if thought and deliberation and intensity are materialized in the form and material of what you hold in your hands. *XX-Die SS Rune als Sonderzeichen auf Schreibmaschinen* by the designers Elizabeth Hinrichs, Aileen Ittner, and Daniel Rother is that kind of project, one that commands your attention because of the thoroughly thought through, obsessively coordinated, and typographically understated approach.

The result is not look-at-me bravura or showmanship, which, given the topic, would be inappropriate, but journalistic and precise. The design of the book is like a skillfully produced documentary, one that is all the more memorable because of its rigor and objectivity, an approach that is all the more effective at revealing itself to the viewer because design seems to recede and content jumps forward.

But, of course, design isn't really receding. It's what is making this book as good as it is—but doing so from underneath and inside the content. For me, this was the revelation of the competition, a book that uses type, scale, structure, and materials to create an indelible document.

Designers' Statement

We focused on the intensive examination of typography and writing in all its social, societal, and aesthetic applications. Using this approach, in 2006 we developed a project on the visual implementation of symbols of power in writing systems under conditions of a totalitarian regime. In particular, we examined the way in which the SS presented and visually legitimated itself by means of a constructed sign. We developed a collection of sources derived from intensive research employing libraries and state archives, the Internet, and interviews with contemporary witnesses. This research was the starting point and the foundation of our 324-page book, *XX- The SS-Rune as a Special Character on Typewriters.*

The book is divided into three chapters—Female (Frau), Sign (Zeichen), and Machine (Maschine). They examine the ways in which administration, communication, and technology were an elementary condition in the functioning of the annihilation apparatus in the Third Reich.

Content: The book consists of visual (from files, advertising and propaganda images of the 30s and 40s) and textual fragments (contemporary, philosophical, sociological statements, plus statements related to cultural studies and encyclopedia entries). The book interprets, displays, and arranges history. In this sophisticated way of dealing with history, which makes the source documents visible and available to use, the book *XX-* questions its sources and their perception. Employing a hybrid composition as both a file and a book, its design uses filing techniques such as a registry, catchwords, numeration, and categorization, and embeds these into a book format.

On one hand, the chapter Female (Frau) recounts the role of a female typist who is subjected to the rationalization and monotony of everyday working life. On the other hand, it questions her status as a subordinate and an accessory in the context of National Socialism.

Sign (Zeichen) first analyses the general structure of signs as a means of communication. Their relevance as symbols of power is elucidated using the example of the SS-rune as a visual medium of ideology. Not least, the Nazis' sway and crimes are also reflected by the SS organization's "rational" labeling of the Nazi's victims.

Machine (Maschine) challenges the neutrality of technology and examines the relationship between the economy and the state using the example of the office as the provider of machines in a dictatorial system. The mechanical aspect is brought out in the same way: The chapter examines the typewriter key as a seemingly marginal activator, and the interchangeability of signs depending on the political system.

The three chapters are supplemented by elements of administration, human mass behavior, and guilt, as well as the idea of an archive as a space for collective memory and history.

Design: *XX-* is designed as the symbiosis of a file and a book cover. It, thus, refers to its sources: archive and literature. Constructed solely of visual and textual fragments, the book uses available literature and images.

The combination of a Swiss soft cover, an open spine, and a cloth binding add an objectlike character to the book. The inside—containing the block, cover, jacket, and a flap like a hard cover—has the outer appearance of a file that reflects its content, extensiveness, and (by means of the chapter cards) taxonomy. The attached book jacket is evocative of such a file's use in libraries. Here, jackets are attached inside and replaced by an imprinting. Because of the title's repetition, the imprinting of a registry number and its appearance—robust and fragile alike, the book defies any fixed ascription and reminds us that every archive can be terminated. The standard format of the registry at the beginning of the twentieth century is reflected in the A4 format

With *XX-* the book as a medium is abrogated in favor of a new perception of historiography. History is interpreted, displayed, and arranged in a reflection of the medium.

Book

Design: Elizabeth Hinrichs, Aileen Ittner, and Daniel Rother, Leipzig, Germany. Editors: Günter Karl Bose and Julia Blume. School: Hochschule für Grafik und Buchkunst (Academy of Visual Arts), Leipzig. Principal Type: DTL Documenta. Dimensions: 8.3 x 11.7 in. (21 x 29.7 cm)

TDC 56 Judge's Choice

Judge's Choice, Henry Sene Yee

Rodney Smith's book of his photography impresses you at first with its beautiful clothbound, slipcased tome and immense 16-inch-by-20-inch size. When you open the book, which is like lifting a door, you see from the first page the 6-inch tall letters of the title, *THE END,* filling the page. The gorgeous typography and its confident placement on the page just grabbed me. The impact was visceral. The type design throughout playfully and elegantly interacted with the stunning photos with generous use of white space and superior printing and production values.

You never see books of this size. I'm so used to viewing publications on a computer screen and on my iPhone. Although I love the convenience of such tools, I realize what we may lose when publishing goes from paper to smaller electronic publishing formats. We'll lose the beauty of a large-size publication, the impact of full-bleed images and large beautiful letterforms, and the contrast in relationships between sizes. We'll no longer have the feel of the bound book form and printing on quality paper. This project is a stunning example of a print publishing field that is rapidly changing.

Designer's Statement

The End is a culmination of the last twenty years of Rodney Smith's career. It is a collection of slightly surreal photographs paired with wry text and design, all of which come together to pose more questions than they answer.

Beginning with a man leaping from the wing of an airplane, the book travels through a photographic world that is somewhat humorous, somewhat enigmatic, and strangely similar to the one in which we live. Circles of text mimic rolling bales of hay, men walk on water, and text blows carelessly in the breeze. The book has been a labor of love over the past five years and is really a cathartic experience as Smith completes this stage of his work and now looks for something else.

Book

Design: David Meredith, New York. Creative Direction: Rodney Smith. Design Office: Pilot New York. Client: Rodney Smith. Principal Type: Hoefler Text. Dimensions: 16 x 20 in. (40.6 x 50.8 cm)

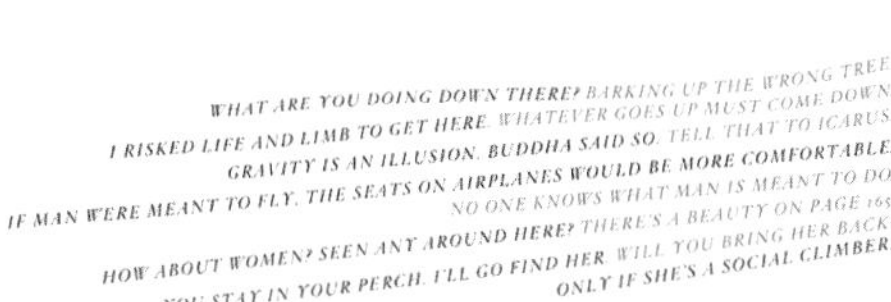

TDC 56 Judge's Choice

Judge's Choice, Joe Duffy

I love the unique simplicity of this design. Everything about it is direct and elegant, while expressing a complete range of meaning; every design decision is measured. The shapes, the color, the type, the production techniques, and the design as a whole all have direct reference to the product; and most important, they all add up to beautiful.

By developing the design from these references, the designer has created something completely original. It is one of those packages that stands apart from all the others on the shelf and becomes a magnet, one that you simply have to pick up and hold in your hands.

A package this beautiful becomes a form of interior design. How could you not display it in a prominent place in your home, or how could you throw it away when the product is gone? There must be some other use for something that looks this good.

In a category where true originality is rare, this design shines like a beacon, representing the power of great design on the shelf. First it attracts, next it informs, and then it sells, all the while doing so in a unique and artful way.

Congratulations to the excellent design team and bravo to the courageous client.

Designers' Statement

The creative concept for the product 52 Liqueur Fusions was centered around the fruit itself. The bottle is slightly rounded in shape, mimicking the blackberry while the color is a dark blue-black. The top was designed to look like a cluster of blackberries, and the label itself was letterpressed to indicate the natural occurrence of pressing that is used in all manners of grapes and berries. The ink used for the letterpress is also a deep blackberry color. However, it is not solid. The intent was to appear as a stain, rather like the experience of picking the actual fruit itself.

Packaging

Design: Peter Pham, San Francisco. Art Direction: Jennifer Sterling. Creative Direction: Jennifer Sterling. Lettering: Peter Pham and Jennifer Sterling. Design Office: Jennifer Sterling Design. Client: 52 Liqueur Fusions. Principal Type: various

TDC 56 Judge's Choice

Judge's Choice, Kristina DiMatteo

It was half past three in the afternoon when I walked into a room ready to discover a new collection of work and was stopped by a glowing light.

Before me was clean modern typography, a symmetrical matrix in motion, and content shown in eight languages, all floating in a brightly lit square. Qlocktwo was, and is, smart, well executed, and beautiful.

I was impressed with this piece's minimalism and elegance, and how, with one click, the display smoothly switched from telling time in full sentences—"It is half past three," in clean-cut DIN—to keeping time with a second hand. The magnetic front surface could also be changed to show eight different languages and five different colors.

I now crave my own qlocktwo. Alas, I'll have to settle for the iPhone app.

Designers' Statement

Qlocktwo allows a different perspective on time—attention is focused on the moment. The typographic clock links time to the written word. This gives it a timeless quality.

A matrix with symmetrically arranged characters forms an additional square on the inside. Some of these characters glow in pure white, thus forming words that describe the time.

The front surface of the qlocktwo is supported by eight magnets. That way, the front surface can be replaced without visible attachments. Users can choose from satin stainless steel or five colors of polished synthetic glass.

When it's switched on, the chronometer adjusts itself to the split second and adapts the brightness of the characters to the ambient light. Whether it's floating on the wall or standing on the sideboard, a fine time will definitely be had by all with the qlocktwo.

Clock

Design: Andreas Funk and Marco Biegert, Schwaebisch Gmuend, Germany. Agency: Biegert & Funk. Principal Type: FF DIN Pro Light. Dimensions: 17.7 x 17.7 in. (45 x 45 cm)

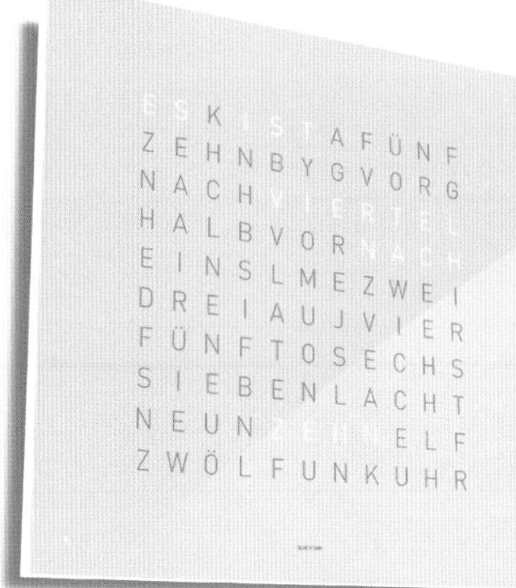

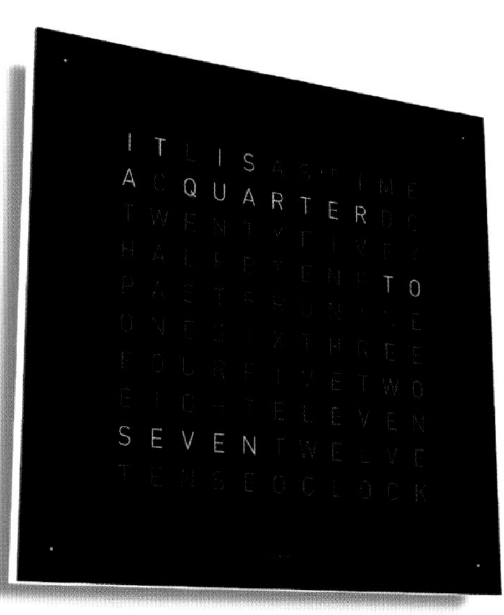

TDC 56 Judge's Choice

Judge's Choice, Michael Riley

The new Avid logo is smart, simple, and clever. I love that the letters, A, V, I, and D are all derived from the "Play" and "Pause" buttons. It's a really clever observation that those letters spell the company name. I like that the graphic language is taken from the very products they create. The typography in this new mark is a big step forward from their previous logos. And it made me laugh when I saw it. Not too many logos do that.

Designers' Statement

Avid has long been known as a pioneer and the creator of an industry standard in nonlinear video editing. What most customers do not know is that other leading audiovisual brands, such as Pro Tools and M-Audio, are also part of Avid. With a change in business strategy to master-brand all of their offerings under the Avid name, Avid needed a new visual identity to unify the portfolio of formerly separate brands, one capable of addressing the needs of enterprise audiences, creative professionals, and home enthusiasts.

Drawing upon their new positioning, which gives them the ability to help people create the most listened to, most watched, and most loved media in the world, the Brand Union created a new logo and visual system for one Avid. Utilizing the buttons, icons, and markers recognized by audiovisual professionals and consumers around the world, the new logo is simultaneously a "wordmark" and a symbol.

Logotype

Design: Sam Becker, New York. Art Direction: Dennis Thomas. Creative Direction: Wally Krantz. Design Office: The Brand Union. Client: Avid Technology. Principal Type: custom

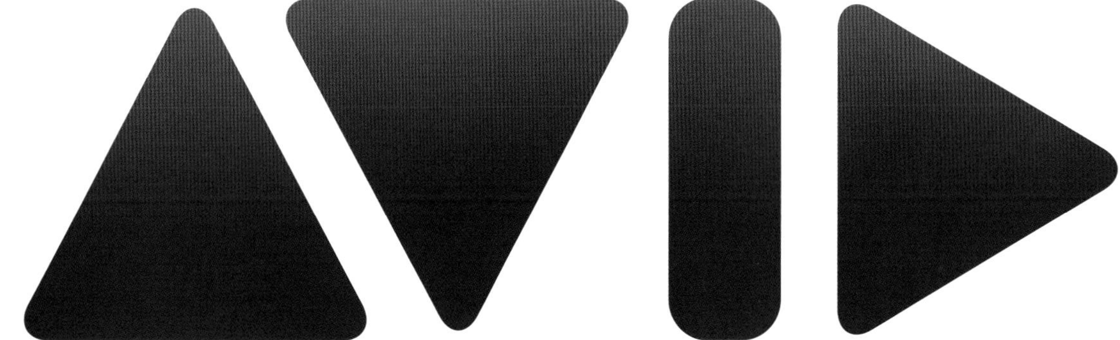

TDC 56 Judge's Choice

Judge's Choice, Brian Collins

This, simply, was my favorite piece of typographic thinking in the show.

And I had many favorite pieces in this show. As you look through this book, you'll see why.

But this solution for Autentic, a German film distribution and production company, is as elegant as it is inevitable.

To say anything more would detract from its effortlessness.

Designers' Statement

When we were asked to develop the logo for Autentic, a newly founded German company that produces and distributes documentary film, the brief was clear: Make it simple; make it open and authentic—a reflection of the enterprise itself.

After a bit of contemplation on the themes of film and vision, we decided to turn the letter A on its side, transforming it into an eye. Afterwards, we developed many alternate variations, experimenting with frames, a sphere, lines, structure. Whatever we tried, we lost either the A or the eye, slipping in the narrow space where one vacillates between seeing two things at once. This experiment with many directions for the visual provided us with the confidence to take the most direct route for the logo signet, where the A for Autentic remains pure, a monogram for the company and a wink to the forward-looking eye.

Logotype

Design: Lutz Widmaier, München, Germany. Creative Direction: Lutz Widmaier and Sabine Schmid. Design Office: Schmid + Widmaier Design. Client: Autentic GmbH. Principal Type: Helvetica Rounded Bold

Book and Related Items

Design: Sharon Werner and Sarah Nelson Forss, St. Paul, Minnesota. Art Direction: Sharon Werner. Creative Direction: Sharon Werner. Studio: Werner Design Werks. Client: Blue Apple Books. Principal Type: ITC Avant Garde, ITC Lubalin, and various others. Dimensions: various

Corporate Identity

Design: Roberto de Vicq de Cumptich, New York. Art Direction: Roberto de Vicq de Cumptich. Creative Direction: Matteo Bologna. Design Office: Mucca Design. Client: Starr Restaurants. Principal Type: various. Dimensions: various

Self-Promotion

Design: Ibán Ramón Rodríguez, Valencia, Spain. Art Direction: Ibán Ramón Rodríguez. Creative Direction: Ibán Ramón Rodríguez. Lettering: Diego Mir, Daniel Requeni, and Ibán Ramón Rodríguez. Studio: Estudio Ibán Ramón. Principal Type: handlettering. Dimensions: 36.8 x 57.2 in. (14.5 x 22.5 cm)

Posters

Design: Hei Yiyang and Liu Zhao, Shenzhen, China. Art Direction: Hei Yiyang. Creative Direction: Hei Yiyang. Photography: Liang Rong. Design Office: SenseTeam. Client: The OCT Art & Design Gallery. Principal Type: DIN. Dimensions: 21 x 30.7 in. (53 x 78 cm)

Exhibition

Design: Ryan Pescatore Frisk, New York; Catelijne van Middelkoop, Rotterdam, Netherlands. Art Direction: Ryan Pescatore Frisk and Catelijne van Middelkoop. Creative Direction: Ryan Pescatore Frisk and Catelijne van Middelkoop. Lettering: Ryan Pescatore Frisk and Catelijne van Middelkoop. Programming/Production: Ryan Pescatore Frisk and Catelijne van Middelkoop. Studio: Strange Attractors Design. Client: Graphic Design Museum, Breda, Netherlands. Principal Type: various and handlettering. Dimensions: various

Catalog

Design: Lucas Badger, Washington, DC. Art Direction: Pum Lefebure. Creative Direction: Pum Lefebure and Jake Lefebure. Design Office: Design Army. Client: Karla Colletto. Principal Type: Berthold Akzidenz Grotesk, Berthold Akzidenz Grotesk Bold, and Berthold Akzidenz Grotesk Bold Condensed. Dimensions: 5 x 7 in. (12.7 x 17.8 cm)

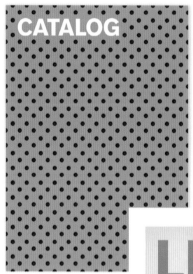

Brochure

Design: René Clément, Montréal. Art Direction: René Clément. Creative Direction: Louis Gagnon. Photography: Monic Richard. Studio: Paprika. Client: Clinique Dr. Mireille Faucher. Principal Type: Berthold Bodoni. Dimensions: 6 x 8 in. (2.4 x 3.1 cm)

Brochure
Design: Johannes Erler and Anne Fischer, Hamburg, Germany. Art Direction: Johannes Erler. Creative Direction: Johannes Erler. Studio: Factor Design. Principal Type: Dolly. Dimensions: 6.3 x 7.9 in. (16 x 20 cm)

Nach fest kommt ab
Von Uwe Melichar, Partner

Es begab sich aber zu der Zeit, als die Menschen hektisch und die Dominosteine ausverkauft waren – am Vormittag des Heiligen Abends. Wie in jedem Jahr hatte mein Vater begonnen, den Weihnachtsbaum in den Weihnachtsbaumständer zu stellen, um ihn für die folgenden Dekoarbeiten zu präparieren. (Aufstellung und Illumination sind seine Aufgabe, seit ich mich zurückerinnern kann. Der Baumschmuck hingegen ist Mama-Sache.) Zu diesem Zweck hatte er sich bisher mit dem klassischen Drei-Halteschrauben-Christbaumständer unter Zuhilfenahme diverser Hilfsholzkeile abgemüht. Das sollte nun endlich anders werden: Im Baumarkt hatte mein Vater ein günstiges Plagiat des bekannten Krinner-Baumständers erstanden, der mit seiner Rundum-Ein-Seil-Technik Bäume bis 4 m Höhe sicher zu fassen versprach.

Ich selbst war es, der den Baum vermeintlich gerade hielt, als mein Vater auf die Fußraste trat, um den Baum zu fixieren. Und der war dann auch fest. Nur leider nicht gerade. Also versuchten wir, die Arretierung wieder zu lösen, zunächst kraft unserer Hände, dann mit leichtem Werkzeug, später mit schwerem Gerät. Doch der Baum war untrennbar mit dem Ständer verbunden.

Also machten wir uns mit Ständer und Baum auf den Weg zum Baumarkt und reklamierten die Sache. Dort gelang es dem Fachpersonal unter größten Mühen und nur mittels totaler Zerstörung des Baumständers, unsere Nordmanntanne zu befreien. Das Angebot eines baugleichen Baumarkt-Austauschständers schlugen wir aus! Stattdessen erfüllte sich mein Vater nun endlich seinen Traum: Für ein paar Euro mehr kaufte er den legendären, den echten Krinner V8. Ein Hightech-Markenprodukt! Den besten Christbaumständer der Welt! So wurde, kurz vor Ladenschluss, doch noch alles gut. Und bei den Melichars konnte es Weihnachten werden.

8 FDMH.18 WEIHNACHTEN MIT PAPA

Wiedervereinigung
Von Olaf Stein, Partner

Als ich meinen Vater nach einer Weihnachtsgeschichte fragte, bei der er eine bemerkenswerte Rolle gespielt hatte, fiel ihm zunächst nichts ein. Dann jedoch entdeckte er dieses Foto. Das ist zwar nicht sonderlich lustig oder originell, die Geschichte dahinter passt jedoch wunderbar zum nun ablaufenden Jahr 2009. Mein Vater schreibt:

Lieber Olaf,
dieses Foto schickte unsere Mutter an die Großeltern, die zu dieser Zeit noch in der DDR wohnten. Unser Vater feierte dieses Weihnachtsfest 1952 das erste Mal zusammen mit seiner Familie. Wir, meine Mutter, meine Schwester und ich, durften in dem Jahr offiziell aus dem Osten in den Westen übersiedeln. Das war unsere Wiedervereinigung vor 57 Jahren. Es war ein schönes Weihnachtsfest.
Gruß, Papa

FDMH.18 WEIHNACHTEN MIT PAPA 9

Booklet

Design: Felix Stumpf, Stuttgart, Germany. Art Direction: Felix Stumpf. Creative Direction: Felix Stumpf. Design Office: Atelier für Gestaltung Felix Stumpf. Principal Type: Rauschen. Dimensions: 5.7 x 8.7 in. (14.4 x 22 cm)

Brochures

Design: Wolfgang Greter, Nicole Klein, Sebastian Schneider, and Barbara Schwitzke, Hamburg, Germany. Art Direction: Nicole Klein and Sebastian Schneider. Creative Direction: Wolfgang Greter and Björn Lux. Copywriting and Proofreading: Frank Wache. Design Office: JUNO. Client: Peyer Graphic. Principal Type: Volume 1, Knockout; Volume 2, Adhesive Black and DIN, Volume 3, Courier and handwriting. Dimensions 4.1 x 5.8 in. (10.5 x 14.8 cm)

Design: Alina Günter and Friedrich-Wilhelm Graf, Zürich, Switzerland. Photography: Cortis & Sonderegger. Design Office: unfolded. Client: Theater der Künste. Principal Type: Lutz and Bodoni Light. Dimensions: unfolded, 23.4 x 16.5 in. (59.4 x 42 cm); folded, 5.8 x 8.3 in. (14.8 x 21 cm)

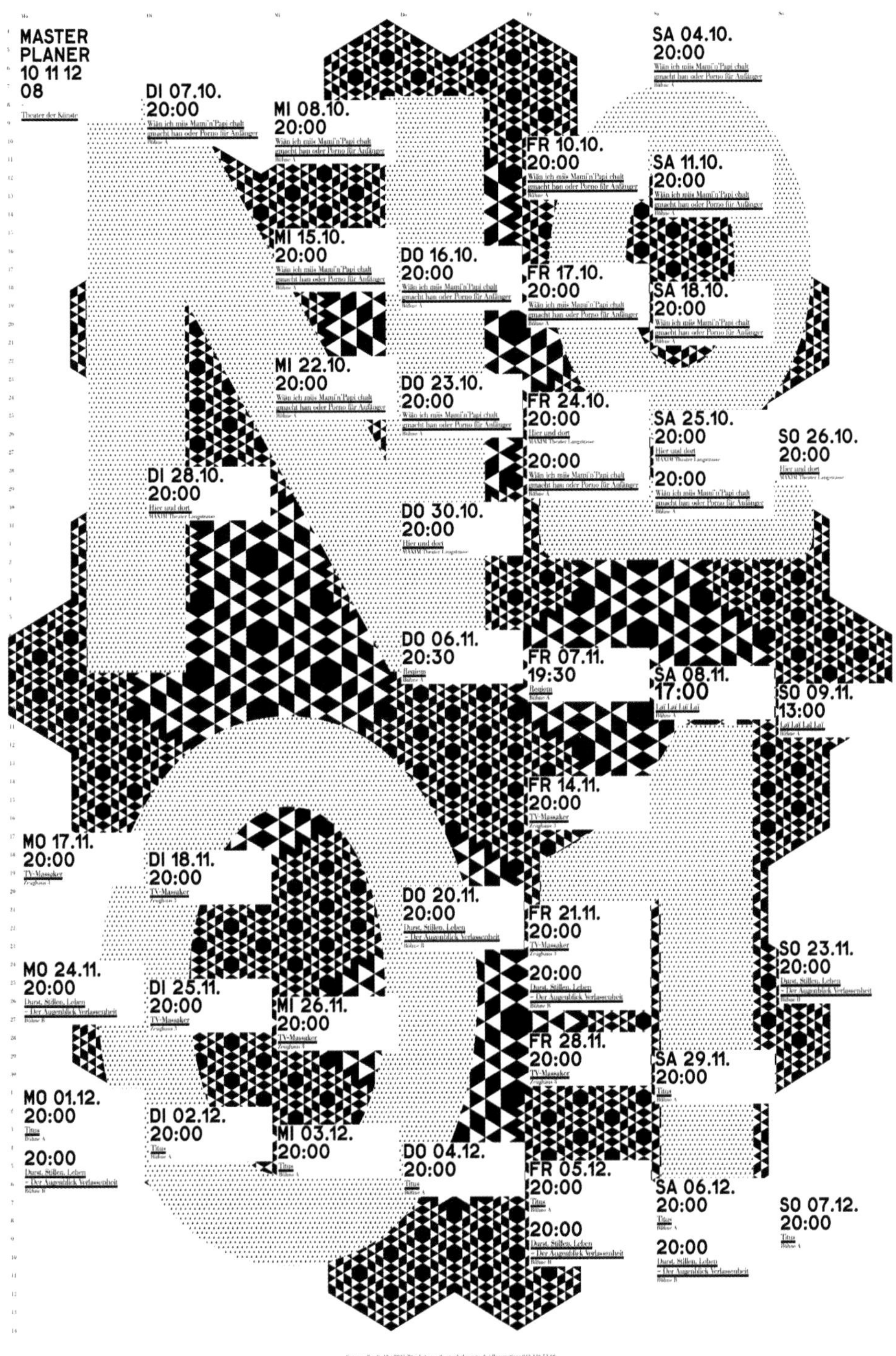

Brochure

Design: François-Xavier Saint-Georges, Montréal. Art Direction: François-Xavier Saint-Georges. Creative Direction: Louis Gagnon. Copywriter: Jimmy Berthelet. Studio: Paprika. Client: Stand. Principal Type: Minion Pro and News Gothic. Dimensions: 5 x 7.75 in. (12.7 x 19.7 cm)

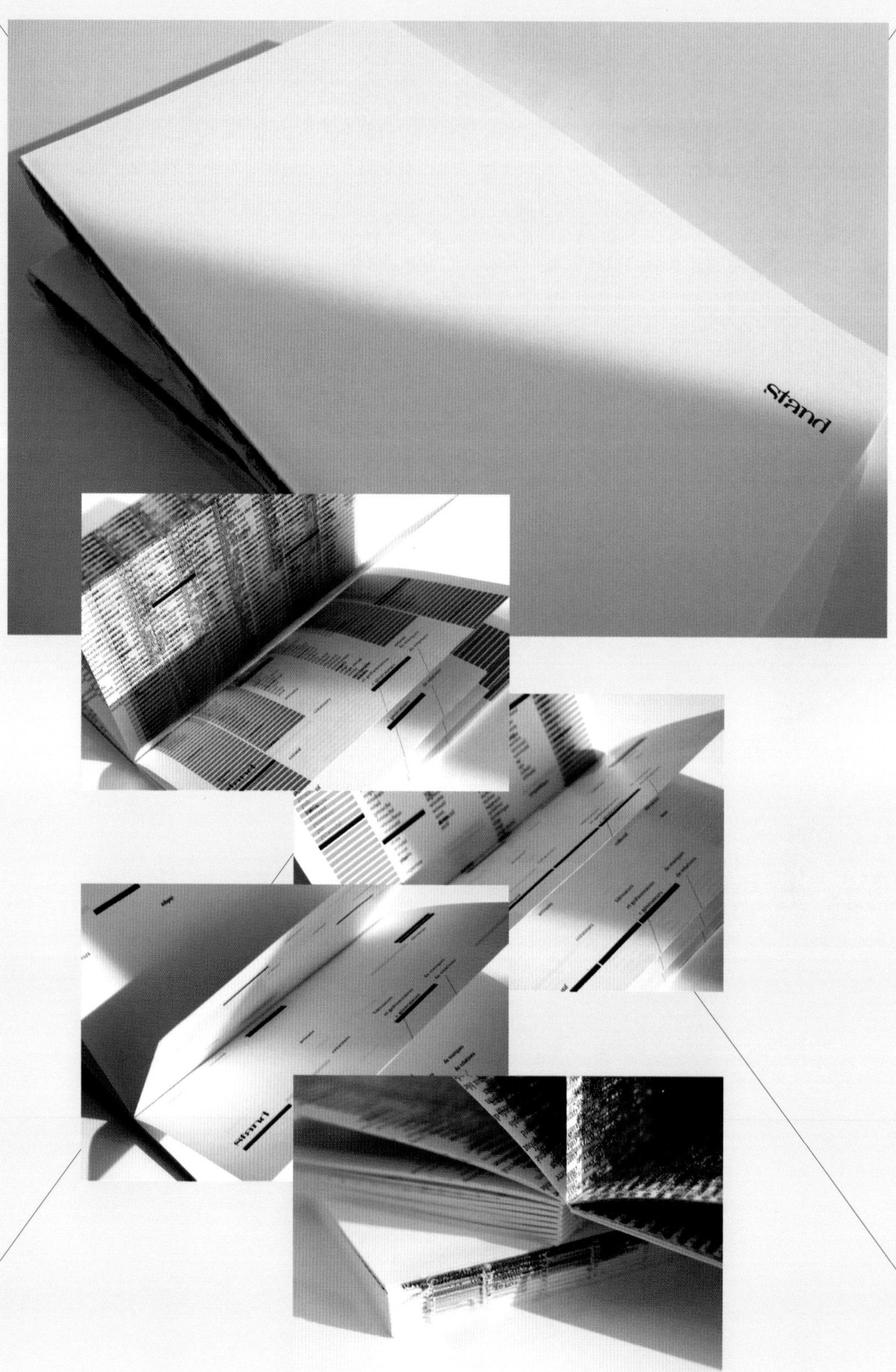

Brochure
Design: Samuel Marty and Irene Bürge Willemse, Zürich, Switzerland. Art Direction: Samuel Marty. Creative Direction: Irene Bürge Willemse. School: Zürcher Hochschule der Künste (ZHdK). Principal Type: Vectora LT Std and Vectora LT Bold. Dimensions: 7.5 in. x 4.3 (19 x 11 cm)

Program

Design: Christine Celic Strohl, New York. Art Direction: Christine Celic Strohl. Creative Direction: Matteo Bologna. Design Office: Mucca Design. Client: American Institute of Graphic Arts (AIGA). Principal Type: custom. Dimensions: 6 x 9 in. (15.2 x 22.9 cm)

Project Documents

Design: Susanna Shannon and Catherine Houbart, Paris. Creative Direction: Susanna Shannon. Design Office: Design Dept. Client : Institut pour la Ville en mouvement. Principal Type: Eclat, Franklin Gothic Extra Condensed, and Times New Roman. Dimensions: 16.5 x 11.7 in. (42 x 29.7 cm)

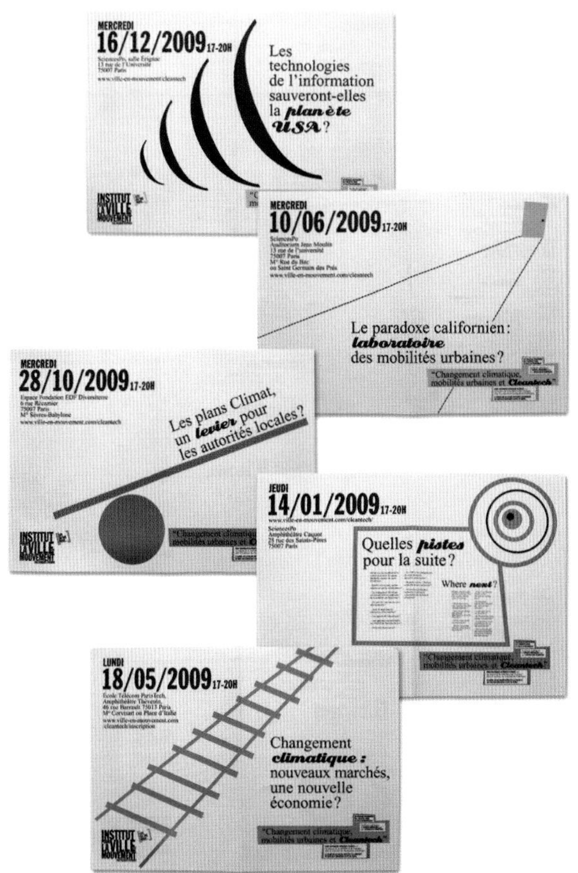

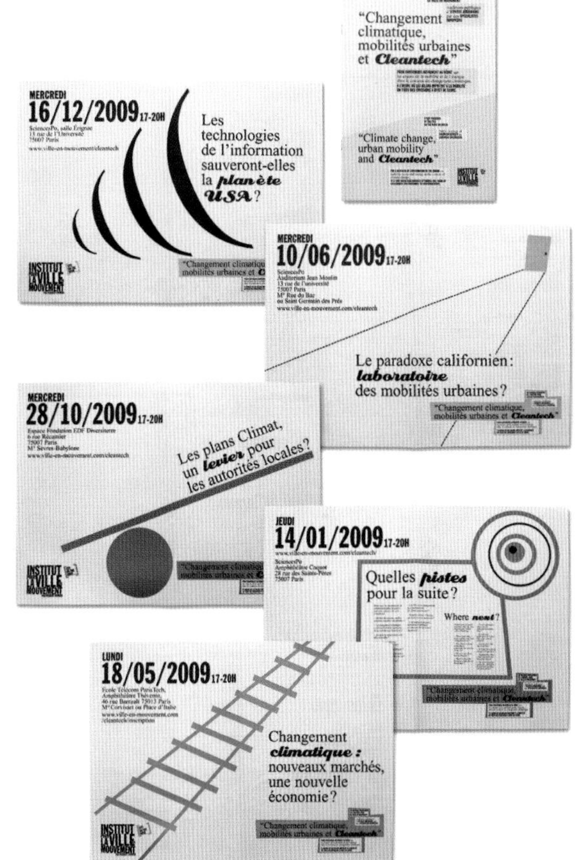

Brochure

Design: Ramon Classen, Thomas Müller, Thomas Neeser, and Daniela Rota, Basel, Switzerland. Art Direction: Thomas Neeser and Thomas Müller. Creative Direction: Thomas Neeser and Thomas Müller. Studio: Neeser & Müller. Client: Verein Neue Musik Rümlingen. Principal Type: Hornet. Dimensions: 8.7 x 11 in. (22 x 28 cm)

Brochure

Design: Helmut Meyer and Thomas Knopf, Frankfurt, Germany. Art Direction: Helmut Meyer and Thomas Knopf. Creative Direction: Helmut Meyer. Lettering: Helmut Meyer and Thomas Knopf. Agency: Ogilvy Frankfurt. Client: Ogilvy Germany. Principal Type: Ogilvy Baskerville and ITC Stone Sans. Dimensions: 9.5 x 13 in. (24 x 33 cm)

Seite 60 / HOW TO

Seite 61 / HOW TO

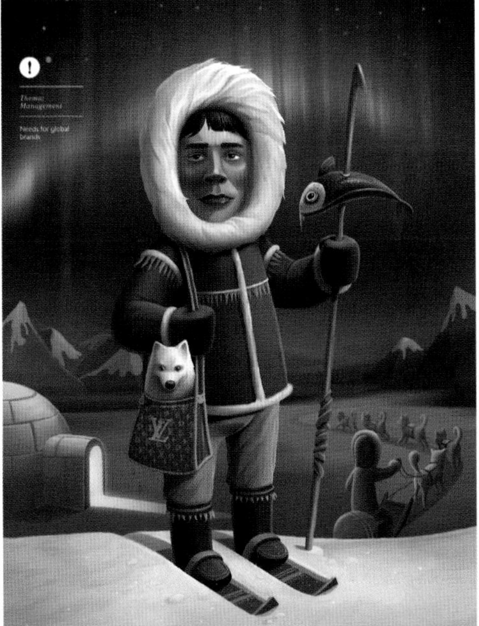

How to manage a global brand account.

AUTOR: *Ulrich Tillmanns, Managing Director, Tillmanns, Ogilvy & Mather Düsseldorf*

ILLUSTRATOR: *Andrey Gordeev*

Catalog

Design: John Hughes, Alexa McNae, and Clive Piercy, Santa Monica, California. Creative Direction: Clive Piercy. Illustration: Ann Field. Design Office: air conditioned. Client: Astani Living. Principal Type: DIN. Dimensions: 11 x 15 in. (27.9 x 38.1 cm)

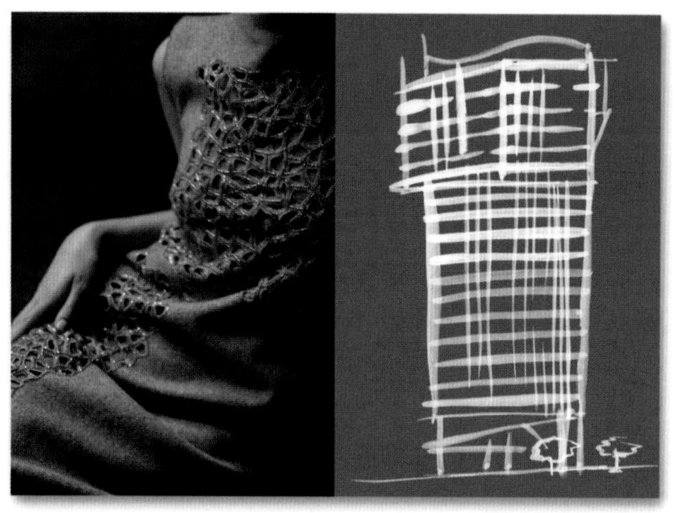

WELCOME
TO THE
NEIGHBOR-
HOOD.

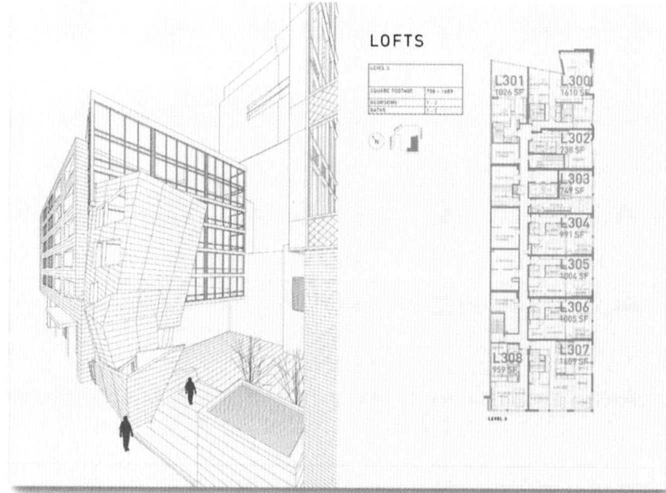

Magazine Cover
Design: Ariane Spanier, Berlin. Art Direction: Ariane Spanier. Studio: Ariane Spanier Design. Client: *FUKT* magazine. Principal Type: custom. Dimensions: 10.4 x 13.6 in. (26.5 x 34.5 cm)

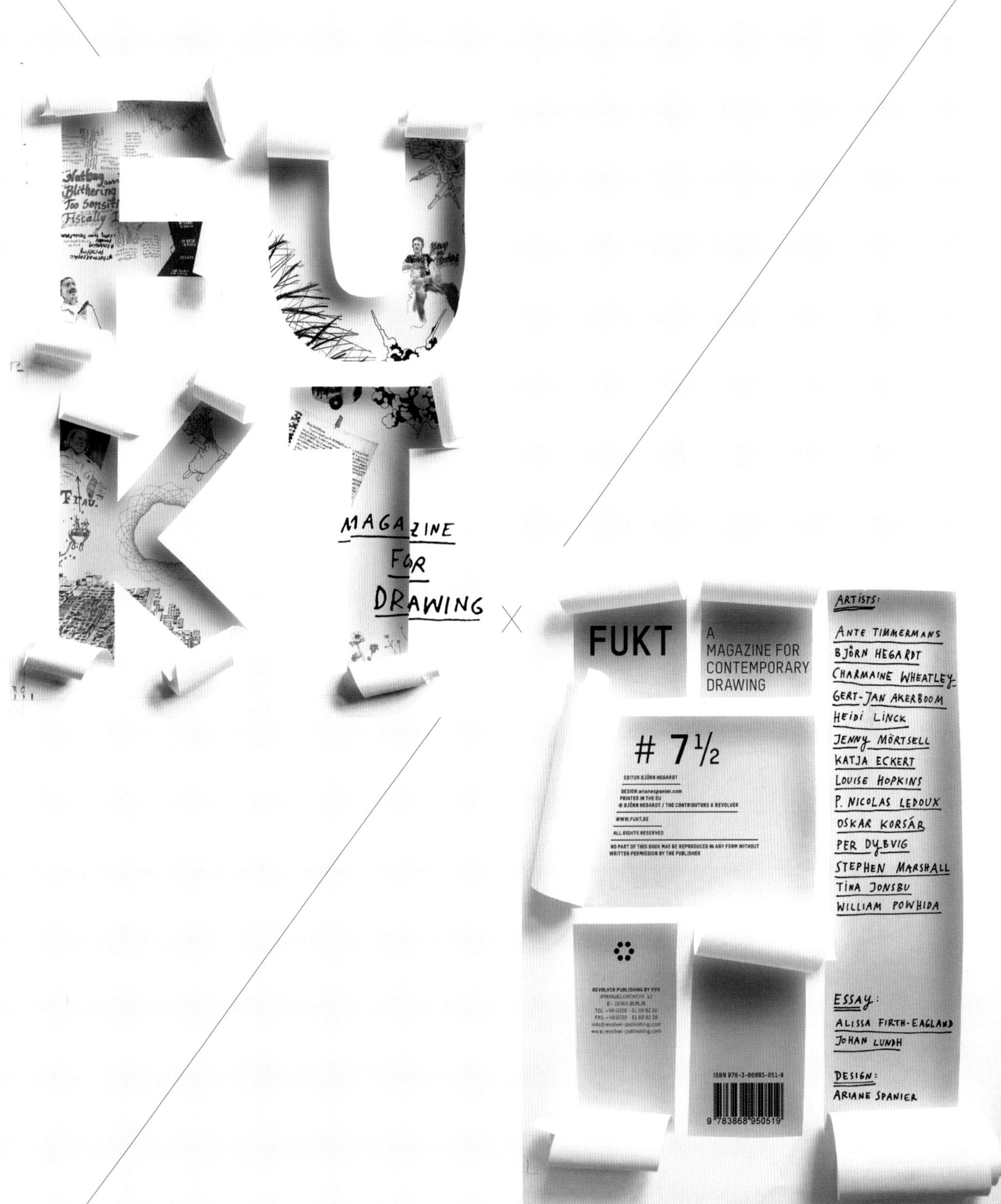

Book Jacket

Design: Carin Goldberg, New York. Art Direction: Rodrigo Corral. Design Office: Rodrigo Corral Design. Client: New Directions Publishing. Principal Type: typewritten. Dimensions: 5.25 x 8 in. (13.3 x 20.3 cm)

Nathanael WEST
MISS Lonelyhearts
The Day of
the LOCUST
introduction BY
Jonathan Lethem

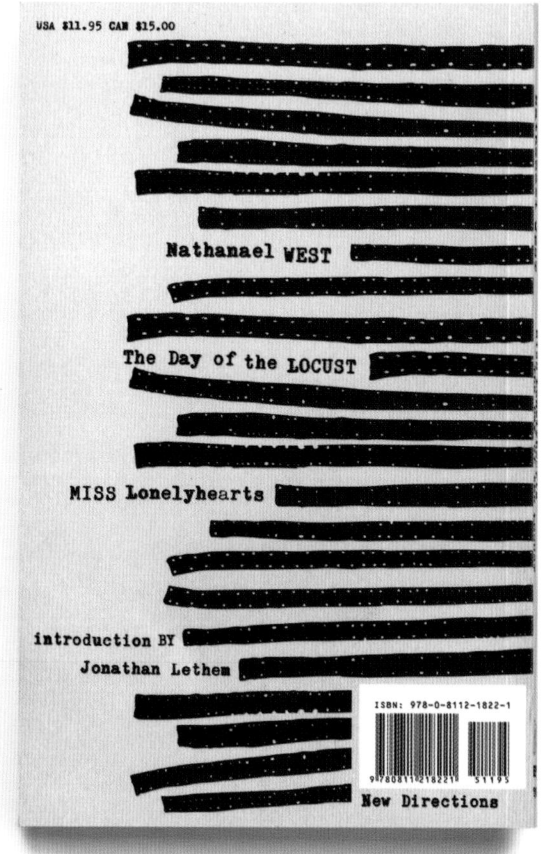

Book Jacket

Design: Tamaye Perry, Brooklyn, New York. Art Direction: Robbin Schiff, New York. Illustration: Tamaye Perry and Christoph Niemann. Design Office: Tamaye Perry Design. Publisher: Random House. Principal Type: Interstate. Dimensions: 5.75 x 8.5 in. (14.6 x 21.6 cm)

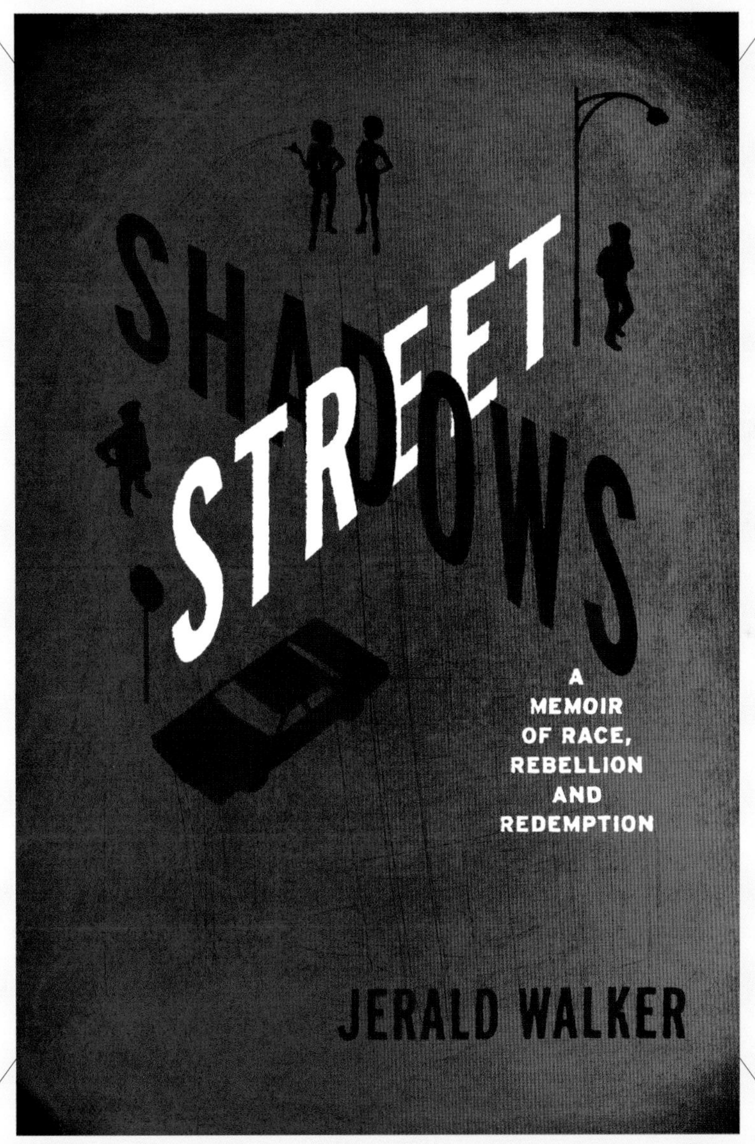

Book Jacket
Design: Peter Mendelsund, New York. Art Direction: Carol Devine Carson. Publisher: Alfred A. Knopf. Principal Type: typewritten (IBM Selectric II). Dimensions: 6.5 x 9.5 in. (16.5 x 24.1 cm)

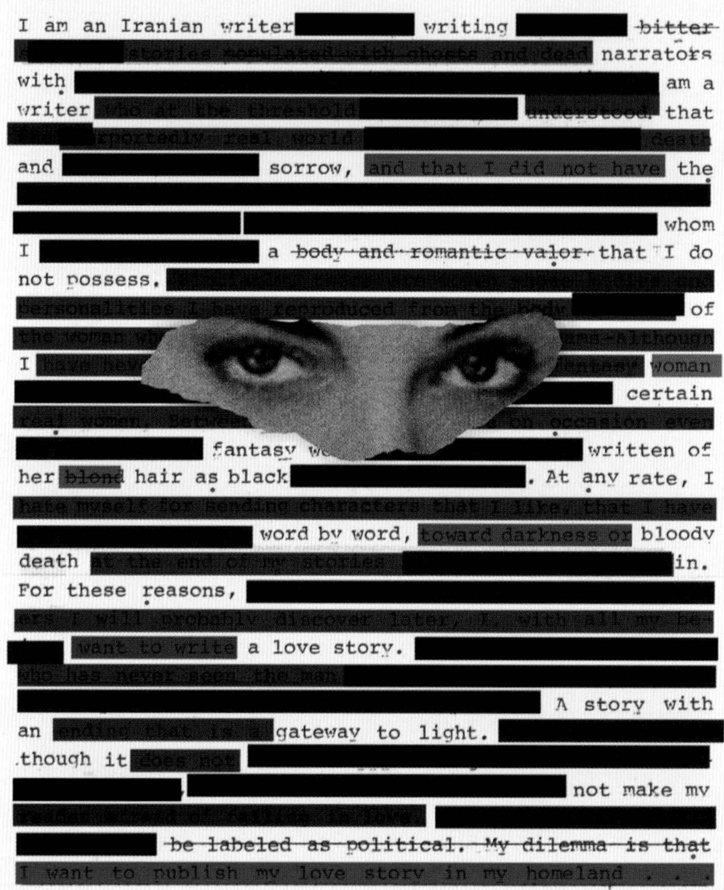

I am an Iranian writer writing bitter
stories populated with ghosts and dead narrators
with am a
writer who at the threshold understood that
purportedly real world death
and sorrow, and that I did not have the
whom
I a body and romantic valor that I do
not possess.
personalities I have reproduced from the body of
woman
certain
real women. on occasion even
fantasy written of
her blond hair as black . At any rate, I
hate myself for sending characters that I like, that I have
word by word, toward darkness or bloody
death at the end of my stories in.
For these reasons,
ers I will probably discover later, I, with all my be-
want to write a love story.
who has never seen the man
A story with
an ending that is a gateway to light.
though it does not
not make my
reader afraid of falling in love.
be labeled as political. My dilemma is that
I want to publish my love story in my homeland . . .
CENSORING AN IRANIAN LOVE STORY.
a novel.
Shahriar Mandanipour.

Book Jacket
Design: Peter Mendelsund, New York. Design Office: Peter Mendelsund Design. Client: Pantheon Books. Principal Type: Baskerville MT. Dimensions: 8.5 x 5.75 in. (21.6 x 14.6 cm)

We Things

See Didn't

ing Com

ven *by* Ste

am Amsterd

Book Jackets

Design: Giona Lodigiani, New York. Art Direction: Matteo Bologna. Creative Direction: Matteo Bologna. Design Office: Mucca Design. Client: Biblioteca Universale Rizzoli (BUR). Principal Type: Mantinia. Dimensions: 4.6 x 7.3 in. (11.7 x 18.6 cm)

Book Jacket

Design: Rex Bonomelli, New York. Art Direction: Rex Bonomelli. Creative Direction: Rex Bonomelli. Publisher: Scribner. Principal Type: Times New Roman and various. Dimensions: 5.75 x 8.7 in. (14.6 x 22.1 cm)

Book Jacket

Design: Rex Bonomelli, New York. Art Direction: Rex Bonomelli. Creative Direction: Rex Bonomelli. Publisher: Scribner. Principal Type: Mrs Eaves (modified). Dimensions: 5.1 x 8.25 in. (13 x 21 cm)

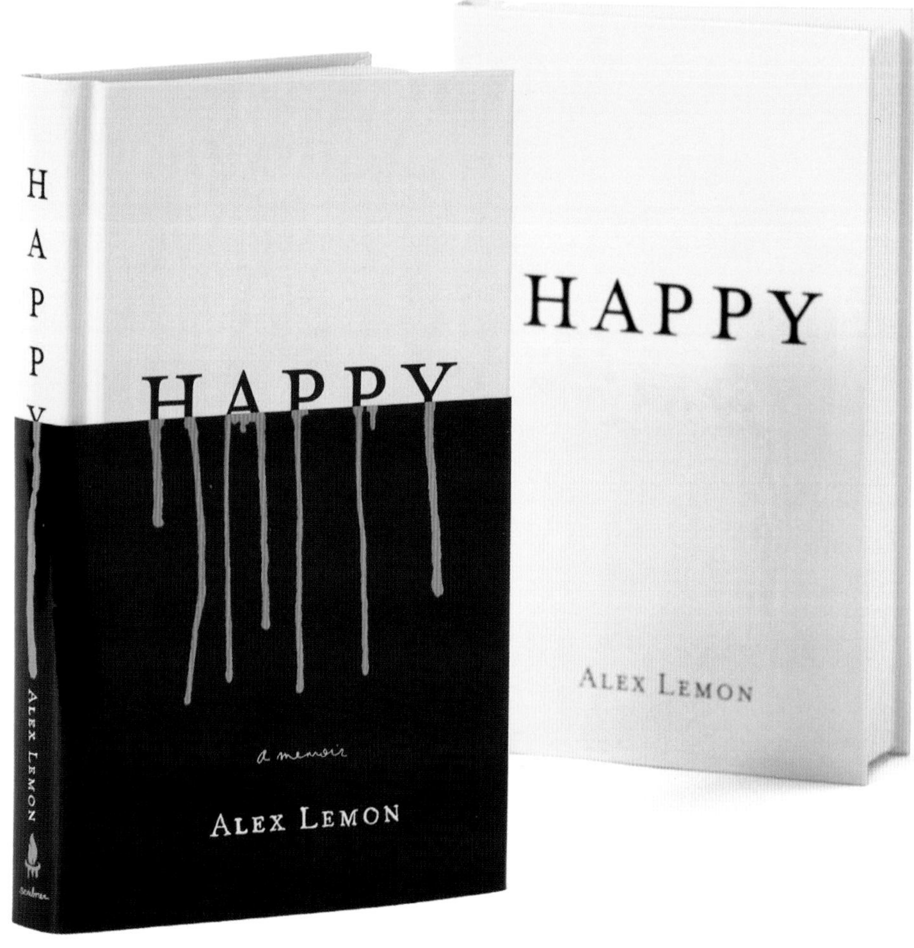

Book Jackets

Design: Scott Williams and Henrik Kubel, London. Creative Direction: Scott Williams and Henrik Kubel. Design Office: A2/SW/HK. Client: Faber & Faber. Principal Type: A2 Beckett. Dimensions: 5.1 x 7.8 in. (13 x 19.8 cm)

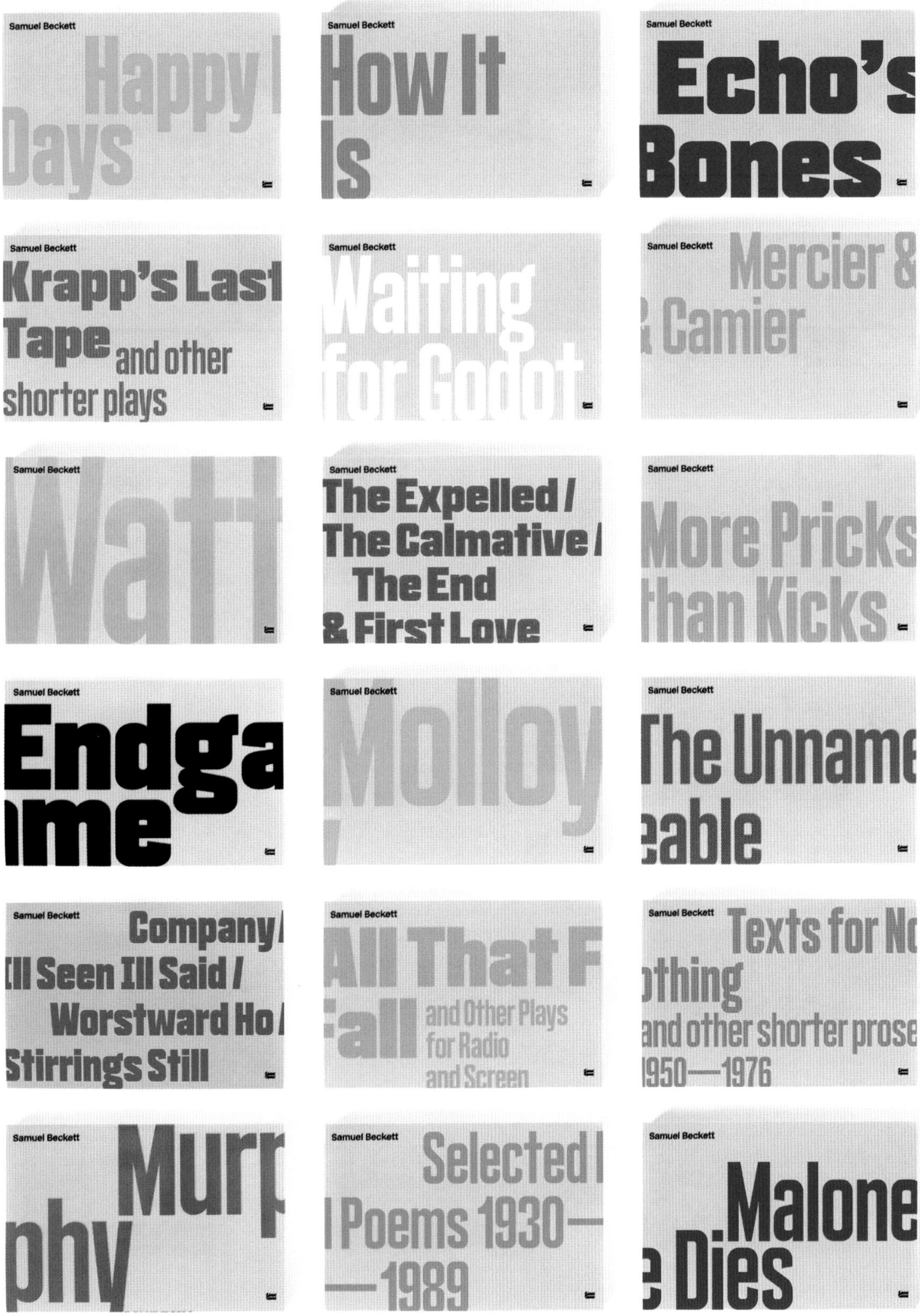

Book Jacket

Design: Ena Cardenal de la Nuez, Madrid. Client: ARTIUM (Centro-Museo Vasco de Arte Contemporáneo), Ayuntamiento de Barcelona, and Lunwerg Editóres. Principal Type: Futura. Dimensions: 9.8 x 11.8 in. (25 x 30 cm)

Book Jackets

Design: Michael Bierut, Barbara de Wilde, Stephen Doyle, John Gall, Chip Kidd, and Peter Mendelsund, New York. Art Direction: John Gall. Publisher: Vintage Books. Principal Type: Hoefler Text. Dimensions: 5.2 x 8 in. (13.2 x 20.3 cm)

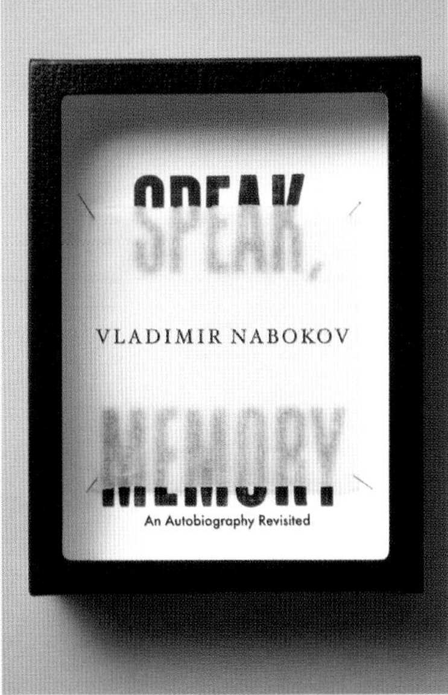

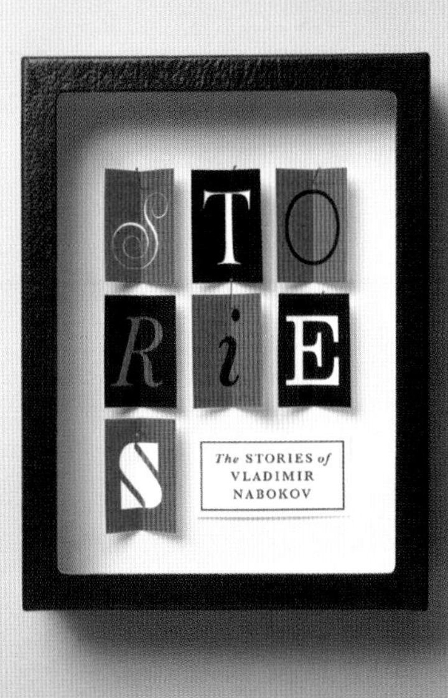

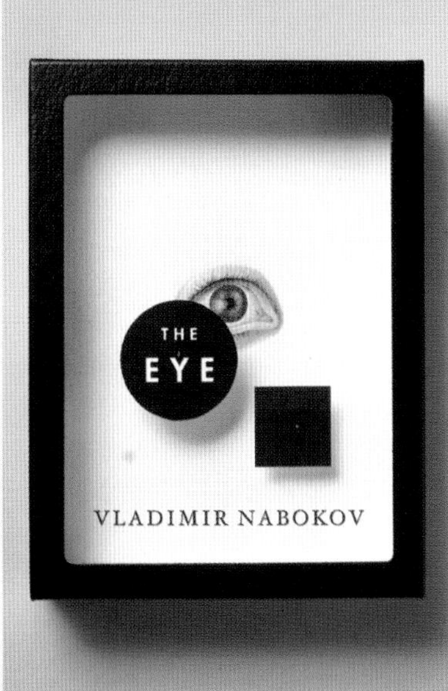

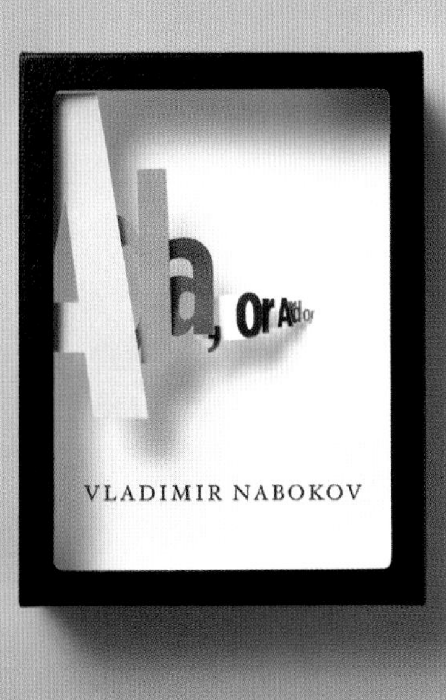

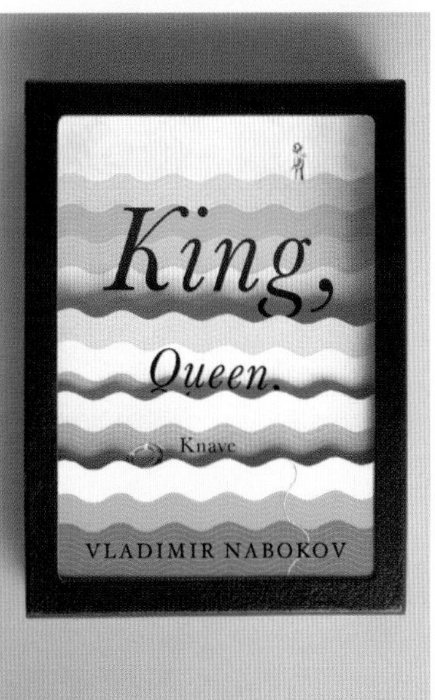

Book Jackets

Design: David Guarnieri, Montréal. Art Direction: David Guarnieri. Creative Direction: Louis Gagnon. Studio: Paprika. Client: Les Allusifs, maison d'édition. Principal Type: Braggadocio and DIN. Dimensions 4.5 x 7.5 in. (11.4 x 19.1 cm)

Book Jackets

Design: Thomas Schrott, Berlin. Art Direction: Fons Hickmann and Gesine Grotrian-Steinweg. Creative Direction: Fons Hickmann and Gesine Grotrian-Steinweg. Lettering: Uma Grotrian-Steinweg and Thomas Schrott. Studio: Fons Hickmann M23. Client: Bavarian State Opera. Principal Type: handlettering. Dimensions: 6.5 x 9.1 in. (16.5 x 23 cm)

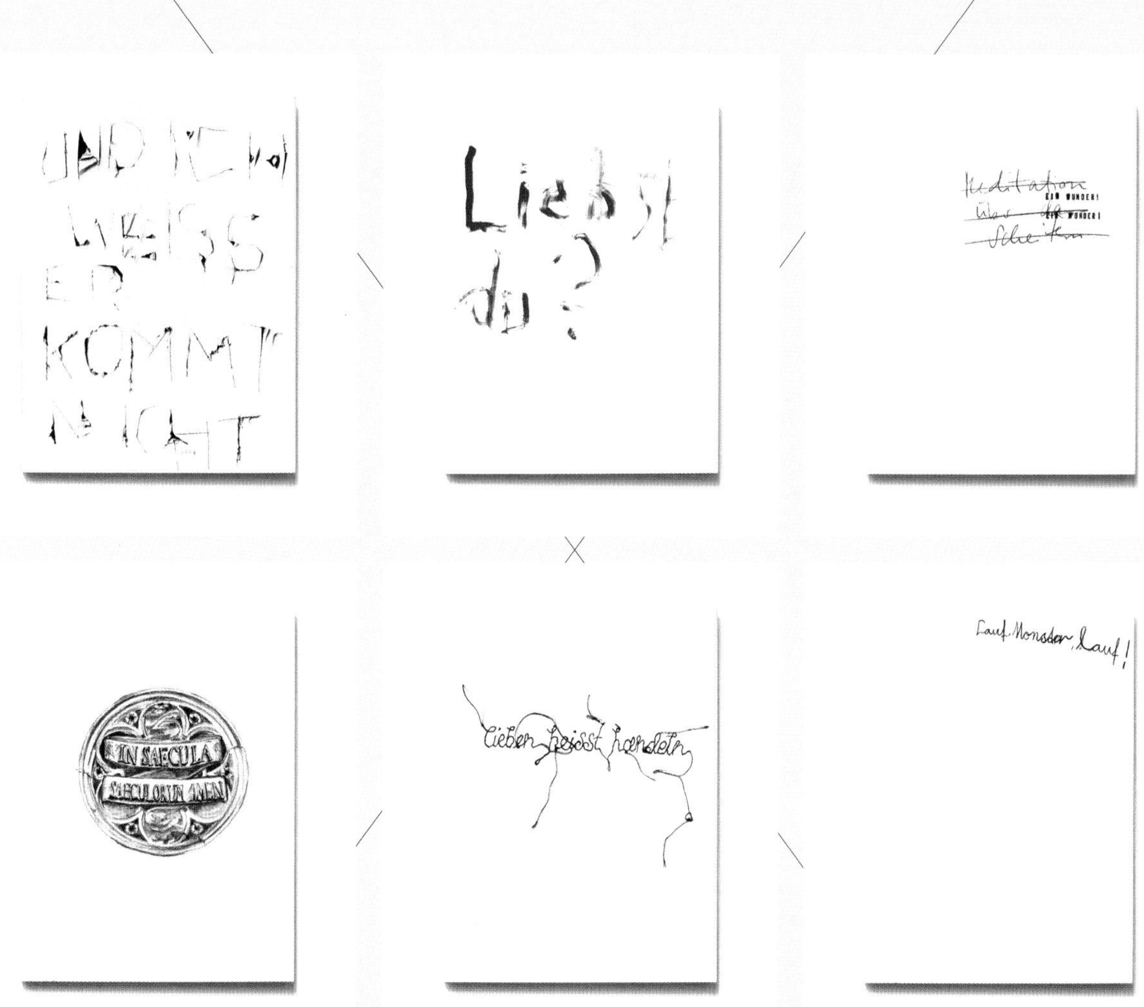

Book Jacket

Design: Florence Chèvre and Giorgio Pesce, Lausanne, Switzerland. Art Direction: Giorgio Pesce. Calligraphy: Giorgio Pesce. Design Office: Atelier Poisson. Client: Editions Cheneau-de-Bourg. Principal Type: Helvetica Neue, Merriam, New Aster, and handlettering. Dimensions: 5.8 x 8.3 in. (14.8 x 21 cm)

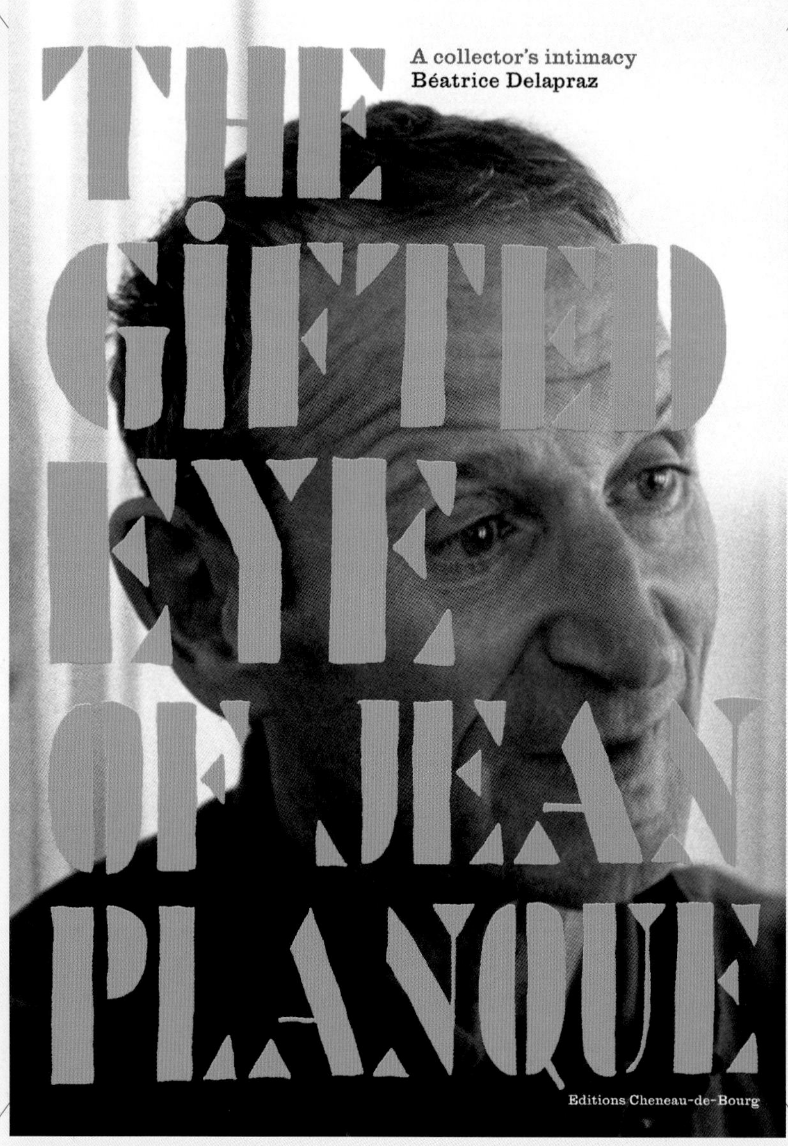

Book Jacket
Design: Stephanie Ising, München, Germany. Creative Direction: Tom Ising and Martin Fengel. Design Office: Herburg Weiland. Client: Kiepenheuer & Witsch Verlag. Principal Type: Poplar. Dimensions: 5.5 x 8.7 in. (14 x 22 cm)

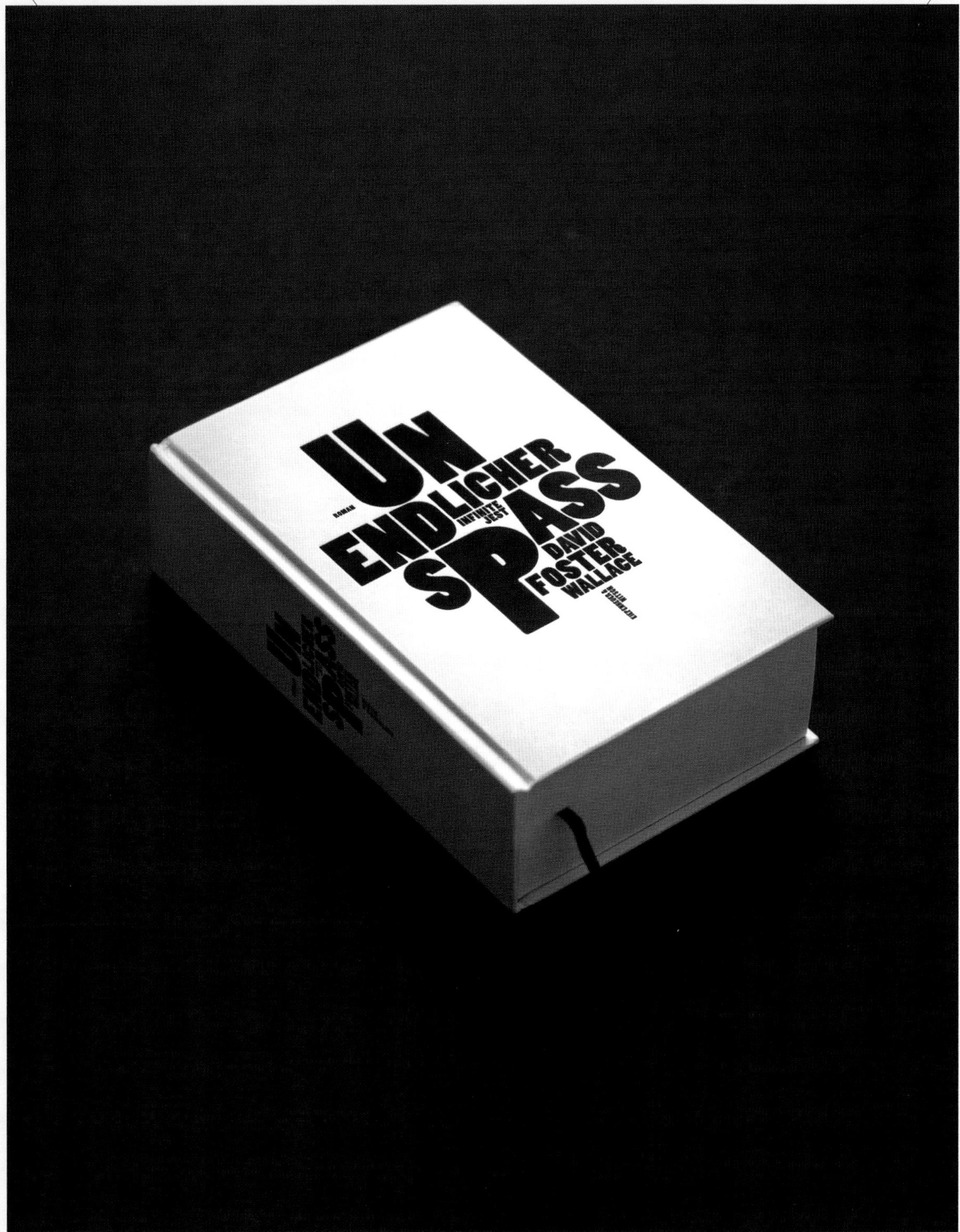

Book Jacket
Design: Roberto de Vicq de Cumptich, New York. Art Direction: Lisa Anoroso. Design Office: de Vicq design. Client: Penguin Press. Principal Type: P22 Kilkenny. Dimensions: 5.6 x 8.5 in. (14.3 x 21.6 cm)

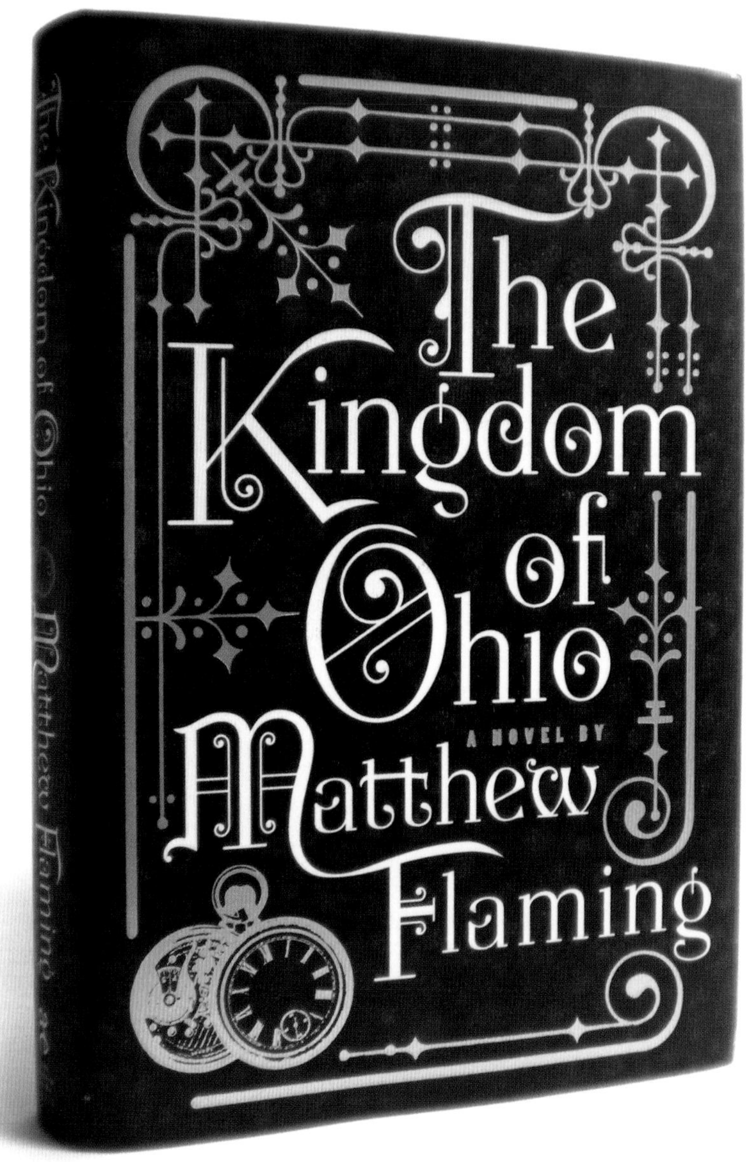

Book Jacket

Design: Michael Bierut and Katie Barcelona, New York. Art Direction: Michael Bierut. Design Office: Pentagram Design, New York. Client: Random House. Principal Type: Swiss 911 and Futura. Dimensions: 5 x 8 in. (12.7 x 20.3 cm)

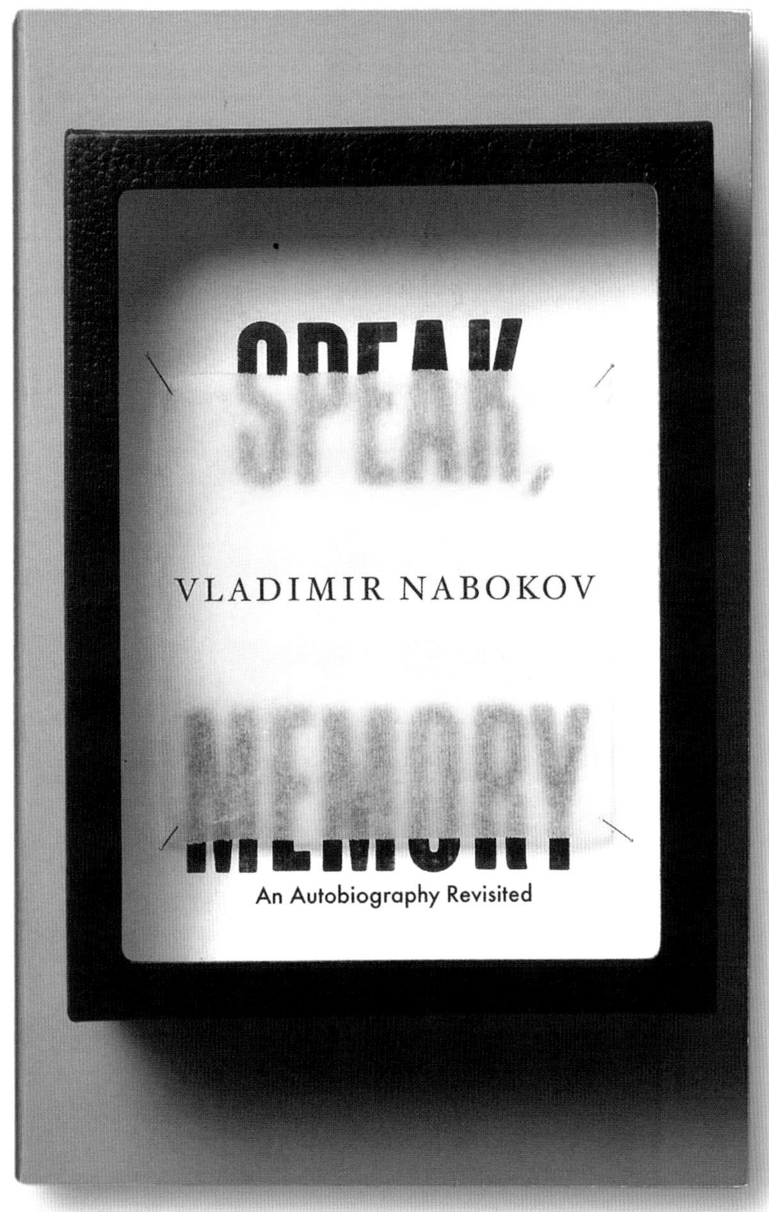

Book Cover
Design: Evan Gaffney, New York. Art Direction: Nicole Caputo. Publisher: Basic Books. Principal Type: Gotham Bold and Adobe Caslon Pro. Dimensions: 5.5 x 8.25 in. (14 x 21 cm)

"Essential reading for people interested in the brain."
—TEMPLE GRANDIN, author of *Thinking in Pictures*

FIXING
MY
GAZE

A SCIENTIST'S JOURNEY into
SEEING in THREE DIMENSIONS

SUSAN R. BARRY

Foreword by OLIVER SACKS

Book

Design: Petra Janssen and Edwin Vollebergh, Den Bosch, Netherlands. Art Direction: Petra Janssen and Edwin Vollebergh. Creative Direction: Petra Janssen and Edwin Vollebergh. Studio: studio Boot. Client: Snor Publishers. Principal Type: Nevermind, Vista Sans, and Vista Slab. Dimensions: 6.7 x 9.1 in. (17 x 23 cm)

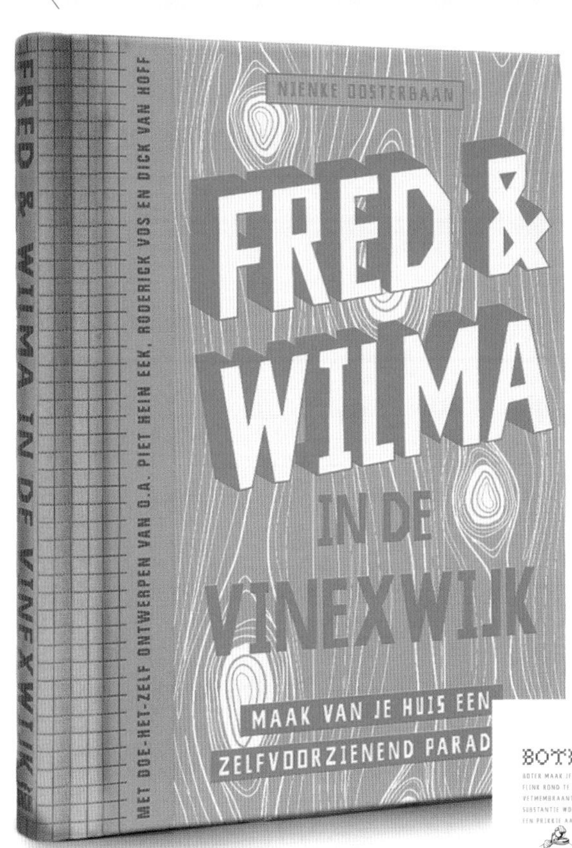

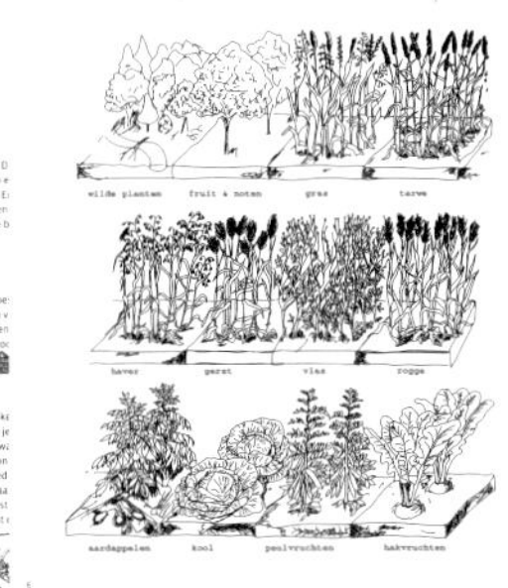

Book

Design: Kathrin Roussel and Jana Aylin Hochmann, Hamburg, Germany. Art Direction: Kathrin Roussel and Jana Aylin Hochmann. Creative Direction: Kathrin Roussel and Jana Aylin Hochmann. Design Office: Hochschule für Bildende Künste, Hamburg. Client: DISKURS 09, Festival for Young Performing Arts. Principal Type: CA Normal. Dimensions: 6.3 x 9.4 in. (16 x 24 cm)

Book

Design: Lars Egert and Jonas Müggler, Zürich, Switzerland; Stefan Fraefel, Zug, Switzerland. Art Direction: Stefan Fraefel, Lars Egert, and Jonas Müggler. Creative Direction: Lars Egert, Stefan Fraefel, and Jonas Müggler. Lettering: Lars Egert. Editor: Pierre Thomé. Publisher: Verlag Niggli. Client: Lucerne University of Applied Sciences and Arts, Illustration Department. Principal Type: DTL Documenta, Monospace 821 BT, and handlettering. Dimensions: 7.9 x 10.4 in. (20 x 26.5 cm)

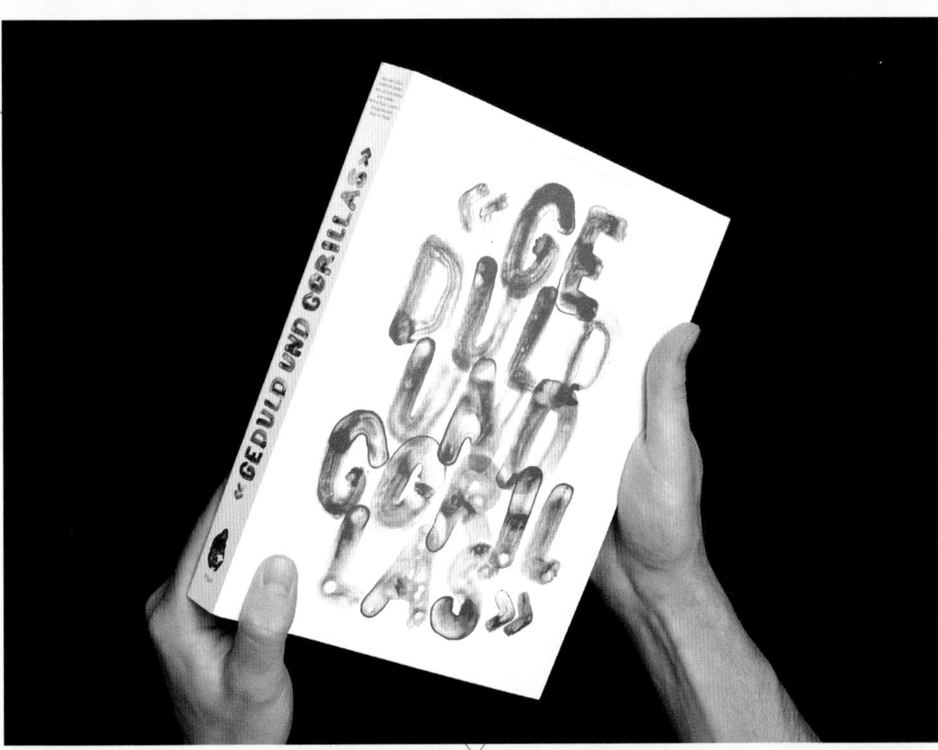

Book

Design: Brandon Downing and Hyun Auh, New York. Art Direction: Emanuela Frigerio. Design Office: C&G Partners. Client: Fence Books. Principal Type: Knockout and Lake Antiquity. Dimensions: 9 x 11 in. (22.9 x 27.9 cm)

Book
Design: Jianping He, Berlin. Art Direction: Jianping He. Creative Direction: Jianping He. Publisher: Hedesign. Principal Type: DIN and Plum BDL. Dimensions: 6.3 x 9.5 in. (16 x 24 cm)

Book

Design: orangetango, Montréal. Printer: Transcontinental Litho Acme. Agency: orangetango. Client: The Montréal Museum of Fine Arts. Principal Type: Arnhem, VT Portable Remington, and wood type. Dimensions: 10 x 12 in. (25.4 x 30.5 cm)

For my nephew Seth Kursman

Crossed Destinies: Manifesting the Paths of Nationhood in the United States and Canada through Landscapes, 1860–1918

Hilliard T. Goldfarb

The years seared at their margins by the experiences of the American Civil War and the First World War witnessed the fulfillment of a transcontinental territorial ambition in the United States that had originated in the early nineteenth century. The fulfillment of this ambition and the changing economic, political and social realities of this epoch fundamentally moulded a sensibility of "American-ness" related to yet quite distinctive from that of the antebellum years, from which a modern national identity emerged. Farther north, events leading to the 1867 Act of Confederation, the integration of territories and provinces into a federal system and a westward expansion (facilitated, as in the United States, by the railroad) also led to changing economic, political and social realities within Canada. The evolution of a more broadly envisioned national identity yet continuing regional tensions, notably among Anglophone, Francophone and Metis constituencies, culminated in the contrasting images of the conflicting and violent domestic reactions to conscription during the First World War between Quebec and the other provinces, and the victory of the Canadian troops at Vimy Ridge. In both countries, regionalism, the powerful assertion of distinct cultural identities and heritages within expanding national frontiers, the mythologizing of history, and the perception and treatment of Native populations were the crucibles through which these national self-consciousnesses were forged.

In the United States, this expansion outward into the North American continent was given conscious expression in the concept of Manifest Destiny, which originally promoted annexation of Texas, the Oregon Territory and territorial appropriations from Mexico, but also encompassed at various historical moments Canada, Mexico itself, Cuba and Central America. The term was coined by the journalist John L. O'Sullivan in 1845, in an article arguing for the annexation of the Republic of Texas. The article, appropriately entitled "Annexation," appeared in the July-August issue of the *United States Magazine and Democratic Review*, of which he was editor. Later that year, in a column that appeared in the December 27 issue of the *New York Morning News*, of which he was also editor, he extended his argument to the Oregon Territory, whose borders were in dispute with the British.

Book

Design: Philipp Hubert, Stuttgart, Germany. Art Direction: Philipp Hubert. Creative Direction: Philipp Hubert. Lettering: Philipp Hubert. Studio: Visiotypen. Principal Type: Champion and handlettering. Dimensions: 11.7 x 16.5 in. (29.7 x 42 cm)

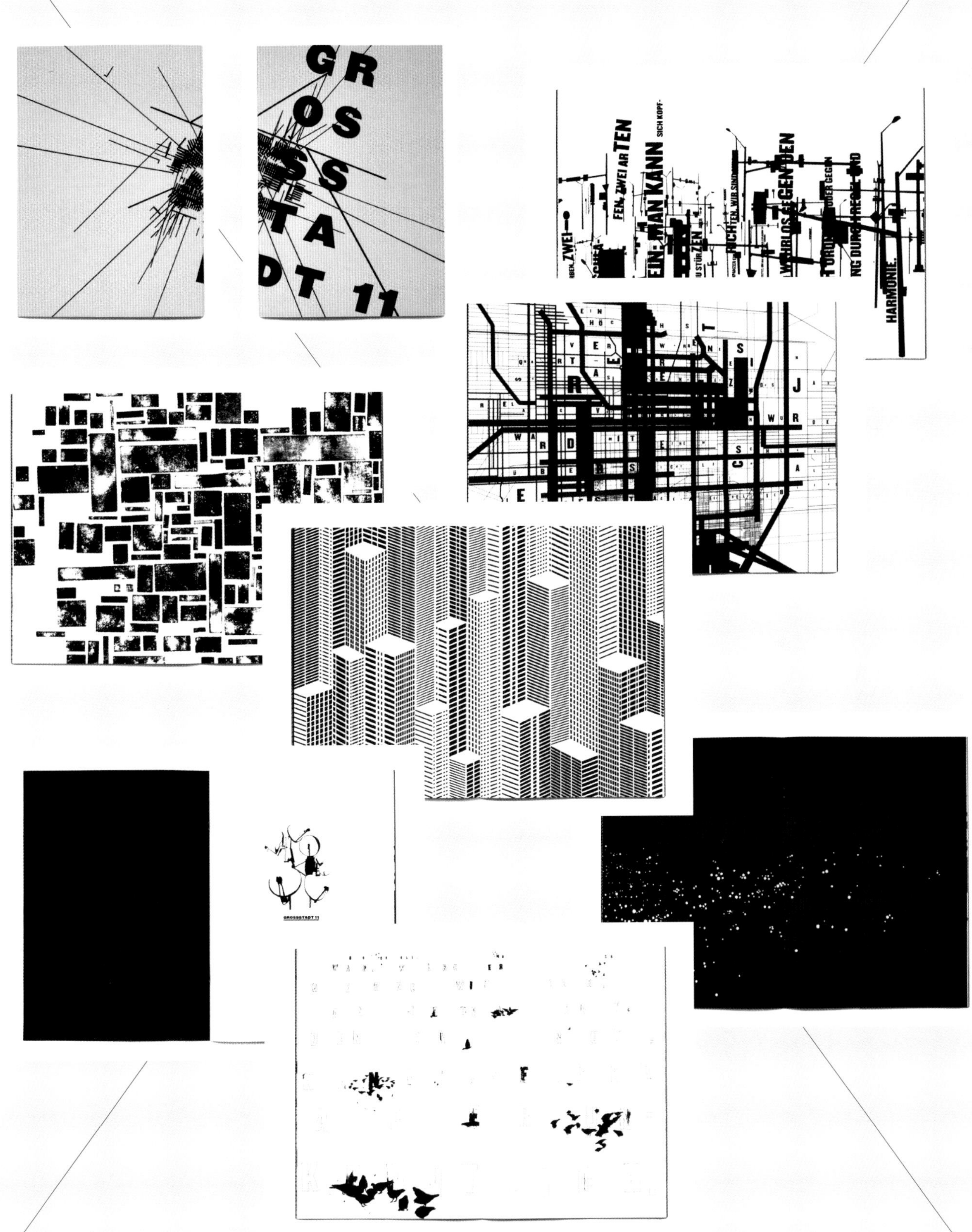

Book

Design: Kuokwai Cheong, Macao, China. Creative Direction: Kuokwai Cheong. Design Office: Cultural Affairs Bureau of the Macao S.A.R. Government. Client: The Macao Orchestra. Principal Type: Courier New and HeiHK W5. Dimensions: 7.3 x 11.6 in. (18.5 x 29.5 cm)

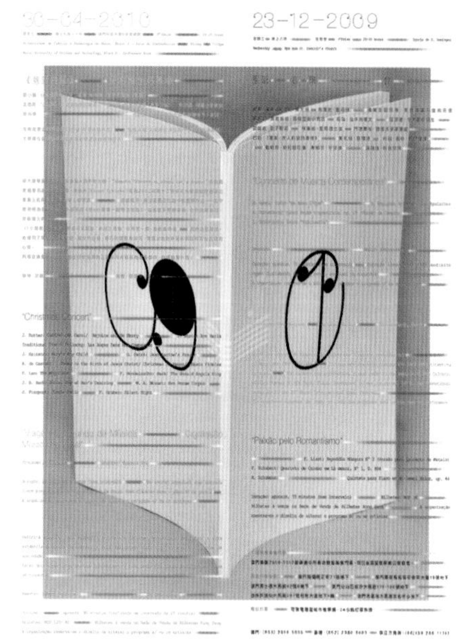

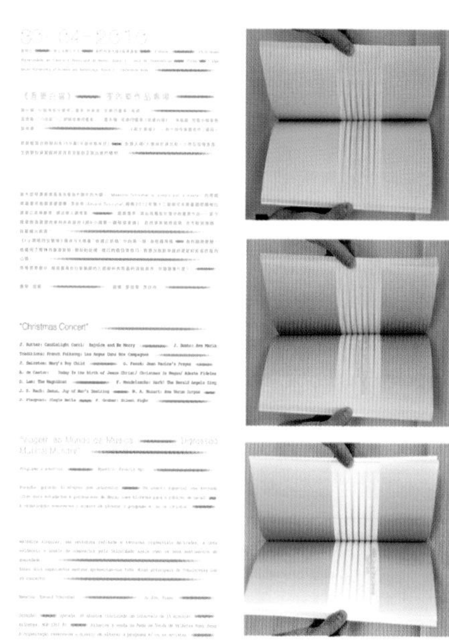

Book
Design: Judith Poirier, Montréal. Principal Type: FF Quadraat and various letterpress. Dimensions: 5.8 x 8.9 in. (14.8 x 22.6 cm)

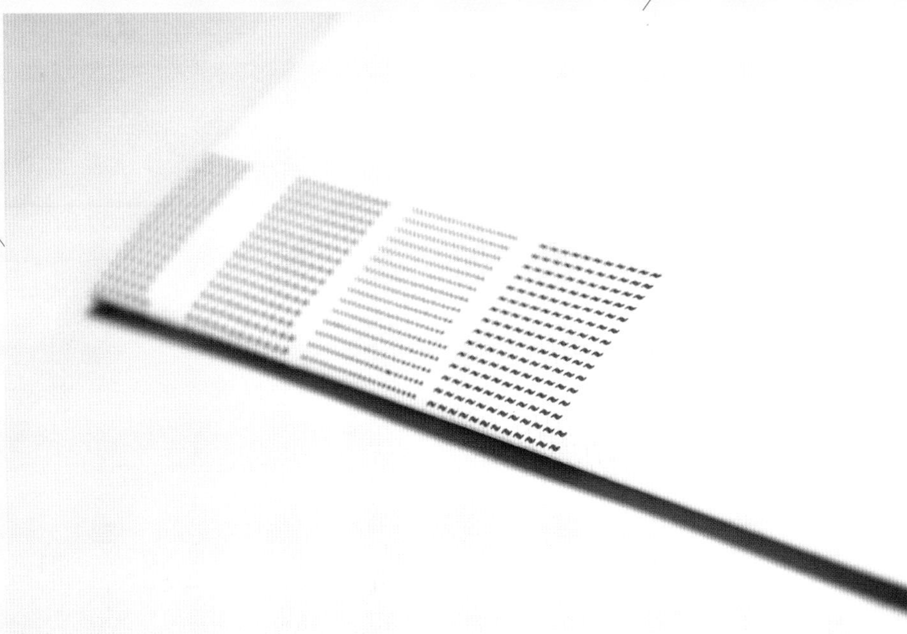

Book

Design: Joep Pohlen, Roermond, Netherlands. Art Direction: Joep Pohlen. Creative Direction: Joep Pohlen. Illustration: Joep Pohlen. Design Office: Polka Design. Client: Fontana Publishers. Principal Type: FF Profile and Interstate. Dimensions: 7.1 x 9.6 in. (18 x 24.5 cm)

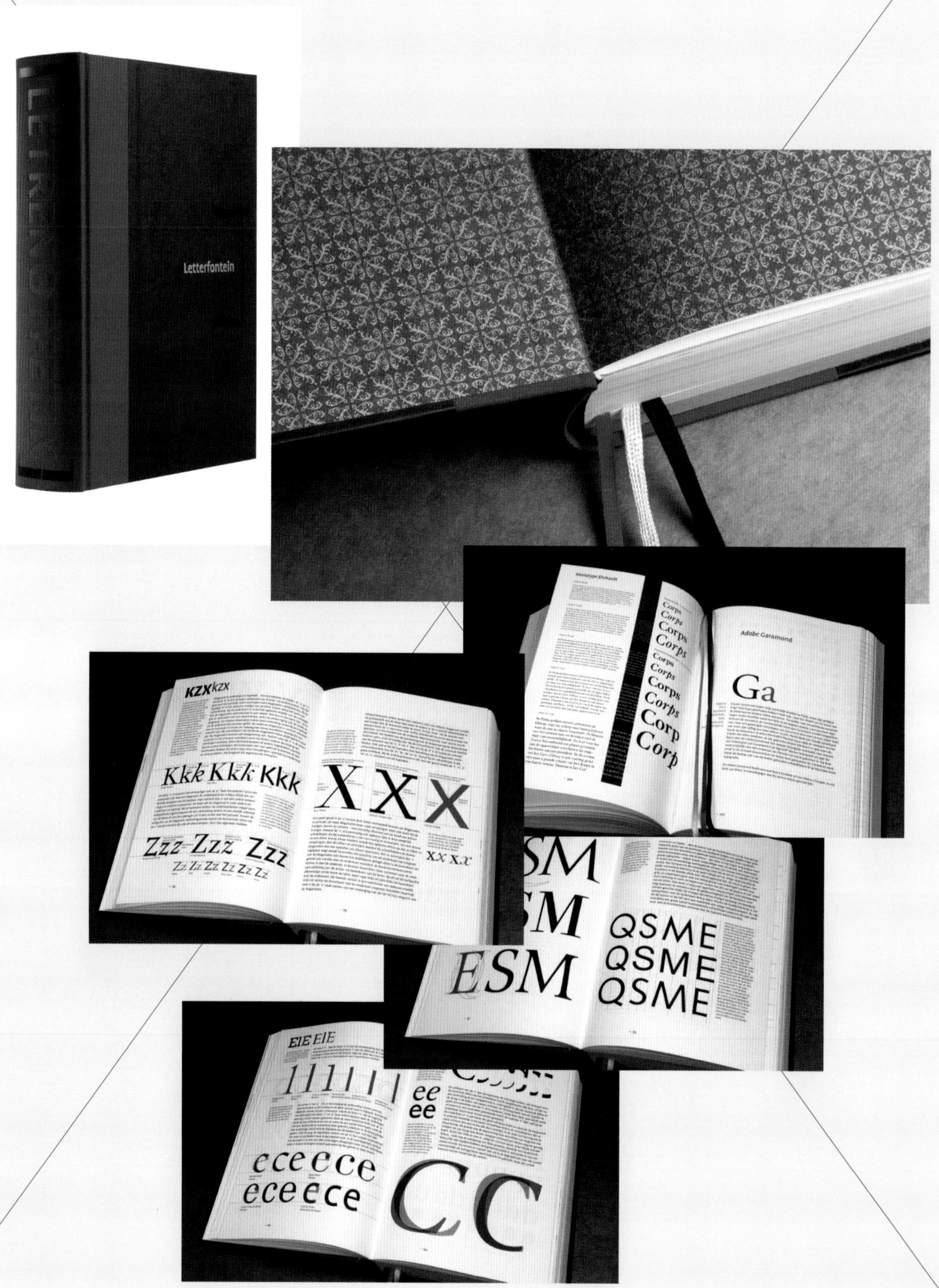

Book

Design: David Jury, Colchester, England. Art Direction: David Jury. Creative Direction: David Jury. Photography: Douglas Sandberg, San Francisco. Studio: Fox Ash. Client: The CODEX Foundation. Principal Type: Adobe Caslon. Dimensions: 9 x 12 in. (22.9 x 30.5 cm)

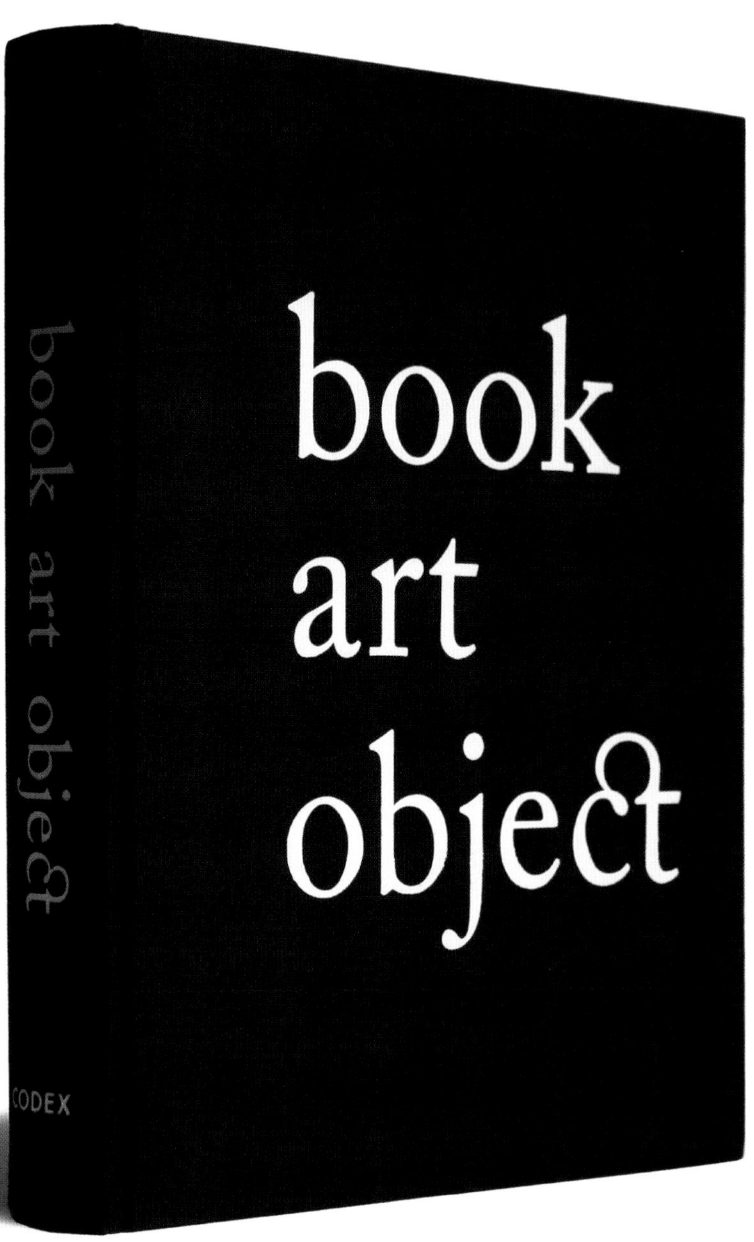

Book

Design: Paul Shaw and Abby Goldstein, New York. Design Office: Paul Shaw Letter Design. Client: Blue Pencil Editions. Principal Type: AG Old Face and Monotype Grotesque. Dimensions: 11.25 x 9.7 in. (28.6 x 24.8 cm)

Book

Design: Steven Jockisch, New York. Art Direction: Steven Jockisch and Giona Lodigiani. Creative Direction: Matteo Bologna. Lettering: Steven Jockisch. Design Office: Mucca Design. Client: Biblioteca Universale Rizzoli (BUR). Principal Type: handlettering. Dimensions: 7.1 x 9.4 in. (18 x 24 cm)

Student Project

Design: Howard Brawidjaya, Chris Lack, Kamil Markowski, Geminesse Padamada, Kate Peters, and Marshall Rake, Pasadena, California. School: Art Center College of Design, Pasadena. Instructor: Lisa Wagner. Principal Type: Arnhem and EF TVNord. Dimensions: 17.5 x 22.75 in. (51.1 x 57.8 cm)

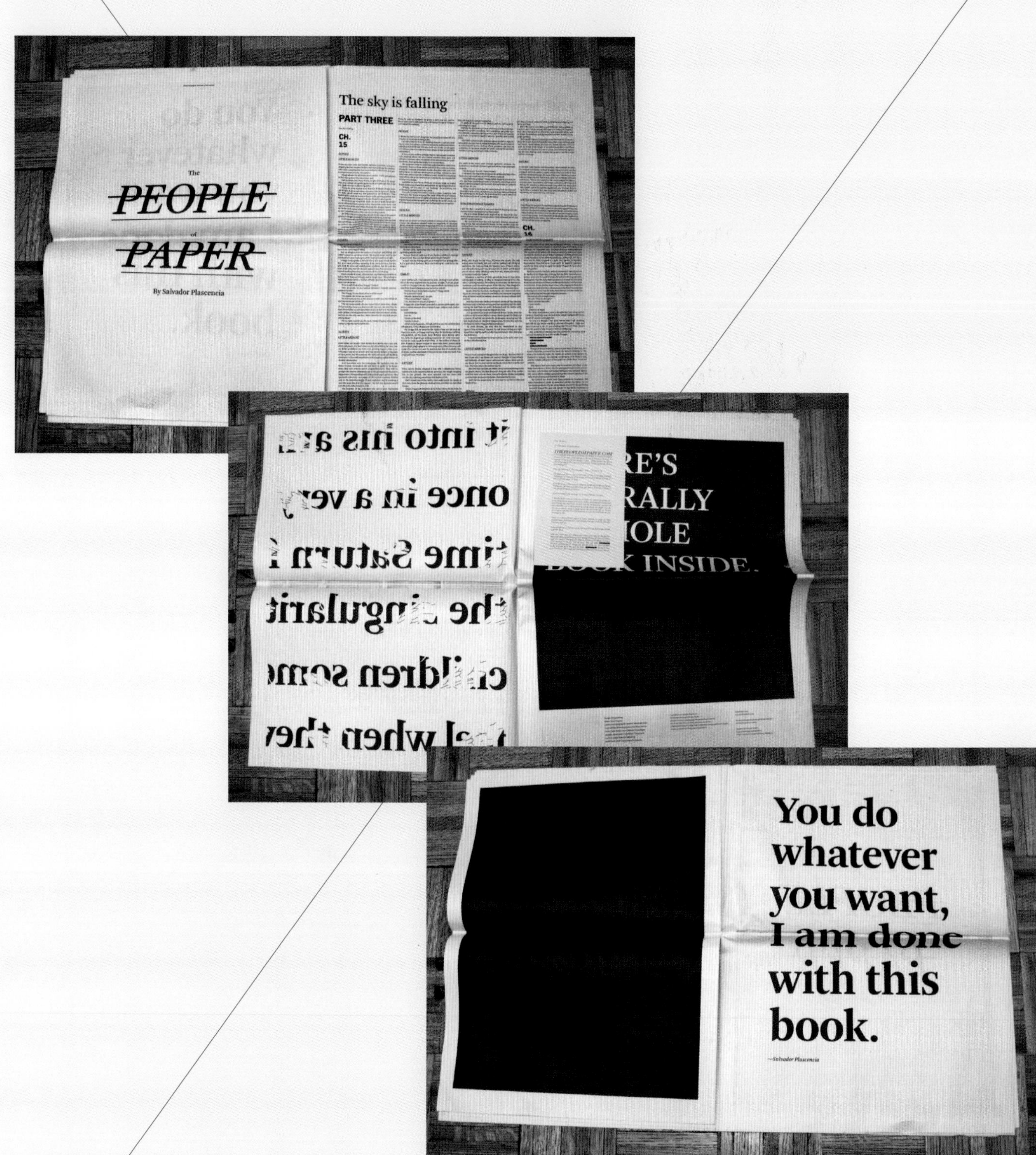

Catalog

Design: Toby Curnow, Max Lozach, and Tony Proffit, Auckland, New Zealand. Creative Direction: Dean Poole. Lettering: Dean Poole. Photography: Alistair Guthrie. Studio: Alt Group. Client: Oakfield Press. Principal Type: Futura and handlettering. Dimensions: 13.1 x 7.3 in. (33.2 x 18.5 cm)

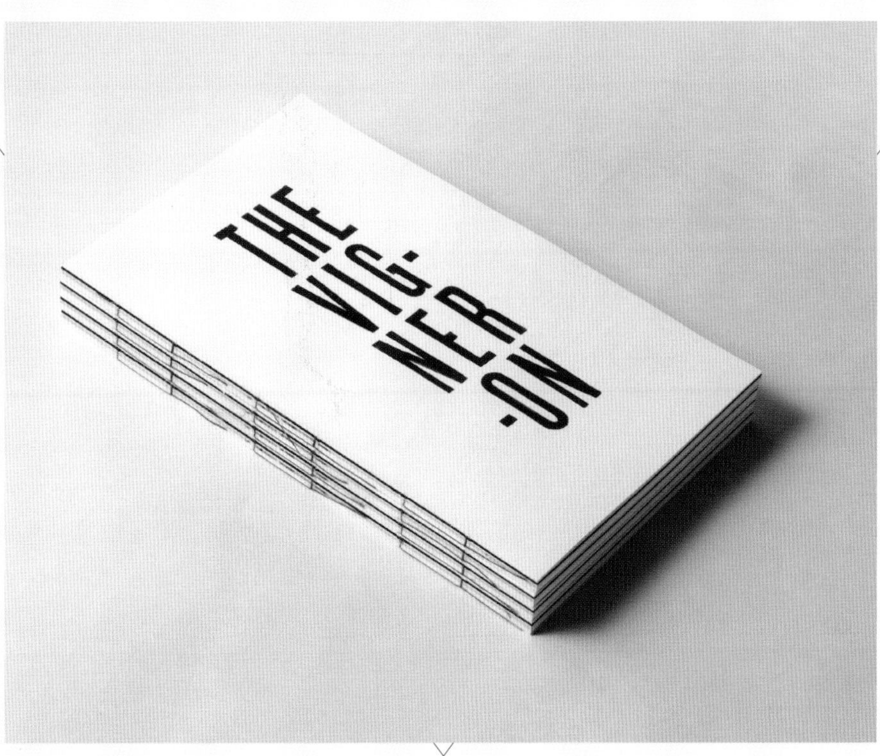

Book
Design: Björn Schwefer, Wuppertal, Germany. Design Office: Boros. Client: DuMont Buchverlag, Köln, Germany. Principal Type: Helvetica. Dimensions: 9.4 x 12.6 in. (24 x 32 cm)

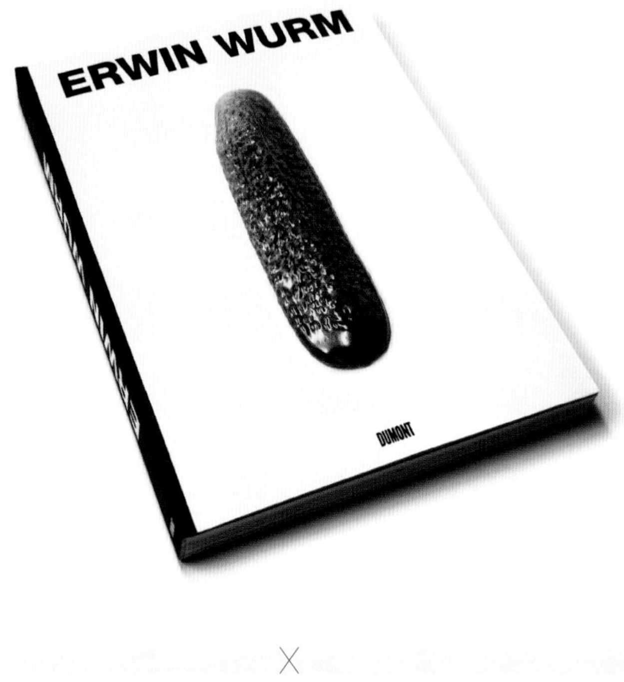

Book
Design: Rita Carvalho, Andrew Howard, and Pedro Pina, Porto, Portugal. Creative Direction: Andrew Howard. Design Office: Studio Andrew Howard. Client: Galeria Municipal de Matosinhos. Principal Type: Akkurat and Jigsaw Stencil. Dimensions: 9.4 x 13.4 in. (24 x 34 cm)

Book

Design: Pieter van Rosmalen, Den Haag, Netherlands. Art Direction: Pieter van Rosmalen. Creative Direction: Pieter van Rosmalen. Design Office: CakeLab. Principal Type: Capibara Classic. Dimensions: 2.4 x 3.1 in. (5.7 x 8 cm)

Books

Design: Veronika Kinczli, München, Germany. Art Direction: Nils Jaedicke. Creative Direction: Annette Häfelinger. Lettering: Nils Jaedicke and Veronika Kinczli. Agency: häfelinger + wagner design. Principal Type: FF Schulbuch Nord, T-STAR Mone Round, and handlettering. Dimensions: large, 8.3 x 10.6 in. (21 x 27 cm); small, 6.1 x 8.3 in. (15.4 x 21 cm)

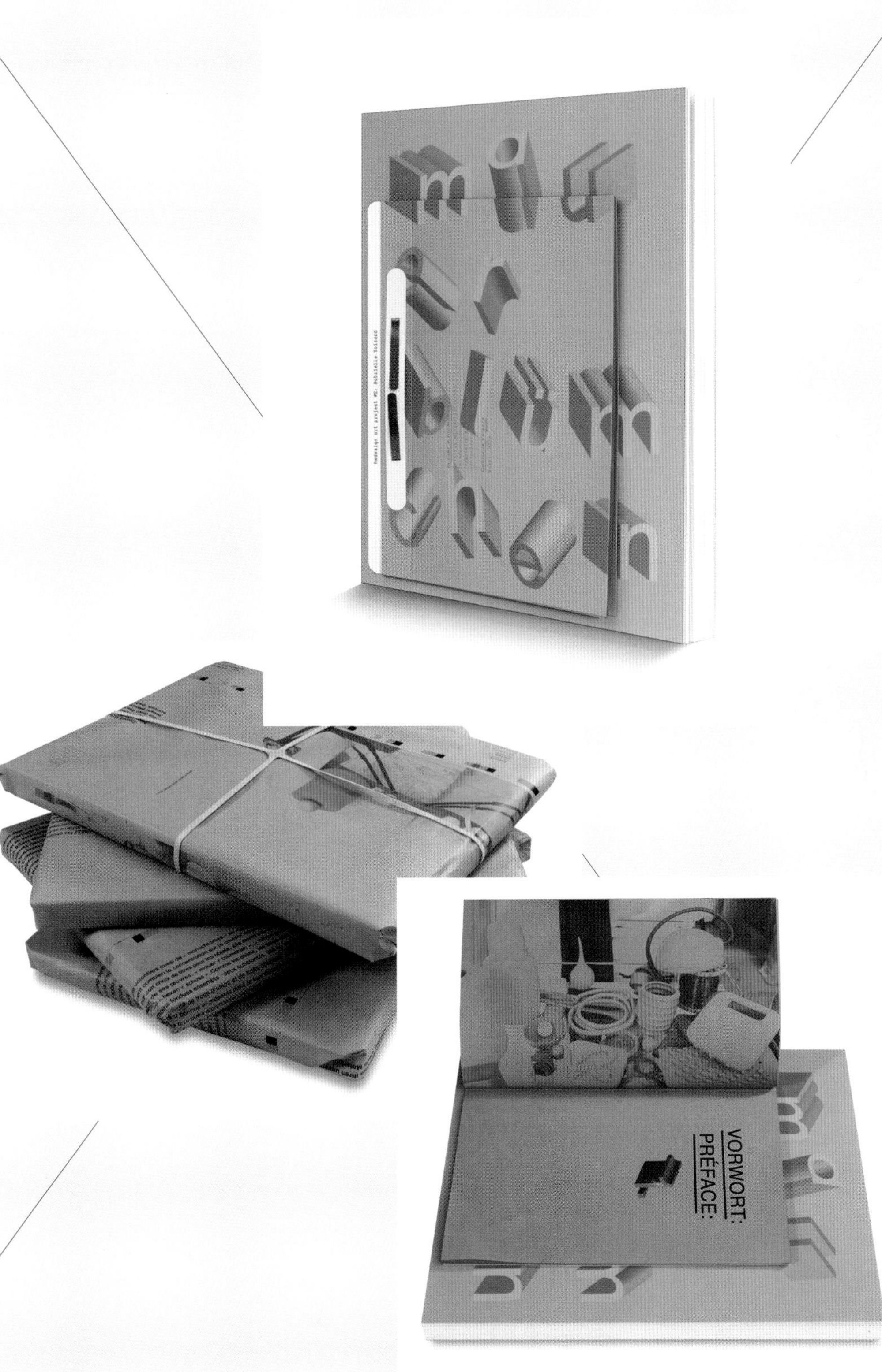

Design: Janice Christie, Scott Christie, Steve Garwood, Sascha Hass, Kevin Hoch, Liam Johnstone, Brian Marchand, Colin Payson, and Robin Smyth, Toronto. Lettering: Hanna Chen. Design Office: Pylon. Principal Type: handlettering. Dimensions: 24 x 22.75 in. (61 x 57.8 cm)

Exhibition
Design: Inva Cota, New York. Art Direction: Ingrid Chou. Creative Direction: Julia Hoffmann. Lettering: Inva Cota. Museum: The Museum of Modern Art (MoMA), Department of Advertising and Graphic Design. Principal Type: Galaxy Polaris and handlettering. Dimensions: various

Posters and Flyers

Design: António Silveira Gomes, Lisboa. Lettering: R. Stevie Moore, M.A. Santos, and Anonymous. Design Office: Barbara Says... Client: OPORTO. Principal Type: Sailor Gothic. Dimensions: posters, 24.4 x 26.4 in. (57 x 67 cm); flyers, various

Brand Identity
Design: Alessandro Argentato and Johannes Herrmann, Hamburg, Germany. Art Direction: Alessandro Argentato and Tom Leifer. Creative Direction: Tom Leifer Photography. Frank Hülsbömer. Agency: Tom Leifer Design. Principal Type: Corporate S. Dimensions: various

Poster and Invitation

Design: Sascha Lobe and Oliver Wörle, Stuttgart, Germany. Creative Direction: Sascha Lobe. Design Office: L2M3 Kommunikationsdesign. Client: Schmuckmuseum Pforzheim. Principal Type: Simple (modified). Dimensions: poster, 23.4 x 33.1 in. (59.4 x 84.1 cm); flyer, 5.8 x 8.3 in. (14.8 x 21 cm); invitation, 4.1 x 5.8 in. (10.5 x 14.8 cm)

Exhibition Collaterals

Design: Jody Work and Jörg Becker, Chicago. Design Office: Products of Poetry. Client: Studio 1 a.m. Principal Type: Utopia Std. Dimensions: wall graphics, 540 x 96 in. (13.7 x 2.4 m); catalog, 38 x 25 in. (96.5 x 63.5 cm)

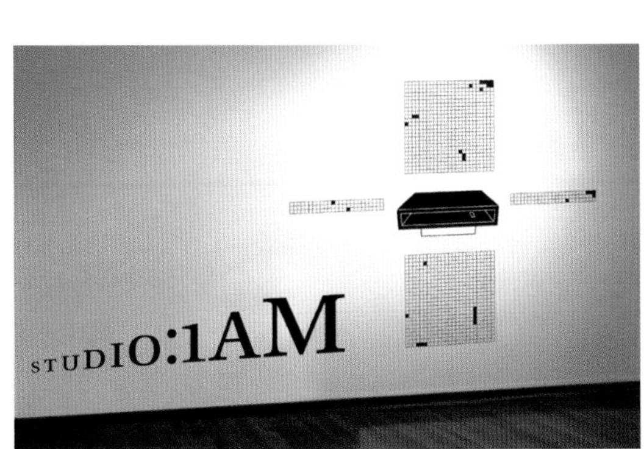

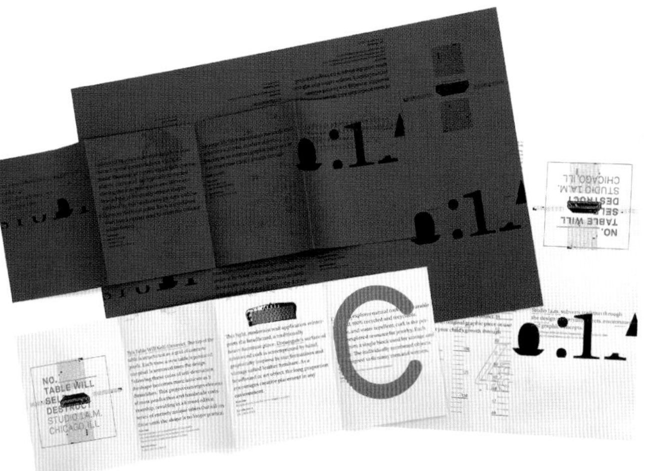

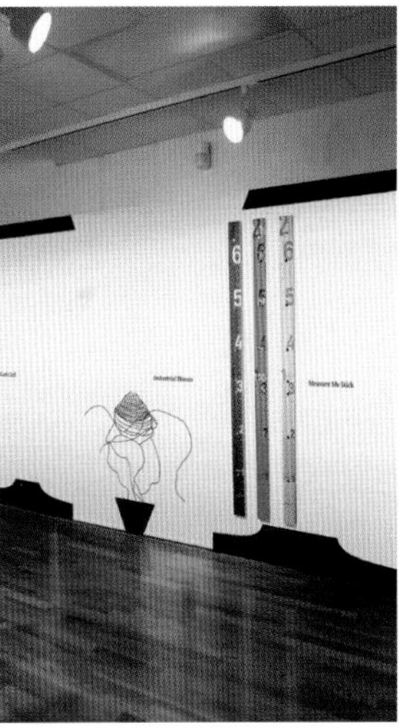

Exhibition

Design: Samuel Sherman, New York. Art Direction: August Heffner and Brigitta Bungard. Creative Direction: Julia Hoffmann. Lettering: August Heffner. Museum: The Museum of Modern Art (MoMA), Department of Advertising and Graphic Design. Principal Type: Knockout and handlettering. Dimensions: various

Design: Ena Cardenal de la Nuez, Madrid. Preprint: Cromotex. Client: Casa Africa. Principal Type: various. Dimensions: various

Posters

Art Direction: Harry Pearce, London. Design Office: Pentagram London. Client: United Nations Office on Drugs and Crime (UNODC). Principal Type: Berthold Akzidenz Grotesk Super. Dimensions: 23.2 x 33.1 in. (59 x 84 cm)

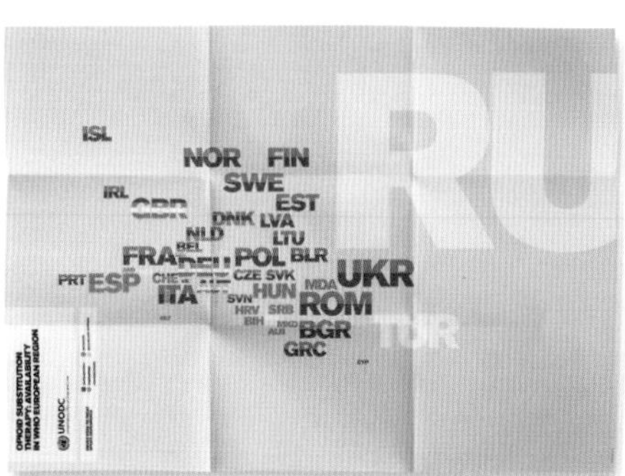

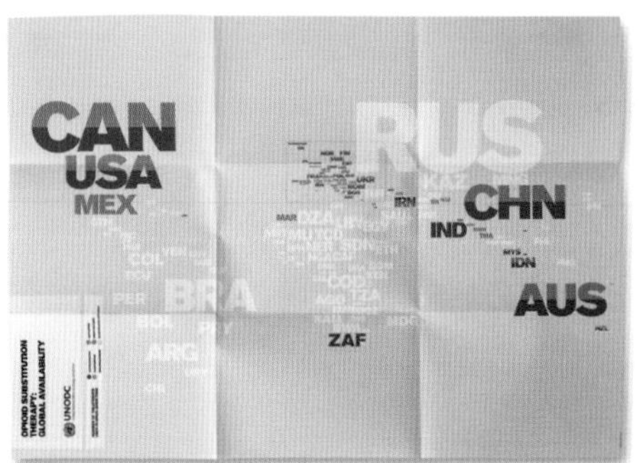

Catalog

Design: Juanma Aznar, Ricardo Cañizares, and Pepe Gimeno, Valencia, Spain. Creative Direction: Pepe Gimeno. Photography: Caparrós Comunicación. Studio: Pepe Gimeno—Proyecto Gráfico. Principal Type: Univers and FB Garamond. Dimensions: 5.9 x 8.3 in. (15 x 21 cm)

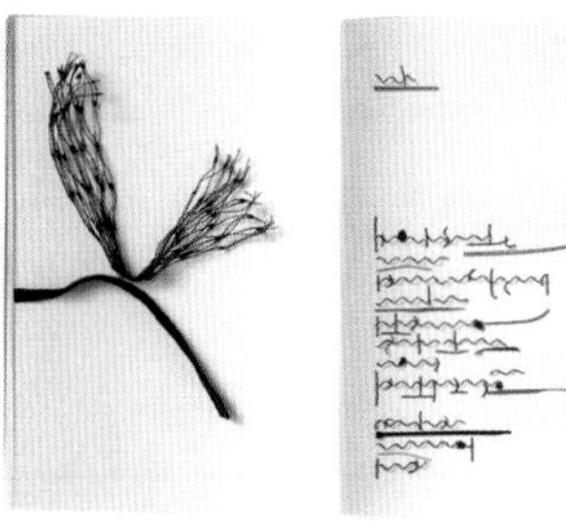

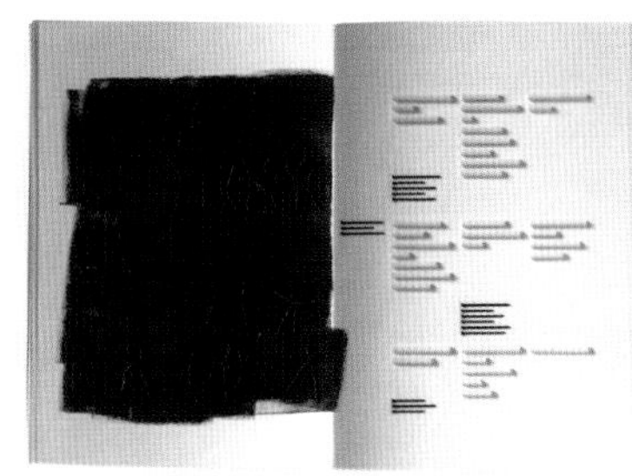

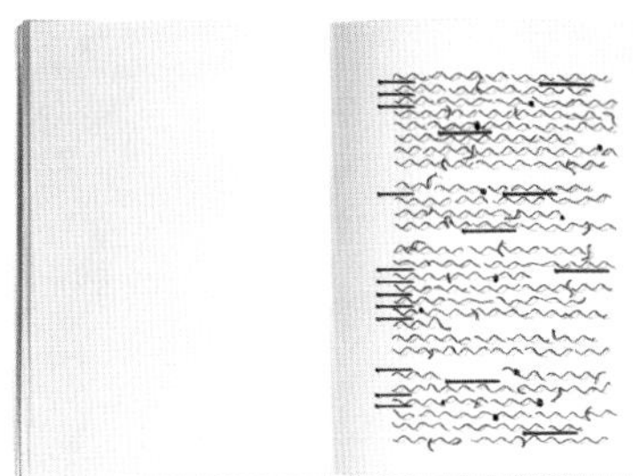

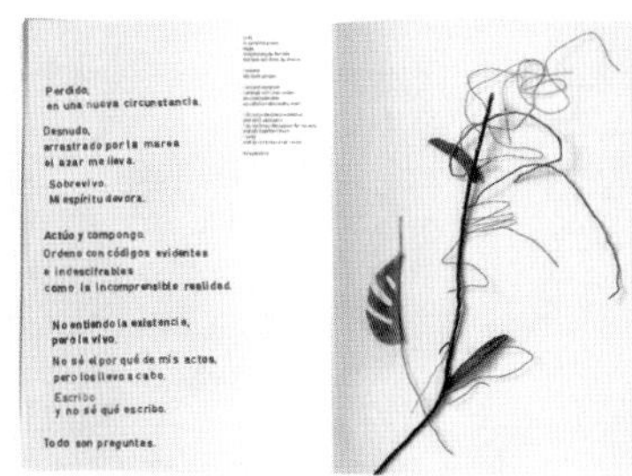

Catalog

Design: Kum-jun Park and Na-won You, Seoul, South Korea. Art Direction: Kum-jun Park. Creative Direction: Kum-jun Park. Photography: Ok-hee Cho. Illustration: Soo-hwan Kim. Coordination: Jong-in Jung. Studio: 601bisang. Principal Type: various. Dimensions: 8.3 x 16.6 in. (21 x 27 cm)

Annual Report

Design: Jason Miller, New York. Art Direction: Jason Miller. Creative Direction: Richard Colbourne. Design Office: Addison. Client: Neenah Paper. Principal Type: Avenir and custom. Dimensions: 8.5 x 11 in. (21.6 x 27.9 cm)

Annual Report
Design: Hugo Goeldner and Martin Christel, Berlin. Design Office: Codeluxe/CDLX. Principal Type: Meta and Meta Serif.
Dimensions: 9.9 x 14.6 in. (25.2 x 37 cm)

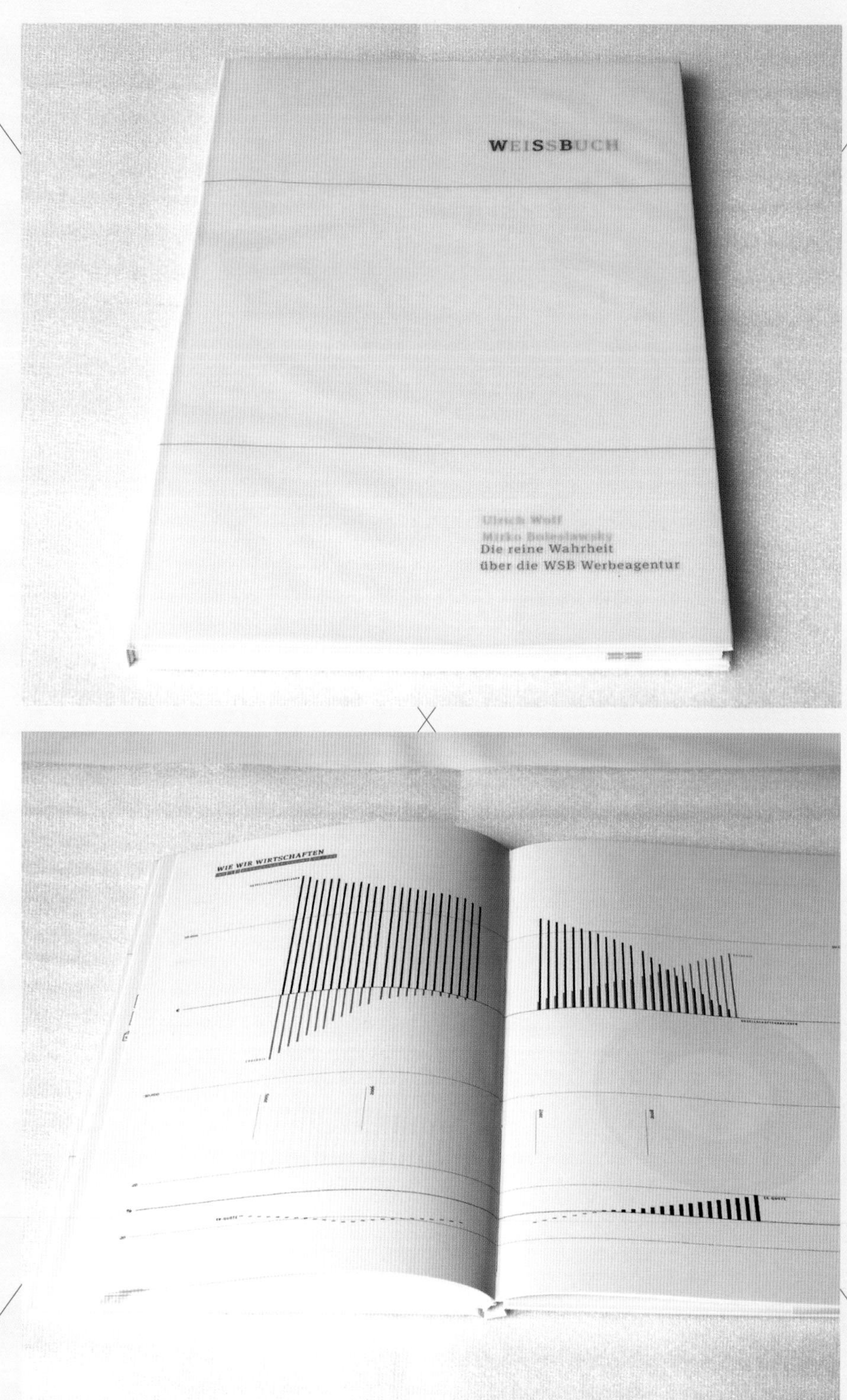

Catalog

Design: Dirk Heine and Cord Warnecke, Hannover, Germany. Art Direction: Dirk Heine. Creative Direction: Dirk Heine. Design Office: Heine Warnecke Design. Client: A.Viani Importe. Principal Type: Filosofia and FTF Morgan Avec. Dimensions: 8.3 x 11 in. (21 x 28 cm)

Catalog
Design: Nicole Jacek, New York. Art Direction: Nicole Jacek. Photography: Jonty Wilde and Ben Blacknell. Illustration and Lettering: Sarah Staton. Production: Darren Pascoe, &coe. Studio: Nicole Jacek™. Client: The Lowry. Principal Type: Baukloetze, FS Sophie, and handlettering. Dimensions: 8.3 x 11.7 in. (21 x 29.7 cm)

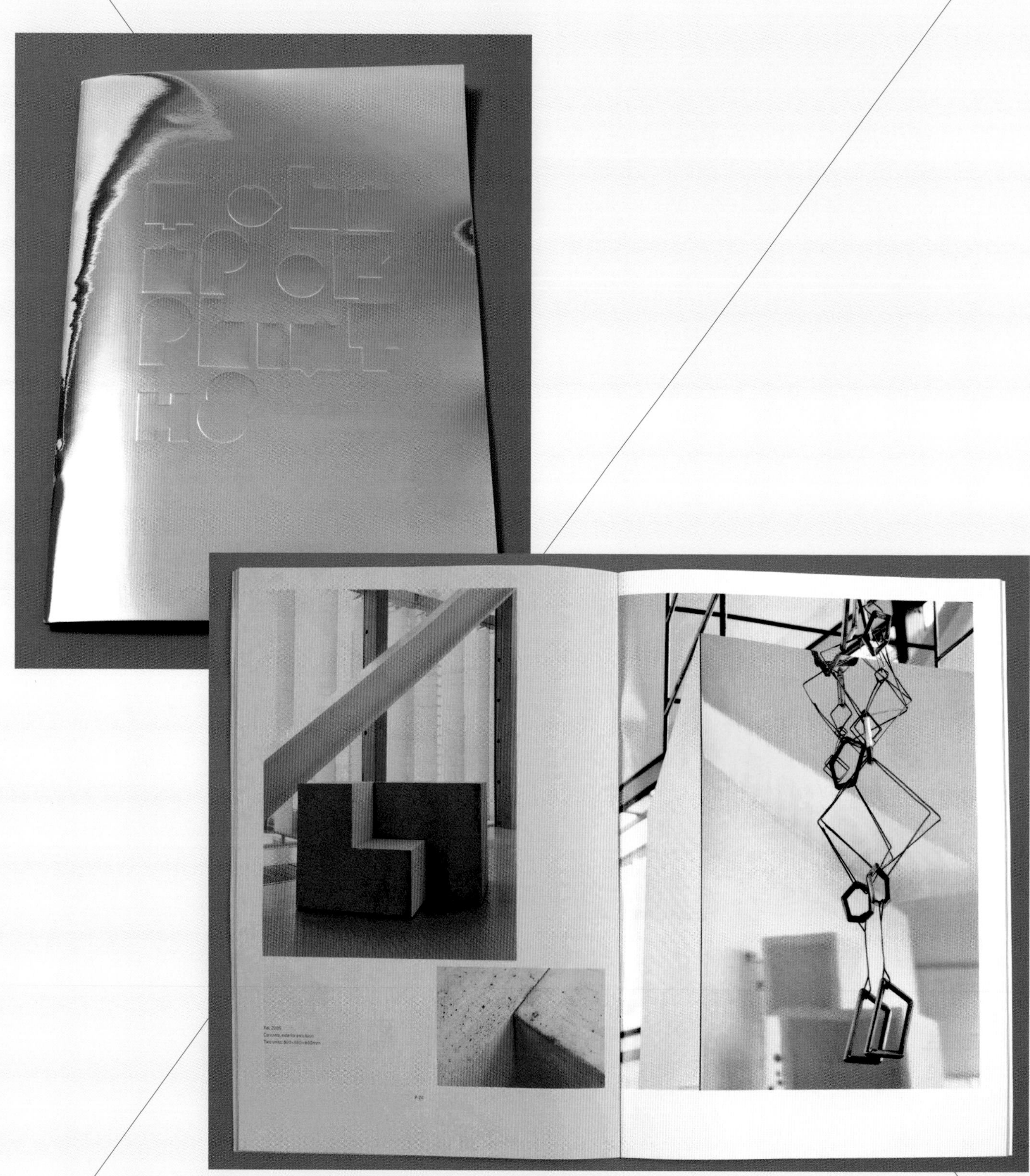

Catalog

Design: Anders Bergesen, Filtvet, Norway; Arne Schneider, Stuttgart, Germany. Studio: Studio Bergesen. Client: Stuttgart State Academy of Art and Design, Department of Industrial Design. Principal Type: Cholla Sans and Adobe Caslon. Dimensions: 8.3 x 10.6 in. (21 x 27 cm)

Annual Report

Design: Tim Bruce and Emilia Klimiuk, Chicago. Creative Direction: Tim Bruce. Calligraphy: Emilia Klimiuk. Photography: Tony Armour. Design Office: LOWERCASE. Client: Chicago Volunteer Legal Services. Principal Type: Trade Gothic and handlettering. Dimensions: 7.5 x 9 in. (19.1 x 22.9 cm)

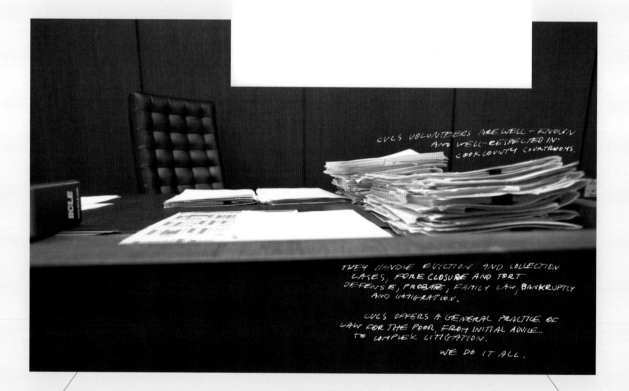

Poster

Design: emerystudio, Southbank, Australia. Art Direction: emerystudio. Creative Direction: emerystudio. Design Office: emerystudio. Client: Australian Department of the Premier and Cabinet. Principal Type: custom. Dimensions: 16.5 x 23.4 in. (42 x 59.4 cm)

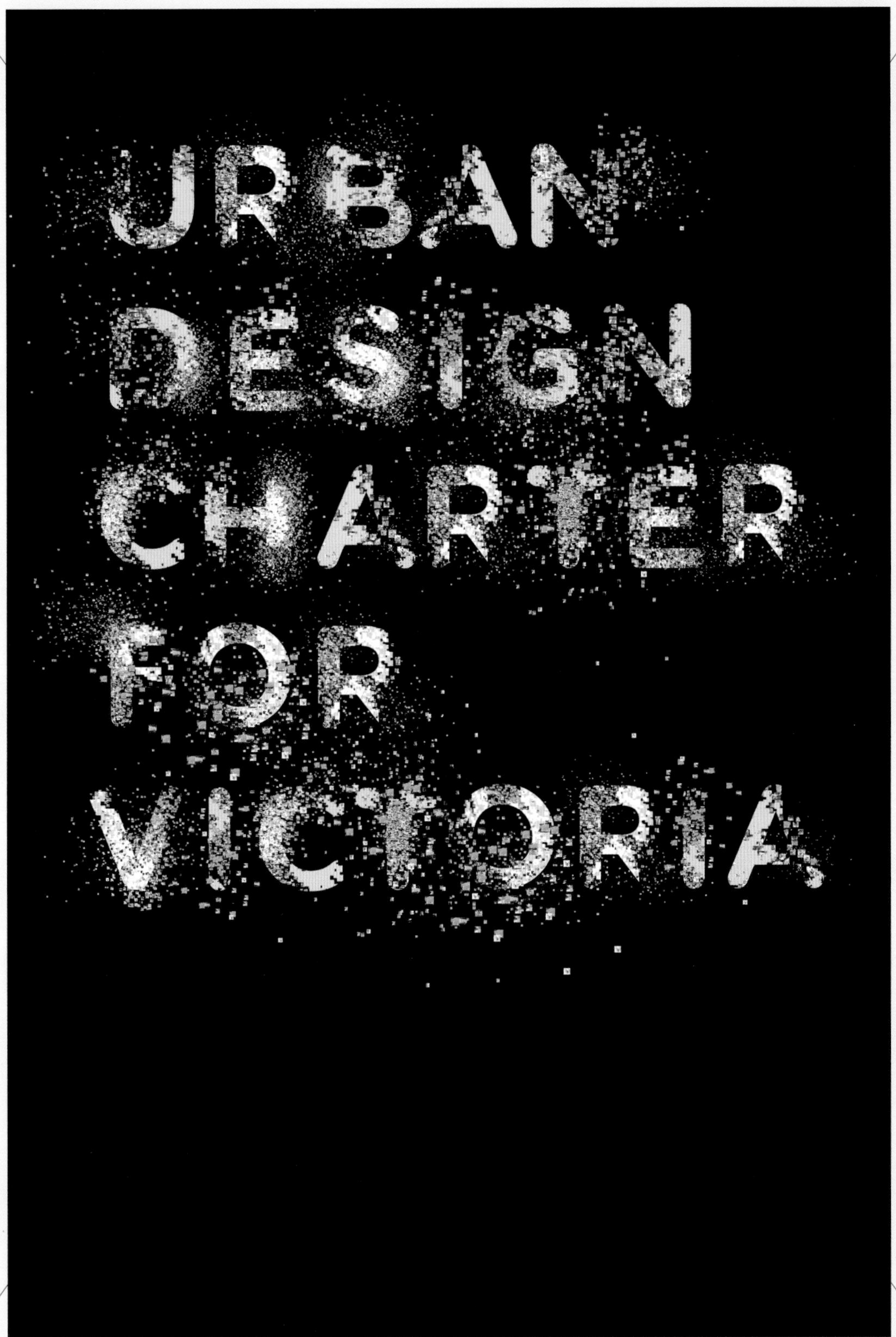

Newspaper

Design: Julia Fuchs, Berlin. Art Direction: Julia Fuchs. Creative Direction: Bastian von Lehsten. Agency: Novamondo Design. Client: Netzwerk Neue Musik. Principal Type: Gotham Rounded and Garamont Amsterdam. Dimensions: 12.4 x 18.5 in. (31.5 x 47 cm)

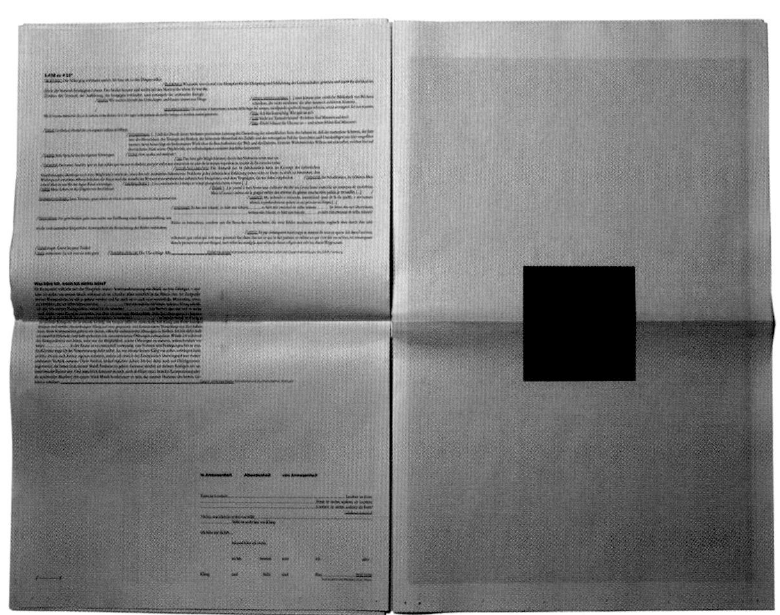

Annual Report

Design: Sucha Becky, Washington, DC. Art Direction: Pum Lefebure. Creative Direction: Pum Lefebure and Jake Lefebure. Design Office: Design Army. Client: Human Rights Campaign. Principal Type: Swiss 721 BT. Dimensions: self-mailer, 9 x 12 in. (22.9 x 30.5 cm); flat, 12 x 18 in. (30.5 x 45.7 cm)

Annual Report

Design: René Clément, Montréal. Art Direction: René Clément. Creative Direction: Louis Gagnon. Photography: Monic Richard and Raphaël Helle. Copywriting: Lefebvre Financial Communications. Studio: Paprika. Client: Boralex. Principal Type: Helvetica Neue. Dimensions: 9.5 x 13 in. (23.6 x 27.9 cm)

Annual Report

Design: Sébastien Bisson, Montréal. Art Direction: René Clément. Creative Direction: Louis Gagnon. Photography: Marcel Lefebvre, Martin Morissette, Sylvie-Diane Rhéault, Monic Richard, and Guillaume Simoneau. Copywriting: Cascades Communication Department. Studio: Paprika. Client: Boralex. Principal Type: Franklin Gothic. Dimensions: 9 x 12 in. (22.9 x 30.5 cm)

Event Publication

Design: Filipe Cergueira, Oscar Maia, Alvaro Martino, and Joáo Martino, Porto, Portugal. Art Direction: Joáo Martino and Alejandro Jaña. Creative Direction: Joáo Martino and Alejandro Jaña. Lettering: Oscar Maia. Studio: Atelier Martino & Jaña. Client: Centro Cultural Vila Flor . Principal Type: Federal (modified), Swift, and United. Dimensions: 14.4 x 16.5 in. (29 x 42 cm)

Catalog
Design: Pia Bardesono, Martin Drozdowski, and Susanne Wagner, Stuttgart, Germany. Creative Direction: Professor Uli Cluss and Oliver A. Krimmel. Design Office: i_d buero + cluss. Client: Galerie Stihl Waiblingen. Dimensions: 10 x 14 in. (25.5 x 35.5 cm)

Magazine Spread

Design: Siung Tjia, New York. Art Direction: Siung Tjia. Creative Direction: Siung Tjia. Publication: *ESPN The Magazine*.
Principal Type: FTF Morgan Avec. Dimensions: 20 x 12 in. (50.8 x 30.5 cm)

NFL PREVIEW 2009

WELL

CONNECTED

BY ALAN GRANT

FAVRE'S A VIKING, VICK'S AN EAGLE AND THE RAMS HAVE HOPE. BUT THE OFF-SEASON'S BIGGEST CHANGES HAPPENED IN INDY. NOT THAT JEFF SATURDAY AND PEYTON MANNING ARE WORRIED. THEY'VE STILL GOT EACH OTHER.

PHOTOGRAPH BY CHRISTOPHER GRIFFITH

55

Magazine Spread

Design: Edward Leida, New York. Design Direction: Edward Leida. Lettering: Edward Leida. Publication: *W* magazine. Principal Type: handlettering. Dimensions: 20 x 13 in. (50.8 x 33 cm)

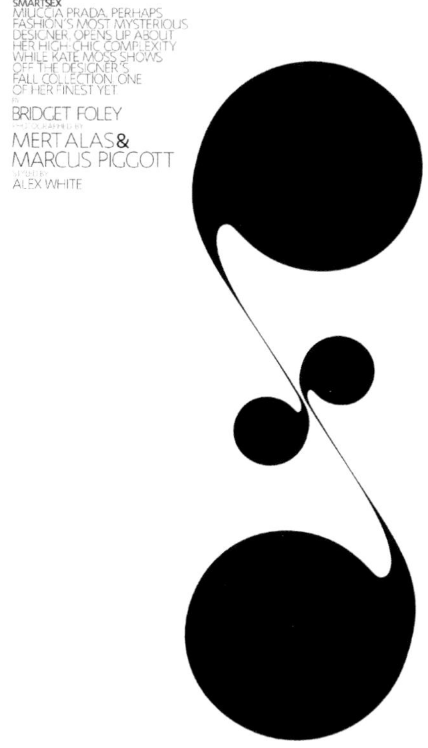

Advertising Campaign
Design: August Heffner, New York. Art Direction: August Heffner. Creative Direction: Julia Hoffmann. Copywriting: Aaron Stern. Museum: The Museum of Modern Art (MoMA), Department of Advertising and Graphic Design. Principal Type: MoMA Gothic. Dimensions: various

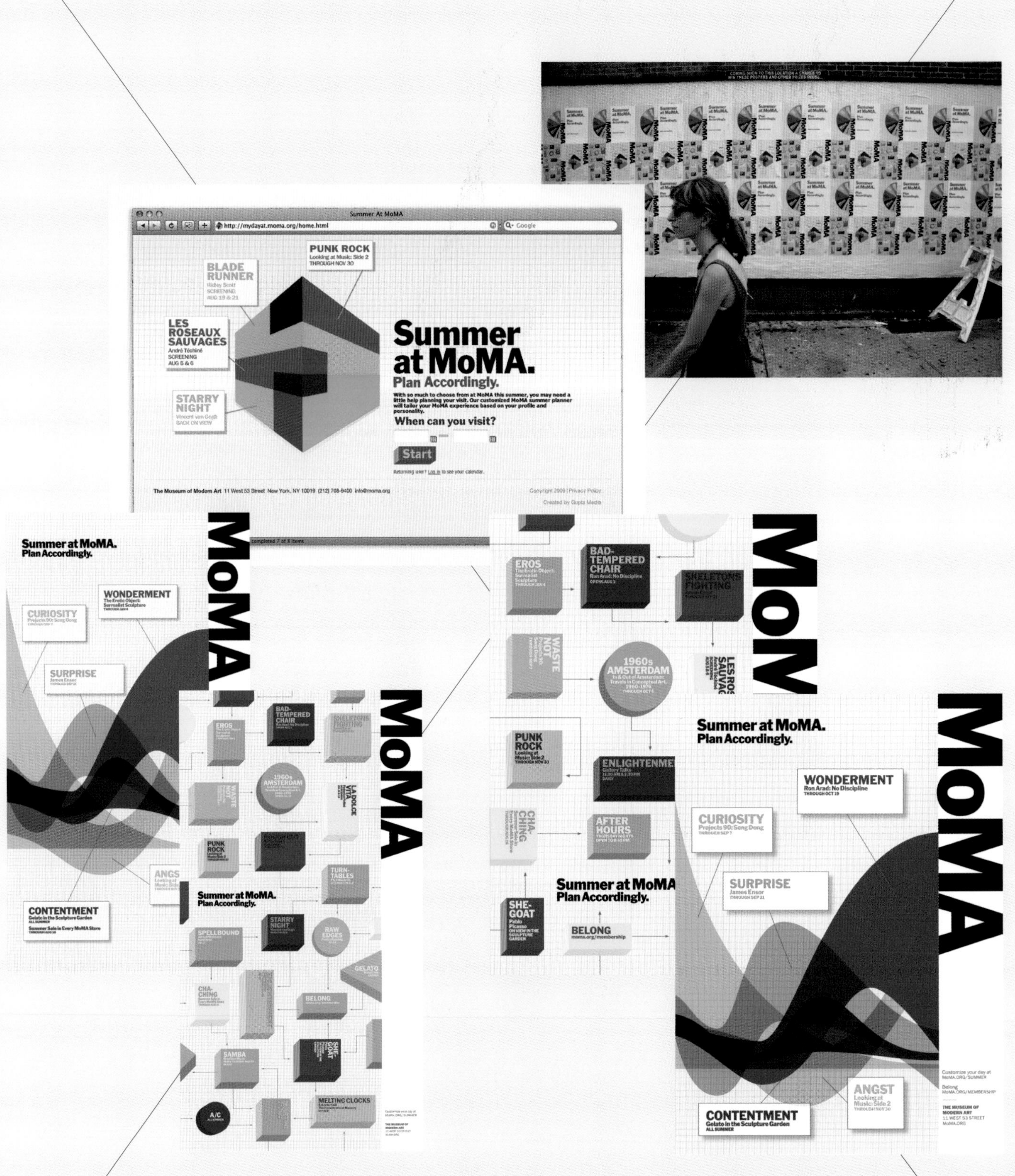

Magazine Pages

Design: Hilary Greenbaum, New York. Deputy Art Direction: Gail Bichler. Design Direction: Arem Duplessis. Lettering: Phantonym—Lowman, Den Haag, Netherlands; Clunkers—Takashi Okada, Tokyo; A-Ha—R.O. Blechman, New York. Publication: *The New York Times Magazine*. Principal Type: handlettering. Dimensions: 8.9 x 10.9 in. (22.6 x 27.6 cm)

Phantonym

Magazine Cover

Design: Nancy Harris Rouemy, New York. Deputy Art Direction: Gail Bichler. Design Direction: Arem Duplessis. Publication: *The New York Times Magazine*. Principal Type: untitled. Dimensions: 8.9 x 10.9 in. (22.6 x 27.6 cm)

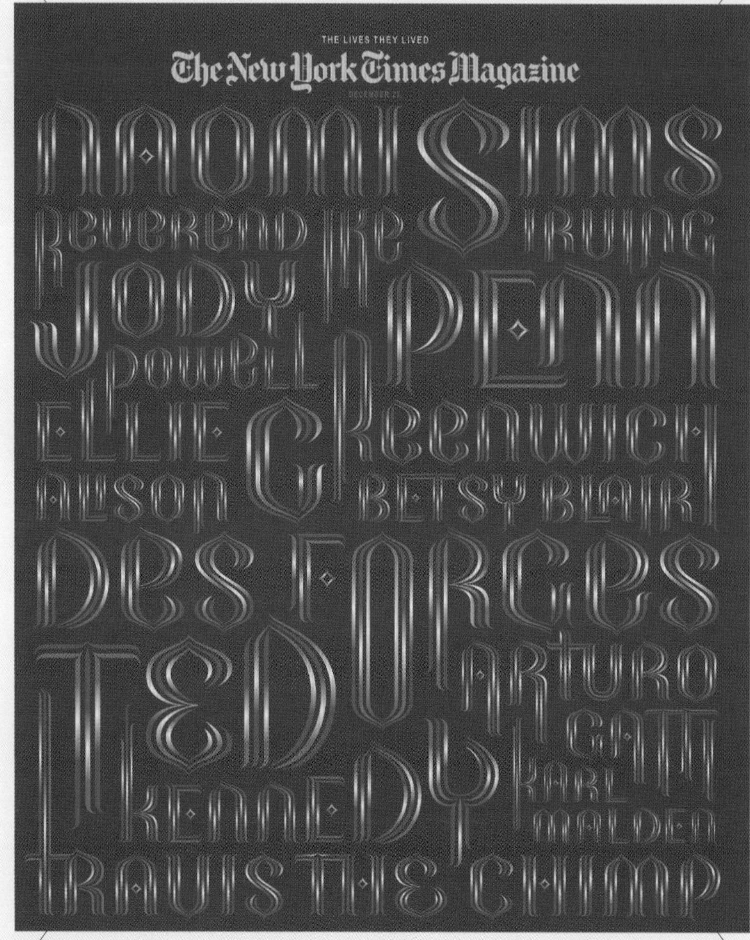

Magazine Spread
Design: Chelsea Cardinal, New York. Design Direction: Fred Woodward. Publication: *GQ*. Principal Type: Titling Gothic FB. Dimensions: 16 x 10.9 in. (40.6 x 7.6 cm)

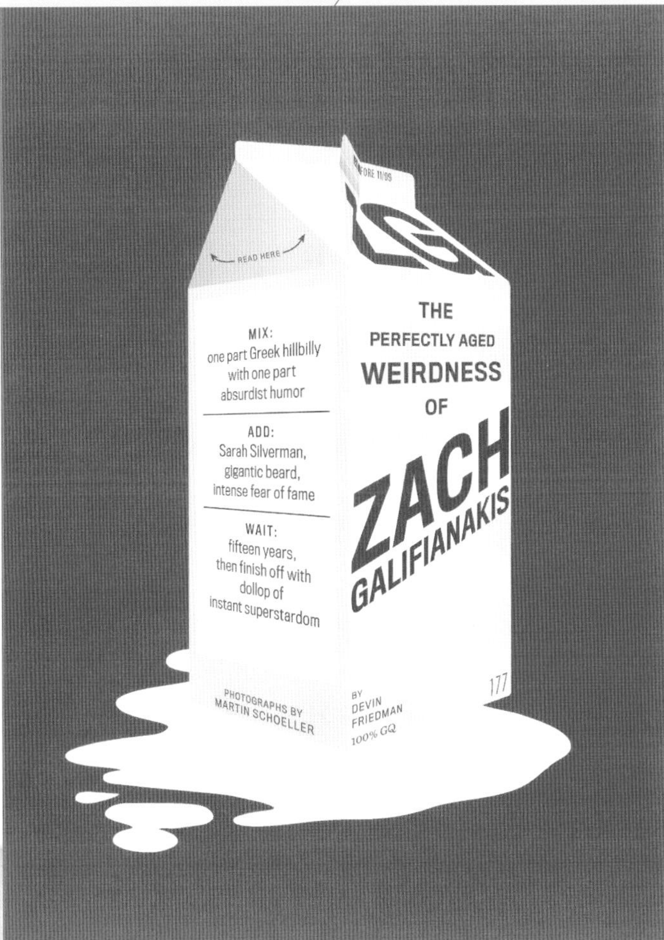

Book

Design: Nadine Hill, Mössingen, Germany. Art Direction: Nadine Hill. Creative Direction: Nadine Hill. Printer: Sautter Repro + Druck. Studio: Nadine Hill Design. Client: Klaus Karl Christmann. Principal Type: Dax Condensed, FF Meta Plus Caps, and various black letters. Dimensions: 6.7 x 9.25 in. (17 x 23.5 cm)

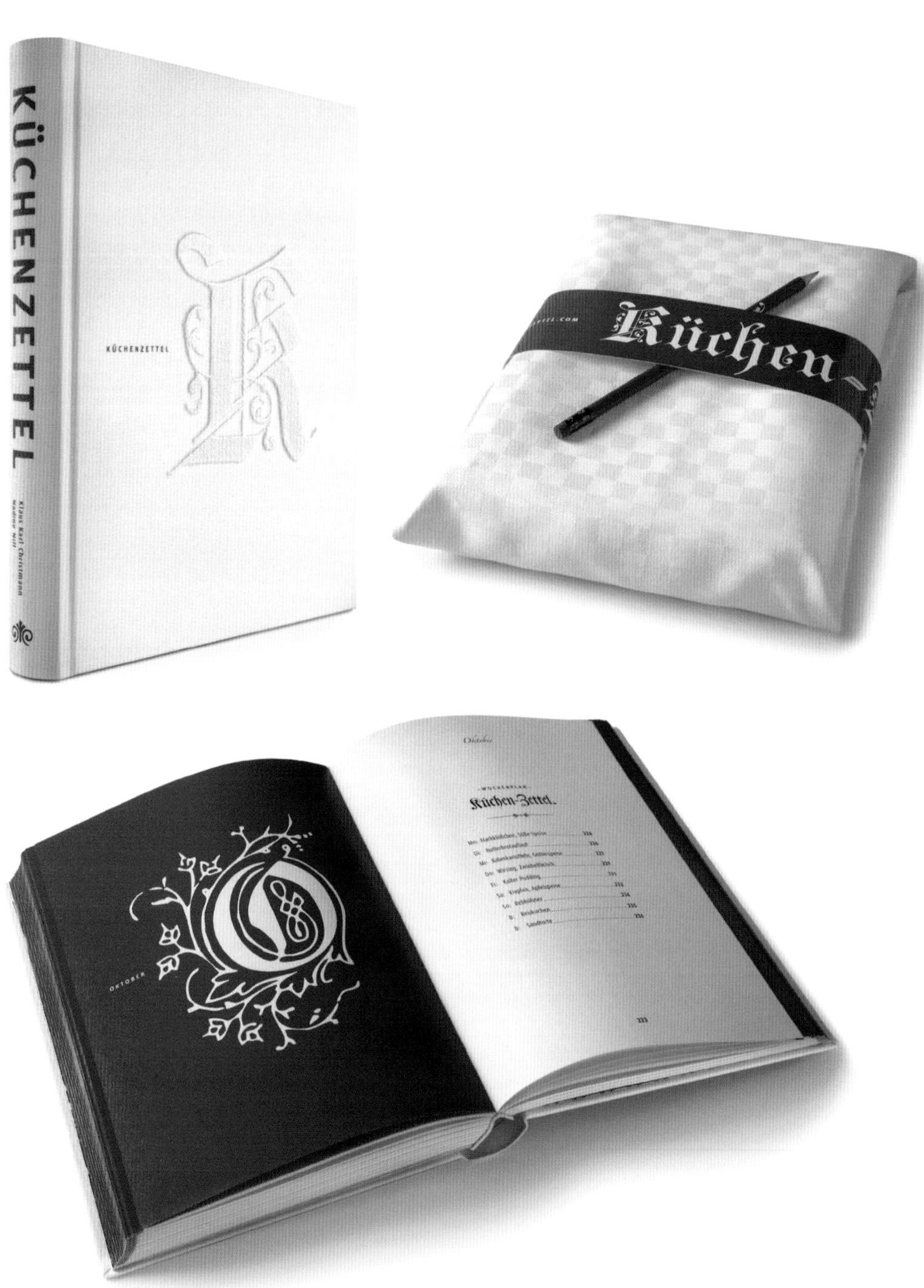

Business Cards

Design: Anna Fahrmaier, Thomas Gabriel, and Michael Hochleitner, Vienna. Lettering: Anna Fahrmaier, Thomas Gabriel, and Michael Hochleitner. Design Office: Typejockeys. Principal Type: handlettering. Dimensions: 2.3. x 3.3 in. (5.9 x 8.5 cm)

Corporate Identity

Design: Stephanie Ising, München, Germany. Creative Direction: Tom Ising and Martin Fengel. Design Office: Herburg Weiland. Client: Lenbachhaus München, Matthias Mühling, and Claudia Weber. Principal Type: Univers. Dimensions: various

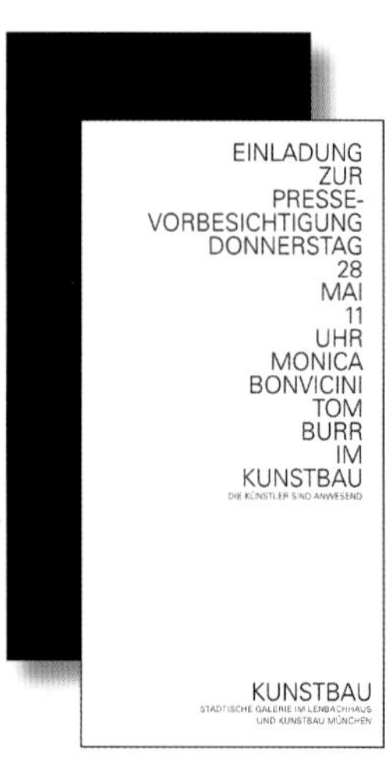

Book

Design: Doug Clouse and Angela Voulangas, New York. Photography: Doug Clouse, Angela Voulangas, and Robert Wright. Authors: Doug Clouse and Angela Voulangas. Publisher: Princeton Architectural Press. Principal Type: various. Dimensions: 8 x 10 in. (20.3 x 25.4 cm)

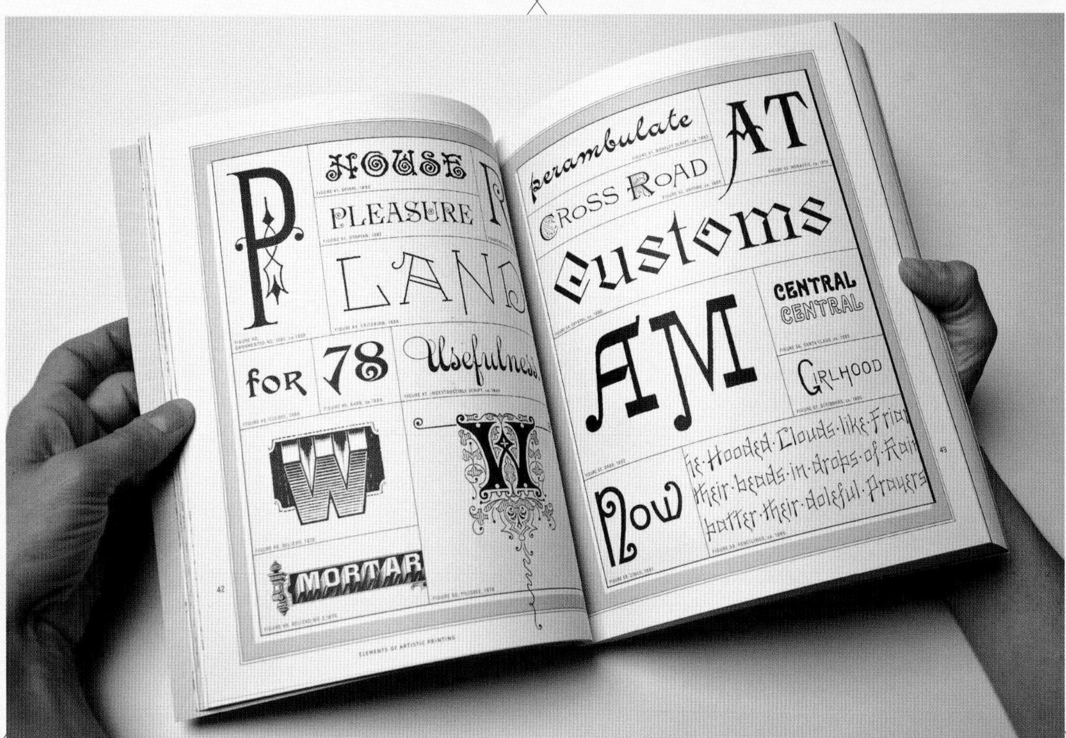

Book

Art Direction: Andrea Moench and Katharina von Hellberg, München, Germany. Creative Direction: Pat Kalt. Agency: Expolab advanced communication and design. Client: BMW. Principal Type: ITC Avant Garde and Baskerville. Dimensions: 7.9 x 10.6 in. (20 x 27 in.)

Corporate Identity

Design: Jamie Paul, Minneapolis, Minnesota. Creative Direction: Derek Sussner. Copywriting: Dave Schutz and Jamie Paul. Design Office: Sussner Design. Client: Pardon My French Café. Principal Type: Filosofia and Trade Gothic. Dimensions: various

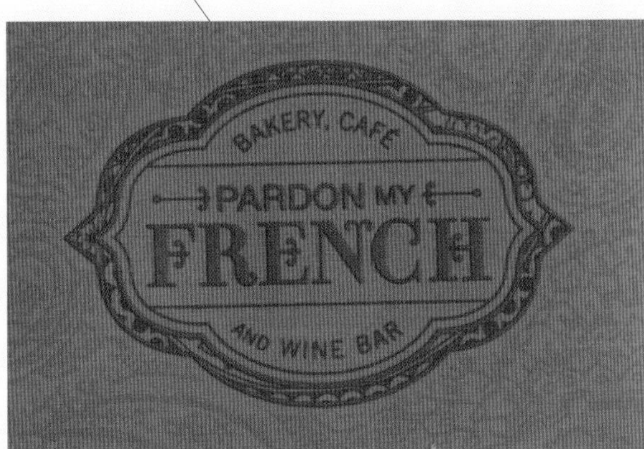

Book

Design: Sonya Dyakova, London. Art Direction: Sonya Dyakova. Creative Direction: Sonya Dyakova. Publisher: Phaidon Press. Principal Type: Didot and Avenir. Dimensions: 10.1 x 11.7 in. (25.7 x 29.7 cm)

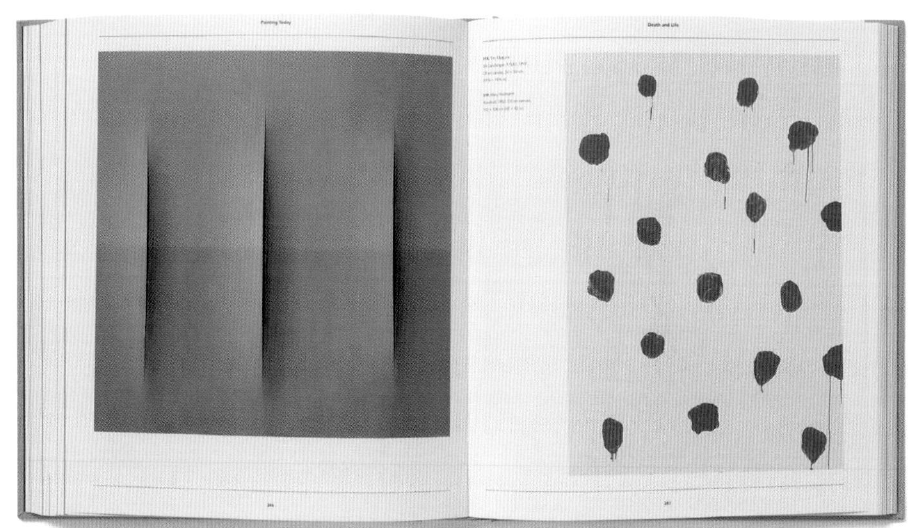

Stationery

Design: Philippe Apeloig, Paris. Art Direction: Philippe Apeloig. Creative Direction: Philippe Apeloig. Calligraphy: Philippe Apeloig. Studio: Studio Apeloig. Client: La Maison de Photo. Principal Type: Deck. Dimensions: various

Self-Promotion

Design: René Clément, Montréal. Art Direction: René Clément. Creative Direction: Louis Gagnon. Lettering: René Clément. Print Producer: Transcontinental Litho Acme. Studio: Paprika. Principal Type: handlettering. Dimensions: 4.25 x 15.5 x 4.25 in. (10.8 x 39 x 10.8 cm)

Self-Promotion

Design: Jed Heuer, Brooklyn, New York. Lettering: Jed Heuer. Principal Type: Arnhem, Blender, and handlettering. Dimensions: 16.5 x 22.5 in. (41.9 x 58.2 cm)

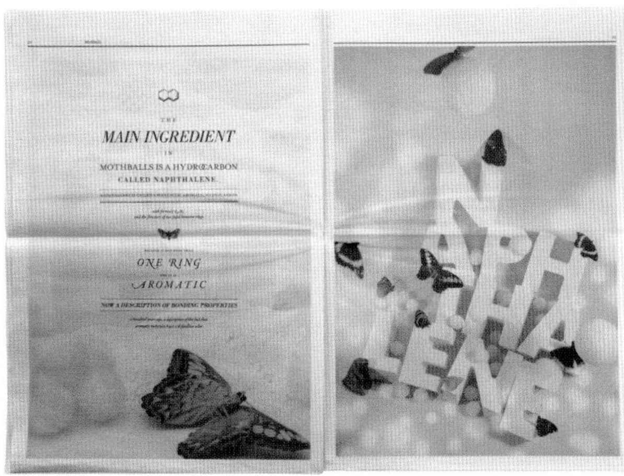

Notebooks

Design: Carrie Solomon, New York. Design Office: Creative Services Department, Bloomberg LLP. Principal Type: Akzidenz Grotesk. Dimensions: 8 x 10 in. (19.4 x 25.4 cm)

Packaging

Design: Joshua Marc Levy, New York. Art Direction: Joshua Marc Levy. Lettering: Joshua Marc Levy. Client: Modest Mouse and Epic Records. Principal Type: wood type and handlettering. Dimensions: 7 x 12 in. (17.8 x 30.5 cm)

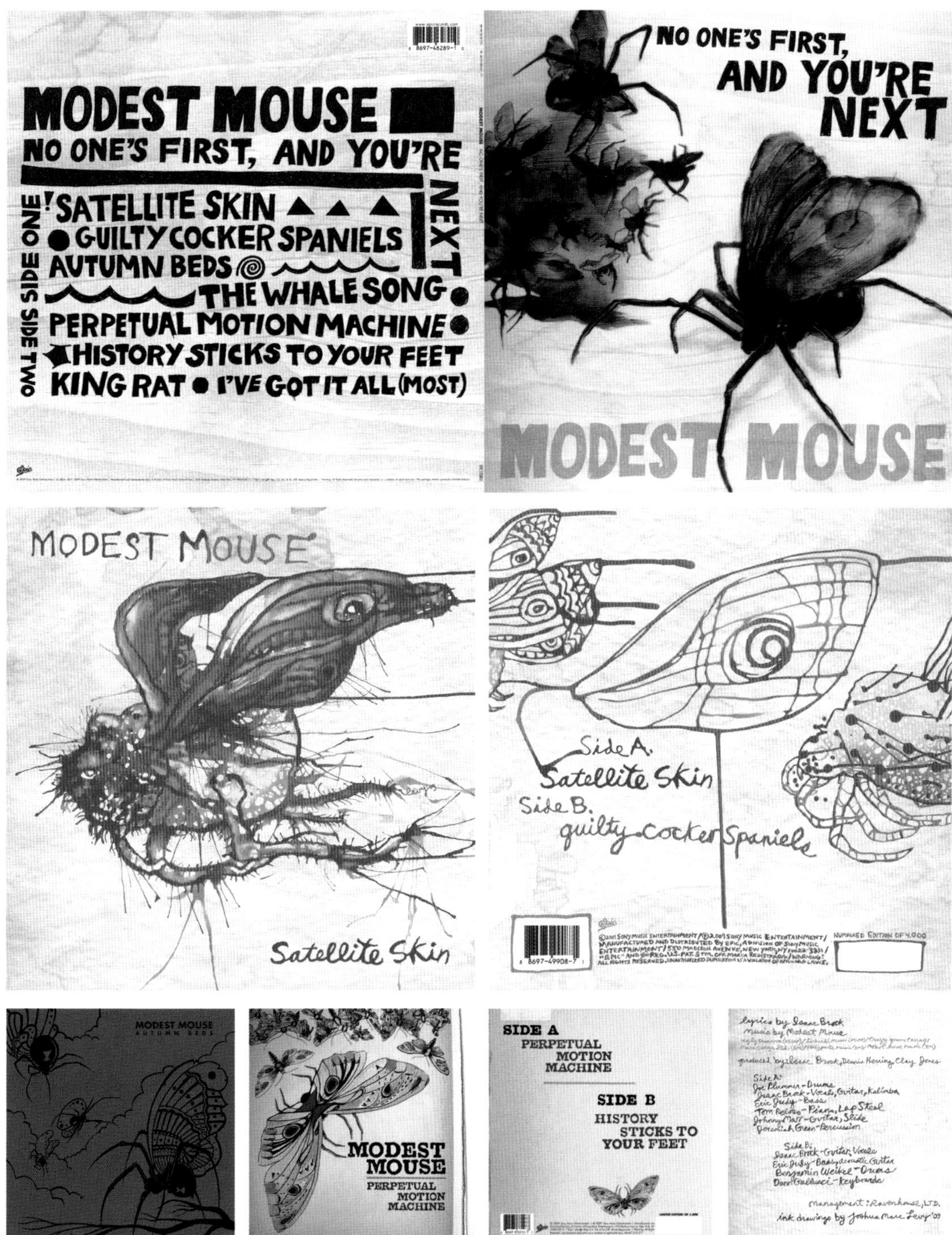

Self-Promotion

Design: Dominic Hofstede and Wendy Ellerton, Prahan, Australia. Creative Direction: Dominic Hofstede. Design Office: Hofstede Design. Principal Type: various. Dimensions: 8.3 x 5.8 in. (21 x 14.8 cm)

Invitation
Design: Dominic Hofstede and Wendy Ellerton, Prahan, Australia. Creative Direction: Dominic Hofstede. Design Office: Hofstede Design. Client: Australian Graphic Design Association. Principal Type: Mercury Text and Mercury Display. Dimensions: 16.5 x 23.4 in. (42 x 59.4 cm)

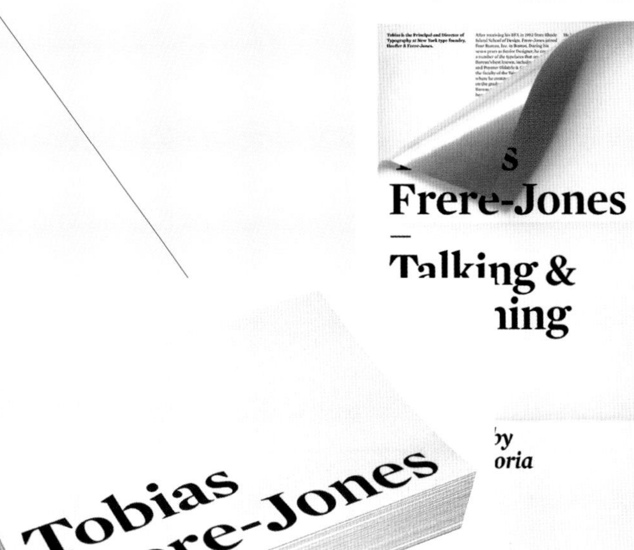

Wrapping Paper

Design: Taylor Buckholz, Washington, DC. Art Direction: Pum Lefebure. Creative Direction: Pum Lefebure and Jake Lefebure. Design Office: Design Army. Principal Type: Akzidenz Grotesk Bold Condensed. Dimensions: 24 x 35 in. (61 x 88.9 cm)

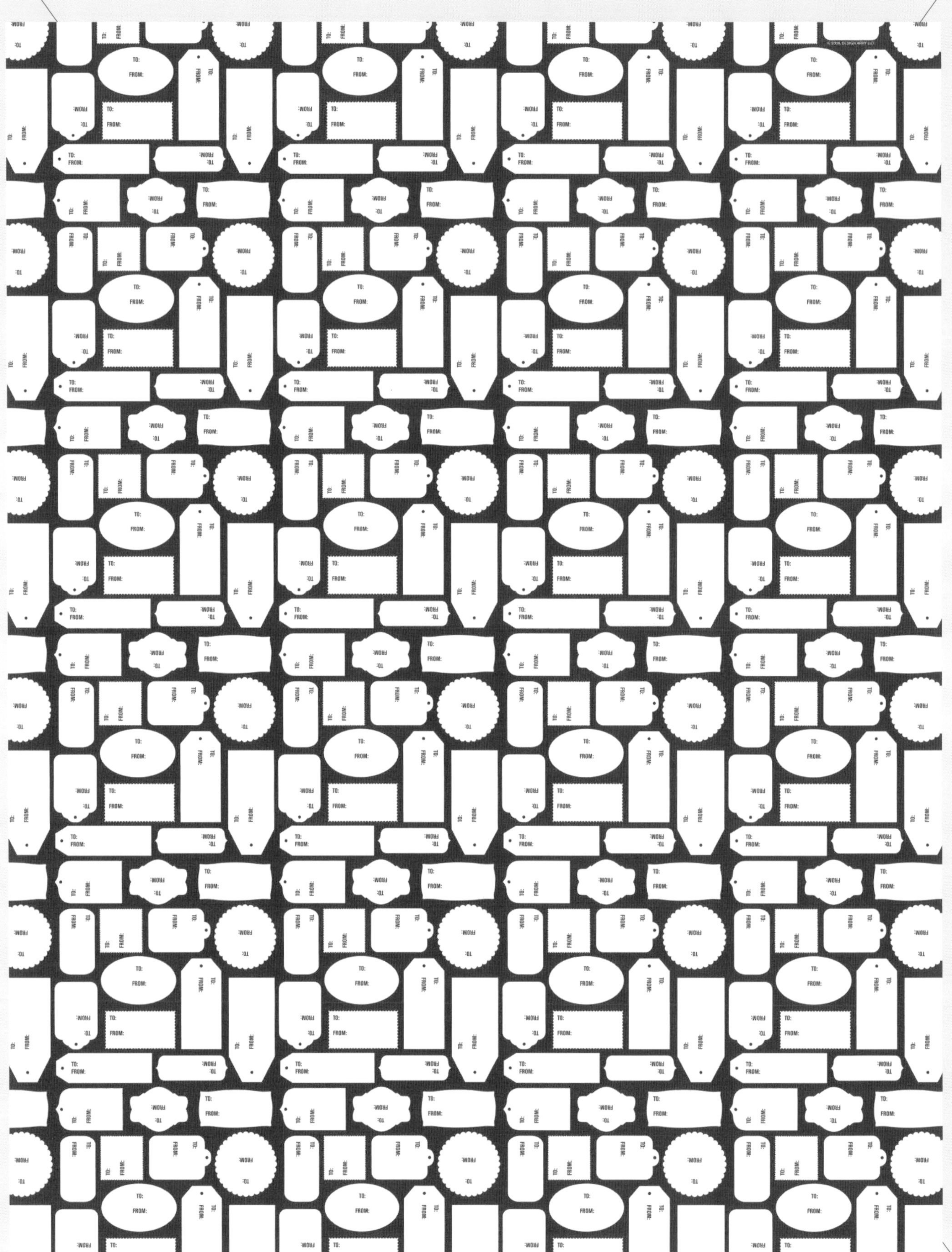

Student Project

Design: Chiharu Tanaka, San Francisco. School: Academy of Art University. Director, MFA Graphic Design Department: Phil Hamlett. Instructors: Rod Cavazos, Carolina de Bartolo, Christian Schwartz, and Erik Spiekermann. Principal Type: NAMI. Dimensions: various

Student Project

Design: Jack Curry, Long Beach, California. School: California State University, Long Beach. Instructor: Andrew Byrom. Principal Type: hand-cut type. Dimensions: various

Student Project

Design: Carolin Lintl and Anne-Katrin Koch, Stuttgart, Germany. Art Direction: Anne-Katrin Koch. Creative Direction: Carolin Lintl. School: Staatliche Akademie der Bildenden Künste Stuttgart. Professor: Niklaus Troxler. Principal Type: handcrafted

Student Project

Design: Helen Hauert, Ramona Heiligensetzer, and Benjamin Kivikoski, Stuttgart, Germany. School: Staatliche Akademie der Bildenden Künste Stuttgart. Professors: Niklaus Troxler and Peter Brugger. Principal Type: Currywurst Display. Dimensions: 7.7 x 10.2 in. (19.5 x 26 cm)

Student Project
Design: Julianne Kim, Los Angeles. School: Art Center College of Design. Instructor: Brad Bartlett. Principal Type: Akkurat and Gotham. Dimensions: 30 x 18 in. (76.2 x 45.7 cm)

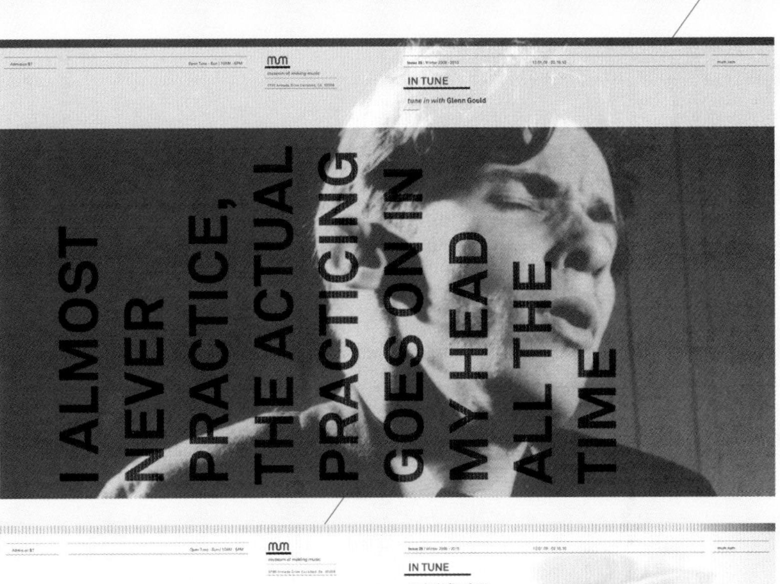

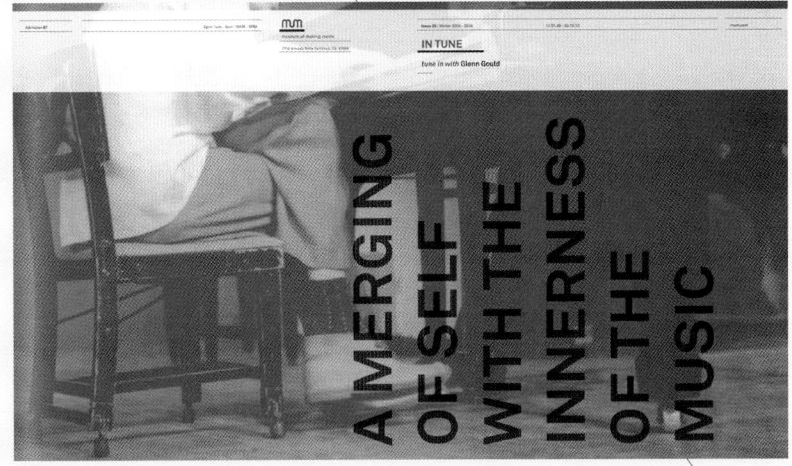

Student Project

Design: Yonghao Yan, Honolulu. School: University of Hawai'i at Mãnoa, Graphic Design Program. Instructor: Anne Bush. Principal Type: Rotis Serif Std and Rotis Sans Serif Std. Dimensions: 8.25 x 5.5 in. (21 x 14 cm)

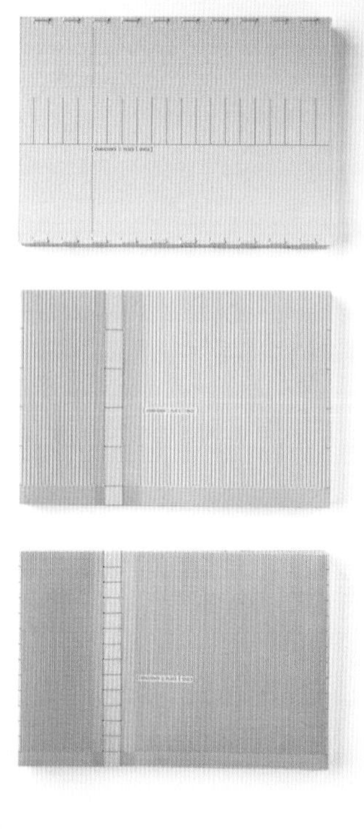

Student Project

Design: James Kyungmo Yang, New York. Photography: Albert Watson. School: School of Visual Arts, MFA Program, New York. Instructor: Howard Reeves. Principal Type: handlettering. Dimensions: 12 x 16 in. (30.5 x 40.6 cm)

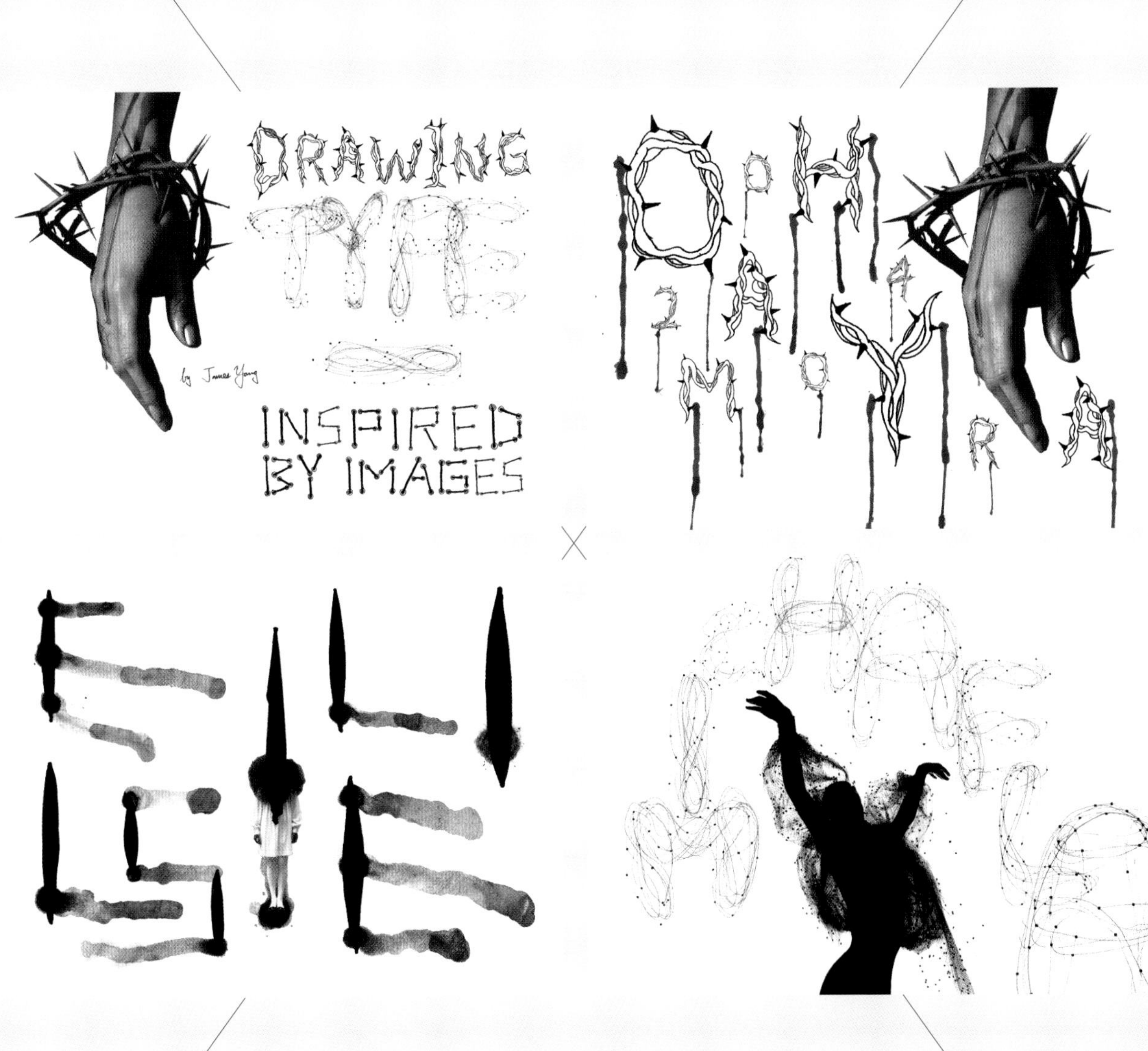

Student Project

Design Sophie Audet Sainte-Marie, Canada. School: Université du Québec à Montréal (UQAM). Instructor: Louis Gagnon. Principal Type: Bodoni, Clarendon, Didot, Folio, Insignia, and Shelley Script. Dimensions 4.9 x 7.7 in. (12.3 x 19.4 cm)

Student Project
Design: Sven Quadflieg, Essen, Germany. School: Folkwang Hochschule. Professors: Thomas Rempen and Uwe Stoklossa.
Client: Sparkasse Essen. Principal Type: various. Dimensions: 5.5 x 4.9 x 3 in. (14 x 12.5 x 7.5 cm)

Student Project

Design: Sangmin Shim, New York. School: Rhode Island School of Design. Instructors: Hans van Dijk and Ernesto Aparacio. Principal Type: Times Ten and Univers. Dimensions: 7 x 9.5 in. (17.8 x 24.1 cm)

Student Project

Design: Ann Im Sunwoo, New York. School: School of Visual Arts, New York. Instructor: Michael Ian Kaye. Principal Type: Neutraface. Dimensions: 9.25 x 11.25 x 2 in. (23.5 x 28.6 x 5.1 cm)

Student Project

Design: Sophie Audet, Sainte-Marie, Canada. School: Université du Québec à Montréal (UQAM). Instructor: Nelu Wolfensohn. Principal Type: DIN Schrift and Bell Gothic. Dimensions: 24 x 36 in. (61 x 91.4 cm)

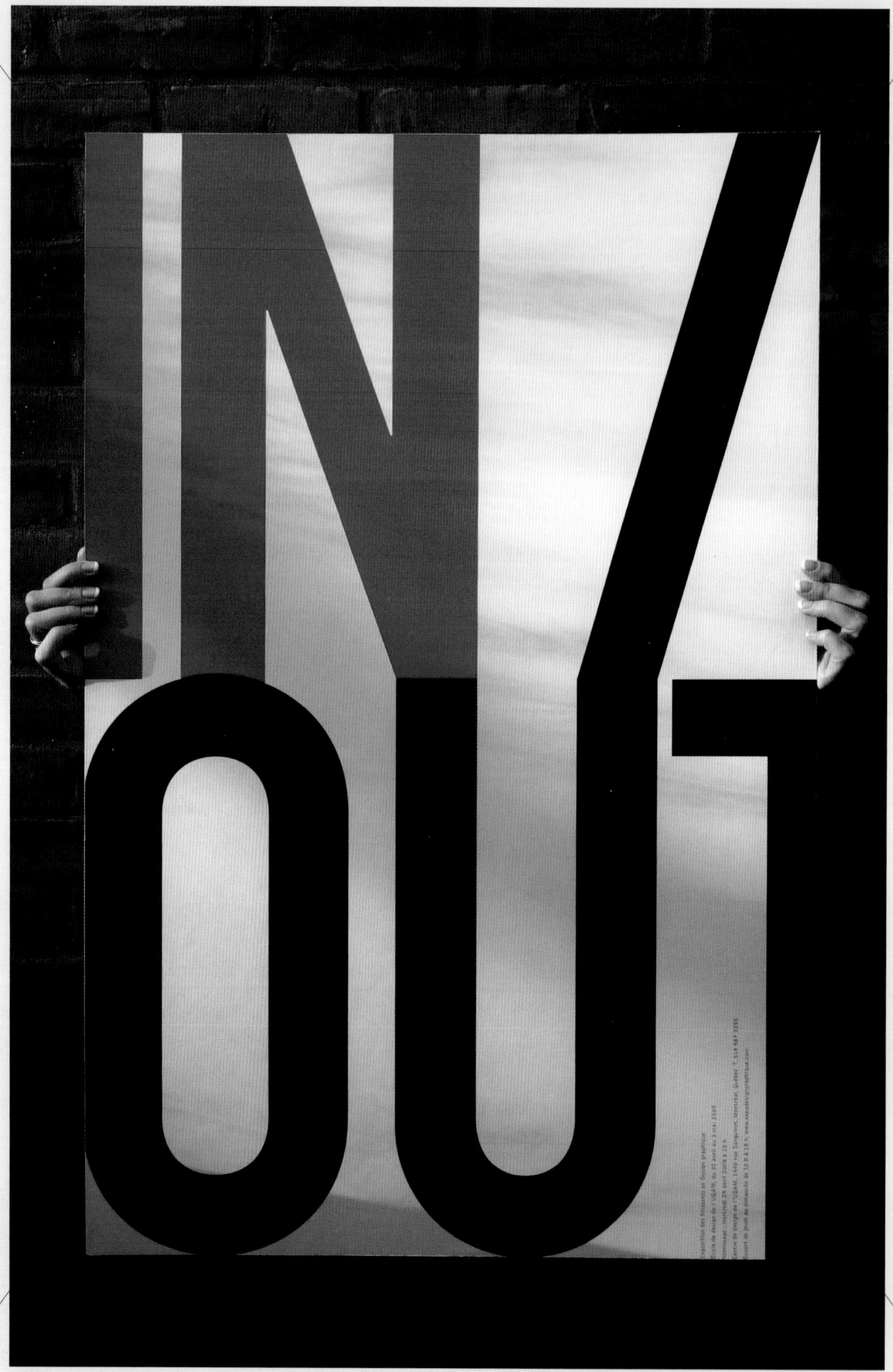

Student Project
Design: Yumi Nakamura, Elmhurst, New York. School: School of Visual Arts, New York. Instructor: Michael Ian Kaye.
Principal Type: Bickham Script. Dimensions: installation, 8.5 x 5 ft. (25.9 x 15.2 m); book, 6.6 x 10 in. (16.8 x 25.4 cm)

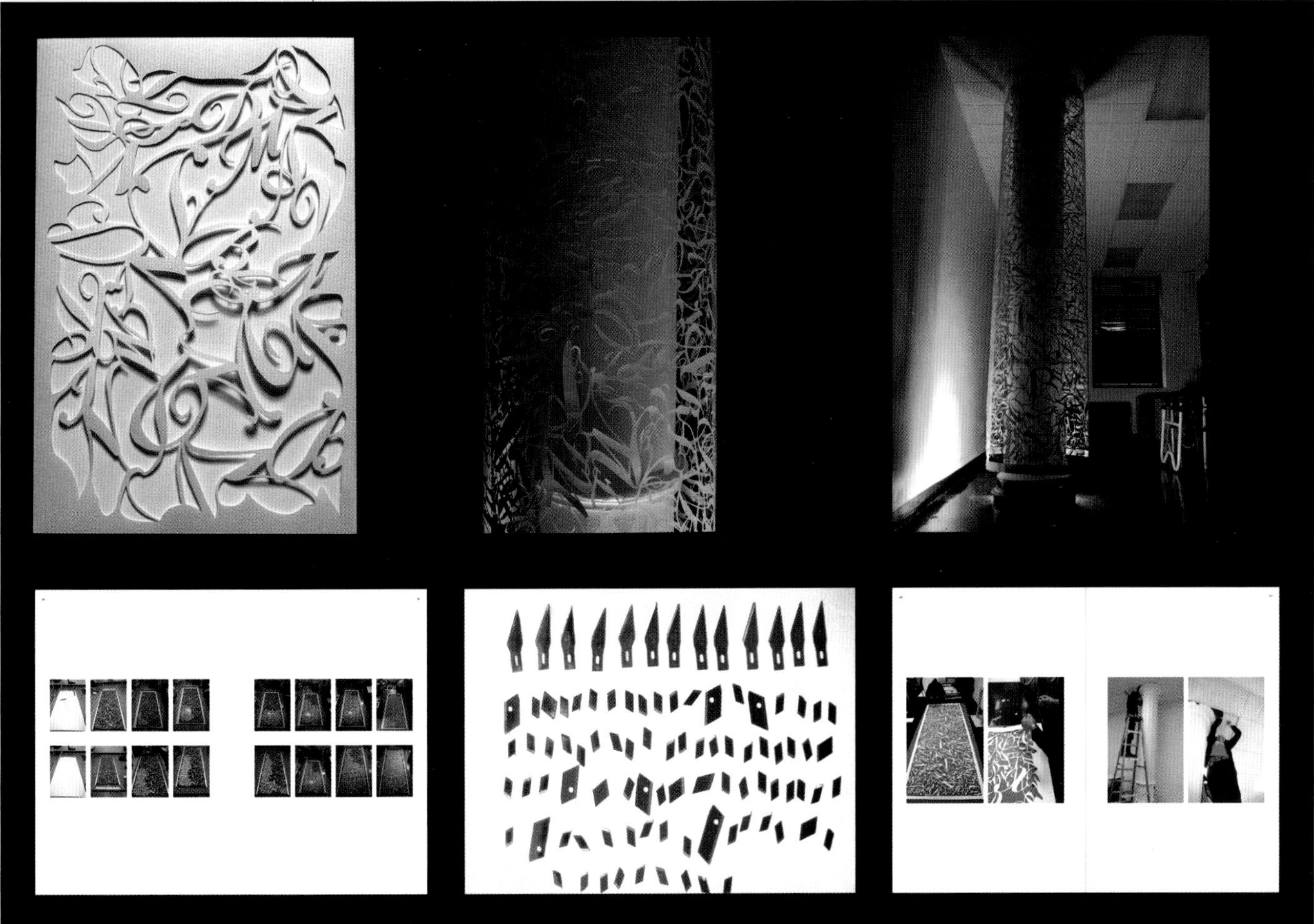

Student Project

Design: Jiwon Park and Jaedeok Yun, Seoul. Art Direction: Jiwon Park. Creative Direction: Jiwon Park. School: EWHA Women's University. Professor: Insohngii Kim. Principal Type: FB Garamond, Helvetica, and custom. Dimensions: various

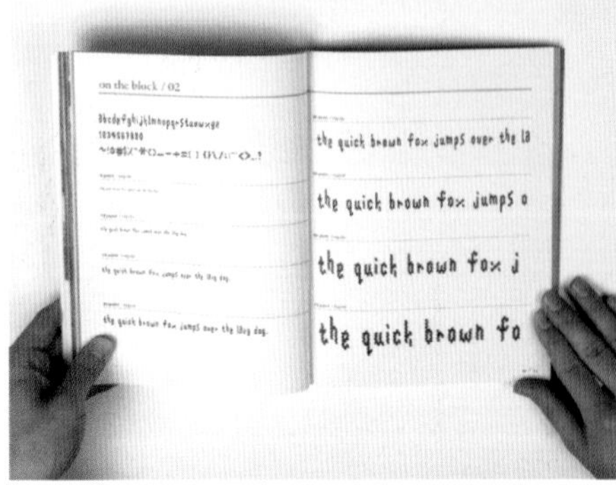

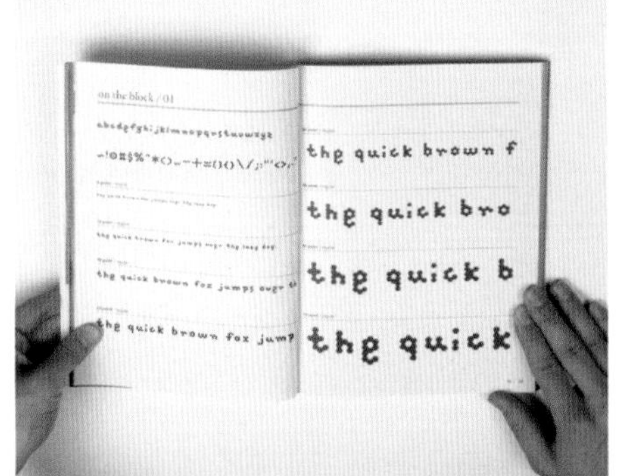

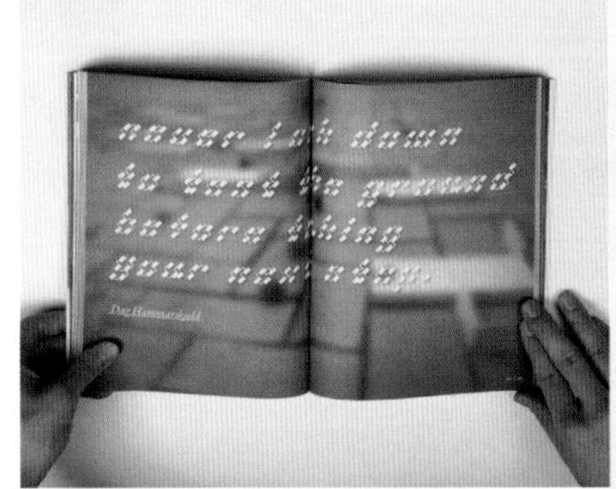

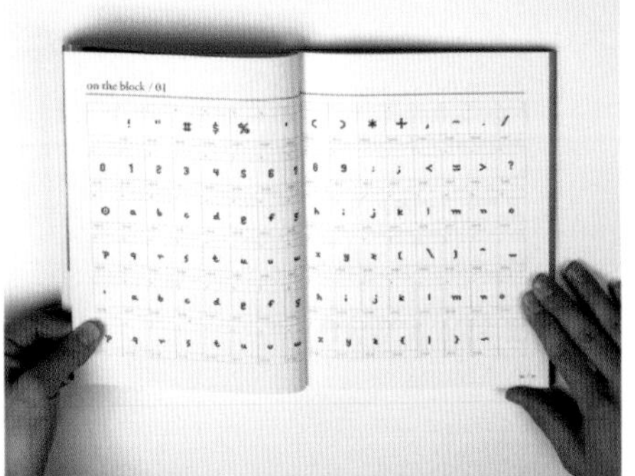

Student Project
Design: Hao In Kuan, Honolulu. School: University of Hawai'i at Mānoa, Graphic Design Program. Instructor: Anne Bush.
Principal Type: Frutiger Light Std. Dimensions: 14.5 x 10.4 x 21.3 in. (5.7 x 4.1 x 8.4 cm)

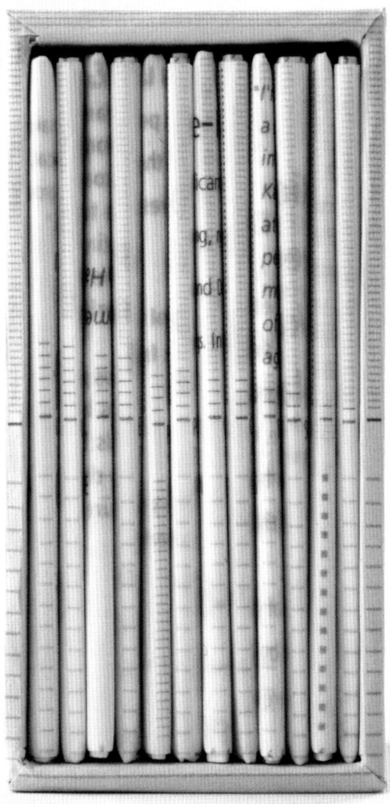

Magazine Spread

Design: Lou Vega, New York. Art Direction: Lou Vega. Creative Direction: Siung Tjia. Lettering: Lou Vega. Publication: *ESPN The Magazine*. Principal Type: Apex New Medium and custom. Dimensions: 20 x 10 in. (50.8 x 25.4 cm)

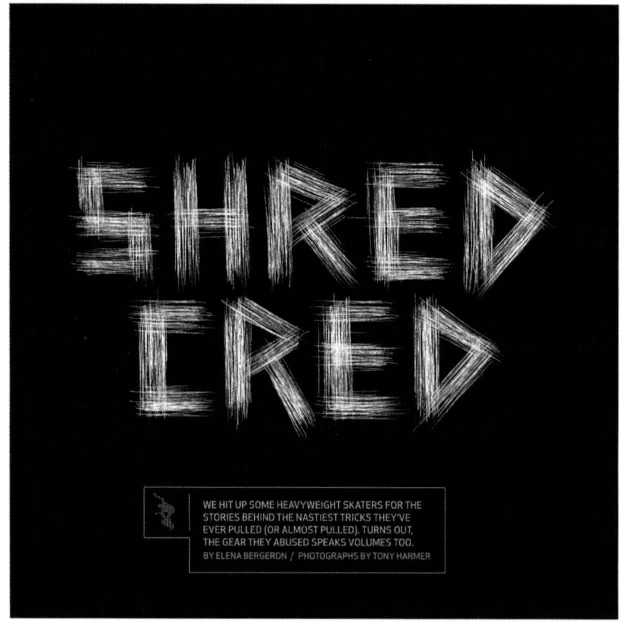

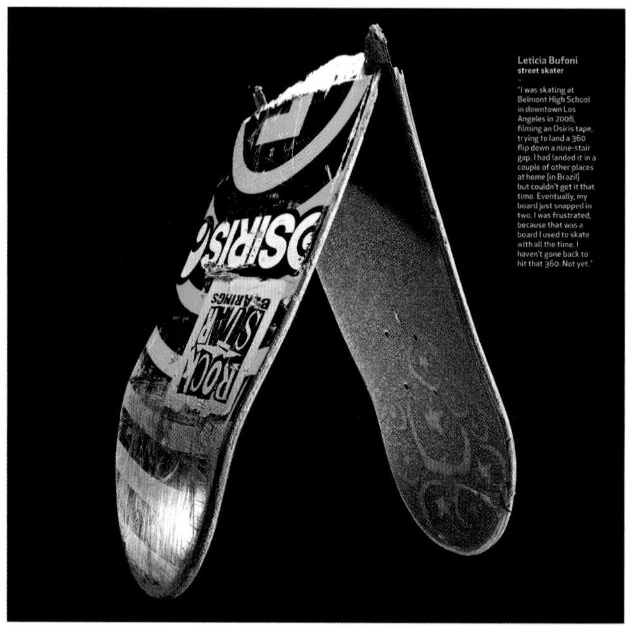

Leticia Bufoni
street skater
"I was skating at Belmont High School in downtown Los Angeles in 2008, filming an Osiris tape, trying to land a 360 flip down a nine-stair gap. I had landed it in a couple of other places at home [in Brazil] but couldn't get it that time. Eventually, my board just snapped in two. I was frustrated, because that was a board I used to skate with all the time. I haven't gone back to hit that 360. Not yet."
EXPN MAGAZINE | 33

Magazine Spread

Design: Chelsea Cardinal, New York. Design Direction: Fred Woodward. Lettering: Chelsea Cardinal. Publication: GQ. Principal Type: handlettering. Dimensions: 16 x 10.9 in. (40.6 x 27.7 cm)

Magazine

Design: Paul Sych, Mississauga, Canada. Art Direction: Paul Sych. Lettering: Paul Sych. Photography: Maude Arsenault. Fashion Director: Serge Kerbel. Studio: Faith. Client: Bassett Media Group. Principal Type: Galaxie Polaris and custom. Dimensions: 9.5 x 13 in. (24.1 x 33 cm)

Magazine Spread
Design: Gail Bichler and Hilary Greenbaum, New York. Deputy Art Direction: Gail Bichler. Design Direction: Arem Duplessis. Lettering: Geoff McFetridge, Los Angeles. Publication: *The New York Times Magazine*. Principal Type: Knockout, Nyte, and custom. Dimensions: 8.9 x 10.9 in. (22.7 x 27.6 cm)

Magazine Spread

Design: Anton Ioukhnovets, New York. Design Direction: Fred Woodward. Lettering: Eve Binder, Chelsea Cardinal, and Drue Wagner. Publication: *GQ*. Principal Type: handlettering. Dimensions 16 x 10.9 in. (40.6 x 27.7 cm)

Magazine Spread

Design: Aviva Michaelov, New York. Deputy Art Direction: Gail Bichler. Design Direction: Arem Duplessis. Lettering: Jacob Magraw-Mickelson, Waldron, Washington. Publication: *The New York Times Magazine*. Principal Type: Futura and handlettering. Dimensions: 8.9 x 10.9 in. (22.7 x 27.6 cm)

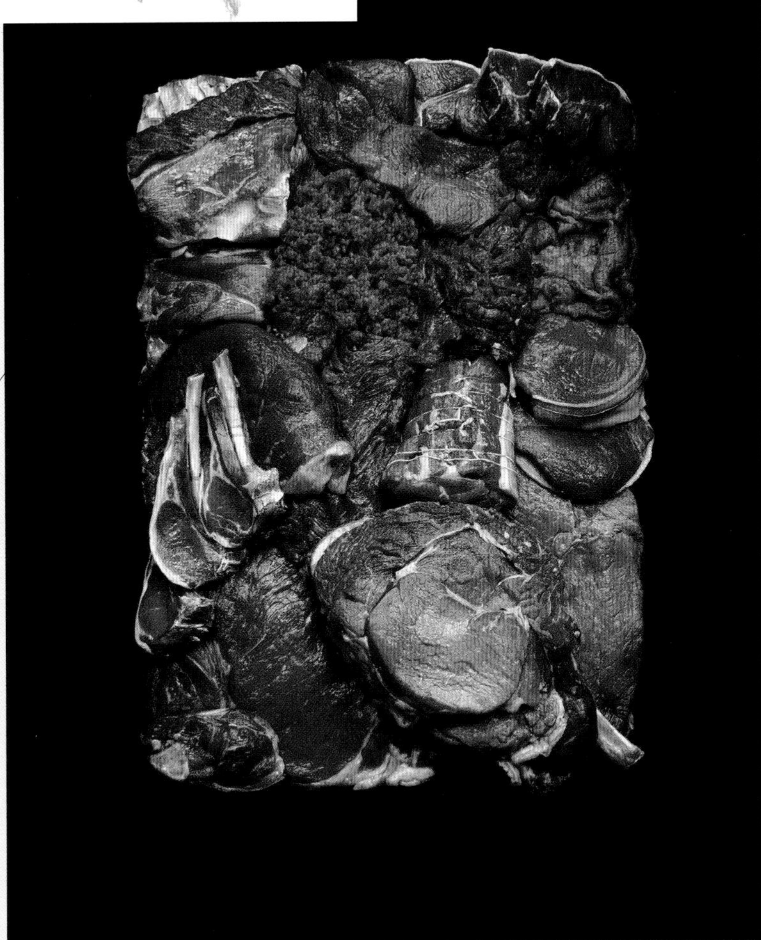

Corporate Identity

Design: Zöe Bather, Studio8 Design, and Joe Sharpe, Applied Works, London. Art Direction: Zöe Bather, Studio8 Design, and Joe Sharpe, Applied Works. Creative Direction: Zöe Bather, Studio8 Design, and Joe Sharpe, Applied Works. Design Offices: Studio8 Design and Applied Works. Client: Dealerworld. Principal Type: Bespoke and Rockwell Light. Dimensions: various

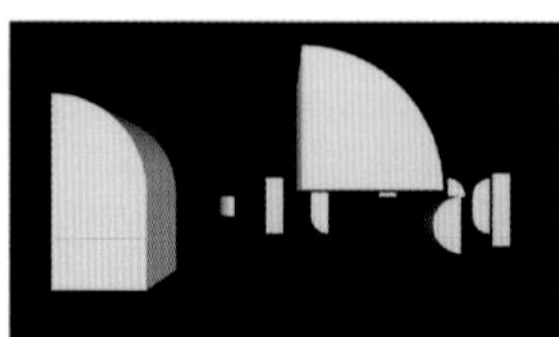

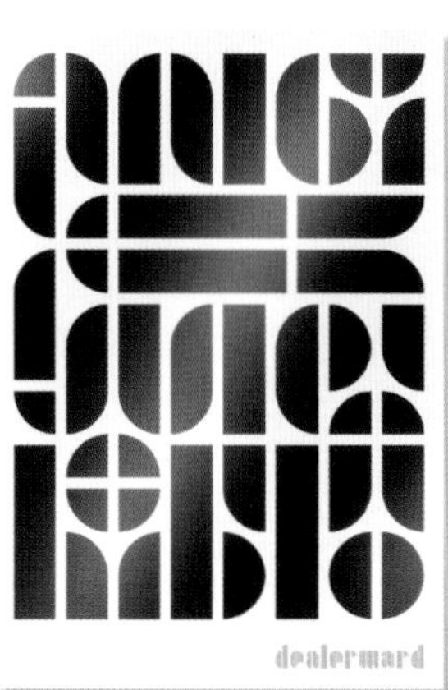

Corporate Identity
Art Direction: Sabine Schoenhaar, Düsseldorf, Germany. Creative Direction: Christian Voettiner. Copywriting: Simone Henke. Design Agency: KW43 BRANDDESIGN. Client: Grey/G2 Group Düsseldorf. Principal Type: Gotham Black and Gotham Extra Light. Dimensions: various

PAIISE

Corporate Identity

Design: Markus Koll, Hamburg, Germany. Art Direction: Markus Koll. Creative Direction: Olaf Stein and Markus Koll. Studio: Factor Design. Client: Thinkprint. Principal Type: Adobe Garamond and various. Dimensions: various

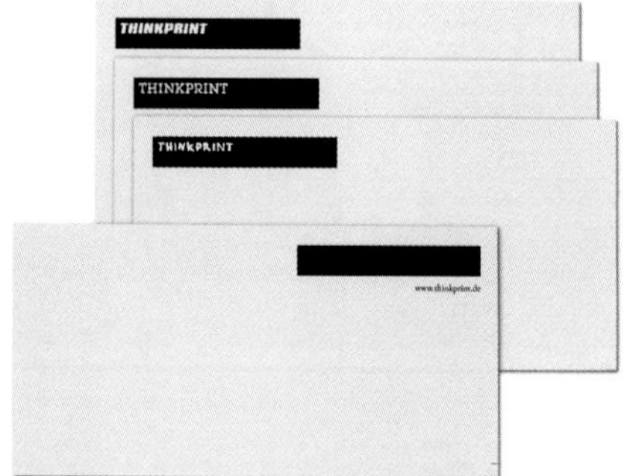

Corporate Identity

Design: Michael Bierut and Yve Ludwig, New York. Art Direction: Michael Bierut. Design Office: Pentagram Design New York. Client: The Oak Room at The Plaza Hotel. Principal Type: Gotham and custom. Dimensions: various

The Oak Room

Corporate Identity

Design: Paula Scher and Lisa Kitschenberg, New York. Art Direction: Paula Scher. Design Office: Pentagram Design New York. Client: The Museum of Modern Art (MoMA). Principal Type: MoMA Gothic. Dimensions: various

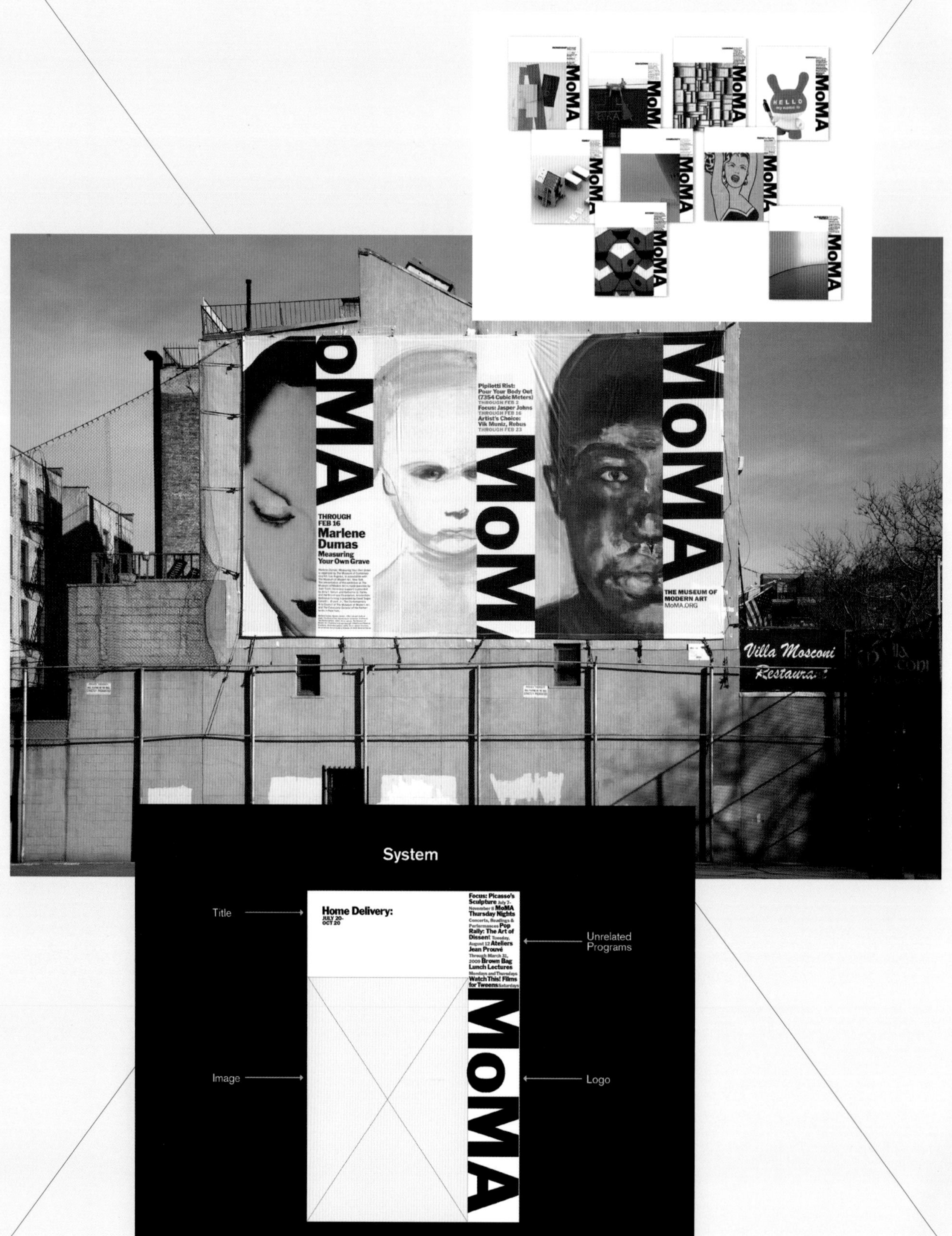

Corporate Identity

Design: Michael Bierut and Joe Marianek, New York. Art Direction: Michael Bierut. Design Office: Pentagram Design New York. Client: Guitar Hero. Principal Type: Hero Bold. Dimensions: various.

Corporate Identity
Design: Frank Viva and Todd Temporale, Toronto. Art Direction: Frank Viva. Lettering: Frank Viva. Design Office: Viva & Co. Client: The Gas Company. Principal Type: FF Scala and handlettering. Dimensions: various.

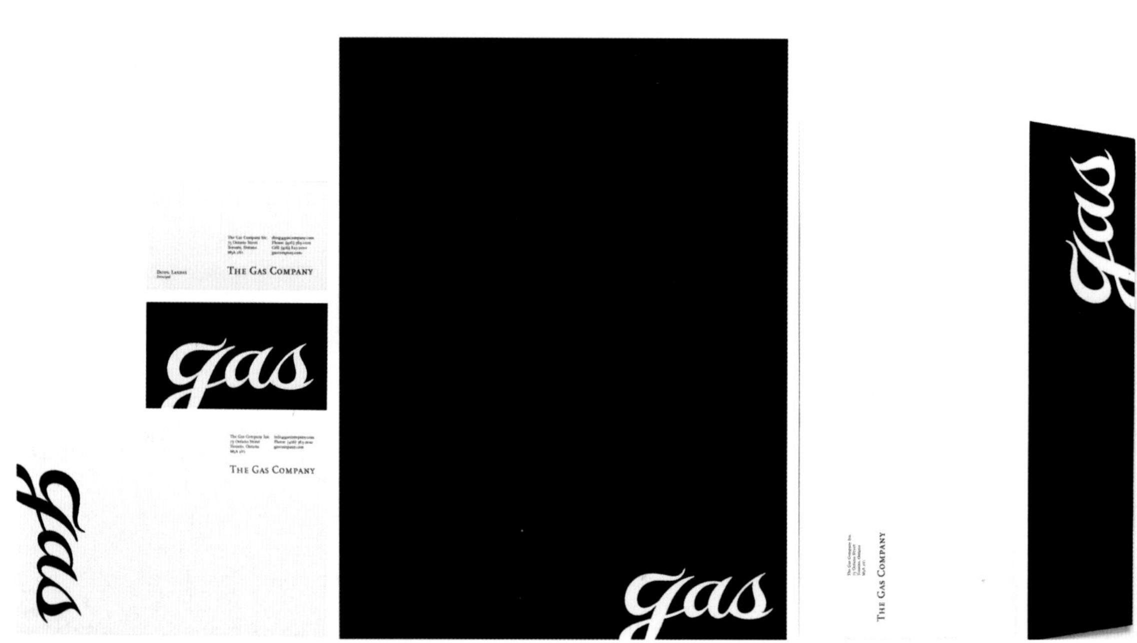

Corporate Identity

Design: Monica Gautier, Montréal. Art Direction: Monica Gautier and Anne Thomas. Creative Direction: Monica Gautier and Anne Thomas. Design Office: Toma Objects. Principal Type: Amplitude and Arnhem. Dimensions: various

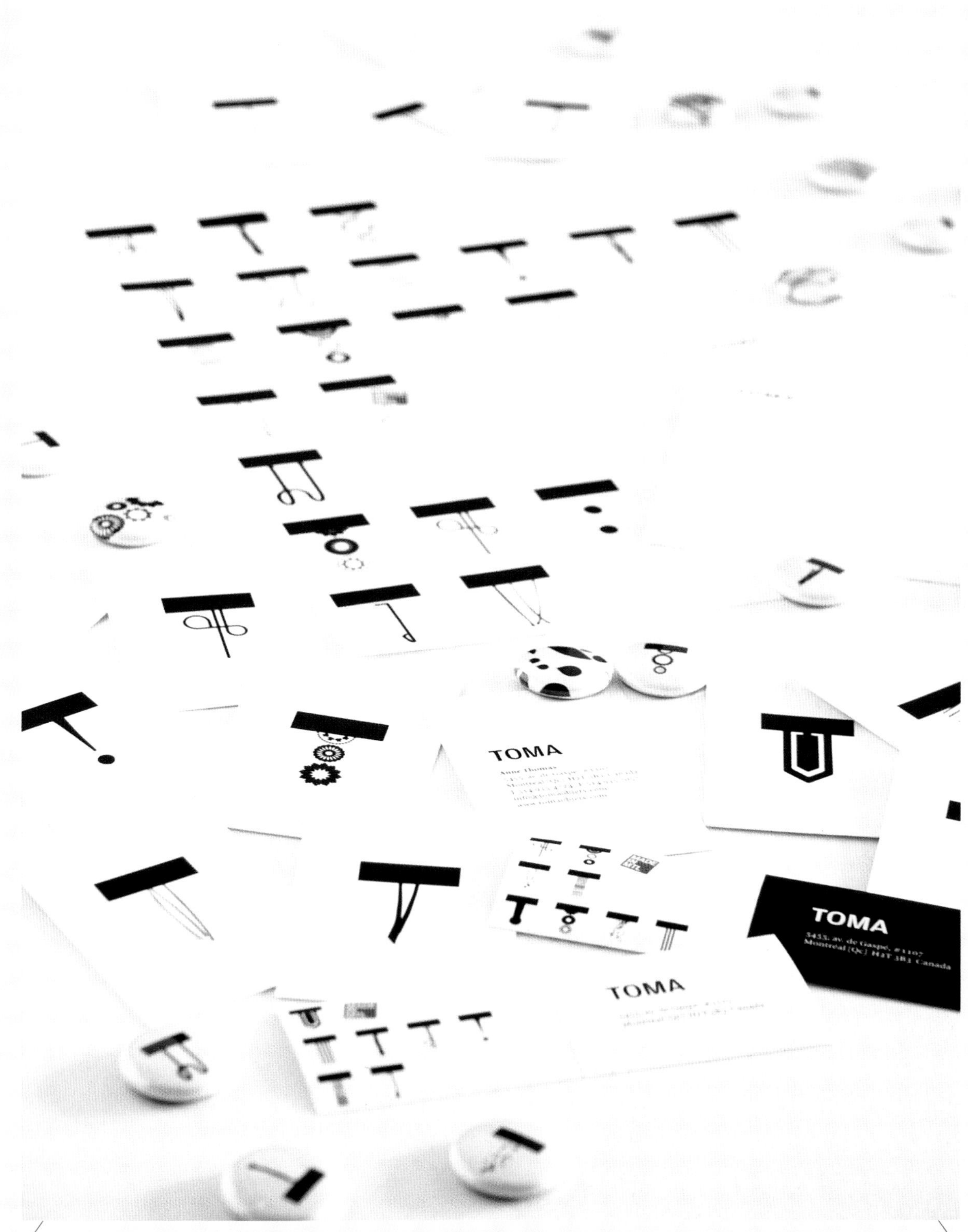

Corporate Identity

Art Direction: Andreas Netthoevel and Martin Gaberthüel, Bern, Switzerland. Communication/PR: Yvonne Uhlig. Studio: secondfloorsouth. Client: Blinden—und Behindertenzentrum Bern. Principal Type: DIN and Braille DIN. Dimensions: various

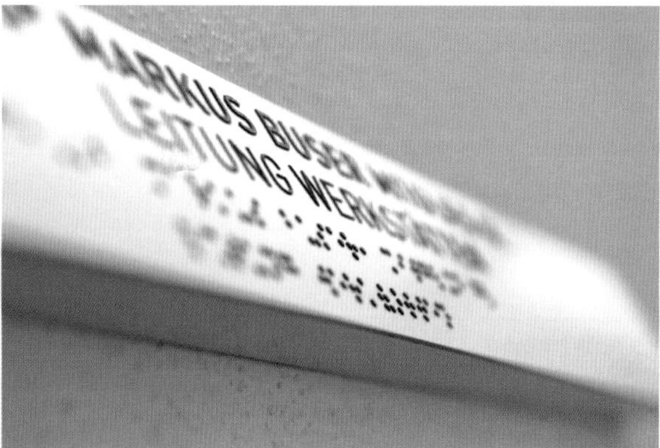

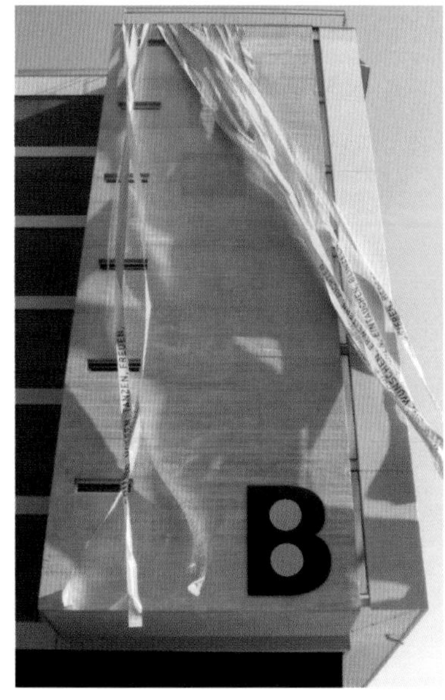

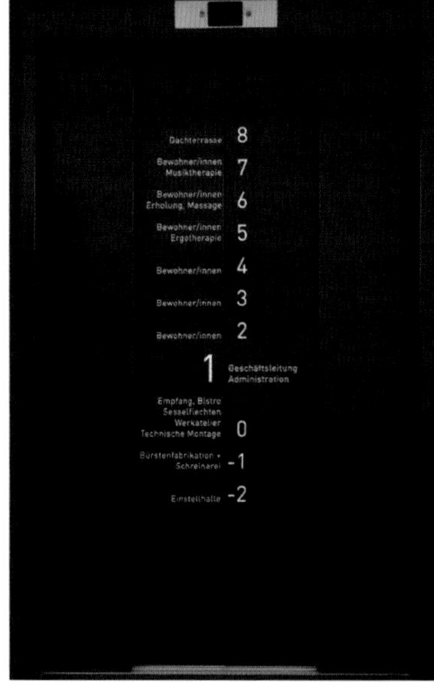

Packaging

Design: Julia Ochsenhirt, Stuttgart, Germany. Art Direction: Kirsten Dietz. Creative Direction: Jochen Raedeker. Agency: Strichpunkt. Client: Weingut Fuerst Lowenstein. Principal Type: Trade Gothic No. 20 and Filosofia. Dimensions: various

Student Project

Design: Nicole Tenbieg, Frankfurt am Main, Germany. School: Frankfurter Akademie. Professors: Udo Herbster, Michaela Kessler, and Dirk Schrod. Principal Type: handlettering. Dimensions: 79 x 156 in. (200 x 400 cm)

Packaging

Design: Louise Fili and Jessica Hische, New York. Art Direction: Louise Fili. Creative Direction: Louise Fili. Lettering: Jessica Hische. Design Office: Louise Fili Ltd. Client: Polaner Selections. Principal Type: Neutraface and handlettering. Dimensions: 3.5 x 4.6 in. (8.9 x 11.7 cm)

Packaging

Design: Aaron Edwards and Max Lozach, Auckland, New Zealand. Creative Direction: Dean Poole. Lettering: Ben Corban. Studio: Alt Group. Client: Oakfield Press. Principal Type: Futura and handlettering. Dimensions 6.2 x 15.4 x 6 in. (15.8 x 39.2 x 15.2 cm)

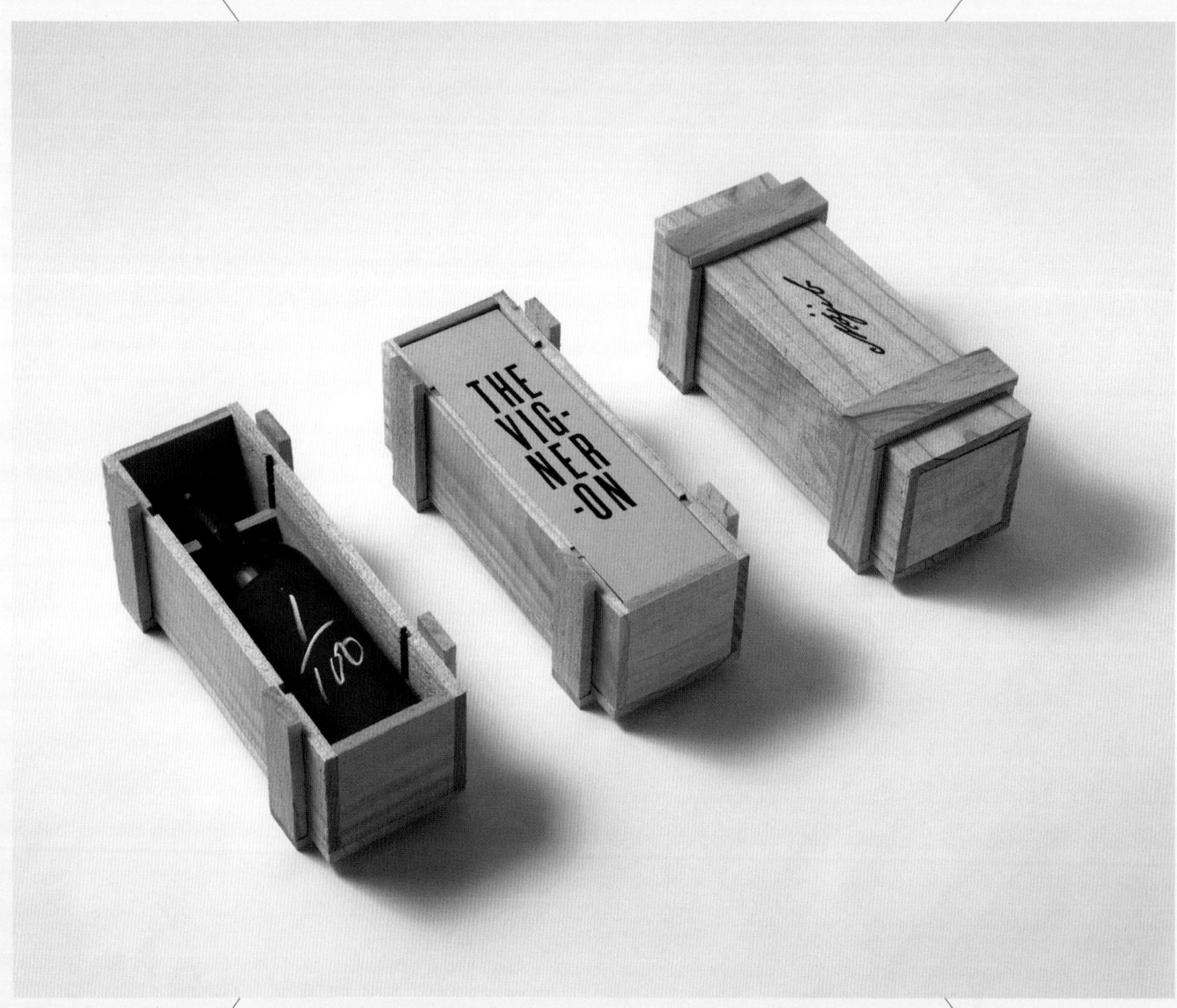

Environmental Graphics

Design: Michael Bierut and Katie Barcelona, New York. Art Direction: Michael Bierut. Design Office: Pentagram Design New York. Client: Harley-Davidson Motor Company. Principal Type: Knockout and Rockwell. Dimensions: various

Signage

Design: Kum-jun Park, Seoul. Art Direction: Kum-jun Park. Creative Direction: Kum-jun Park. Lettering: Kum-jun Park. Coordination: Jong-in Jung, Seung-youn Nam, Hae-rang Park, and Na-won You. Studio: 601bisang. Dimensions: various

Installation
Design: Lizá Ramalho and Artur Rebelo, Porto, Portugal. Art Direction: Lizá Ramalho and Artur Rebelo. Creative Direction: Lizá Ramalho and Artur Rebelo. Design Office: R2 Design. Client: Ermida Nossa Senhora da Conceição. Principal Type: Neutraface Slab. Dimensions: 19.7 x 51.2 ft. (50 x 130 m)

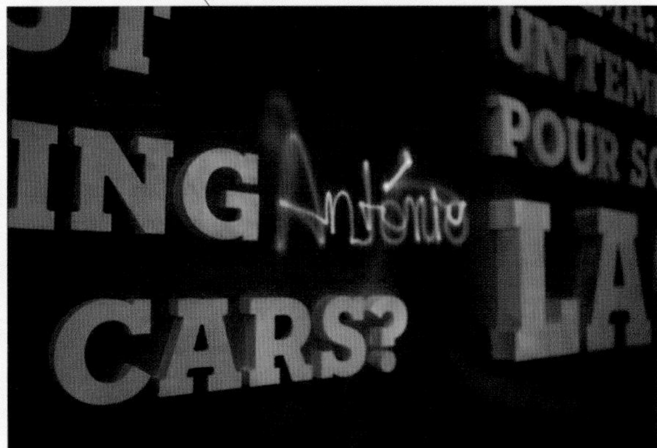

Exhibit

Design: Tanja Devetak and Eduard Cehovin, Ljubljana, Slovenia. Art Direction: Tanja Devetak and Eduard Cehovin. Creative Direction: Tanja Devetak and Eduard Cehovin. Design Office: Design Center. Principal Type: custom. Dimensions: 27.6 x 39.4 in. (70 x 100 cm)

Exhibition

Design: Hanif Kureshi, New Delhi. Art Direction: Hanif Kureshi. Creative Direction: V. Sunil. Agency: Wieden+Kennedy, Delhi. Principal Type: 23,000 pencils. Dimensions: 20 x 9 ft. (6.1 x 2.7 m)

Posters

Design: Kota Sagae and Tatsunori Kuroki, Tokyo. Art Direction: Kota Sagae. Creative Direction: Kota Sagae. Design Office: SAGA. Client: Nippon Bartenders Association. Principal Type: Bauer Bodoni. Dimensions: 28.7 x 40.6 in. (72.8 x 103 cm)

Posters
Design: 2xGoldstein, Karlsruhe, Germany. Client: Adam Seide Archiv. Principal Type: Akzidenz Grotesk. Dimensions: 24.4 x 35 in. (62 x 89 cm)

1/11/2009
4. Adam Seide
Literaturtag
Vortrag
Günter Müller
Lesungen
Reinhard Jirgl
Angelika Overath
Peter Weber
Musikalische
Interpretation
Helmut
Bieler-Wendt
HfG Karlsruhe
Lorenzstraße 15
Ab 11 Uhr
Eintritt frei
www.
adamseide.de

Poster
Design: Rocco Piscatello, New York. Lettering: Rocco Piscatello. Design Office: Piscatello Design Centre. Client: Fashion Institute of Technology. Principal Type: Futura and custom. Dimensions: 23.4 x 33.1 in. (59.4 x 84.1 cm)

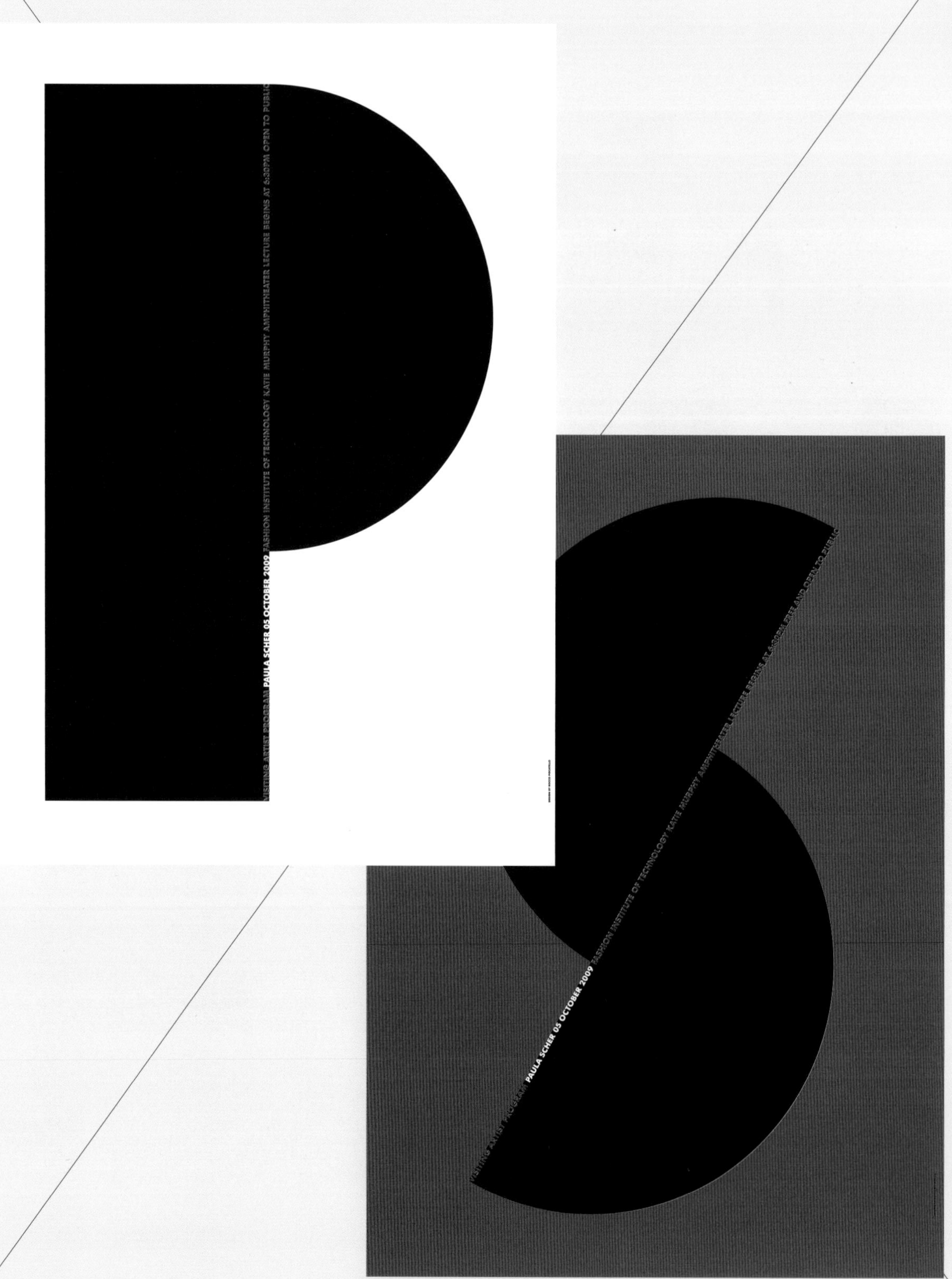

Exhibition Signage

Design: Masayoshi Kodaira and Yukiharu Takematsu, E.P.A., Tokyo. Art Direction: Masayoshi Kodaira. Photography: Mikiya Takimoto and Fumihito Katamura. Producer: Soichiro Fukutake. Studio: FLAME. Client: Fukutake Foundation for the Promotion of Regional Culture. Principal Type: Trade Gothic. Dimensions: various

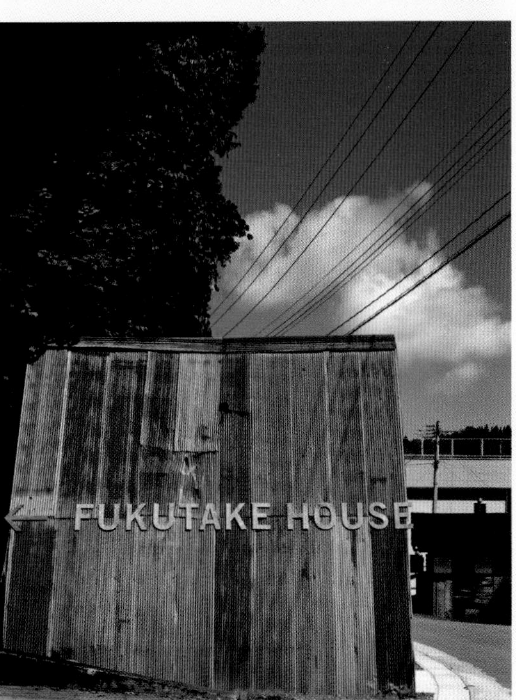

Poster

Design: Paul Garbett, Rushcutters Bay, Australia. Creative Direction: Paul Garbett. Lettering: Paul Garbett. Design Office: Naughtyfish Design. Client: Australian Graphic Design Association. Principal Type: handlettering. Dimensions: 33.1 x 46.8 in. (84 x 118.8 cm)

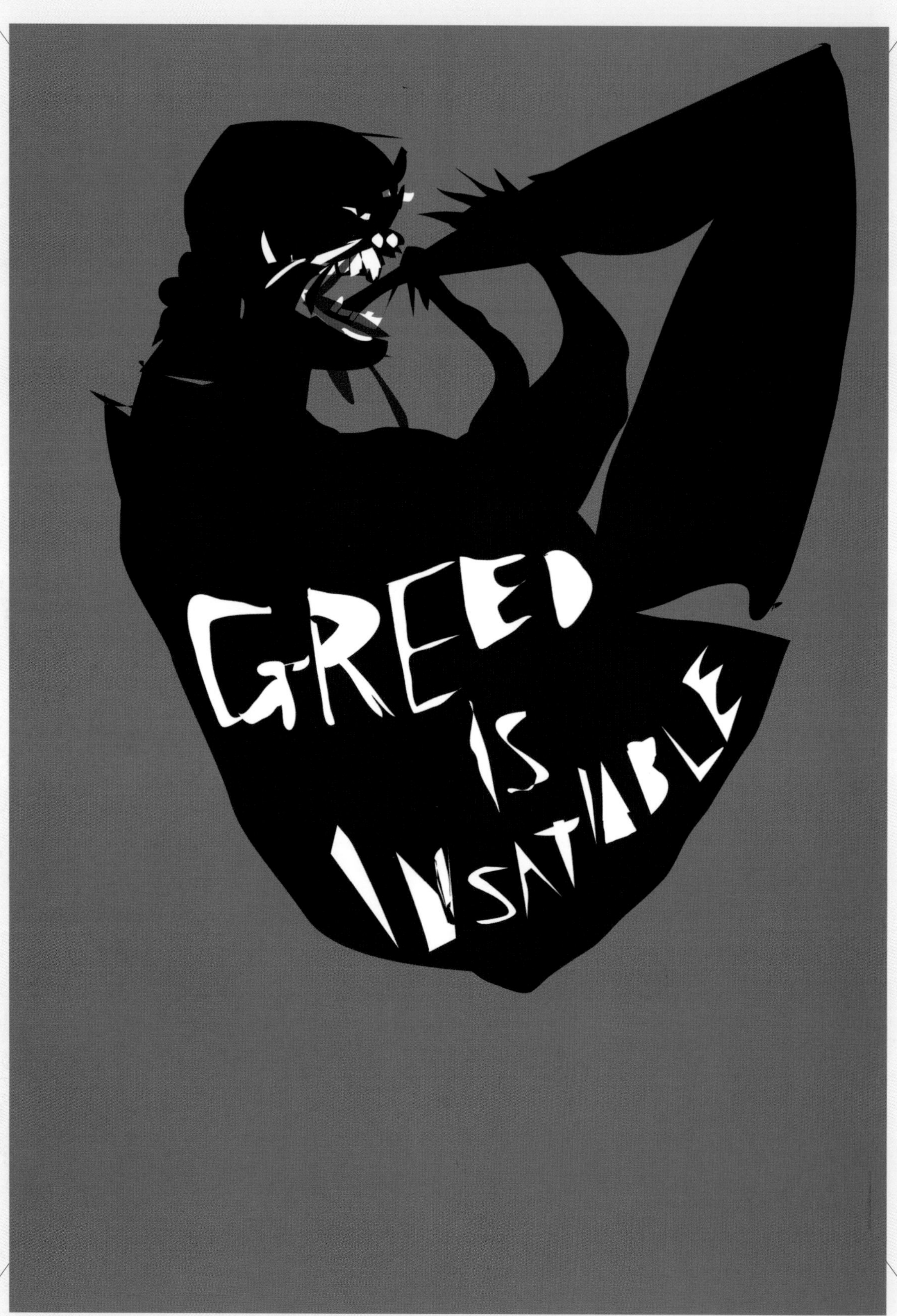

Poster

Design: Kum-jun Park and Na-won You, Seoul. Art Direction: Kum-jun Park. Creative Direction: Kum-jun Park. Illustration: Kum-jun Park. Coordination: Jong-in Jung. Studio: 610bisang. Principal Type: various. Dimensions: 27.6 x 39.4 in. (70 x 100 cm)

Posters
Design: Frank Viva, Toronto. Lettering: Frank Viva. Design Office: Viva & Co. Client: Whigby. Principal Type: handlettering.
Dimensions: 19.5 x 26.5 in. (49.5 x 67.3 cm)

Membership Kit

Design: James Wai Mo Leung, Hong Kong. Art Direction: James Wai Mo Leung. Creative Direction: James Wai Mo Leung. Lettering: James Wai Mo Leung. Photography: Eva Chan. Design Office: Genemix. Client: Hong Kong Designers Association. Principal Type: ITC American Typewriter, Myriad Pro, and custom. Dimensions: various

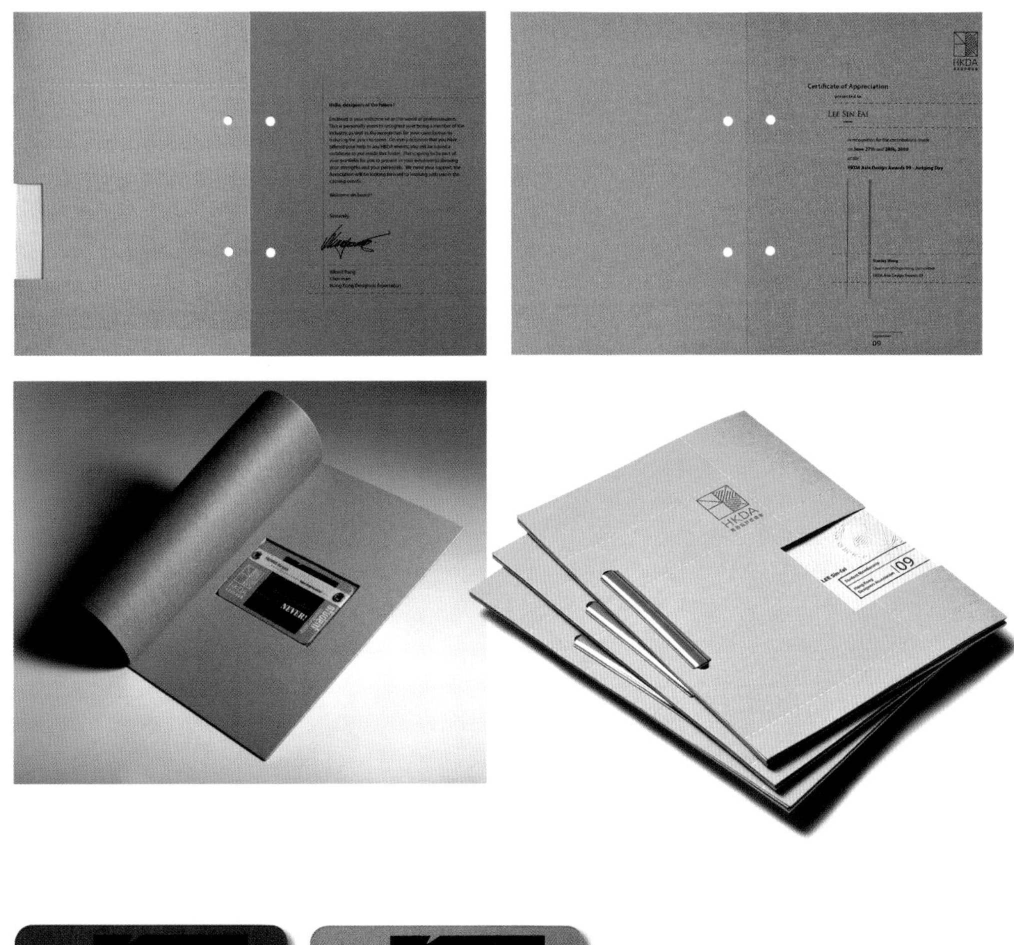

Exhibits

Design: Elliot, Montréal. Creative Direction: Elliot. Collaborators: Mélanie Boucher and Pierre-Luc Faubert. Studio: Elliot. Client: Bibliothèque et Archives Nationales du Québec. Principal Type: Univers and Caslon. Dimensions: panel, 8.9 x 7.25 ft. (2.7 x 2.2 m); wall, 4 x 40 ft. (1.2 x 12.2 m)

Calendar

Design: Linda Ritoh and Chica Yoshizawa, Osaka, Japan. Art Direction: Linda Ritoh. Creative Direction: Linda Ritoh and Yoshihiro Miura. Photography: various. Design Office: LINDA GRAPHICA & LIBIDO. Client: Pantone Hexachrome Consortium. Principal Type: Helvetica and MB31. Dimensions: 28.7 x 40.6 in. (72.8 x 103 cm)

Student Project

Design: Miriam Magdalena Rockel, Berlin. School: Hochschule Augsburg. Professors: Robert Rose and Jürgen Hefele. Principal Type: custom. Dimensions: various

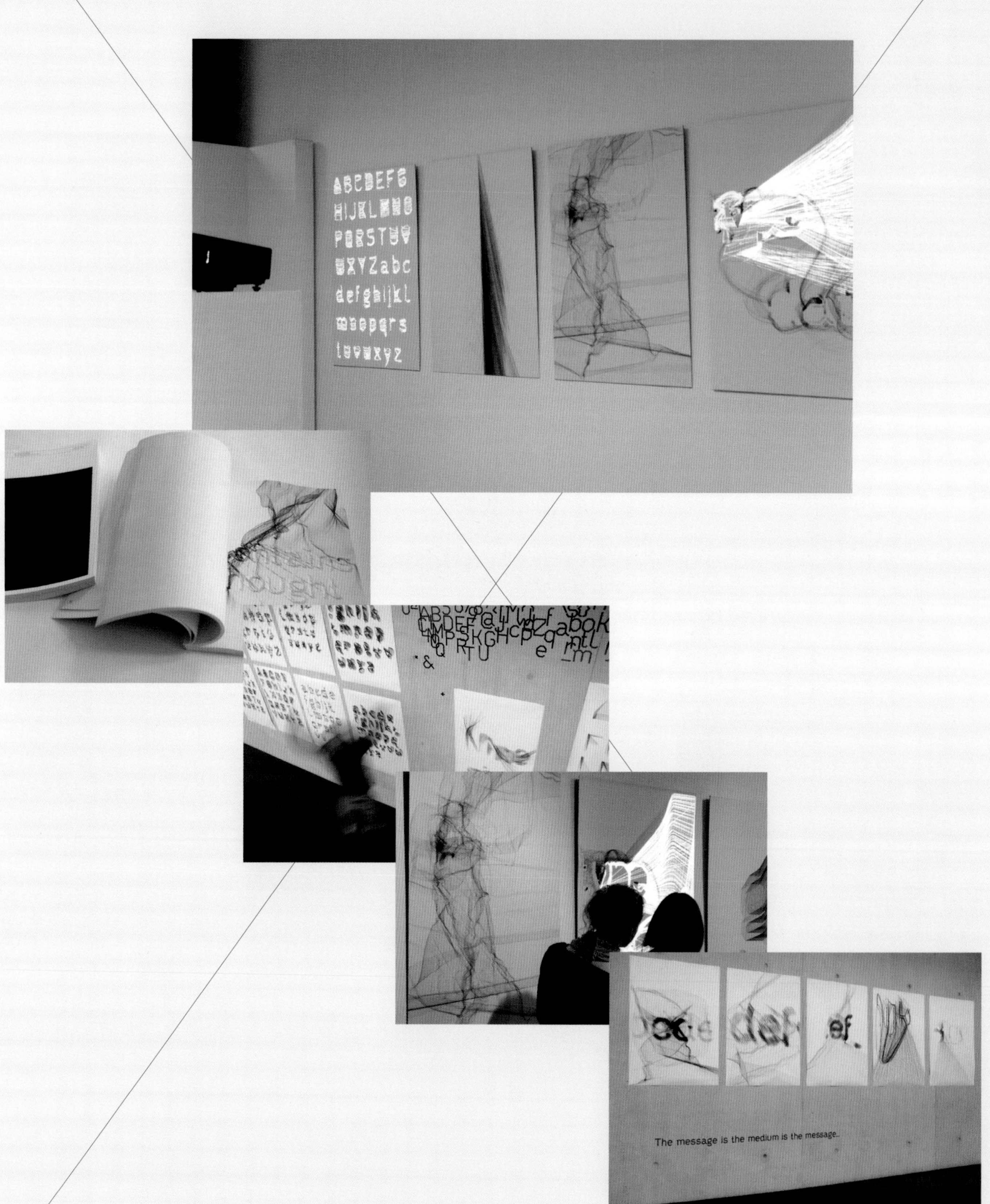

Student Project

Design: Jessica Scholz, Wuppertal, Germany. Art Direction: Professor Heribert Birnbach and Jessica Scholz. Creative Direction: Professor Heribert Birnbach, Bonn, Germany. Schools: Bergische Universität Wuppertal, Campus Wuppertal, and Folkwang Universität. Principal Type: FF DIN. Dimensions: 8 x 11.2 in. (21 x 28.5 cm)

Packaging

Design: Anthony De Leo, Adelaide, Australia. Creative Direction: Anthony De Leo. Studio: Voice. Client: Back Label Wines. Principal Type: Helvetica Neue. Dimensions: 4.5 x 4.6 in. (11.5 x 11.6 cm)

Calendar
Design: Hugo Goeldner and Martin Christel, Berlin. Design Office: Codeluxe/CDLX. Client: WSB Werbeagentur, Leipzig.
Principal Type: Akkurat Mono. Dimensions: 23.6 x 34.1 in. (60 x 86.6 cm)

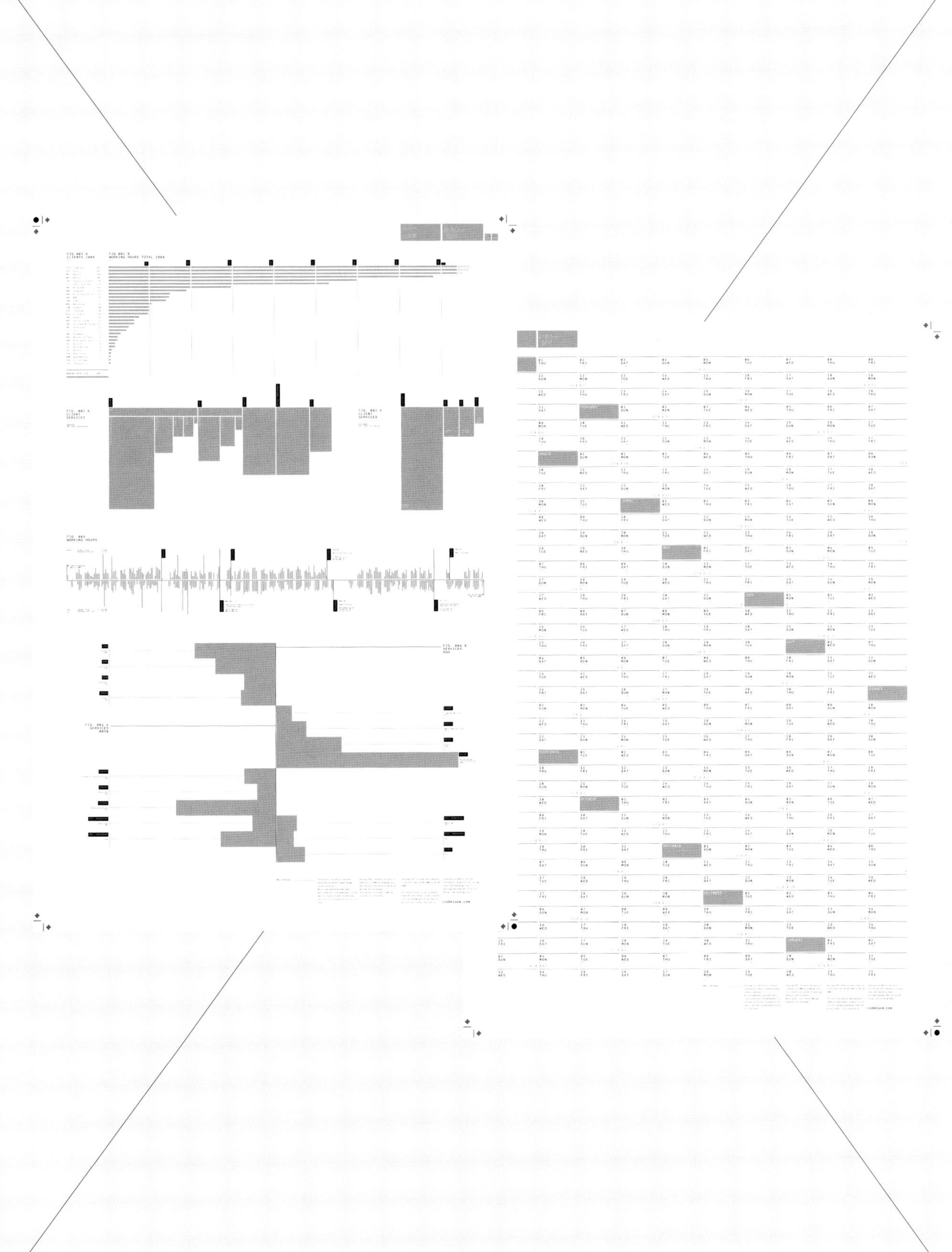

Invitation

Design: Shingo Noma, Tokyo. Art Direction: Shingo Noma. Photography: Koji Udo. Principal Type: Mona Regular and Mona Regular Stressed. Dimensions: 16.5 x 23.4 in. (42 x 59.4 cm)

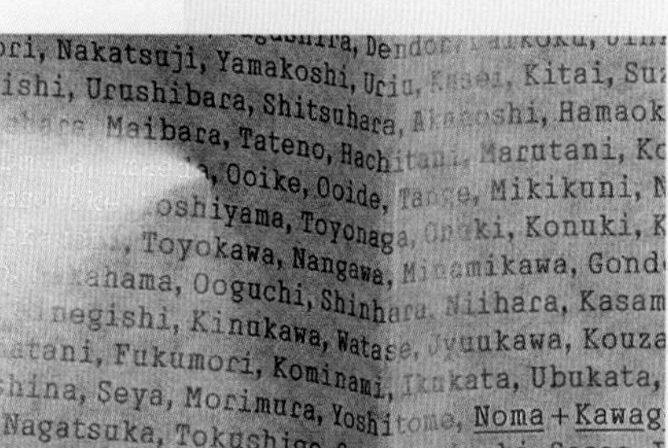

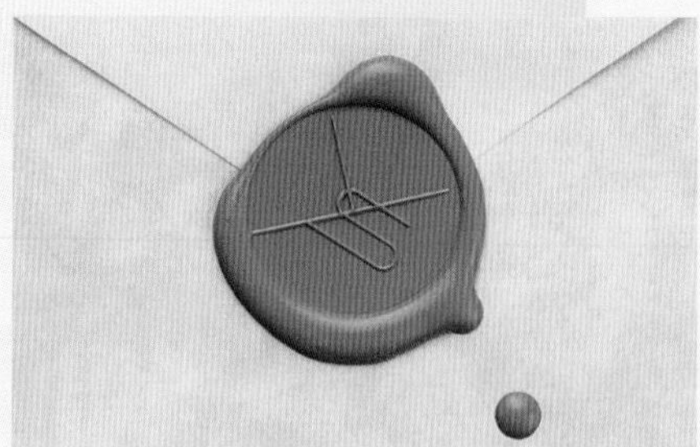

Student Project
Design: Ihn Sun Kim, New York. School: School of Visual Arts, New York. Instructors: Carin Goldberg and Timothy Samara.
Principal Type: We R.1. and OCR-A. Dimensions: 18 x 26.3 in. (45.9 x 66.8 cm)

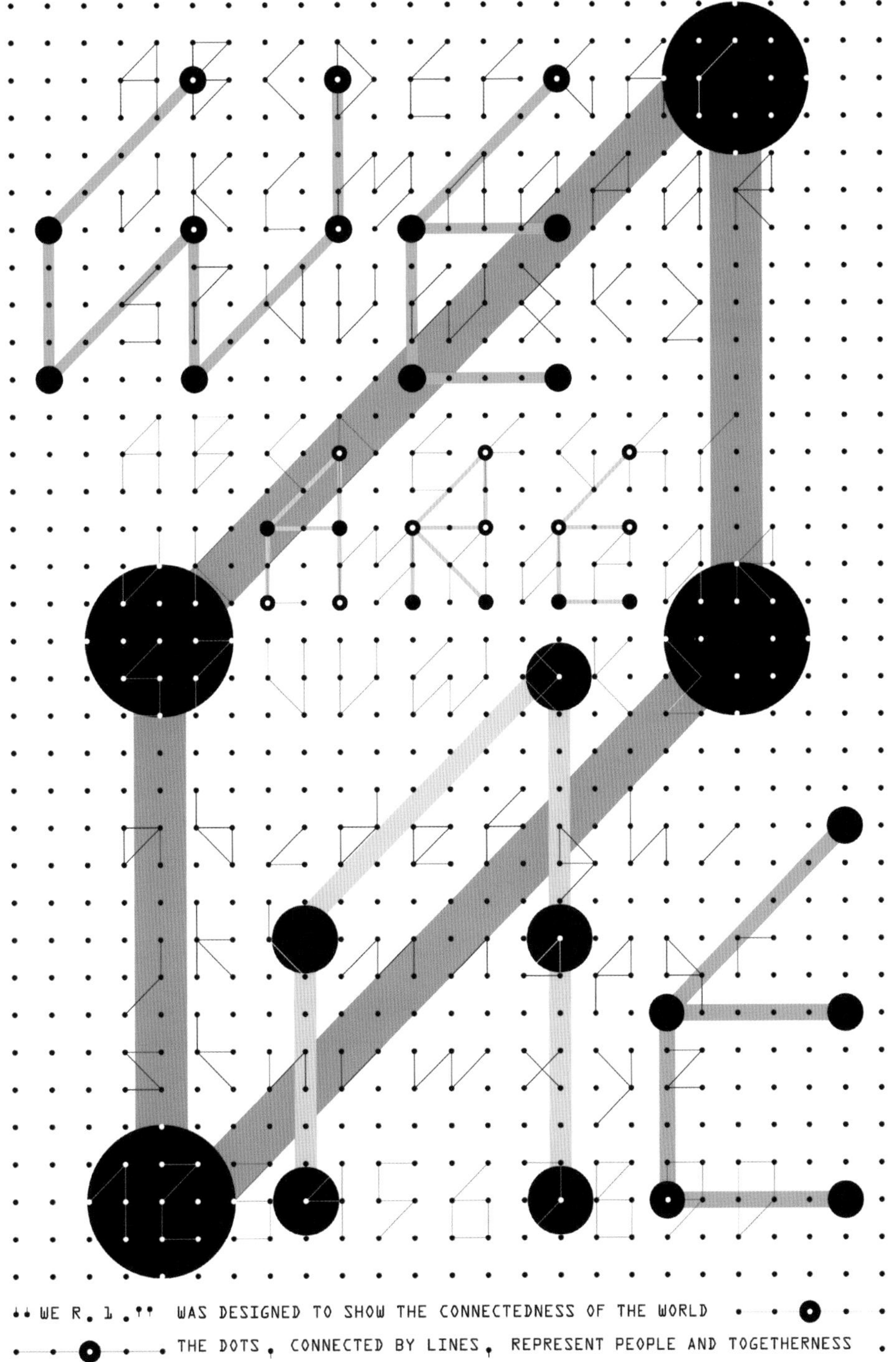

Student Project

Design: Jiwon Kim, New York. School: School of Visual Arts, New York. Instructors: Paula Scher and Lisa Kitschenberg. Principal Type: custom. Dimensions: various

GRAMERCY
FLOWER
SHOP

260 THIRD AVE
NEW YORK
NY 10010

ABCDEFGHIJKLMN
OPQRSTUVWXYZ

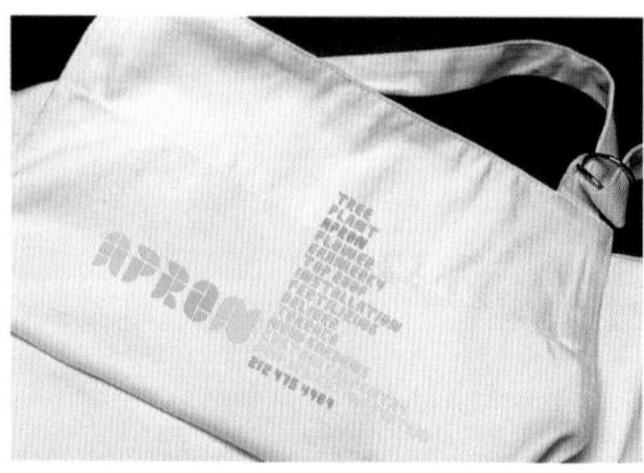

Student Project

Design: Joey Flynn, Seattle. School: University of Washington. Instructor: Annabelle Gould. Principal Type: Helvetica.
Dimensions: 33.1 x 46.8 in. (84.1 x 118.9 cm)

A conversation
on color perception
and deficiency.

Keigo Hirakawa
Alex Byrne
David Hilbert
Todd Zickler

14 October 2009
7 pm

Walker Art Center
1750 Hennepin Ave
Minneapolis, MN

Poster 1 of 8
Tritanopia: a total absence of blue retinal receptors.

www.walkerart.org

Ro G. Roy G.
Biv Biv

A conversation
on color perception
and deficiency.

Keigo Hirakawa
Alex Byrne
David Hilbert
Todd Zickler

14 October 2009
7 pm

Walker Art Center
1750 Hennepin Ave
Minneapolis, MN

Poster 7 of 8
Typical Monochromacy: the complete inability to perceive color.

www.walkerart.org

Ro G. Roy G.
Biv Biv

Student Project
Design: Gabrielle Lamontagne, Montréal. School: Université du Québec à Montréal (UQAM). Instructor: Judith Poirier. Principal Type: Filosofia, FF Info Office, Mrs Eaves, and ITC Officina Sans. Dimensions: 20 x 30 in. (50.8 x 76.2 cm)

Student Project

Design: Eunjung Yoo, New York. School: School of Visual Arts, New York. Instructor: Skip Sorvino. Principal Type: custom using kitchen forks. Dimensions: 6 x 10 in. (15.2 x 25.4 cm)

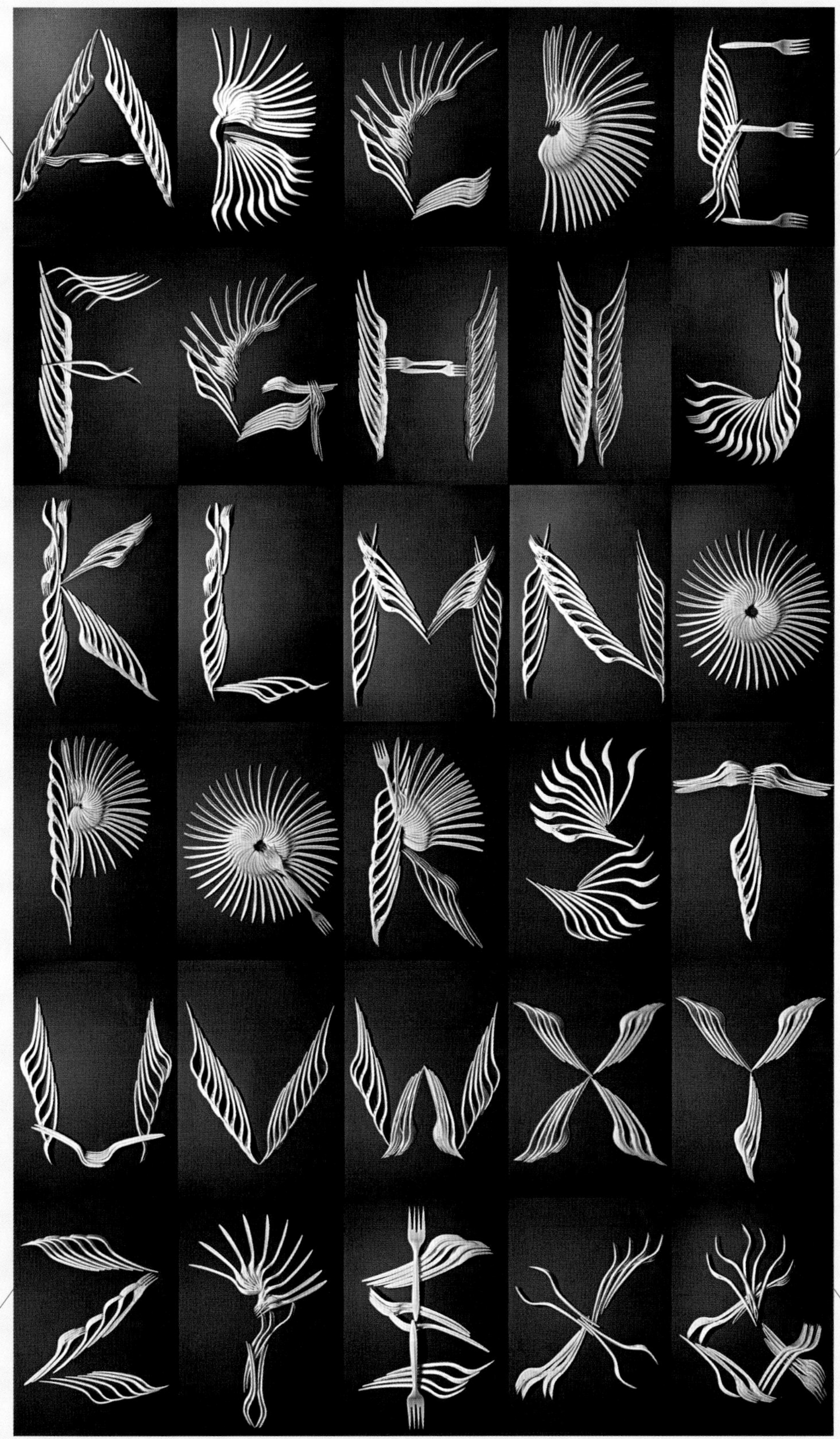

Student Project

Design: Thomas Losinski, Spotswood, New Jersey. School: School of Visual Arts, New York. Instructor: Henrietta Condak. Principal Type: Cloister Black, Futura, and black letter. Dimensions: 13 x 19 in. (33 x 48.3 cm)

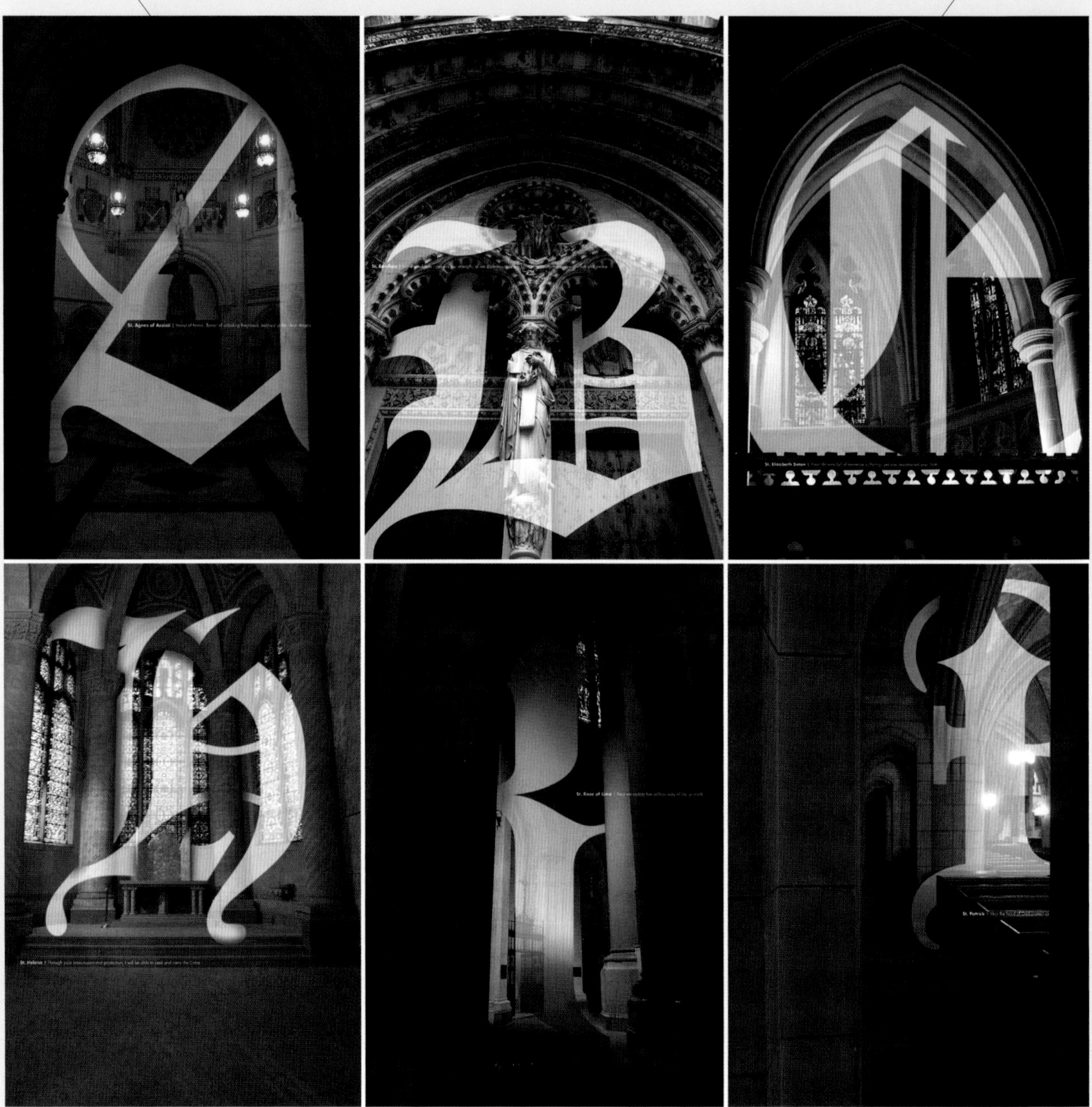

Student Project

Design: James Kyungmo Yang, New York. School: School of Visual Arts, MFA Program, New York. Instructor: Stephen Doyle. Principal Type: various. Dimensions: 18 x 24 in. (45.8 x 61 cm)

MUST
SEE
THINGS
FROM
ALL
ANGLES

SEE
ANGNES

Student Project

Design: James Kyungmo Yang, New York. School: School of Visual Arts, MFA Program, New York. Instructor: Kevin O'Callaghan. Principal Type: custom. Dimensions: 4 x 4 x 8 ft. (12.2 x 12.2. x 24.4 m)

Student Project

Design: Tom Grunwald, New York. School: School of Visual Arts, New York. Instructor: Genevieve Williams. Principal Type: Nemek Regular. Dimensions: 24 x 36 in. (61 x 91.4 cm)

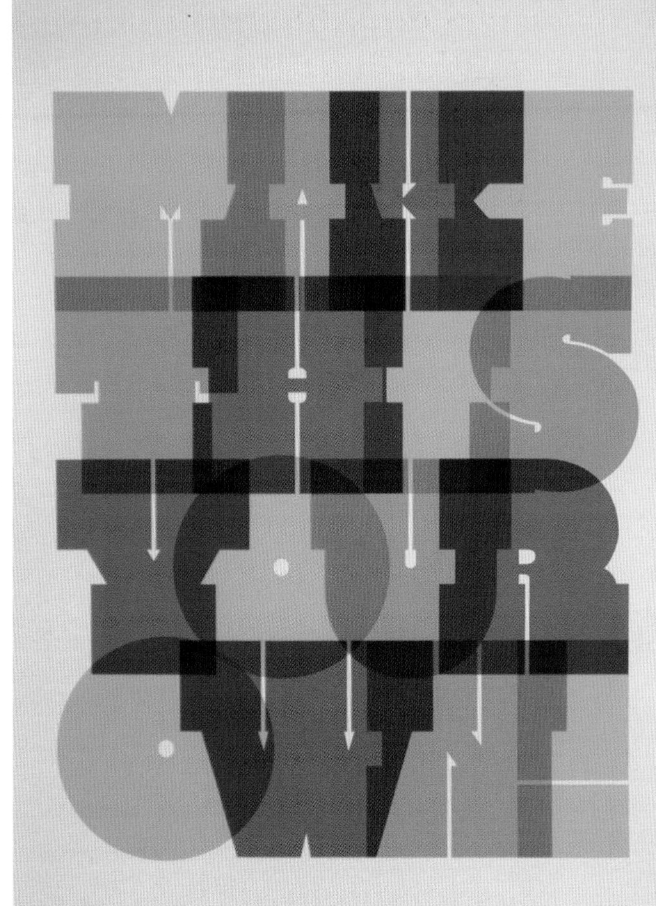

Corporate Identity
Design: Jeeyoon Rhee, New York. Art Direction: Jeeyon Rhee. Creative Direction: Jeeyon Rhee. Design Office: PastPresentFuture. Client: Fragmental Museum, New York. Principal Type: Helvetica and Glypha (modified). Dimensions: various

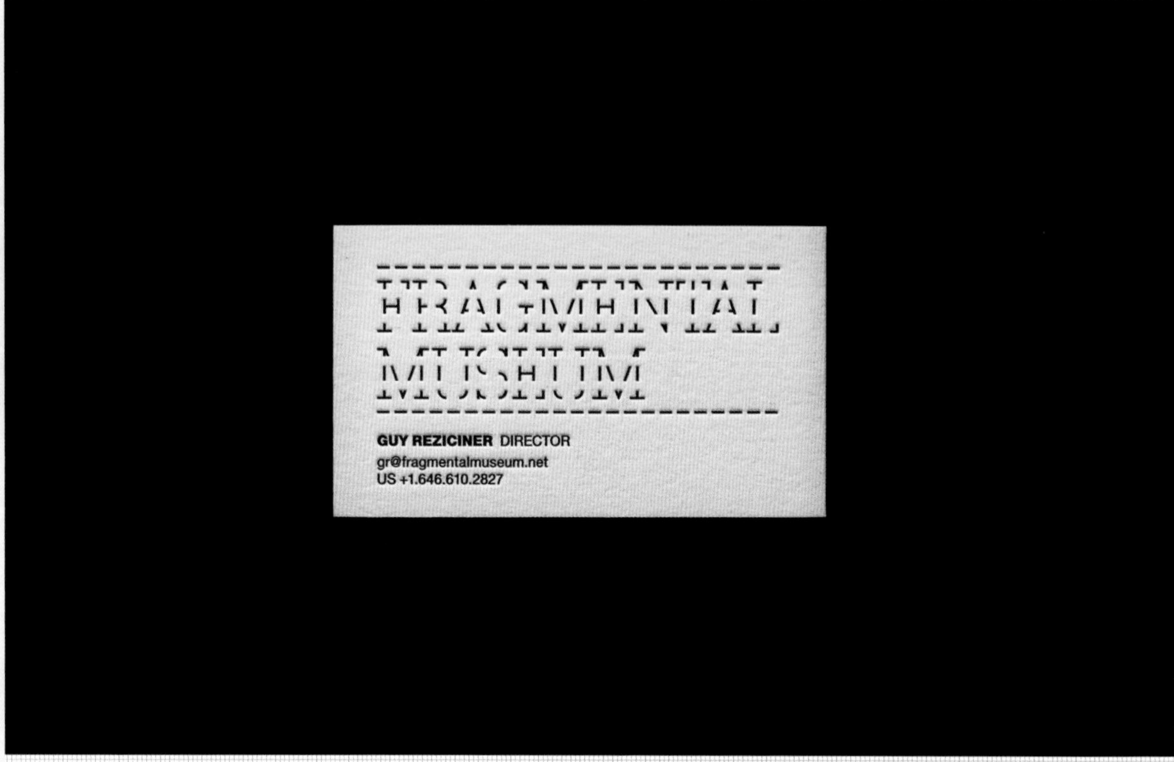

Corporate Identity

Design: Edwin Vollebergh and Petra Janssen, Den Bosch, Netherlands. Art Direction: Edwin Vollebergh and Petra Janssen. Creative Direction: Edwin Vollebergh and Petra Janssen. Lettering: studio Boot. Studio: studio Boot. Principal Type: Stella. Dimensions: various

WWW.STUDIOBOOT.NL

STUDIO BOOT
ONTWERP

CREATIEF DIRECTEUR
EDWIN VOLLEBERGH
ADRES
LUIJBENSTRAAT 40/42
5211 BT
'S-HERTOGENBOSCH
PHONE
+31(0)73 - 614 35 93
MOB
+31(0)6 - 5111 56 18
MAIL
EDWIN@STUDIOBOOT.NL
WIL JE MEER ZIEN ?
KIJK DAN OP WWW.STUDIOBOOT.NL

STUDIO BOOT • grafische & illustratieve vormgeving / GRAPHIC & ILLUSTRATIVE DESIGN | uijbenstraat 40 • 5211 BT 's-Hertogenbosch TEL. (+31) 073 - 614 35 93 | FAX.(+31) 073 - 613 31 90 | ISDN 073 - 612 98 65 | rek.nr.: 52.43.10.076 | BTW.nr: NL.1225.61.922.B.01 van / FROM: Petra Janssen (petra@studioboot.nl) | Edwin Vollebergh (edwin@studioboot.nl) | kijk ook op www.studioboot.nl ALLE OPDRACHTEN WORDEN UITGEVOERD CONFORM DE ALGEMENE VOORWAARDEN VAN DE BNO (BEROEPSVERENIGING NEDERLANDSE ONTWERPERS). ZOALS GEDEPONEERD TER GRIFFIE VAN DE ARRONDISEMENTSRECHTBANK TE AMSTERDAM • brief / LETTER • factuur / INVOICE (rek.nr.: 52.43.10.076) begroting / ESTIMATE • opdrachtbevestiging / CONFIRMATION • fax / FAX (aantal pagina's / NUMBER OF PAGES) datum / DATE : betreft / CONCERNING :

INDIEN ONBESTELBAAR RETOUR AFZENDER:
STUDIO BOOT | Luijbenstraat 40 | 5211 BT | 's-Hertogenbosch

Poster

Design: Christian Rüther, München, Germany. Art Direction: Darius Gondor. Creative Direction: Annette Häfelinger. Lettering: Darius Gondor and Christina Rüther. Agency: häfelinger + wagner design. Principal Type: Akkurat Regular, Letter Gothic, and handlettering. Dimensions: 23.4 x 33.1 in. (59.4 x 84.1 cm)

Logotype
Design: Keita Shimbo and Misako Shimbo, Tokyo. Art Direction: Keita Shimbo and Misako Shimbo. Creative Direction: Takaaki Murase. Design Office: nanilani co. Client: The Organizing Committee of the International Festival for Arts and Media Yokohama 2009. Principal Type: custom

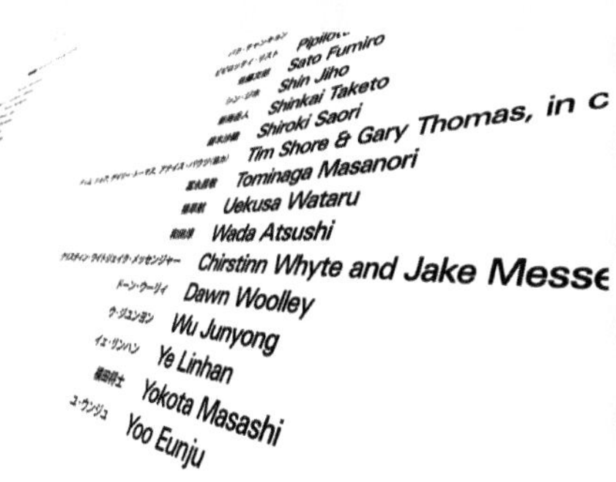

Student Project

Design: Benjamin K. Shown, Seattle. School: University of Washington. Instructor: Annabelle Gould. Principal Type: Red October and Fedra Serif. Dimensions: 22 x 17 in. (55.9 x 43.2 cm)

Television Commercial

Design: Why Not Associates, London. Art Direction: Why Not Associates. Creative Direction: Brian Harrington and Why Not Associates. Design Office: Why Not Associates. Client: Channel 4. Principal Type: Impact

Exhibition

Design: René Clément and François-Xavier Saint-Georges, Montréal. Art Direction: René Clément. Creative Direction: Louis Gagnon. Studio: Paprika. Client: Montréal Museum of Fine Arts. Principal Type: Interstate. Dimensions: various

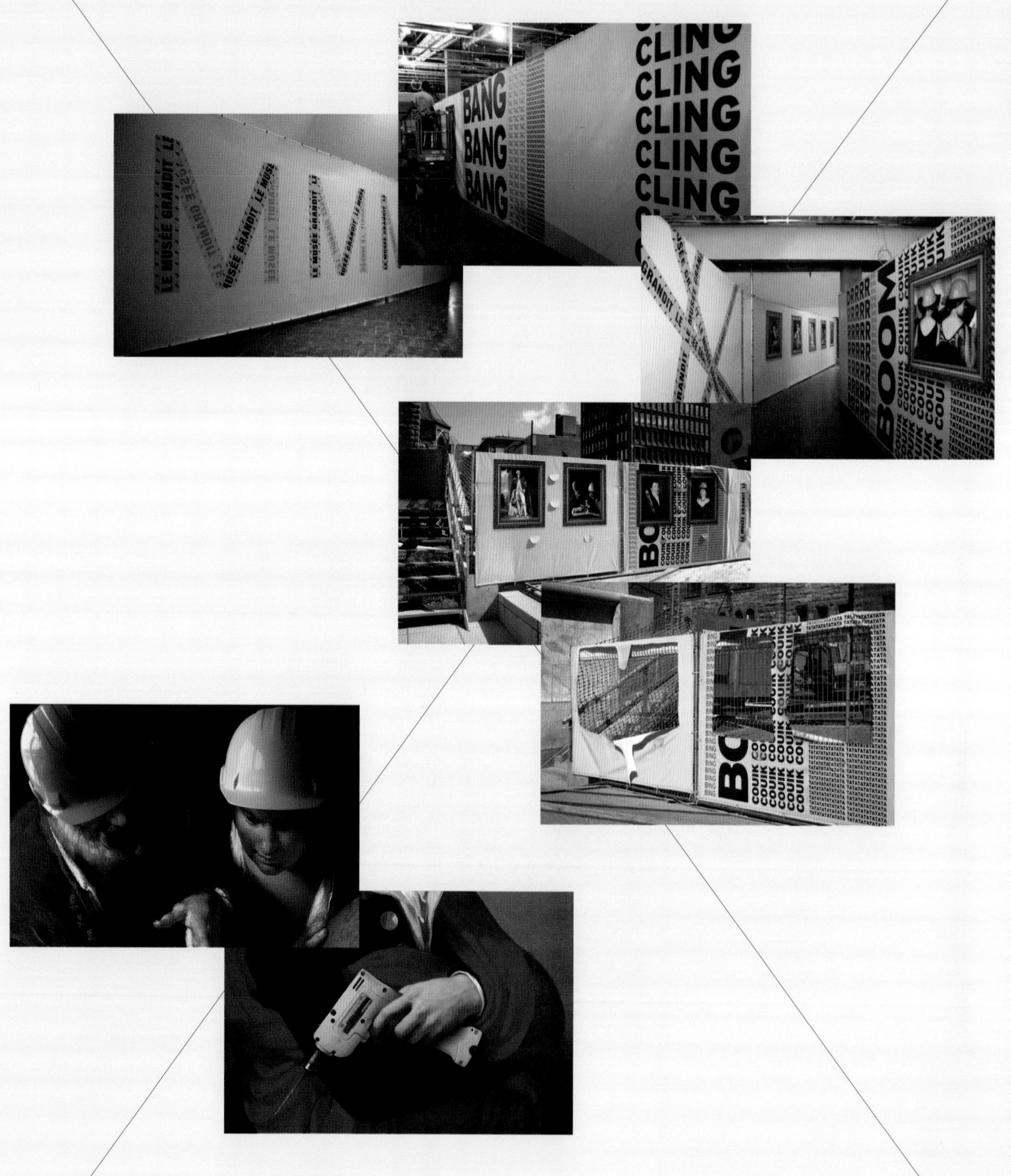

Packaging

Design: Lisa Rienermann, Berlin. Art Direction: Anne-Lene Proff. Creative Direction: Peter Bünnagel, Barbara Kotte, and Anne-Lene Proff. Studio: Scrollan. Client: Heimat Werbeagentur. Principal Type: ITC Conduit. Dimensions: 3.1 x 8.7 in. (8 x 22 cm)

Exhibition

Design: Gordon Young and Why Not Associates, London. Art Direction: Gordon Young and Why Not Associates. Creative Direction: Gordon Young and Why Not Associates. Design Office: Why Not Associates. Client: West Sussex County Council. Principal Type: various. Dimensions: various

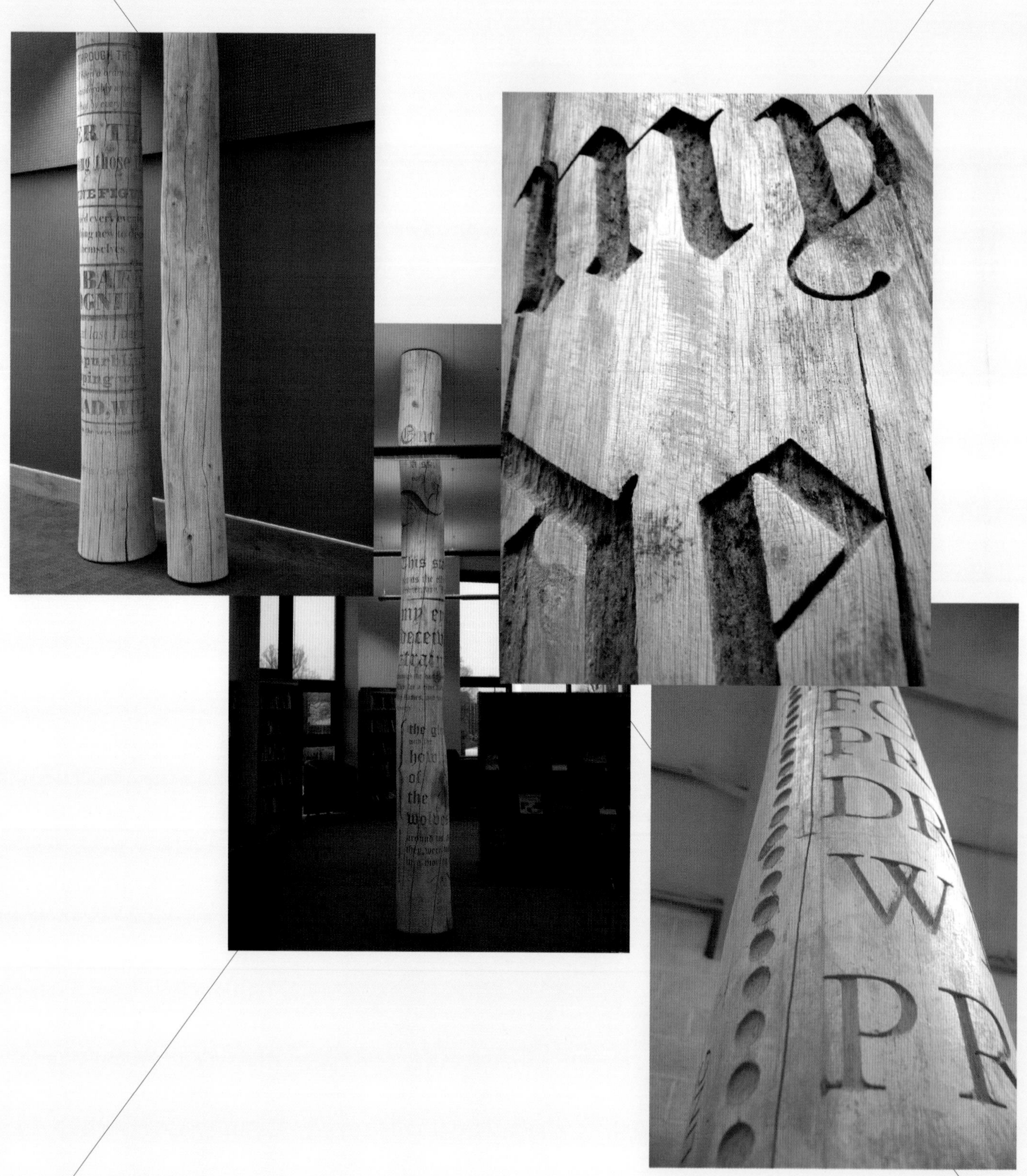

Poster

Design: Stefanie Schwarz, Stuttgart, Germany. School: Fakultät für Gestaltung, Hochschule Pforzheim. Principal Type: Trade Gothic. Dimensions: 23.4 x 33.1 in. (59.4 x 84.1 cm)

27.05.2009

ROBERT

KLANTEN

18 UHR – VORTRAG

„IDENTITÄT UND MATERIALISIERUNG“

19 UHR – DISKUSSION

„KNISTERN VS. KLICKEN – ZWISCHEN BILDSCHIRM UND PAPIER“

WEITERE TEIL-NEHMER:

PETER BÜNNAGEL
SCROLLAN, BERLIN

LARS HARMSEN
MAGMA BRAND DESIGN, KARLSRUHE

WOLFGANG HENSELER
PROF, PFORZHEIM
SYZYGY, BAD HOMBURG

MARIO LOMBARDO
BUREAU MARIO LOMBARDO, BERLIN

DESIGN PF

STUDIENGANG VISUELLE KOMMUNIKATION . ÖSTLICHE KARL-FRIEDRICH-STRASSE 24 . 75175 PFORZHEIM . IM 4. OG

HOCHSCHULE PFORZHEIM
FAKULTÄT FÜR GESTALTUNG
WWW.GESTALTUNG.HS-PFORZHEIM.DE

Poster

Design: Klaus Hesse, Düsseldorf, Germany. Lettering: Klaus Hesse. Design Office: Hesse Design. Client: Hochschule für Gestaltung Offenbach am Main. Principal Type: Corporate S and handlettering. Dimensions: 27.6 x 39.4 in. (70 x 100 cm)

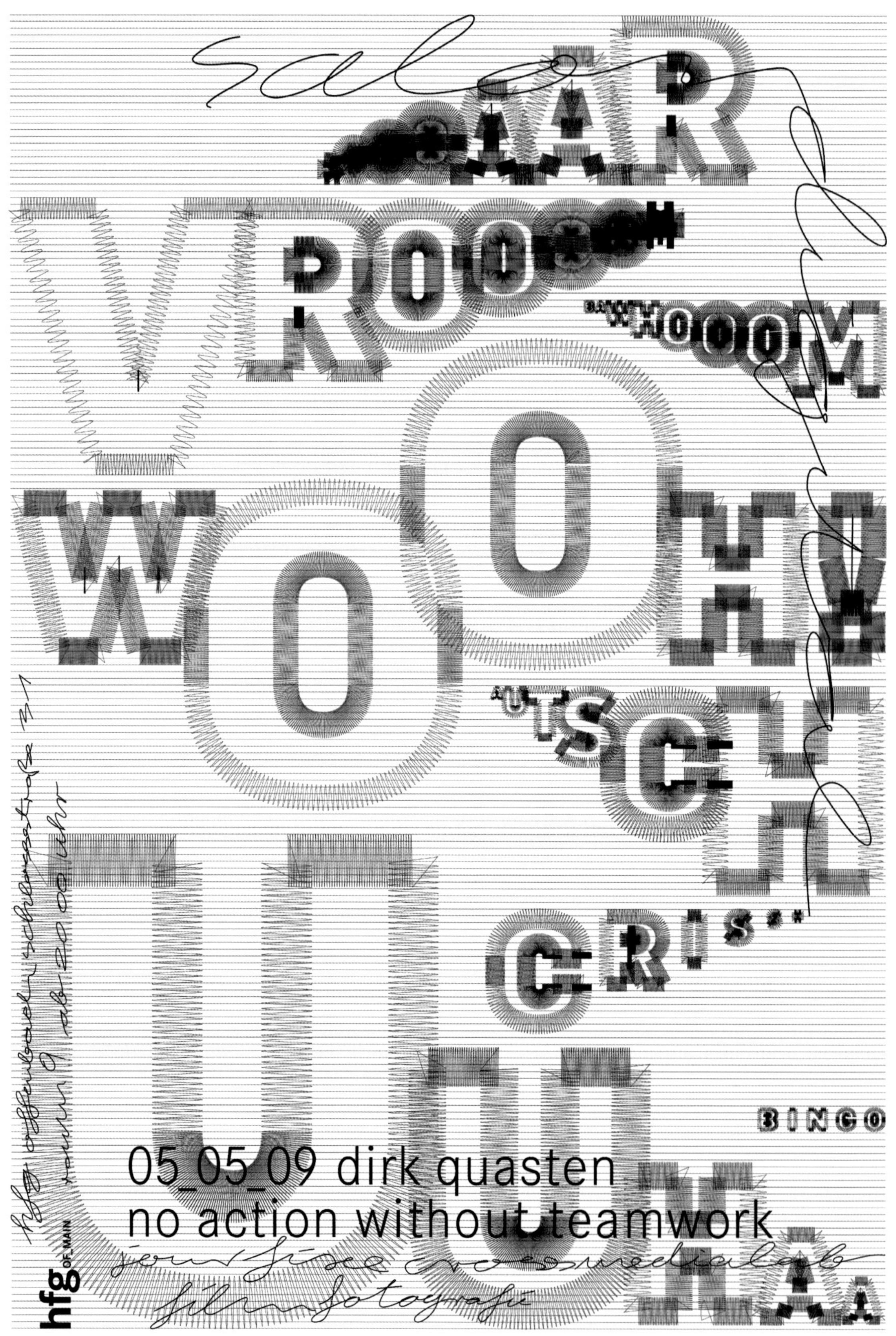

Poster

Design: Mark Gowing, Sydney, Australia. Creative Direction: Mark Gowing. Lettering: Mark Gowing. Design Office: Mark Gowing Design. Client: Hopscotch Films. Principal Type: Impact and custom. Dimensions: 27.2 x 39.4 in. (69 x 100 cm)

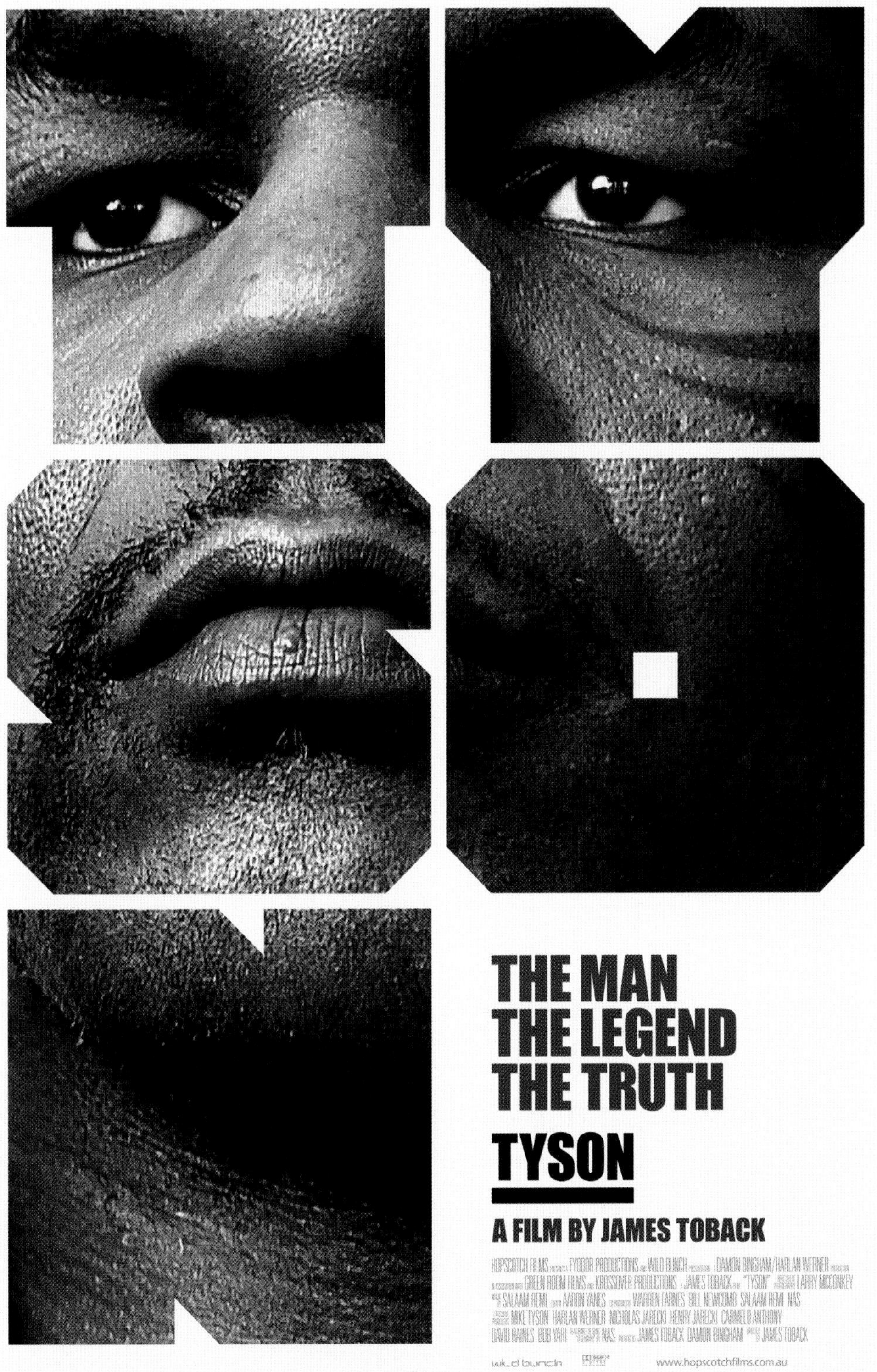

Poster

Design: Jason Little, Sydney, Australia. Art Direction: Jason Little. Creative Direction: Jason Little. Agency: Landor Associates. Client: Australian Graphic Design Association. Principal Type: Courier and custom. Dimensions: 23.4 x 33.1 in. (59.4 x 84 cm)

AGDA

DESIGNER DINNER #1
ESKIMO DESIGN
OTTO RISTORANTE
WOOLLOOMOOLOO
THURSDAY 19 MARCH '09
RSVP ANITA LYONS
NSW@AGDA.COM.AU

Poster

Design: Mike Hart, Jason Little, Ivana Martinovic, Sam Pemberton, and Jefton Sungkar, Sydney, Australia. Creative Direction: Jason Little. Lettering: Jefton Sungkar. Photography: Mike Hart. Props and Models: Chenying Hau, Malin Holmstrom, Sandra Kelso, and Pan Yamboonruang, Landor Associates. Client: Australian Graphic Design Association. Principal Type: Helvetica Neue Bold Condensed and Helvetica Neue Heavy Condensed. Dimensions: 23.4 x 33.1 in. (59.4 x 84 cm)

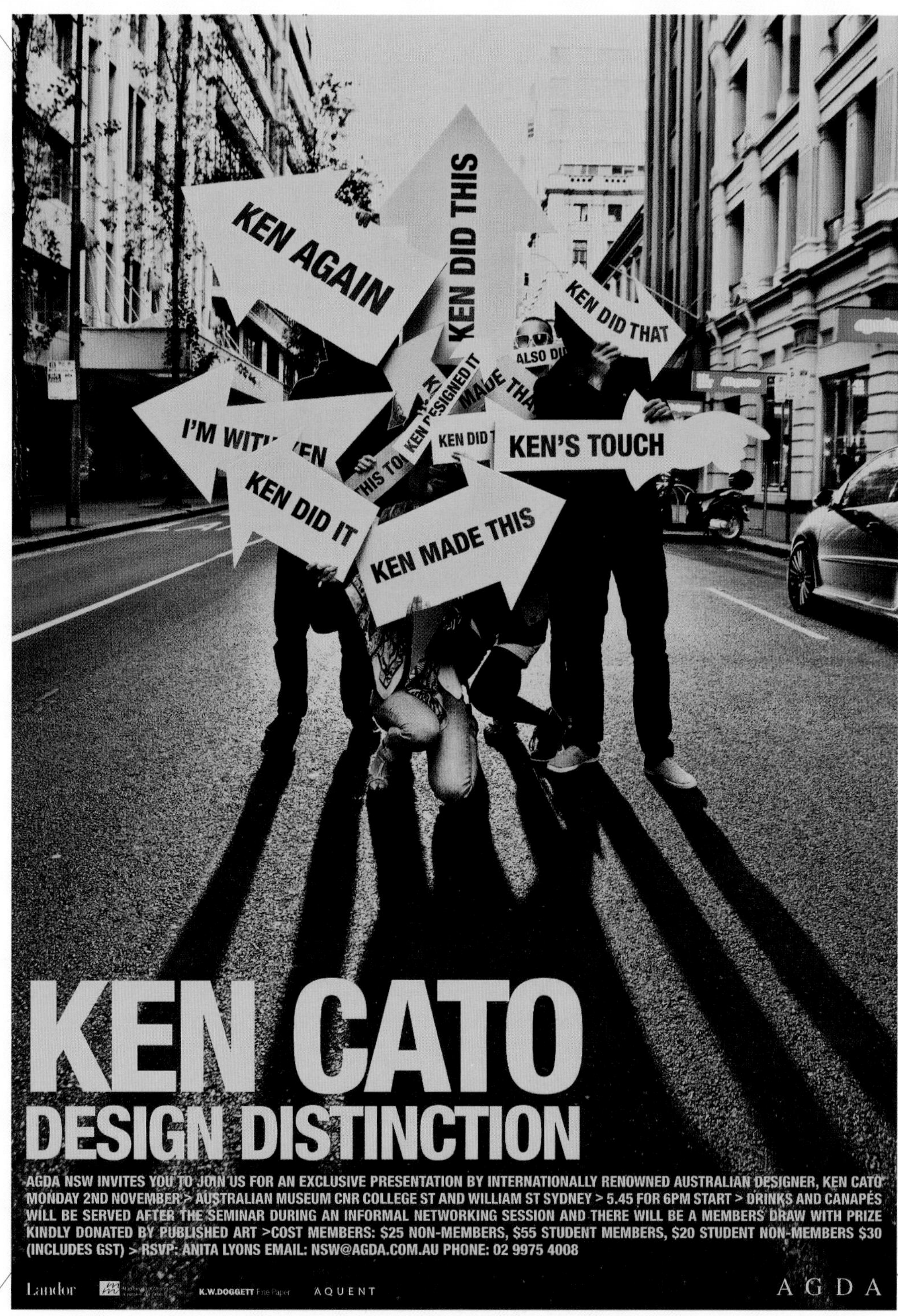

Poster

Design: Markus Koll, Hamburg, Germany. Art Direction: Markus Koll. Creative Direction: Olaf Stein and Markus Koll. Studio: Factor Design. Client: Thinkprint. Principal Type: Adobe Garamond and various. Dimensions: 23.4 x 33.1 in. (59.4 x 84 cm)

Packaging

Design: Helen Hacker, Düsseldorf, Germany. Creative Direction: Helen Hacker. Design Office: Büro Grotesk. Client: MMacarons and Caroline Gruss. Principal Type: Alpha Headline, Bickman Script Pro, and Univers. Dimensions: various

Signage
Design: Katy Fischer, St. Louis. Art Direction: Eric Thoelke. Creative Direction: Eric Thoelke. Lettering: Katy Fischer and Noah Woods. Illustration: Noah Woods. Design Office: TOKY Branding + Design. Client: St. Louis Public Library Foundation. Principal Type: handlettering. Dimensions: various

Exhibition

Design: Steff Geissbuhler and Mariano Desmaras, New York. Art Direction: Steff Geissbuhler. Lettering: Steff Geissbuhler. Design Office: C&G Partners. Client: Radio Free Europe and Radio Liberty. Principal Type: custom. Dimensions: 10 ft. (3 m) tall

Exhibit

Design: Motoyasu Hojo, Sentaro Miki, and Ken Morigaki, Tokyo. Art Direction: Ken Morigaki. Creative Direction: Ken Morigaki. Photography: Takumi Ota. Client: Association of Mukojima Studies, Tokyo Metropolitan Foundation for History and Culture, and Tokyo Metropolitan Government. Principal Type: Interstate and custom. Dimensions: 43.3 x 70.9 x 94.5 in. (110 x 180 x 240 cm)

Posters
Design: Steve Cullen, Seattle. Creative Direction: Matt Peterson and Jim Haven. Lettering: Dave Kaul. Print Production: Dave Kaul. Printer: D & L Screenprinting. Design Office: Creature. Client: Velo Bike Shop. Principal Type: handlettering. Dimensions: 18 x 24 in. (45.7 x 61 cm)

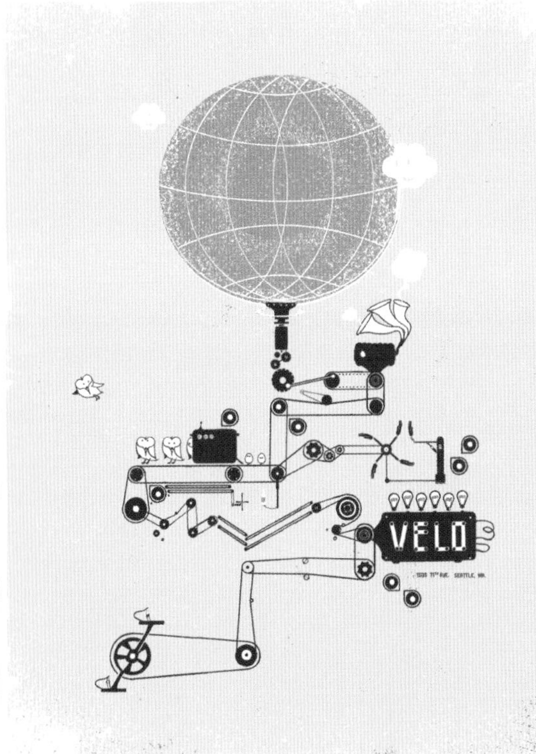

Poster

Design: Chris Silas Neal, Brooklyn, New York. Lettering: Chris Silas Neal. Studio: Chris Silas Neal Studio. Client: The Fillmore, San Francisco. Principal Type: handlettering. Dimensions: 13 x 19 in. (33 x 48.3 cm)

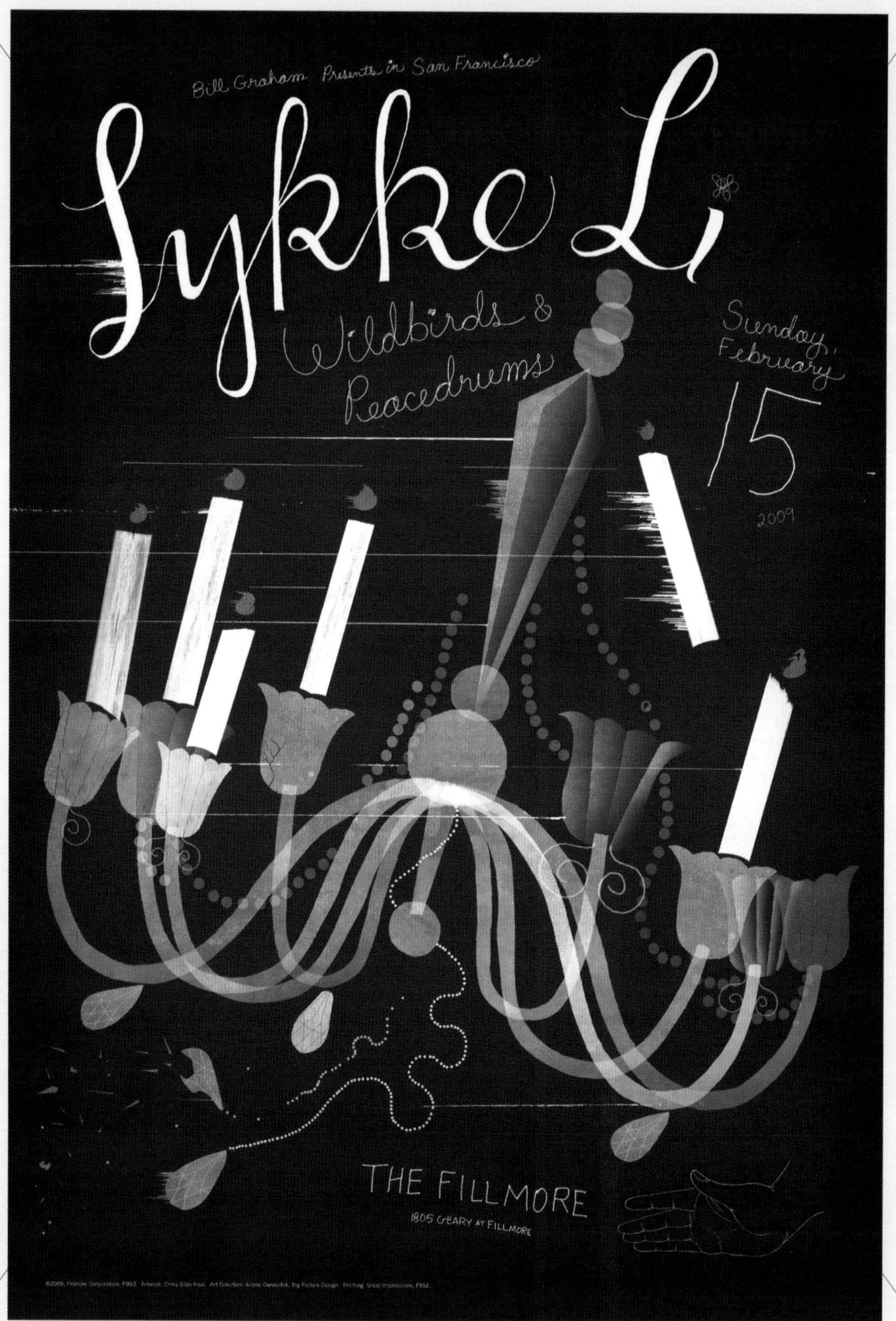

Posters

Design: Kevin Brainard (Anne Frank), Timothy Goodman (I Do! I Do!), Jamus Marquette (Happy Days), and Naomi Mizusaki (She Loves Me), New York. Art Direction: Kevin Brainard and Darren Cox. Creative Direction: Kevin Brainard and Darren Cox. Lettering: Bill Brown, Seattle. Illustration: Bill Brown (She Loves Me). Studio: Pleasure. Client: Westport Country Playhouse. Principal Type: Century Schoolbook, Franklin Gothic Extra Condensed, Nobel, and handlettering. Dimensions: 14 x 22 in. (35.6 x 55.9 cm)

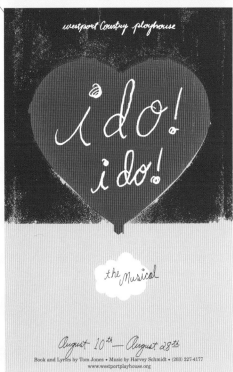

Poster

Design: Julie Savarsky, Austin, Texas. Art Direction: DJ Stout. Photography: Randal Ford. Design Office: Pentagram Design Austin. Principal Type: Akkurat. Dimensions: 24 x 34 in. (61 x 86.4 cm)

Poster

Design: Paul Belford, London. Creative Direction: Paul Belford. Agency: This is Real Art. Principal Type: Helvetica. Dimensions: 18.4 x 27.6 in. (46.7 x 70 cm)

We made this poster for Bruno Maag. He hates it.

This is the world's most popular typeface. What's wrong with it? Come to a lecture by type designer Bruno Maag to find out. 7pm, Thursday 26th March at This is Real Art, 2 Sycamore Street, London EC1.

abcdefghijklmnopqrstuvwxyzáçèøî¢öž*&ñ?,ß'#;!

Poster

Design: Michael Strassburger, Seattle. Art Direction: Michael Strassburger. Creative Direction: Michael Strassburger. Lettering: Michael Strassburger. Studio: Modern Dog Design. Client: Seattle Theatre Group. Principal Type: handlettering. Dimensions: 18 x 24 in. (45.7 x 61 cm)

Poster

Design: Ariane Spanier, Berlin. Art Direction: Ariane Spanier. Photography: Theo Agren. Studio: Ariane Spanier Design. Client: Björn Hegardt and Theo Agren. Principal Type: Cambria and custom. Dimensions: 26.8 x 38.6 in. (68 x 98 cm)

Poster
Design: Niklaus Troxler, Willisau, Switzerland. Art Direction: Niklaus Troxler. Creative Direction: Niklaus Troxler. Lettering: Niklaus Troxler. Design Office: Niklaus Troxler Design. Client: Jazz in Willisau. Principal Type: handlettering. Dimensions: 35.4 x 50.4 in. (90 x 128 cm)

Poster

Design: Niklaus Troxler, Willisau, Switzerland. Art Direction: Niklaus Troxler. Creative Direction: Niklaus Troxler. Lettering: Niklaus Troxler. Design Office: Niklaus Troxler Design. Client: Jazz in Willisau. Principal Type: handlettering. Dimensions: 35.4 x 50.4 in. (90 x 128 cm)

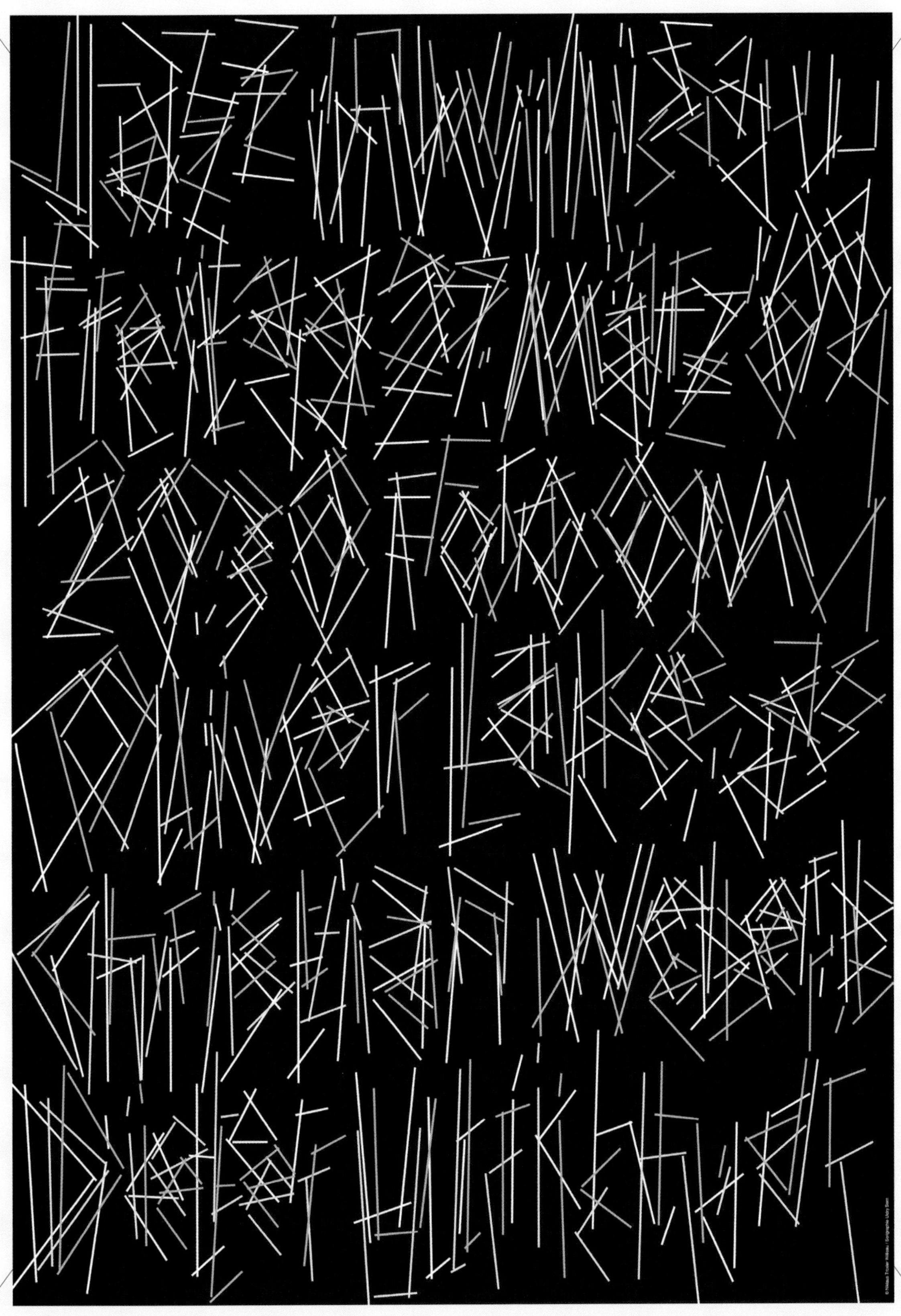

Poster

Design: Giorgio Pesce, Lausanne, Switzerland. Art Direction: Giorgio Pesce. Calligraphy: Giorgio Pesce. Photography: Giorgio Pesce. Design Office: Atelier Poisson. Client: Musée Historique Lausanne. Principal Type: handlettering. Dimensions: 35.2 x 50.4 in. (89.5 x 128 cm)

Poster
Design: Niklaus Troxler, Willisau, Switzerland. Art Direction: Niklaus Troxler. Creative Direction: Niklaus Troxler. Lettering: Niklaus Troxler. Design Office: Niklaus Troxler Design. Client: Boesch Silkscreen, Stans, Switzerland. Principal Type: handlettering. Dimensions: 35.4 x 50.4 in. (90 x 128 cm)

Poster
Design: Mitsunori Taoda, Osaka, Japan. Art Direction: Mitsunori Taoda. Creative Direction: Mitsunori Taoda. Hair Products Manufacturer: Number Three, Inc. Client: Jyunin-Toiro. Principal Type: Braggadocio Regular and Gothic MB101 B. Dimensions: 28.7 x 40.6 in. (72.8 x 103 cm)

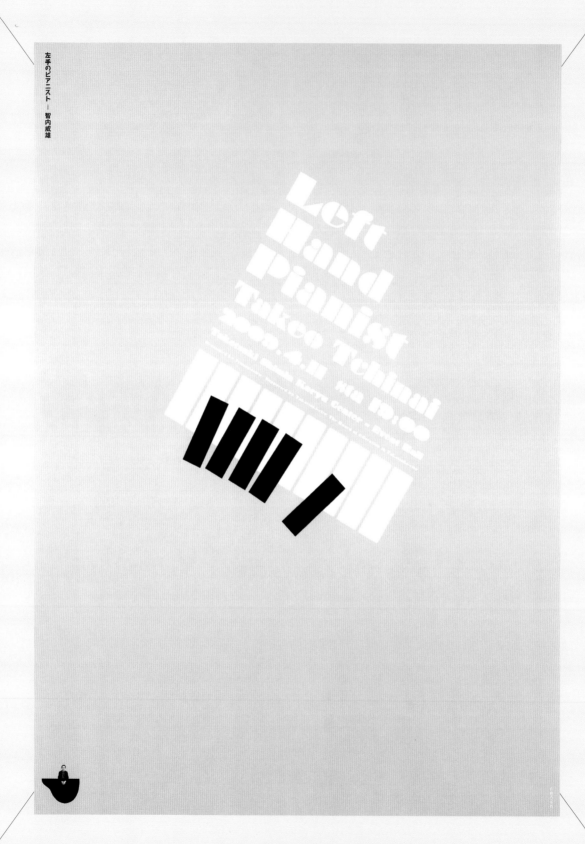

Posters

Design: Kazuto Nakamura and Miyuki Kurata, Hiroshima, Japan. Art Direction: Kazuto Nakamura and Tomiko Nakamura. Creative Direction: Kazuto Nakamura. Design Office: Penguin Graphics. Client: Uemoto Wasabi Honpo. Principal Type: ITC Garamond Light. Dimensions 40.6 x 28.7 in. (103 x 72.8 cm)

Poster

Design: Aaron Edwards and Max Lozach, Auckland, New Zealand. Creative Direction: Dean Poole. Studio: Alt Group.
Principal Type: font created by magnification and burning. Dimensions: 48.2 x 34.1 in. (122.5 x 86.5 cm)

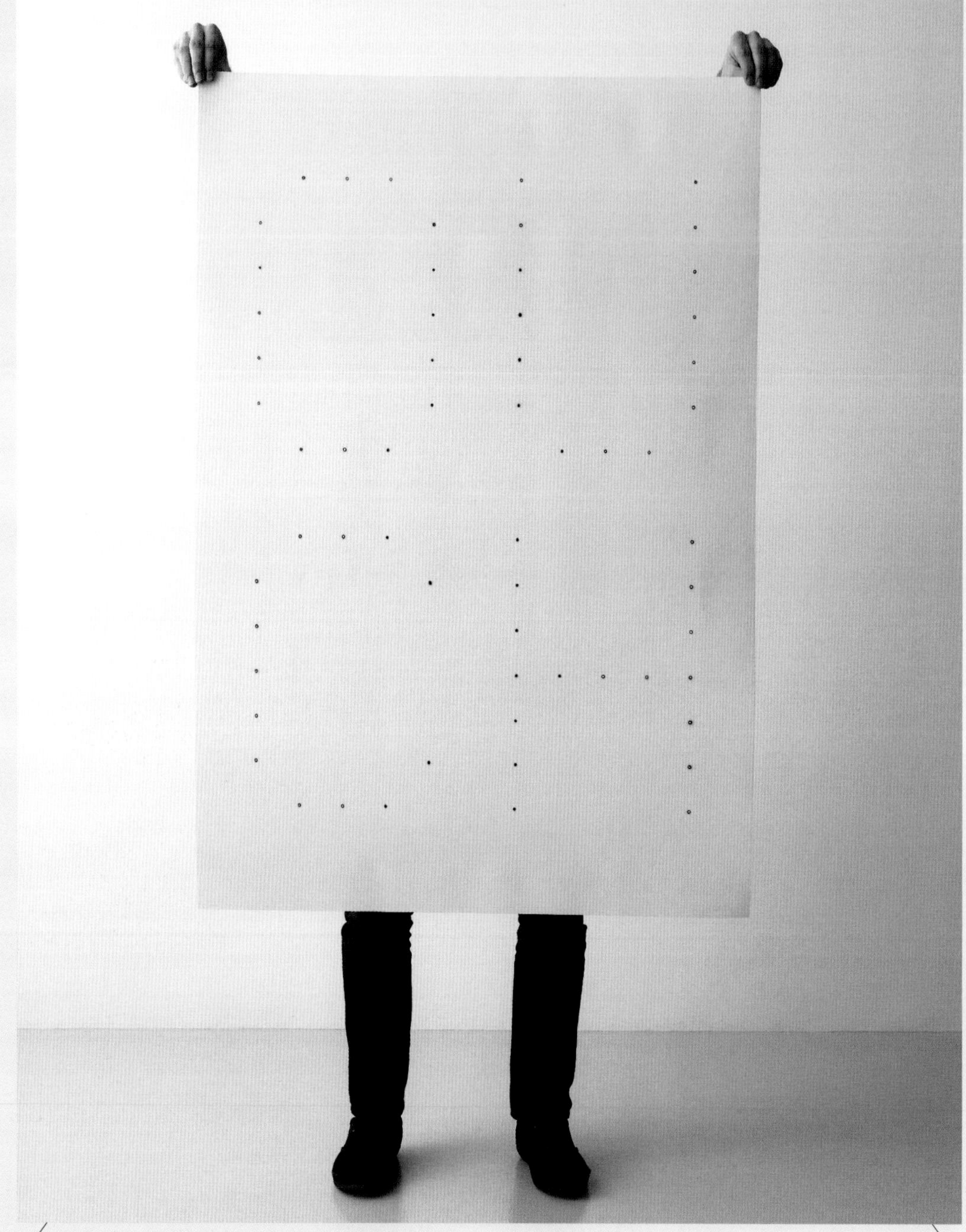

Poster
Design: Philippe Apeloig, Paris. Art Direction: Philippe Apeloig. Creative Direction: Philippe Apeloig. Calligraphy: Philippe Apeloig. Studio: Studio Apeloig. Client: Association des Bibliothécaires de France. Principal Type: Akkurat. Dimensions: 47.2 x 69.3 in. (120 x 176 cm)

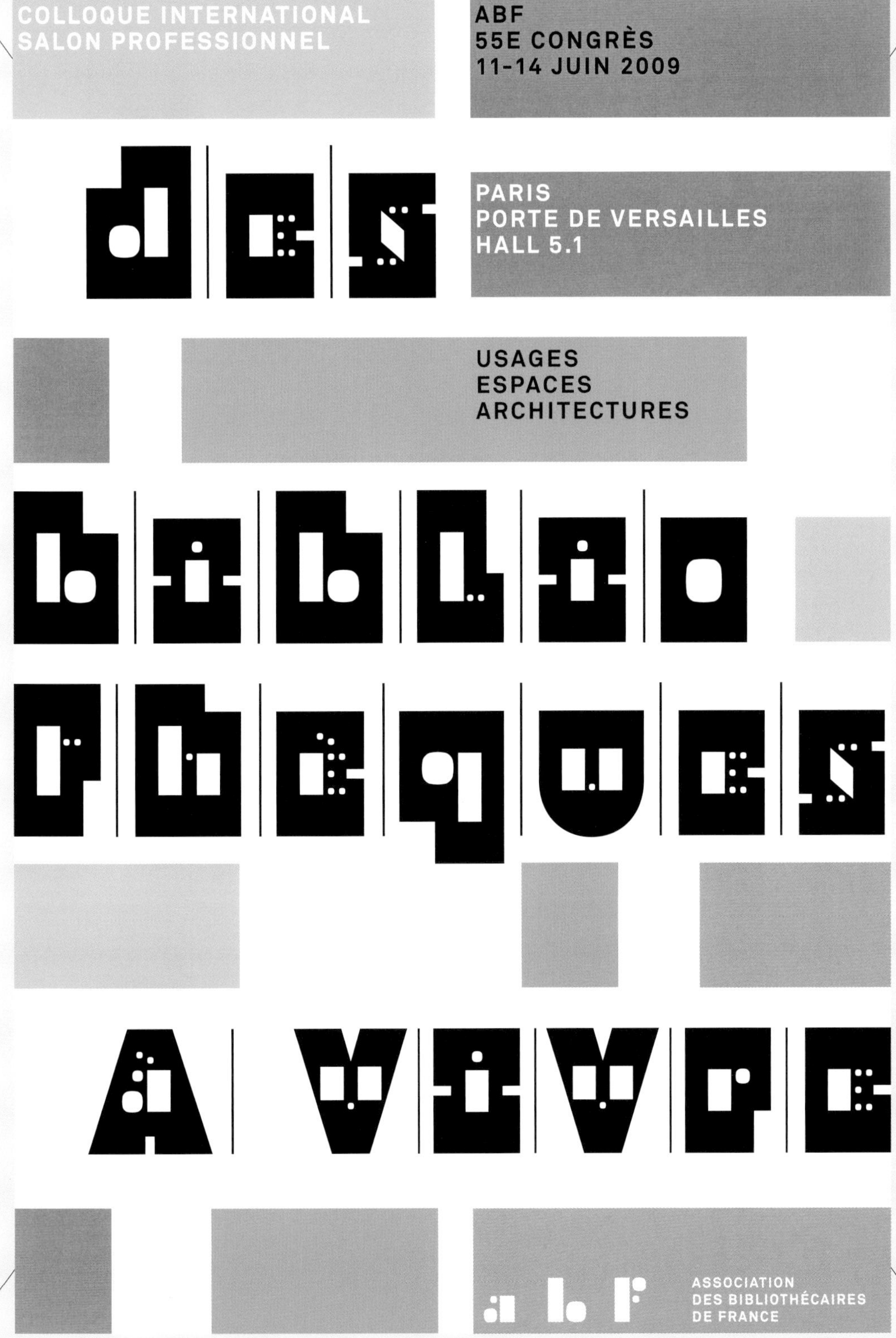

Posters

Design: Hong Chong Ip and Victor Hugo Marreiros, Macau, China. Lettering: Hong Chong Ip. Illustration: Hong Chong Ip and Ha Tin Cheong. Client: Cultural Affairs Bureau of the Macau S.A.R. Government. Principal Type: custom. Dimensions: 27.6 x 39.4 in. (70 x 100 cm)

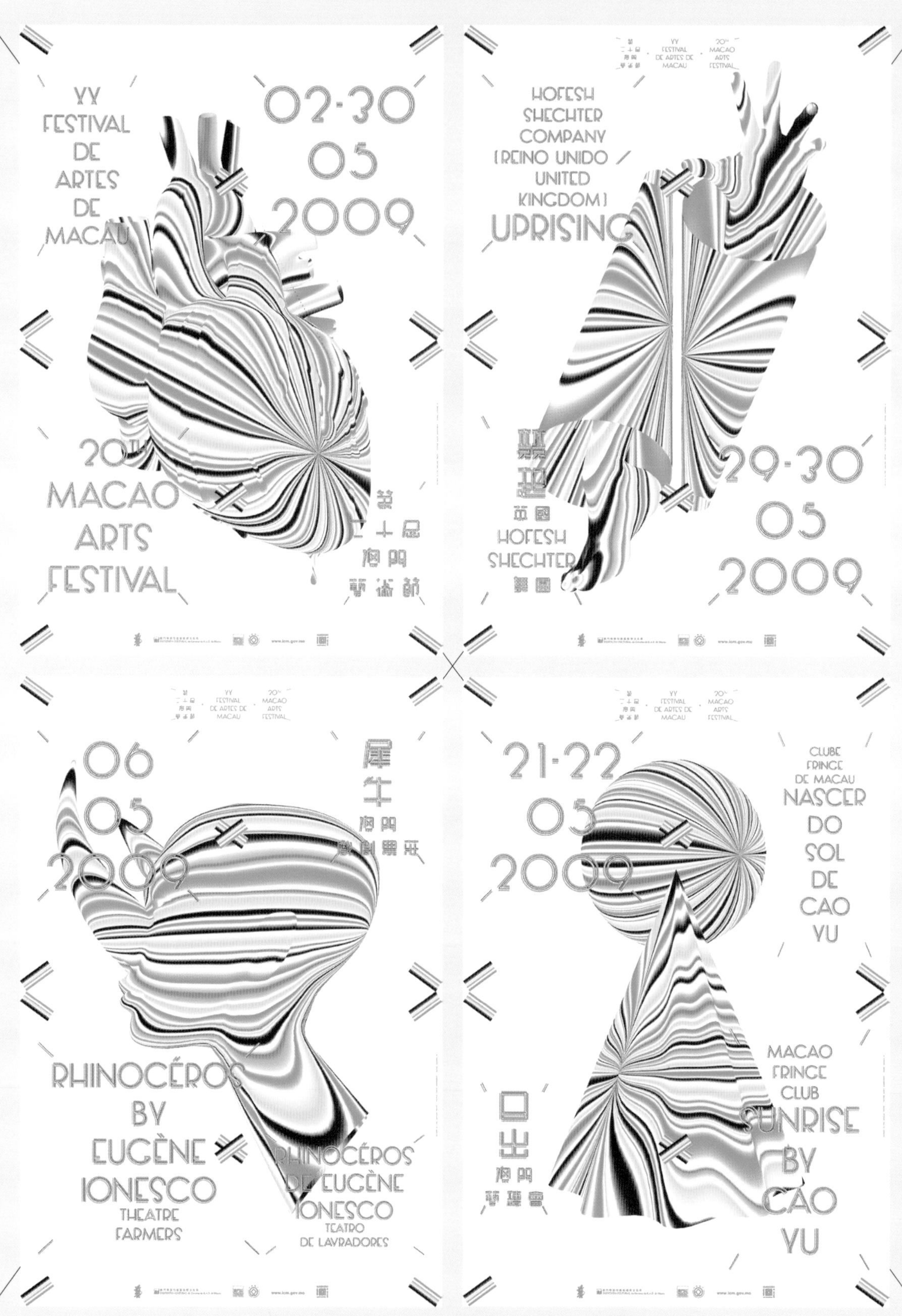

Posters
Design: Akiko Masunaga, Osaka, Japan. Art Direction: Akiko Masunaga. Creative Direction: Akiko Masunaga. Photography: Tomokazu Nishizawa. Design Office: Masunaga Design Team. Client: Heiwa Paper Co. Principal Type: custom. Dimensions: 28.7 x 40.6 in. (72.8 x 103 cm)

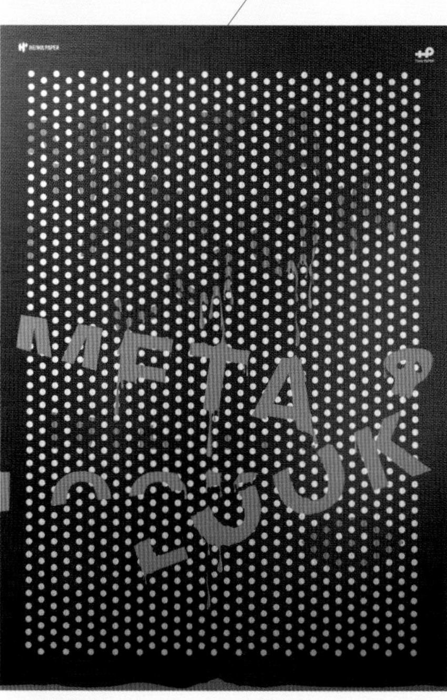

Posters

Design: Akiko Masunaga and Kazumi Sugimoto, Osaka, Japan. Art Direction: Akiko Masunaga. Creative Direction: Akiko Masunaga. Photography: Tomokazu Nishizawa. Illustration: Yusuke Mashiba. Design Office: Masunaga Design Team. Client: Heiwa Paper Co. Principal Type: custom. Dimensions: 28.7 x 40.6 in. (72.8 x 103 cm)

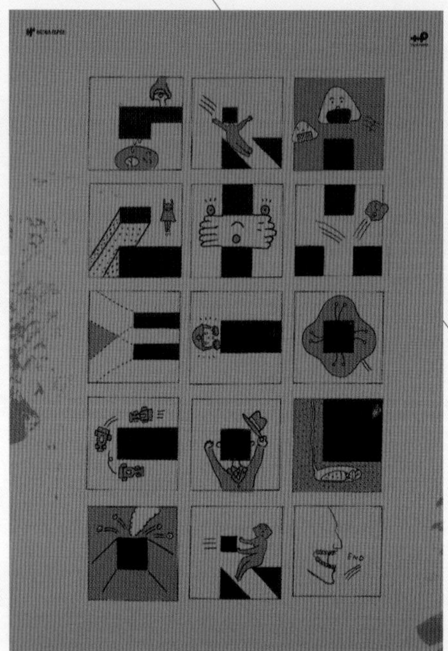

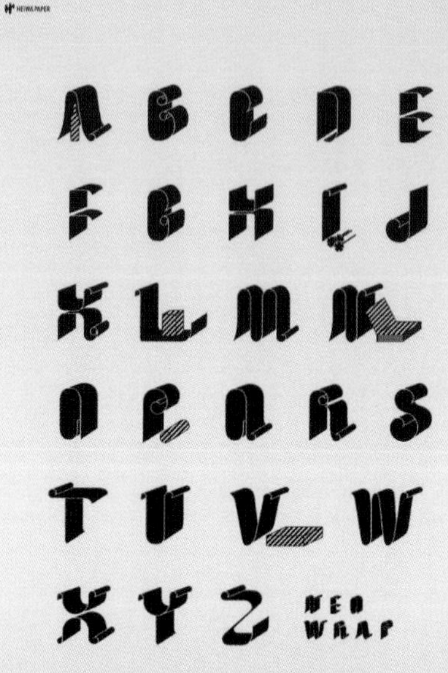

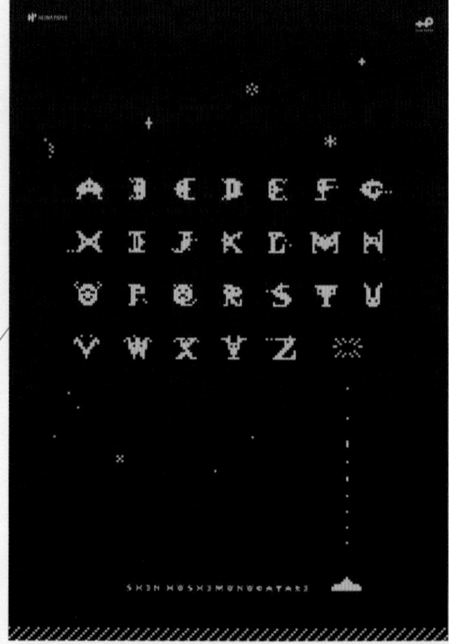

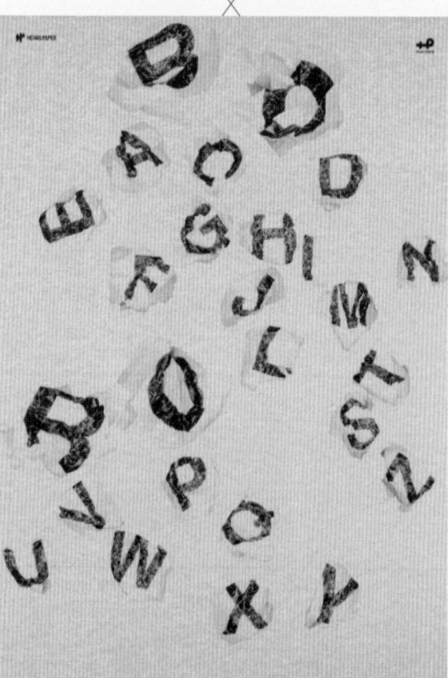

Posters
Design: Hideyuki Fukuda, Tokyo. Art Direction: Hideyuki Fukuda. Studio: Studio Fuku-De. Client: Japan Graphic Designers Association. Principal Type: letters formed from rice. Dimensions: 28.7 x 40.6 in. (72.8 x 103 cm)

Posters
Design: Mitsunori Taoda, Osaka, Japan. Art Direction: Mitsunori Taoda. Creative Direction: Mitsunori Taoda. Hair Products Manufacturer: Number Three, Inc. Principal Type: Berthold Akzidenz Grotesk Light. Dimensions: 28.7 x 40.6 in. (72.8 x 103 cm)

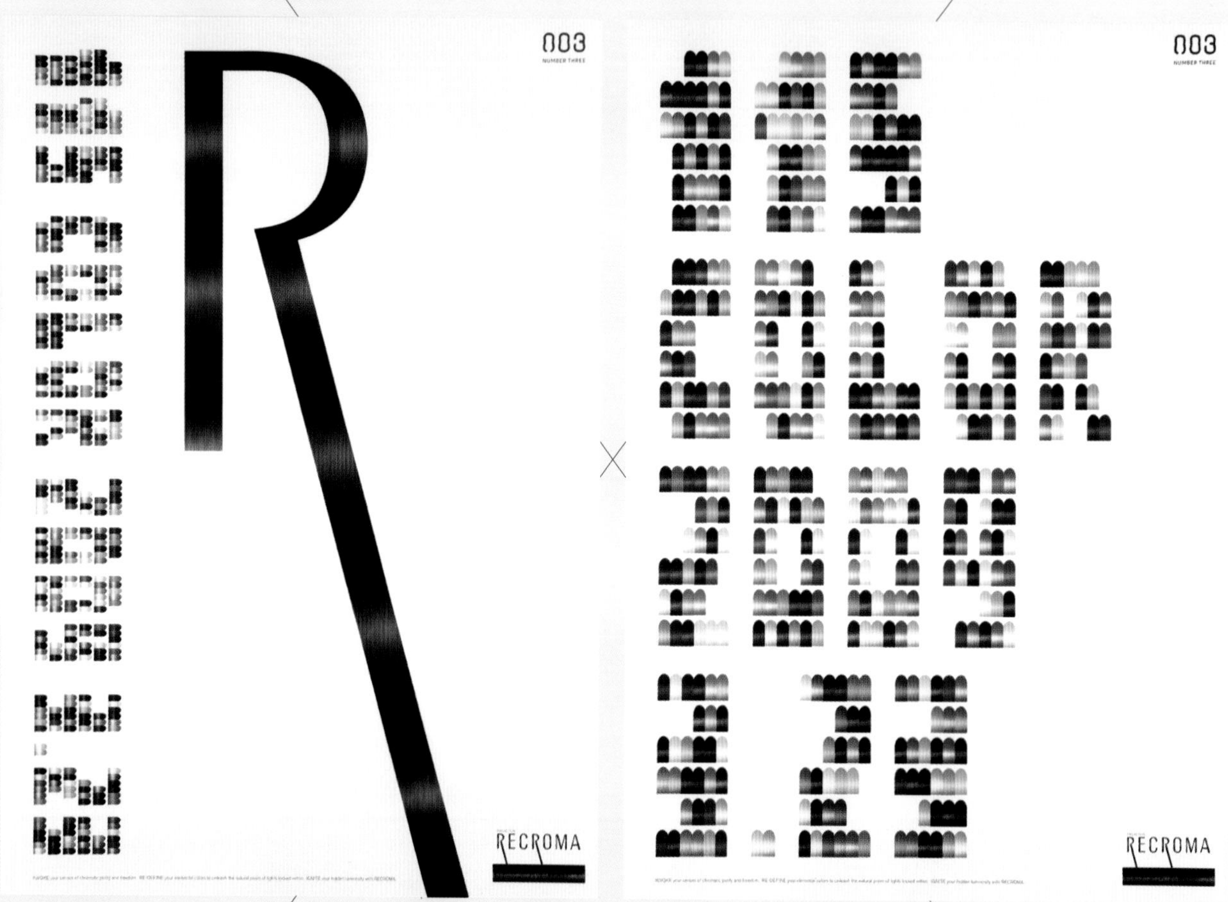

Poster
Design: orangetango, Montréal. Printer: K2 Impressions. Agency: orangetango. Client: Université du Québec à Montréal (UQAM), Centre de Design. Principal Type: Knockout. Dimensions: 24 x 36 in. (61 x 91.4 cm)

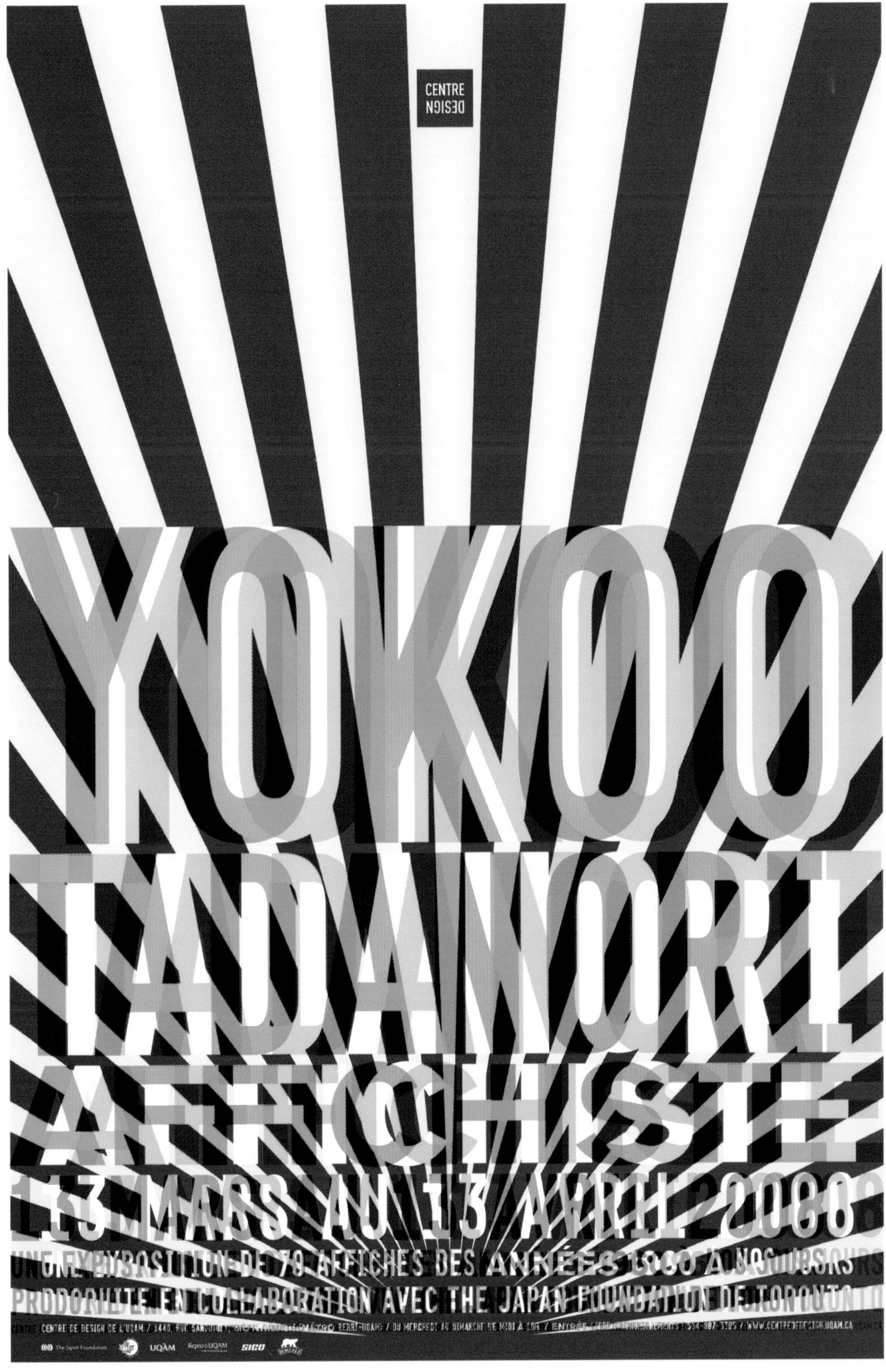

Posters

Design: Linda Ritoh, Osaka, Japan. Art Direction: Linda Ritoh. Creative Direction: Linda Ritoh. Lettering: Linda Ritoh. Photography: Linda Ritoh. Sculptor: Linda Ritoh. Design Office: LINDA GRAPHICA & LIBIDO. Client: P Gallery SOCO. Principal Type: FB Garamond, OCR-A, and Shinseikaiyotai. Dimensions: 28.7 x 40.6 in. (72.8 x 103 cm)

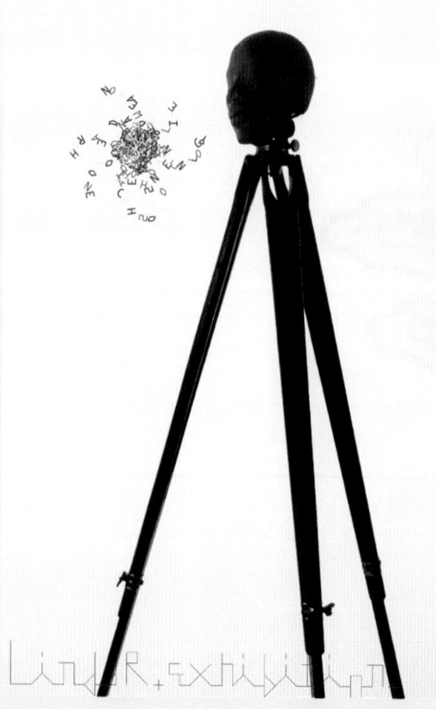

Exhibition

Design: Arata Maruyama, Brusino Arsizio, Switzerland. Art Direction: Arata Maruyama. Photography: Mitsumasa Fujitsuka. Printing Director: Kinji Watanabe. Client: DNP Art Communications Co. and Ginza Graphic Gallery. Principal Type: Akzidenz Grotesk, Linotype Didot, Honmincyo, and woodblock. Dimensions: various

Poster

Design: Alex Trochut, Barcelona, Spain. Art Direction: Alex Trochut. Lettering: Alex Trochut. Client: The Decemberists. Principal Type: handlettering. Dimensions: 11.8 x 16.5 in. (30 x 42 cm)

THE DECEMBERISTS
WITH BLIND PILOT
AUGUST 10, 2009 • W.L. LYONS BROWN THEATRE • LOUISVILLE, KY

Poster
Design: Eike Dingler, Berlin. Client: Peter Behrens School of Architecture. Principal Type: Moiré. Dimensions: 23.4 x 33.1 in. (59.4 x 84 cm)

Poster

Design: Kali Nikitas, Los Angeles. Studio: Graphic Design for Love (+$). Client: Otis College of Art and Design, Communication Arts Department. Principal Type: Playbill and Clarendon Condensed. Dimensions: 15 x 20 in. (38.1 x 50.8 cm)

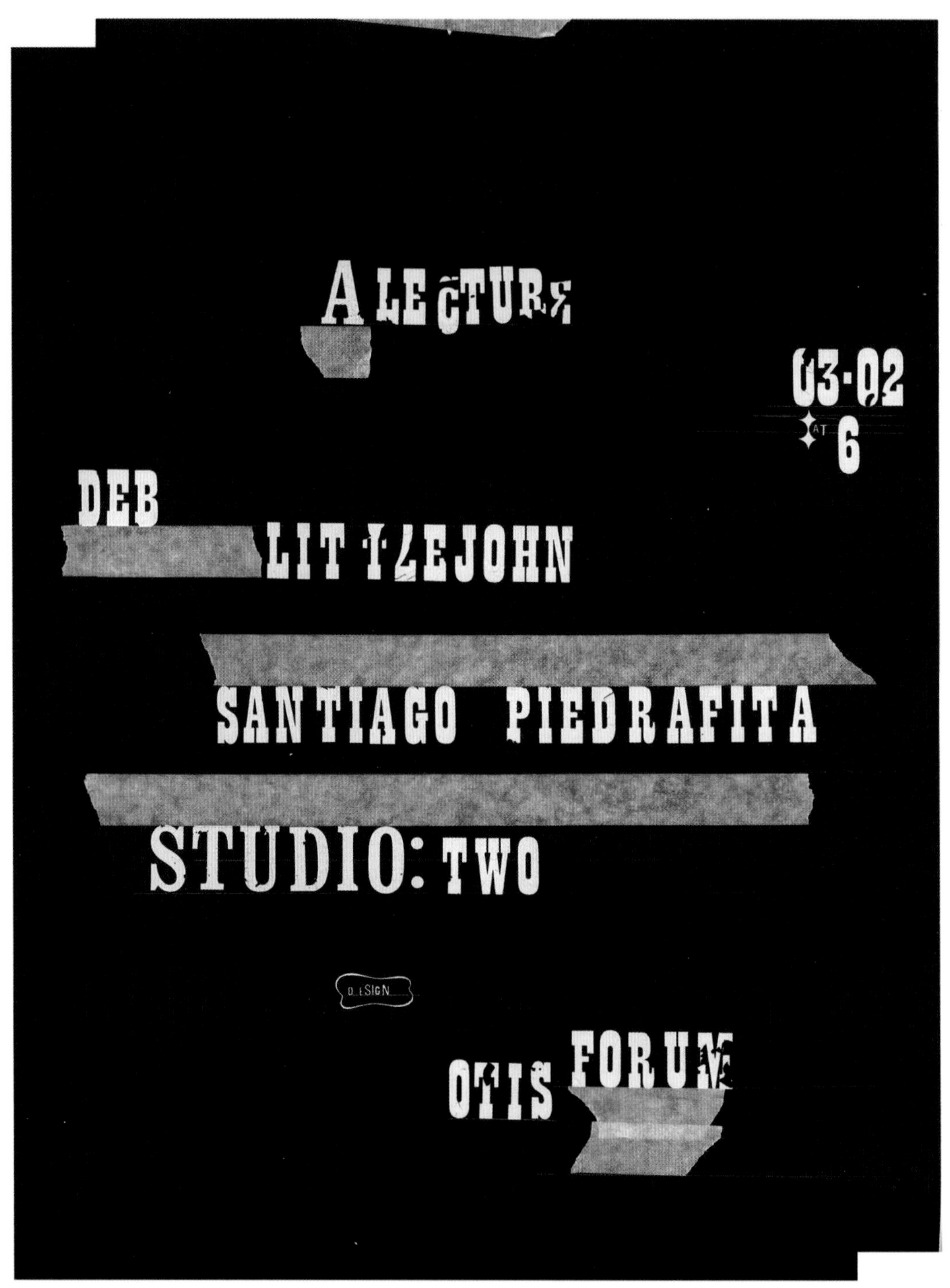

Posters

Art Direction: Iri Fussenegger. Creative Direction: Peter Bünnagel, Barbara Kotte, and Anne-Lene Proff, Berlin. Studio: Scrollan. Client: Hochschule für Angewandte Wissenschaft und Kunst (HAWK). Principal Type: Gotham Ultra and Bodoni Poster. Dimensions: 27.6 x 39.4 in. (70 x 100 cm)

Posters

Design: Arata Maruyama, Brusino Arsizio, Switzerland. Art Direction: Arata Maruyama. Photography: Saji Yasuo. Printing Director: Takeshi Kitagawa, Taiyo Printing Co. Client: Gallery 5610. Principal Type: Akzidenz Grotesk, Koburina Gothic, and woodblock. Dimensions: various

Student Project
Design: Erica Yujin Choi, New York. School: Rhode Island School of Design. Instructors: Krzysztof Lenk and Hoon Kim.
Principal Type: Futura Maxi and News Gothic. Dimensions: 28 x 40 in. (71.1 x 101.6 cm)

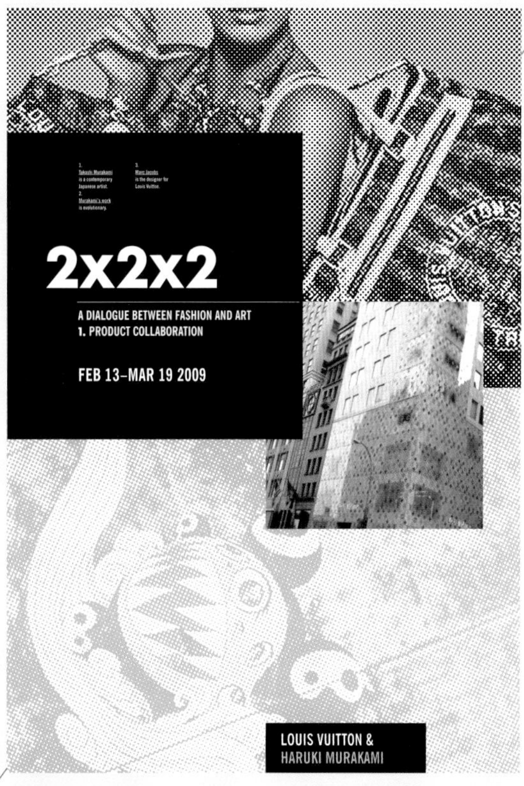

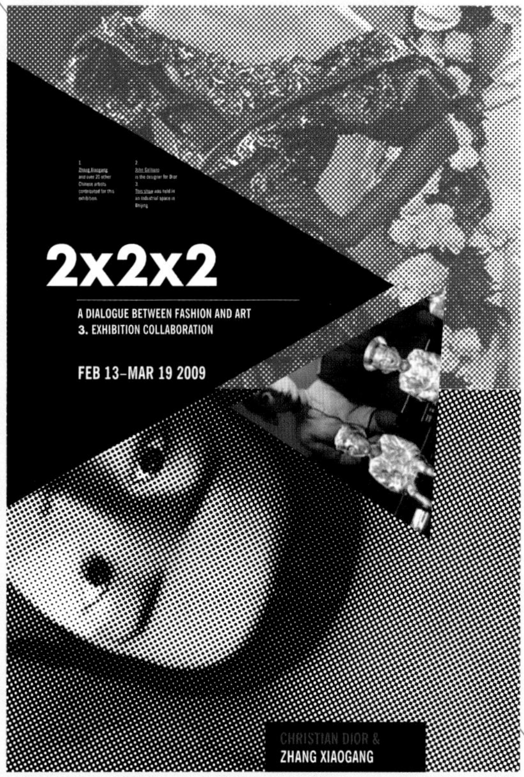

Poster

Design: Tetsuya Namaizawa and Gaku Ohsugi, Tokyo. Art Direction: Gaku Ohsugi. Creative Direction: Fumiko Shirahama. Design Office: 702 Design Works. Client: WA Ltd. Principal Type: Resource SSK Regular. Dimensions: 28.7 x 40.6 in. (72.8 x 103 cm)

Poster

Design: Mélanie Zentner and Nicolas Zentner, Lausanne, Switzerland. Design Office: enzed. Client: Ville de Pully. Principal Type: Helvetica. Dimensions: 35.4 x 50.4 in. (90 x 128 cm)

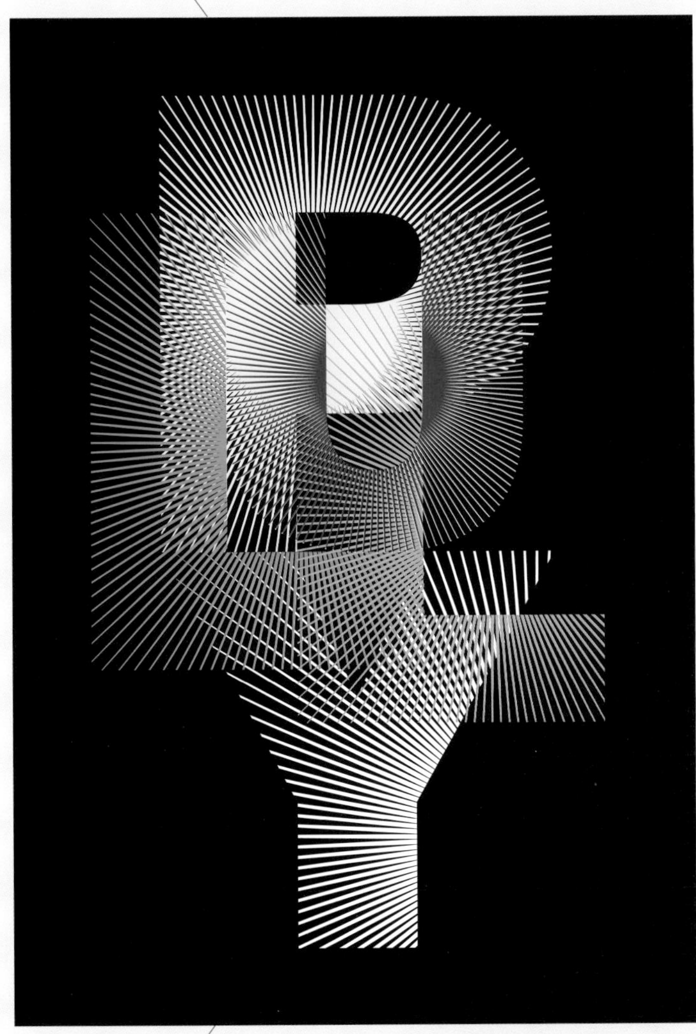

1ER AOÛT 2009
FÊTE NATIONALE
DÈS 18H00
PORT DE PULLY
www.pully.ch

1ER AOÛT 2009
FÊTE NATIONALE
PORT DE PULLY

Poster

Design: ping-pong Design, Rotterdam, Netherlands. Creative Direction: ping-pong Design. Studio: ping-pong Design.
Client: Drang theatre group, Den Haag. Principal Type: Birch Std and handlettering. Dimensions: 33.1 x 46.8 in. (84.1 x 118.9 cm)

Posters

Art Direction: Kaoru Morimoto, Tokyo. Studio: Migration. Client: SAN SAN FARM Co. Principal Type: font made with photographs. Dimensions: 57.7 x 40.6 in. (145.6 x 103 cm)

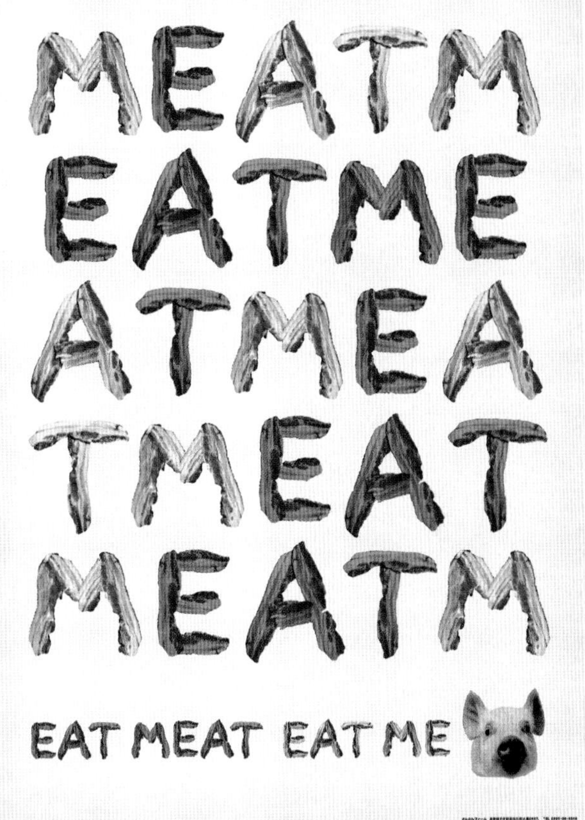

Poster

Design: Ramon Classen, Thomas Müller, Thomas Neeser, and Daniela Rota, Basel, Switzerland. Art Direction: Thomas Neeser and Thomas Müller. Creative Direction: Thomas Neeser and Thomas Müller. Studio: Neeser & Müller. Client: Verein Neue Musik Rümlingen. Principal Type: Hornet and TripleMassive. Dimensions: 35.2 x 50.4 in.(89.5 x 128 cm)

Poster
Design: Melchior Imboden, Buochs, Switzerland. Art Direction: Melchior Imboden. Creative Direction: Melchior Imboden. Design Office: Graphic Atelier Imboden. Client: Galerie Reussbad, Lucern. Principal Type: custom. Dimensions: 35.6 x 50.4 in. (90.5 x 128 cm)

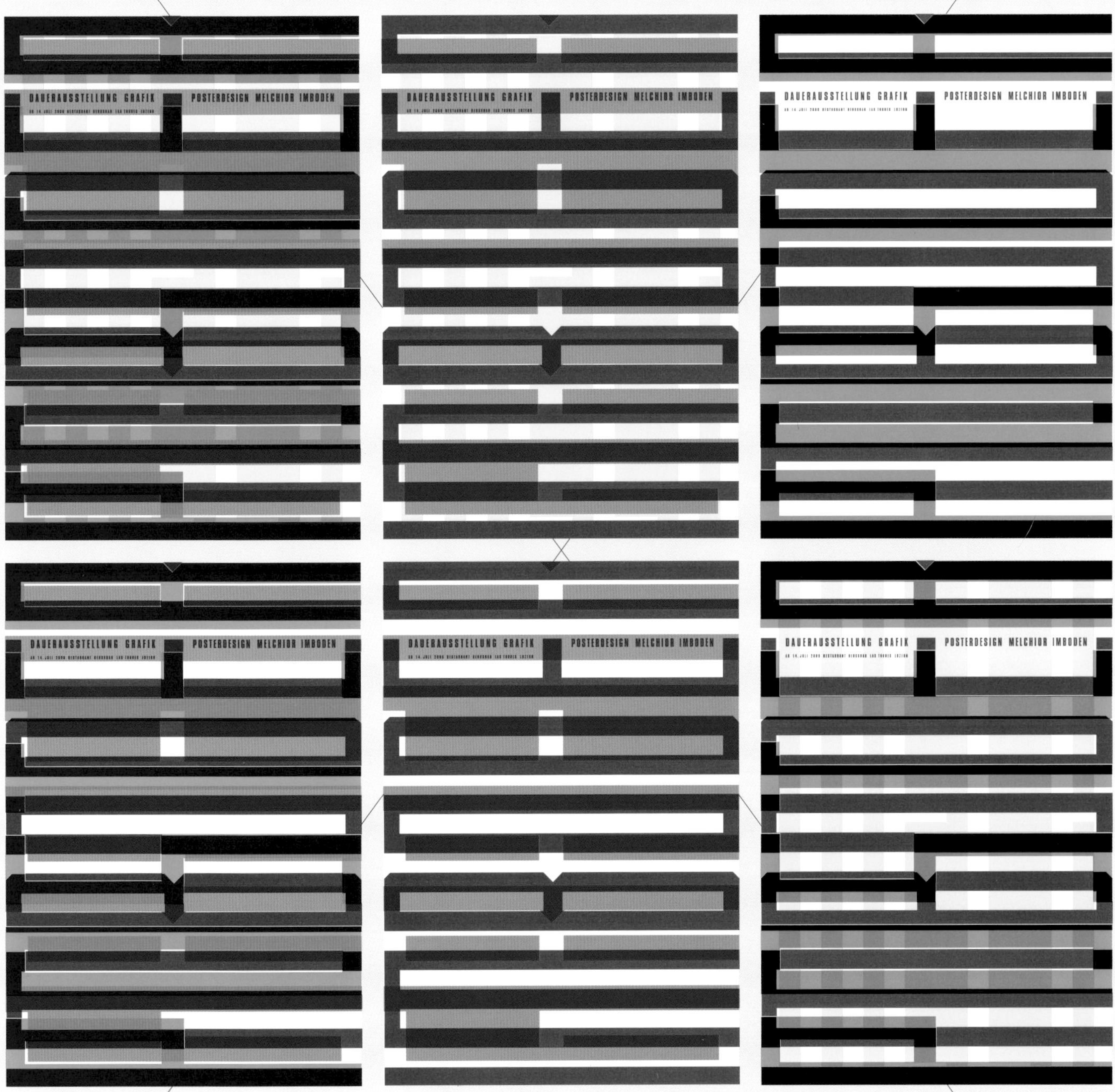

Poster

Design: Stephan Bundi-Bonjour, Bern, Switzerland. Art Direction: Stephan Bundi-Bonjour. Studio: Atelier Bundi AG. Client: Theater Biel-Solothurn. Principal Type: Simple Bold. Dimensions: 35.2 x 50.4 in. (89.5 x 128 cm)

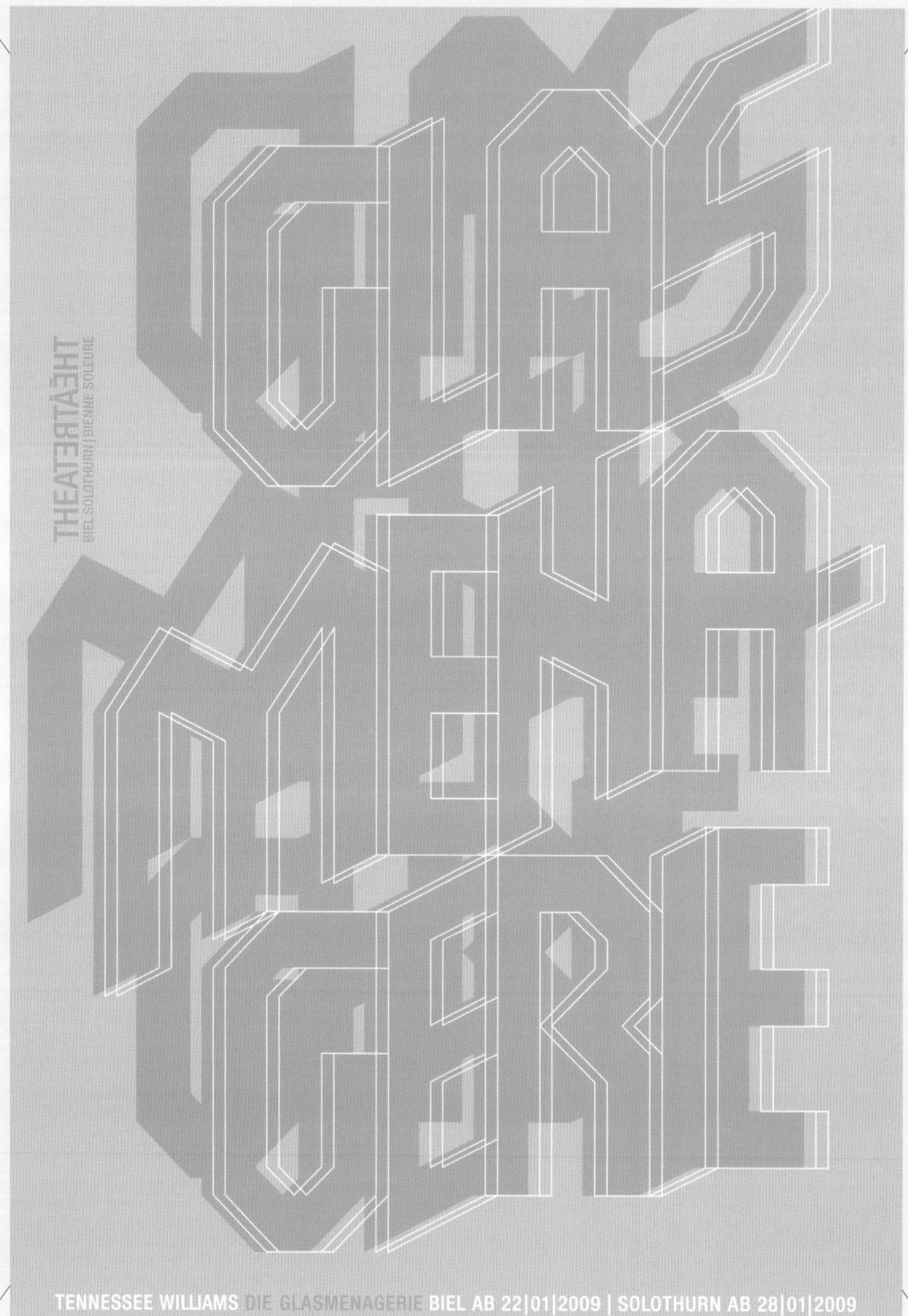

Poster

Design Lizá Ramalho and Artur Rebelo, Porto, Portugal. Art Direction: Lizá Ramalho and Artur Rebelo. Creative Direction: Lizá Ramalho and Artur Rebelo. Design Office: R2 Design. Client: Good 50x70. Principal Type: font handmade from headless dolls. Dimensions: 27.6 x 39.4 in. (70 x 100 cm)

Poster

Design: Cybu Richli and Fabienne Burri, Lucerne, Switzerland. Studio: C2F. Art Direction: Cybu Richli and Fabienne Burri. Creative Direction: Cybu Richli and Fabienne Burri. Client: Museum of Art Lucerne. Principal Type: Patience. Dimensions: 35.2 x 50.4 in. (89.5 x 128 cm)

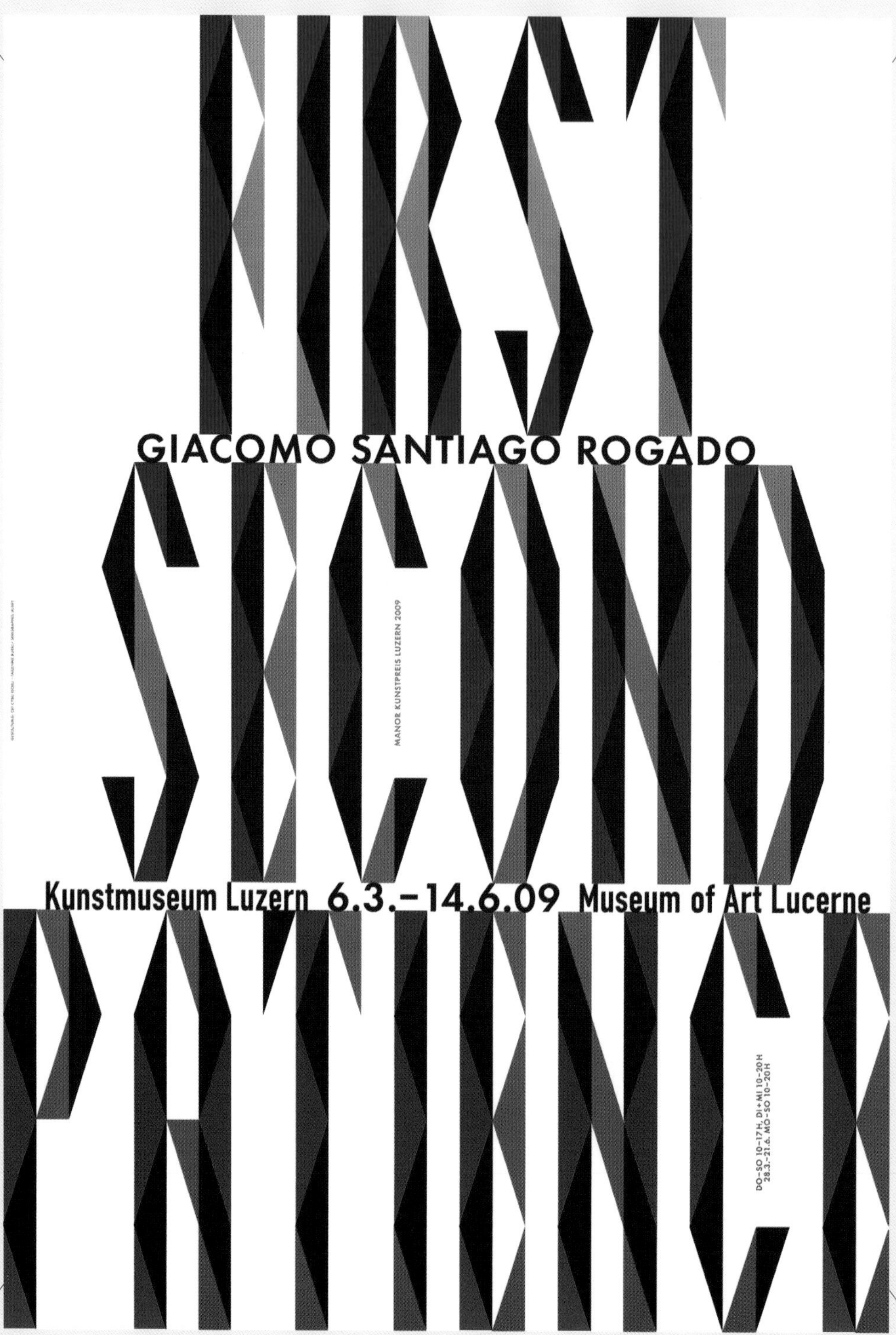

Posters
Design: Gail Anderson, New York. Art Direction: Michael J. Walsh. Creative Direction: Anthony P. Rhodes. Illustration: Terry Allen. School: School of Visual Arts, New York. Principal Type: various. Dimensions: 29.8 x 45 in. (75.6 x 114.3 cm)

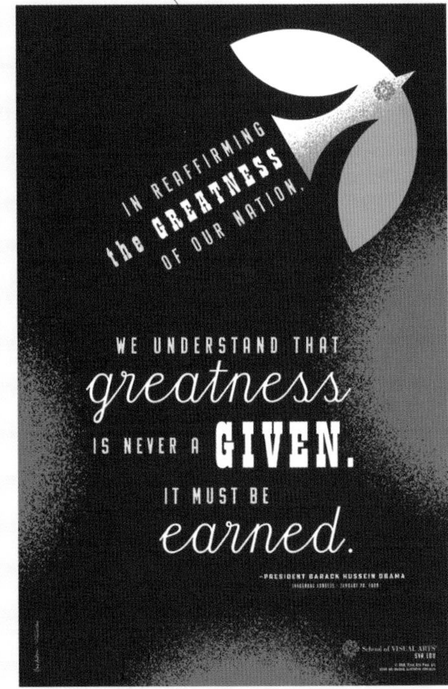

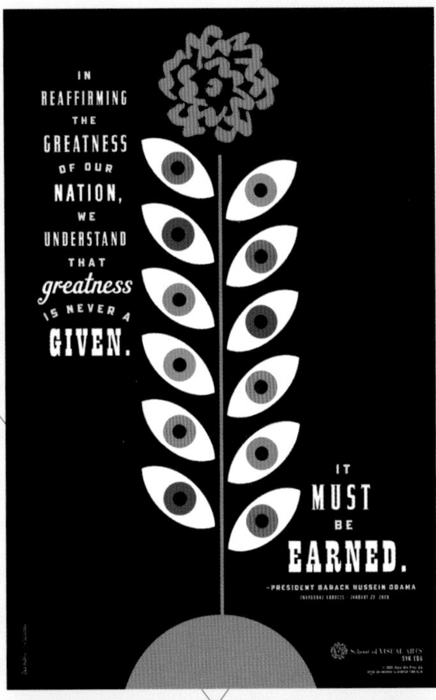

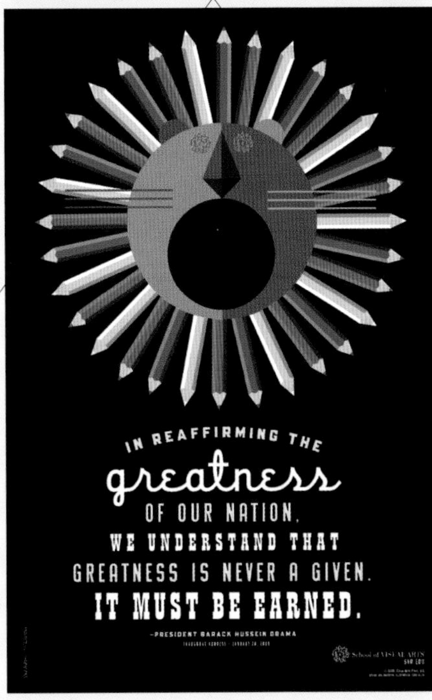

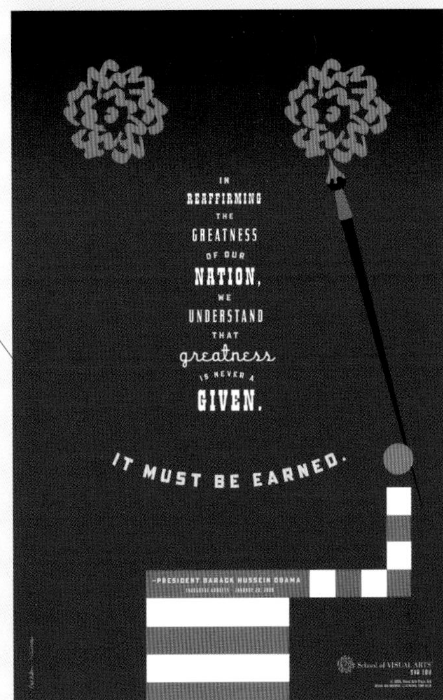

Posters

Design: Namoo Kim, Seoul. Art Direction: Namoo Kim. Creative Direction: Namoo Kim. Studio: GT. Client: Korea Design Foundation. Principal Type: FF OCR-F. Dimensions: 27.6 x 36.1 in. (70 x 92.5 cm)

Posters

Design: Namoo Kim, Seoul. Art Direction: Namoo Kim. Creative Direction: Namoo Kim. Studio: GT Client: RISD Alumni Association in Korea. Principal Type: custom. Dimensions: 27.6 x 27.6 in. (70 x 70 cm)

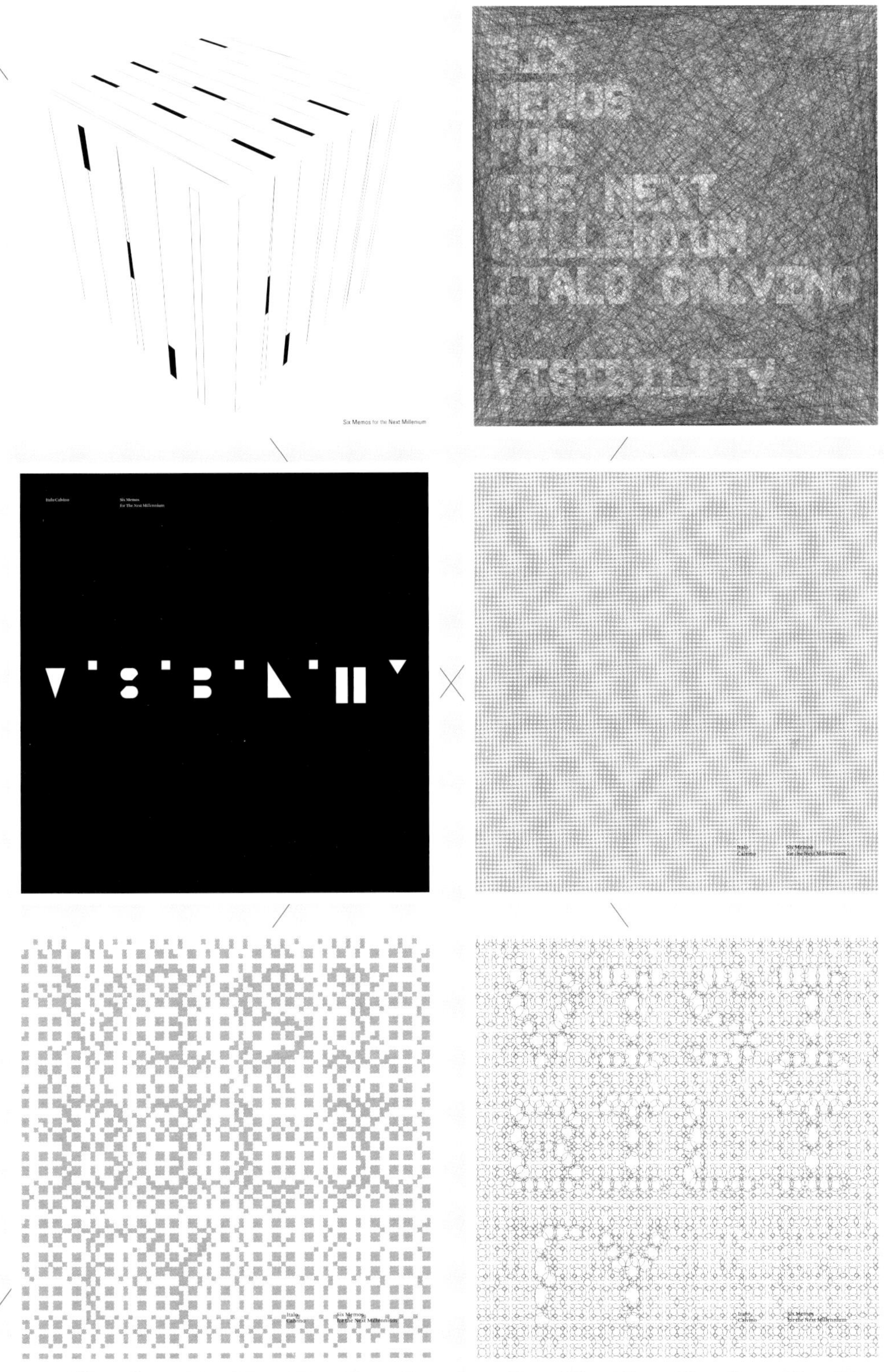

Music Video

Design: Tamara Gildengers Connolly and Joshua Hester, Brooklyn, New York. Art Direction: Tamara Gildengers Connolly and Joshua Hester. Creative Direction: Tamara Gildengers Connolly and Joshua Hester. Client: RedBull Records. Principal Type: Various

Student Project

Design: Marian Chiao, Los Angeles. Animation: Andrew Tan. School: Art Center College of Design. Instructor: Simon Johnston. Principal Type: Gotham

Student Project
Design: Ke Cao, New Haven, Connecticut. School: Yale University, School of Art. Instructors: Karin Fong and Todd St. John.
Principal Type: handlettering

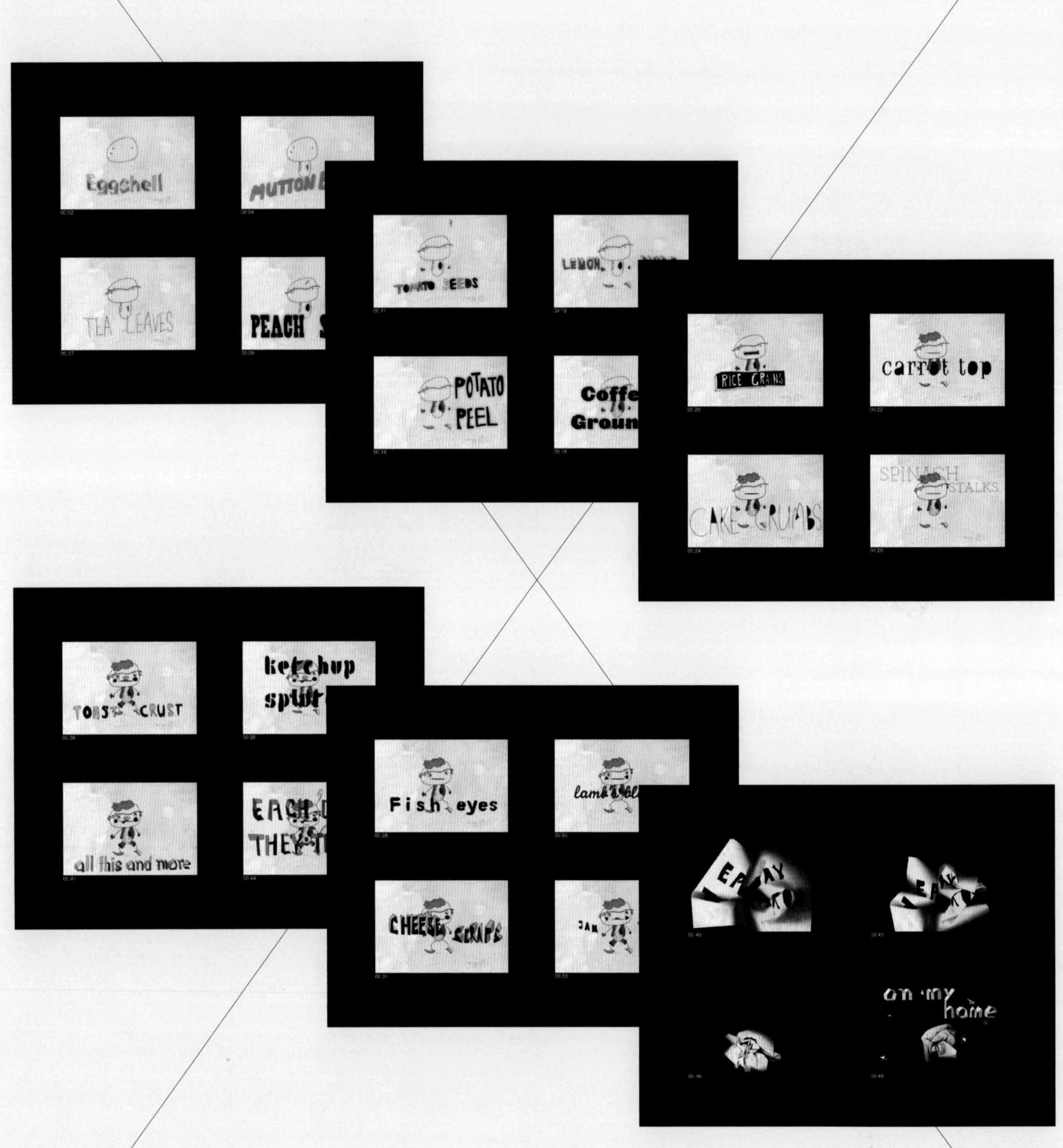

Student Project

Design: Rosina Bosco, New York. School: School of Visual Arts, MFA Program, New York. Instructor: Stefan Sagmeister. Principal Type: after Foundry Gridnik Light

Film Trailer

Design: Sam Brynes, Sharon Lee, and Julian Melhuish, Sydney, Australia. Creative Direction: Julian Melhuish. Design Office: Saatchi Design, Sydney. Client: Sydney Writers' Festival 2009. Principal Type: Serifa Black.

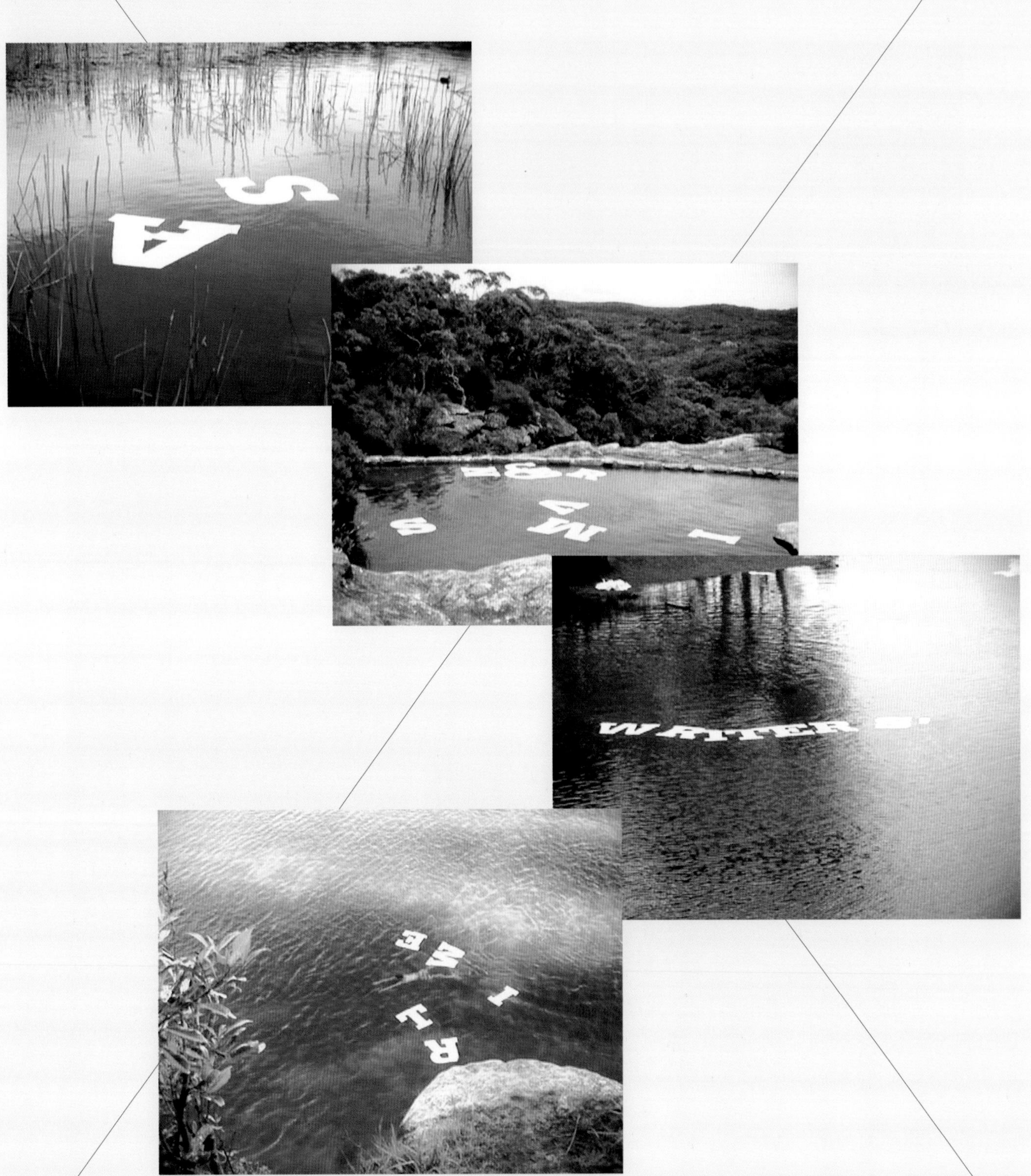

Student Project

Design: Karin Soukup, New York. Musician/Song: Wax Tailor "Que Sera, Sera." School: School of Visual Arts, MFA Program, New York. Instructor: Gail Anderson. Principal Type: various

Website

Design: Lisa Strausfeld and Nina Boesch, New York. Creative Direction: Lisa Strausfeld. Design Office: Pentagram Design New York. Client: WNET. Principal Type: Gotham

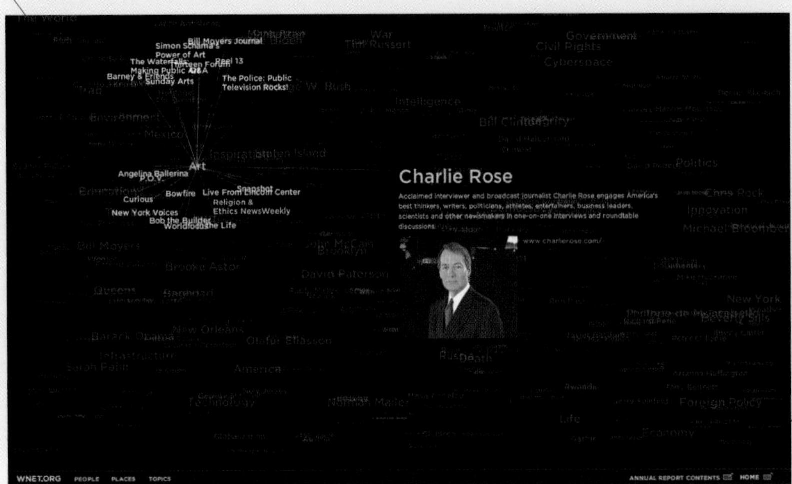

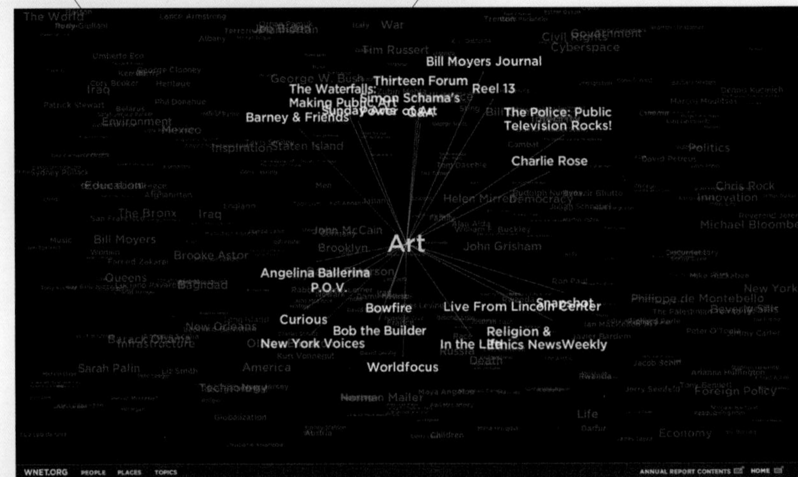

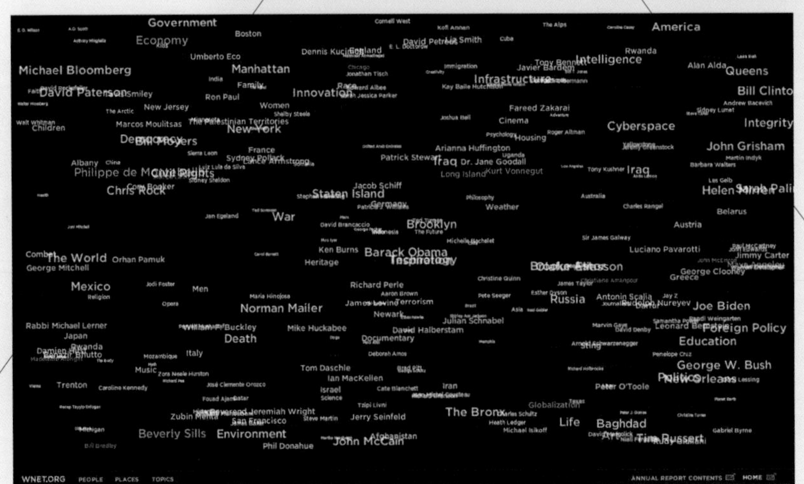

Television Commercial

Design: Why Not Associates, London. Art Direction: Why Not Associates. Creative Direction: Why Not Associates and Brian Harrington. Lettering: Why Not Associates. Design Office: Why Not Associates. Client: Channel 4. Principal Type: ITC American Typewriter, Helvetica, and handlettering

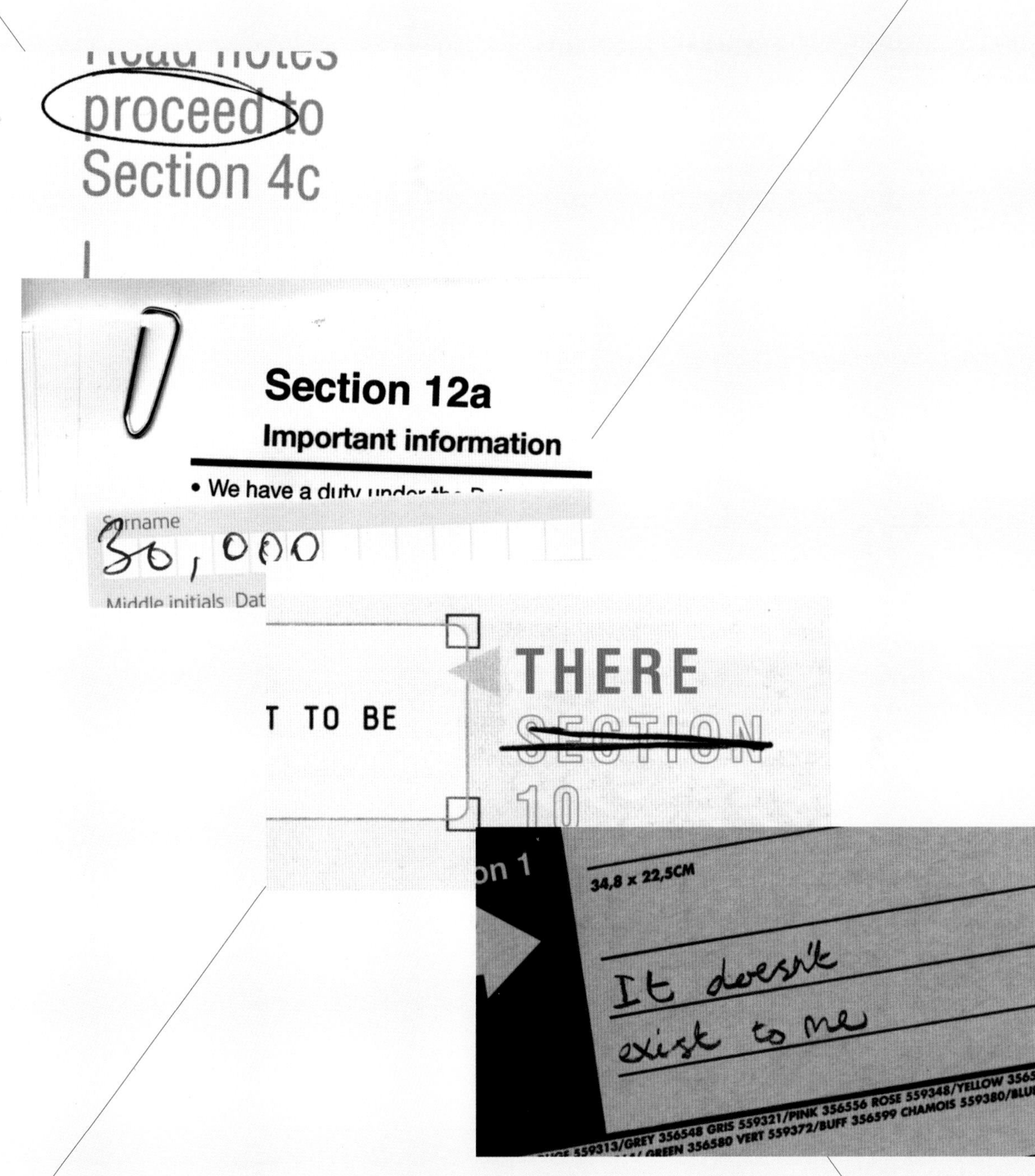

Television Commercial

Creative Direction: Julia Hoffmann, New York. Lettering: Tim Burton, London. Director: Tim Burton. Animator: Chris Tichborne, Manchester, England. Sound: Danny Elfman, Los Angeles. Studio: Mackinnon and Saunders, Manchester. Museum: The Museum of Modern Art (MoMA). Principal Type: MoMA Gothic

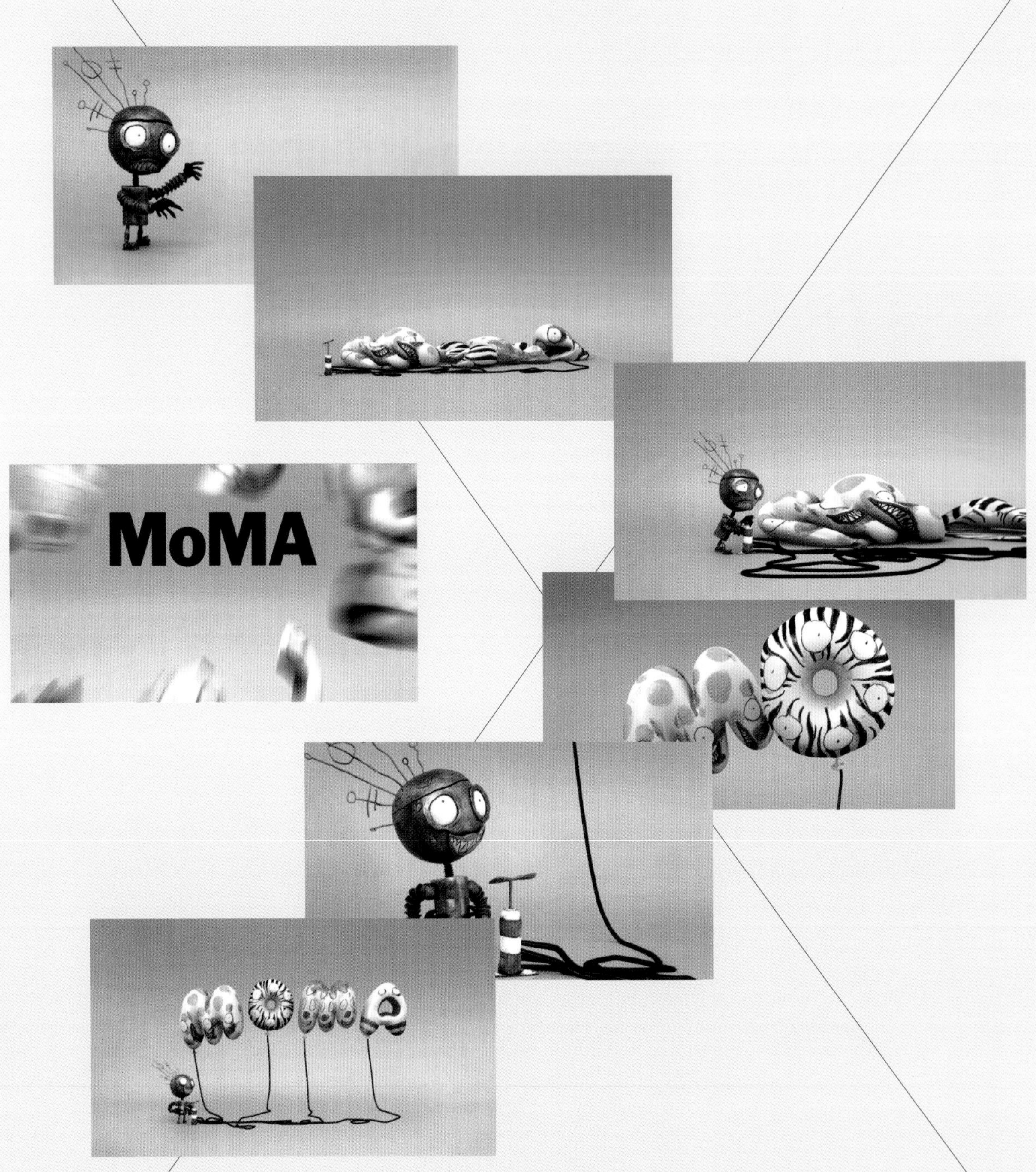

Student Project

Design: Young Bum Kim, New York. School: School of Visual Arts, New York. Instructor: Ori Kleiner. Principal Type: Times New Roman.

Student Project

Design: Jules Tardy, Brooklyn, New York. School: School of Visual Arts, MFA Program, New York. Instructor: Gail Anderson. Principal Type: Courier New and DIN

Website

Design: Georgina Clarke and Megan Paradise, New York. Creative Direction: Georgina Clarke. Lettering: Georgina Clarke. Client: Flight of the Conchords. Principal Type: handlettering

Student Project
Design: Wesley Gott, New York. School: School of Visual Arts, MFA Program, New York. Instructor: Gail Anderson.
Principal Type: Housecut and Amanda

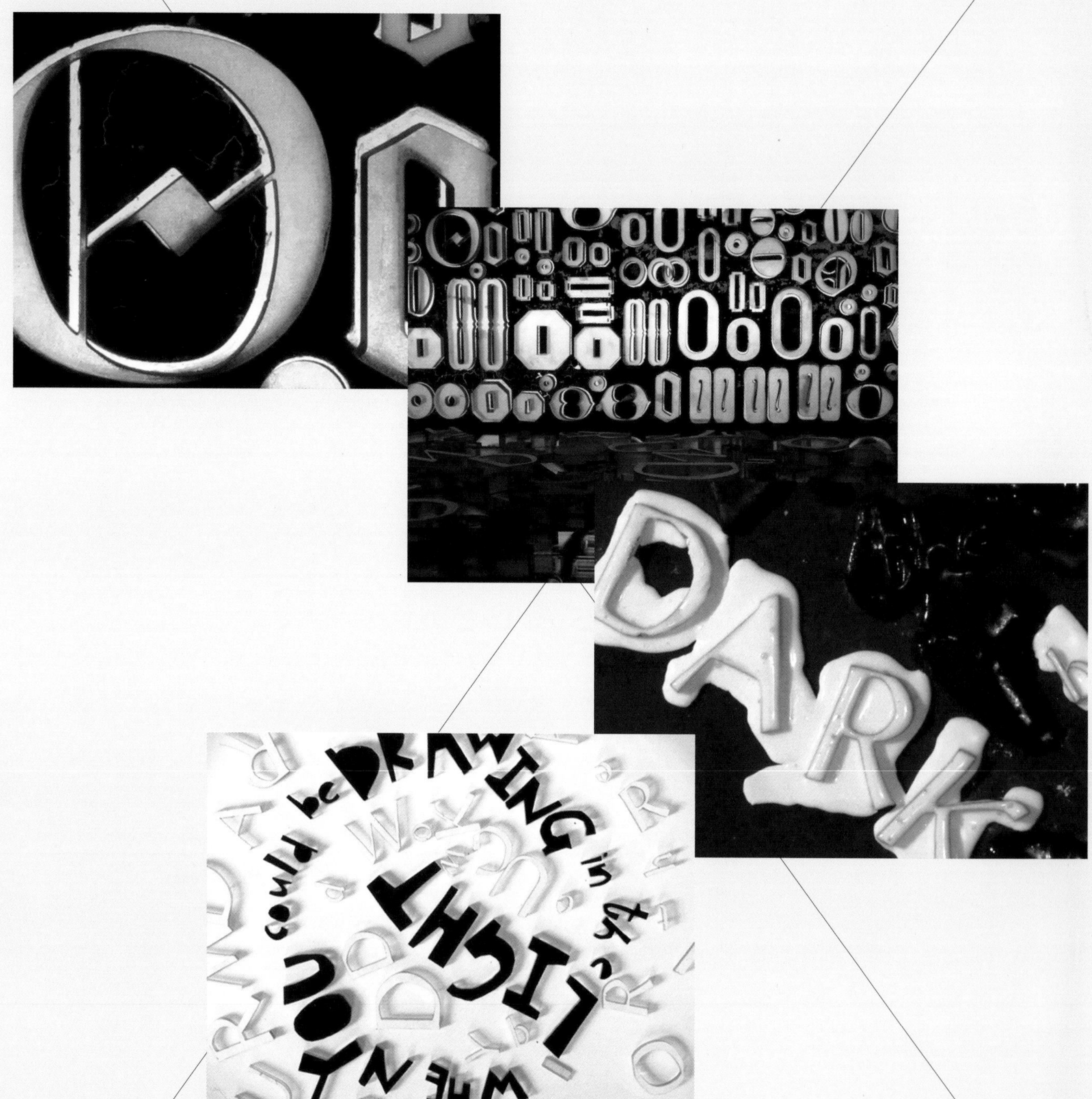

TDC² 2010

Chairman's Statement

By now—the thirteenth year TDC² has been included in the annual TDC competitions—the designers who submited their fonts for judging by a panel of their peers will know the level of ingenuity and standards of design that are expected, simply by the quality of the winners that preceded them. It's interesting to take a look back, as I did when I was asked to chair TDC² 2010, at both the judges' choices over the previous twelve years and their selections, to see if they have actually attained any popularity or usage. At the same time, have any new type designer stars been added to the firmament? The answer is a qualified yes in both cases, but this, of course, is not really objective, because over the years the judges, along with their chairpersons—some sixty or so—have considered more than 1,500 fonts and have collectively chosen in excess of 200 winners from more than thirty countries.

This year had the highest number of entries ever, 176 from twenty-nine countries, and the judges (Gail Anderson, Doyald Young, Daniel Pelavin, and Gary Munch) selected sixteen, with 80 percent coming from outside the United States. This percentage has only been beaten once before: in 2005, another record-breaking year for entries, with less than 15 percent of the winners coming from the U.S.

The judges started by whittling down the anonymous font submissions from the variety of type classifications, which were not as ruthlessly expunged as I expected. It took them a while to get into their stride and bring the numbers down by around half. But then I wasn't a judge, and it was only their opinions that mattered; they carefully considered the proportions, substance, and flexibility of each and every font. It was stimulating to see such a wide range of new styles across the categories, particularly the non-Latin fonts, bringing a diversity of scripts and nonalphabetical systems.

So it will be interesting in the coming months and years to see how many of these fonts make an impression in the real world, validating or otherwise the judges' selections. I think they will perform, in general, very well. There is a good cross section of text and display fonts, and if they live up to the previous twelve years' selections, then they do stand at least a 50 percent chance of making an impression—short or long, only time will tell.

I'm sure you will appreciate, as I do, the designers' skill and creativity in developing these fonts, and maybe you will have an opportunity to make use of them. But you can also thank the judges. They brought their selections forward as a collection, making a typographic pattern out of a jigsaw, the pieces of which have come together randomly from around the globe.

—Dave Farey

TDC² 2010 Judges

Dave Farey

Gail Anderson

Gary Munch

Daniel Pelavin

Doyald Young

Dave Farey, Chairman, TDC² 2010

Dave Farey's type designs now tend toward multilingual and multimedia challenges, both as commissions and for general release. Print and graphic design technologies have changed dramatically during his working life, as he has been able to design alphabets and letterforms for metal typesetting, transfer, and photosetting, and for the alternative arenas that wander the ether in search of hard drives or digital chips.

At HouseStyle Graphics in London, Farey has worked with Richard Dawson, reviving iconic British typefaces, notably from Eric Gill and Edward Johnston, and creating original fonts that now, fortunately, can be placed in the "twentieth century" category.

Newspapers and magazines are facing robust competition but, surprisingly perhaps, are not only holding their own but are collectively increasing circulations worldwide. Nevertheless, the end of print is inevitable, and editorial designers of publication titles have become active in parallel websites that need visual harmony. And where there's a need to revitalize editorial fonts and the paraphernalia of nameplates and mastheads, Farey is more than happy to contribute.

Gail Anderson, Judge

Gail Anderson is the creative director of design at SpotCo. From 1987 to early 2002, she served as senior art director at *Rolling Stone* magazine.

Anderson's work, which has received numerous awards, is in the permanent collections of the Cooper-Hewitt, National Design Museum; the Milton Glaser Design Study Center and Archives; and the Library of Congress. She is coauthor, with Steven Heller, of six design books, including *New Ornamental Type.*

She teaches in New York City's School of Visual Arts MFA and undergraduate design programs and currently serves on the advisory boards of Adobe Partners by Design and the Society of Publication Designers.

Anderson is the recipient of the 2008 American Institute of Graphic Arts Medal, and the 2009 Richard Gangel Art Director Award from the Society of Illustrators.

Gary Munch, Judge

Gary Munch is a type designer as well as a professor at the University of Bridgeport in Connecticut. He has designed typefaces for Linotype (Ergo, Really) and for Microsoft's ClearType project (Candara). He has a long-standing interest in non-Latin scripts, and he has designed award-winning typefaces in Cyrillic and Greek.

From 2001 to 2008, Munch was on the board of the Type Directors Club, where he served as president and chairman. He also chaired the TDC² 2002 type design competition and the TDC50 typography competition in 2004.

He speaks occasionally at TypeCon, the annual type design conference of the Society of Typographic Aficionados. At the University of Bridgeport, he teaches graphic design, typography, and type design in the design programs.

Daniel Pelavin, Judge

This is Daniel Pelavin's fourth decade of transforming and melding the images and cultural ephemera of our times into cogent and compelling messages for publishing, advertising, and communication design.

Working his way up through the ranks in the legendary art studios of Detroit, in the halcyon days of the early 1970s, Pelavin apprenticed with artists from the entire gamut of graphic arts professionals, including decorative, fashion, product, and technical illustrators as well as letterers, typographers, and designers. Following the completion of a Master of Fine Arts degree, he taught college courses in design, lettering, and illustration before moving to New York City in hopes of pursuing his career in art.

More than 30 years later, Pelavin has honed and polished his craft to become a celebrated illustrator and typographic designer with national and international clients. He has become, as well, an educator who shares his knowledge and experience with students and fellow professionals alike, and he continues to play a pioneering role in the evolution of digital art and the seamless merging of design and illustration.

Doyald Young, Judge

Doyald Young was born in Holliday, Texas, on Sept 12, 1926. He attended Los Angeles City College, the Los Angeles Trade-Technical College, Chouinard School of Art, and the Art Center College of Design in Pasadena, California. Among his many and varied clients are the California Institute of Technology; Henry Dreyfuss Associates; University of California, Los Angeles; Max Factor cosmetics; and Sassoon. With Don Bartels, he designed the GE logo font for General Electric's worldwide identity program. He is an associate of International Design Associates and Bikohsha Inc., of Japan.

Young has served as typographical consultant to Xerox Corporation, Southern California Edison Company, and Bechtel Corporation, and consulted with Emerson Stern and the Salk Institute on development of a written American Sign Language alphabet for the National Institutes of Health. He has designed fonts for Max Factor, the International Typeface Corporation, Compugraphic Corporation, Teletype Corporation, and Prudential Insurance Company of America. Fonts he has designed include: Eclat, Home Run, Young Gallant, ITC Young Baroque and ITC Young Finesse, and a formal script.

He is an international lecturer and has taught lettering, logo design, and typography basics at the Art Center College of Design for 27 years. The Art Center in 2001 named him Inaugural Master of the School for teaching and for his contribution to the field of art and design. In 2009, he was an American Institute of Graphic Arts Medalist.

He is the author of *Logotypes & Letterforms, Fonts & Logos, The Art of the Letter,* and *Dangerous Curves,* and he is working on *Learning Curves.*

TDC² 2010 Judge's Choice

Judge's Choice, Gail Anderson

I stuck a notebook in my pocket as I headed out to the judging so I could jot down the names of fonts I hoped to purchase later on. I've got many, many wish lists on scraps of paper and in assorted Molskines, but if I'd had actual gold stars on me that Saturday, Ingeborg most certainly would have received five. It's got everything I love, including a unicase and a sexy, quirky ital. Ingeborg is both classic and contemporary, and I can tell that the display weights are going to be a lot of fun to work with. I got a kick out of the chunky numbers and even the crazy Ingeborg Block weight (though I usually prefer to make my own outlines and drop shadows). I claimed this one early on as my Judge's Choice and made sure it would be my first post-TDC² purchase. It's just plain fun and looks as though it was designed by someone who really enjoyed the effort.

Designer's Concept

The Ingeborg family was designed to produce a readable modern face. Its roots might be historical, but its approach is contemporary. Ingeborg's text weights are functional and discreet. This was achieved without losing any of the classic characteristics of a Didone typeface, which are vertical stresses and high contrast. The display weights, on the other hand, are designed to fulfill their job and will catch the reader's eye by individual form language and a whole lot of ink on the paper. Nevertheless, both are of one origin and work together in harmony.

Typeface: Ingeborg

Typeface Designer: Michael Hochleitner, Vienna, Austria. Foundry: Typejockeys, www.typejockeys.com. Members of Typeface Family/System: Regular Italic, Bold, Bold Italic, Heavy, Heavy Italic, Fat, Fat Italic, and Block Concept

Now from and in

Vienna City

SQUARE

Rocket №5

Regular, Bold, Heavy & Fat

INCLUDING UNICASE

INGEBORG

A new kind of Modern Face

Whoever thought that Modern Faces were not readable should now know better. Ingeborg's text weights combine everything a "Didone" should be, without being inferior to the common oldstyle faces used for copy text setting.

TDC² 2010 Judge's Choice

Judge's Choice, Gary Munch

The entire jury was entranced by this entry, a Japanese kanji typeface in a very calligraphic style. The sample presentation as a text was impeccable, featuring flowing lines of brushwork that recall a very fine personal calligraphy. So different from the tradition of European calligraphy, the trace of the brush here is not at all compromised by the narrow requirements of type founding, and the energy inherent in a moving brush is made particularly evident: pressing, rising, turning, flicking, and dabbing.

The characters have been ingeniously allowed their own height or depth, and together avoid the perhaps overly regular sense in Japanese type of many small blocks assembled together on a Cartesian grid. The effect is one of graceful speech pausing or lengthening a sound for poetic or rhetorical effect, and it is quite as engaging as it is innovative.

Designer's Concept

After several revisions of this typeface design, which started as my 1995 graduation thesis from an art university, I was able to turn it into a working font. A fully proportional Japanese typeface design is not only about the design, and turning it into a working font is not possible without help from technology. By defying the boundaries of traditional Japanese type design, I think I was able to create a freely flowing design.

Typeface: Kazuraki

Typeface Designer: Ryoko Nishizuka, Tokyo. Foundry: Adobe Systems, Inc. URL: http://store1.adobe.com/cfusion/store/html/indextn?store+OLS-US&event=displayFont&code=KORK10005000. Language: Japanese. Members of Typeface Family/Superfamily: Single, Display, and True Proportional Calligraphic Type

懐石のコースもございます
おしながき　日本料理
新鮮なお造りに焼物と煮物を
車海老の天ぷら　栗きんとん
市場から直送の新鮮なお魚をご賞味ください
個室もご用意いたします　白アスパラガス
日本酒も揃えております
蕪蒸し　和風のカルパッチョ
鯛のあら炊き　手打ちのお蕎麦
江戸前寿司　百合根団子
サヨリの塩焼き　海胆焼き
甘鯛の飯蒸し　焼き鳥
ワイン・焼酎・ウィスキーその他

プロポーショナルかな書体
＋字種限定漢字追加

かづらき®

TDC² 2010 Judge's Choice

Judge's Choice, Daniel Pelavin

In viewing the submissions to TDC² 2010, I was impressed by the collections of families, superfamilies, monster families, and mega-gigundo families, and wondered to myself, "How many angels can fit on the head of a pin?" For me, apparently, the thrill of admiring the minute twitch of a serif or the subtle curve of a counter has faded.

I was, however, awed and honored to be in the company of esteemed colleagues who judged the entries, supervised the competition, and helped me understand the distinction between a good "Zhe" and an insufficient one. Still, I have to say that using leading-edge technology to generate fonts that mimic relics of bygone ages seems not so unlike Johannes Gutenburg, who used his own version of OpenType alternate glyphs to basically "forge" handwritten manuscripts (this, from one who regularly uses leading-edge technology to effect historical idiom).

Then I came upon Urbana, and though my first thought was this was 80s "innovative" typography redux, I was less puzzled by the eccentricity of its letterforms than I was intrigued by the process through which they emerged. There was something beyond rebelling against one's parents or excluding those who don't get it. The fact of these characters being abstracted from the very pathways of people's daily existence imbues them with a charm and cogency that justifies further exploration by some of today's "innovators."

Designer's Concept

Designing Urbana Lnd was mostly about looking very closely at something that already existed, extracting parts, and then transferring them into a new context. I was not even aware that I was designing a font when I first started engaging myself with its forms. I found them in the road network of London, which is full of beautiful little ornaments when seen from above. It was important to me not to add any streets or change the course of the roads, but I allowed myself to leave out streets and proportion the ones I kept. What I like most is that the output shows a very particular design process, which is more related to exploring that it is to inventing.

Typeface: Urbana Lnd
Typeface Designer: Birgit Mayer, Vienna

FT
ABOVE GROUND LEVEL
LON
DON, UK!
THE QUICK BROWN FOX
JUMPS OVER A LAZY DOG.

TDC² 2010 Judge's Choice

Judge's Choice, Doyald Young

In 1948 Joe Gibby, my lettering teacher, introduced me to Jenson's type. There have been a number of versions based on the original: The Golden Type, Centaur, Cloister, Eusebius, Robert Slimbach's version for Adobe, and the latest version, Ronald Arnholm's Legacy. It is a large family that includes his square-serif version, my favorite member of this family. Type preference is personal, and after the designer has done the necessary homework on proportion, color, fit, and kerning, what remains is style or concept. A text face by nature should exercise restraint. Legacy square serif does this, and exhibits great style also. It is a highly legible font, useful and welcome.

Designer's Concept

Rounding out my ITC Legacy family is the square serif version, begun as pencil sketches on tracing vellum. I worked both on serif and sans serif specimens, with the square serif concept being my hypothetical interpolation between the two styles. Final sketches, scanned and brought into Photoshop for editing, allowed me to work in a manner similar to that of precomputer days, before moving to Fontographer.

At a microscopic level, the serif corners create a very strong definition to the edge of the baseline, x-height, and cap height, giving it a crisp color on the page; both the bracketing and tapering of some serifs prevent it from being overly assertive. The diagonal humanist stress creates interlacing between letters, and along with the serif asymmetry, produce forward momentum, a feeling of warmth, readability, and legibility on both paper and screen. Sentences are like a braided rope, rather than a chain of beads. In text sizes, the font does not assert itself as a square serif, since it is not seen as that style, meshing perfectly with the serif. But at display sizes, it is definitely a square serif.

Typeface ITC Legacy Square Serif Pro

Typeface Designer: Ronald Arnholm, Athens, Georgia. Foundry: International Typeface Corporation. URLs: www.itcfonts.com, www.fonts.com, www.linotype.com, www.faces.co.uk. Members of Typeface Family/System: Book, Light, Extra Light, Medium, Bold, Bold Italic, and Ultra Foundry

ITC® Legacy®
Square Serif Pro
EXTRA LIGHT | LIGHT | BOOK
MEDIUM | BOLD | ULTRA
EXTRA LIGHT | LIGHT | BOOK
MEDIUM | BOLD
Square Serif Pro
Designed by Ronald Arnholm

A QUICK BROWN FOX JUMPS OVER **THE LAZY DOG**
All questions asked by five watch experts *amazed the judge.*
Oozy *quivering* jellyfish expectorated by the mad hawk.
The five amazing boxing *wizards* jumped very quickly?
Many victors flank the *Egyptians* who mixed a job quiz.
Wolves exit quickly as the six *fanged zoo chimps* jabber.
Quickly wafting zephyrs did vex a very poor Jim!
The War in Afghanistan

U.S. SPY AGENCIES FAILED TO COLLATE CLUES ON TERROR

High Quality
Low Cost
Free Shipping

NOW ONLY $25.37

English Lavender Facebook ?

Floral Bath & Body Gels ***Upgrade now and save!***

THE ELEMENTS OF Typographic Style Robert Bringhurst ¶

1 2 3 4 5 6 7 8 9 0

Supercalifragilistic**expialidocious** @
*Supercalifragilistic**expialidocious***

IN THE BEGINNING God created the heaven and the earth. And the earth *was* without form, and void, and darkness was upon the face of the deep. And the Spirit of God moved upon the face of the waters. And God said, Let there be light: and there was light. And

Apple's fusion of hardware and software design

"Earthquake!"

Typeface: Deliscript

Typeface Designer: Michael Doret, Hollywood, California. Members of Typeface Family/System: Upright and Slant

Designer's Concept Although initially inspired by the neon sign in front of Canter's Deli in Los Angeles, the design of Deliscript soon took on a life of its own, such as the variable-length tails, which can be accessed in six different styles, and the crossbars, which can be extended outward from the lowercase *t* in either direction. These unusual features only became possible after enlisting OpenType programming assistance from Patrick Griffin of CanadaType, and they help make possible typesetting that approaches the look and feel of handlettering.

Typeface: Joos

Typeface Designer: Laurent Bourcellier, Scherwiller, France. Foundry: typographies.fr. URL: http://www.typographies.fr/index.php?page=fontes&s=Joos. Members of Typeface Family/System: Classic and Pro

Designer's Concept Joos is a revival of an upright italic created in 1536 in Gent. This work is not a formal revival; rather, it was faithfully fit into the scheme of Joos Lambrecht's (punchcutter) thinking, which was to idealize roman types by bringing together the characteristically graceful shapes of italics and the angles of romans. In order to make the character optically vertical, it was necessary to work on each character with a specific angle, which was defined notably by its structure and dimension. Capitals have geometric, vertical stems, while lowercase letters have an angle that varies from zero to two degrees.

This poster was setted in Joos, a revival of an

upright italic

created in sixteenth century,

→ precisely in 1536 in Gent.

This work is not a formal revival, but faithfully fit into the scheme of the

Punchcutter's thought,

which was to idealize roman types by bringing together

the characteristic

gy

graceful ſhapes of italics and the angle of romans.

ǺBÇĐĘFĞĦĪĴĶŁMŊØP
QŔŠŢŰVẄXŶŻ
ǺBÇĐĘFĞĦĪĴĶŁMŊǾP
QŔŠŢŰVẄXŶŻ
aqbčđěfģhħĩjķłmńøp
qřşŧůvẅxỳzẓ
æœfiflßfygjctðĳ þqſpſ&
0123456789&0123456789
$¥€£ƒ@!?([{/%½¼«"#¶§†‡❦*
and many others...

In order to make the character

optically vertical,

it was necessary to work on each character

with a ſpecific angle,

which was defined notably by its structure & dimension.

Capitals have a geometrical vertical ſtem, while the lowercases have an angle which vary

BETWEEN 0 & 2 DEGREES.

Typeface: Espinosa Nova
Typeface Designer: Cristobal Henestrosa, Mexico City. Members of Typeface Family/System: Regular, Italic, Bold, Rotunda (Bold Alt), Titling, and Ornaments

Designer's Concept This revival is based on the types used by Antonio de Espinosa, the most important Mexican printer of the sixteenth century and very probably the first native-born punchcutter on the American continent.

ESPINOSA NOVA

Titling

is a Mexican revival

Regular

from the 16th Century

Italic

based on the work

Bold

of Antonio de Espinosa

Rotunda (Bold Alt)

Ornaments

Typeface: Lavigne Display
Typeface Designer: Ramiro Espinoza, Amsterdam. Foundry: ReType. Members of Typeface Family/System: Regular, Italic, Light, Light Italic, Bold, and Bold Italic

Designer's Concept Lavigne Display is the first release of a type family for magazines and other publications requiring a touch of distinction. The goal: the high contrast and other refinements of classic modern serif typefaces. Pointed-pen calligraphy and sketching were the main sources of inspiration. Lavigne was planned as a family with Display and Text. The range will cover every type hierarchy used in modern magazines. The six styles of Display are published in OpenType format, with small caps, four sets of numbers (proportional old style, tabular old style, proportional lining, and tabular lining), and currency symbols.

Sexism

A fresh graphic to lighten wardrobes

longchamp

THE CHICEST WAY TO WARD OFF WINTER CHILLS

nice & twice

Fashion trends and hairstyle resources

mulberry

The prettiest—and cosiest—look of the season

ABCDEFGHIJKLMNOPQRSTUVWXY&Z

abcdeffiflghijklmnopqrstuvwxyz@ß?!¶†‡§

ABCDEFGHIJKLMNOPQRSTUVWXYZµπ∂∞

$£¥€01234567890—$£¥€0123456789

Typeface: Retiro

Typeface Designer: Jean François Porchez, Clamart, France. Members of Typeface Family/System: Regular and its extensions

Designer's Concept A daring interpretation of Spanish typography—severe, austere, and yet full of life—Retiro is named after a lovely park in Madrid. *Madriz* magazine wanted stereotypical Didot as in the masthead of the women's magazines *L'Officiel, Vogue,* and *Harper's Bazaar.* The result is an imaginary Castilian and Andalusian vernacular Didot, because such typefaces don't exist in the history of Spanish typography. Retiro was commissioned by a publisher rather than an art director, thus the project started as an unusual collaboration. During the summer of 2009, the designers finalized the typeface, adding many additional glyphs and removing undesired ones. *Madriz* magazine, a witness to the contrasts between the city's modernization and its traditions, is a biannual, bilingual city magazine that was first published in 2007.

Retiro

abcdefghijklmnopqrstuvwxyz

RAEILO (calt) acdefgjkmnprsyz (swsh–ss1) abnqu (ss2)

ABCDEFGHIJKLMNOPQRSTUVWXYZ

ACEFGHJKMNSR (swsh–ss1) A (ss2) AZ (ss4) AMN (ss5)

ABCDEFGHIJKLMNOPQRSTUVWXYZ (ss3)

–@№0123456789 ([{#€¥$¢ƒ£ ¶&!?,.»”-

GUÍA ¶ FORO ‡ BEBE

aaabbccctcddeefffiggkkjj

LLORCA † ALLOA * CALOR

nnnppqqrrststssuuuyyzz

Typeface: Narziss
Designer: Hubert Jocham, Lautrach, Germany. Foundry: Hubert Jocham Type. URL: www.hubertjocham.de. Members of Typeface Family/System: Regular, Drops, and Swirls

Designer's Concept Hubert Jocham was always fascinated by Tony DiSpigna's lettering in *U&lc*. So he designed Mommie with very high contrast. Narziss is an upright neoclassic serif with very high contrast, too. In the swirls version, Jocham wanted the swirls to overlap with the neighboring characters.

Typeface: Rieven Uncial
Designer: Steven Skaggs, Louisville, Kentucky. Foundry: Delve Fonts. URL: www.delvefonts.com. Members of Typeface Family/System: Uncial and Italic

Designer's Concept Rieven Uncial retains the richnes of traditional uncial forms, but it has been carefully tempered to be much more versatile. Uncial Italic works perfectly with Uncial Regular, despite being structurally distinct. The trick is to make the contrast between regular and italic one of narrow-to-wide rather than straight-to-slanted; the italic slants only five degrees. The italic relates to the regular form with "knuckles" that suggest the branching direction of the uncial (it actually branches from the bottom like a cursive). The Rieven Uncial family possesses the flexibility needed for general text work.

DANTE
ALIGHIERI

Typeface: Fugu
Designer: Neil Summerour, Jefferson, Georgia. Foundry: Positype. URL: TypeTrust.com, MyFonts.com, veer.com, FontShop.com

Designer's Concept Fugu is not intended to be perfectly flowing or over-the-top. It is the product of sumi brush on cotton paper and is written at an intentionally casual pace. Each letterform created relies on how the hand reacts from character to character. The interplay is instinctual and deliberate with resulting forms taking a more visceral appearance on the page and screen. The texture is devoid of software trickery or plug-ins. The casual style is refreshing and contemporary—further expanded by alternate glyphs, swashes, and ligatures found in both the type and glyph palettes.

A dangerous but amazing
tetrodotoxin
starts paralyzing muscles
suffering from asphyxiation & striking pain
a paper-thin
Delicacy
with no known antidote
fugu

Typeface: Ysobel

Typeface Designers: Robin Nicholas, Alice Savoie, and Delve Withrington. Foundry: Monotype and fonts.com. URLs: MonotypeImaging.com and Fonts.com. Members of Typeface Family/System: Regular, Italic, Light, Light Italic, Semi Bold, Semi Bold Italic, Bold, Bold Italic, Display, Display Italic, Display Light, Display Light Italic, Display Semi Bold, Display Semi Bold Italic, Display Bold, Display Bold Italic, Display Extra Bold, Display Extra Bold Italic, Display Thin, and Display Thin Italic

Designers' Concept The design started when Robin Nicholas was asked to develop a custom Century Schoolbook. He wanted a more contemporary feel, but the client kept their typeface closer to the original. That project provided ideas for a new design. Ever since designing Nimrod 30 years ago, Nicholas wanted to make a modern typeface for newspapers and magazines. Ysobel has the soft, inviting letter shapes of Century Schoolbook, with more incised serifs and terminals. Its capitals are also narrower, and they were harmonized with the lowercase. Ysobel's x-height is full-bodied without disrupting lowercase proportions.

Ysobel Pro Wins Much Coveted TDC² 2010 Typography Award

The Ysobel family is an elegant, versatile graphic communicator. Designed for newspapers and periodicals, it is equally at home anywhere that easy reading and economy of space are important.

NEW YORK, NY – The Ysobel™ typeface family is not only elegant, but also exceptionally legible and space economical. A collaborative design effort between Robin Nicholas as lead designer and project director, Alice Savoie of Monotype Imaging, as well as typeface designer Delve Withrington, the project had the primary goal of creating a typeface family for setting text in newspapers and periodicals. The resulting type family, however, is also ideal for any application that requires quick and easy assimilation of text.

According to Nicholas, "The idea for the design started when I was asked to develop a custom version of Century Schoolbook. I wanted to give the design a more contemporary feel, although the client ultimately decided to keep their typeface closer to the original. The project gave me

The subtle yet important differences between Ysobel Pro and Ysobel Display Pro can be seen above.

"I am very conscious of type usage in signage, advertising, etc. This gets in the way of the message sometimes, but I guess that is the price for spending a lifetime working in type."

❧ DESIGNER ROBIN NICHOLAS

Typeface: Rum Black
Typeface Designer: Trine Rask, Copenhagen. Foundry: Types United. URL: www.myfonts.com

Designer's Concept Rum, which means "space" in Danish, is designed inside out, focusing on the counters. The counters are repeated throughout the typeface, which gives a strong text image in small and especially in display sizes. It is both very simple and very delicate in detail. It has a large character set with alternative characters that make it possible to create a softer and rounder text image. It has very delicate swashes that work like a discreet period after a word.

Szőlőlé
cœūŗ çiåő ģřœş pölśę ğyš Þórfrónsvé Óháði straße
orange
»§012#34567±89&012¥34€567$89« ©TRask
panqueques
rødgrød med fløde&råcreme på pæretærte
hedelmäkori
gâteau avec un glaçage
súkkulaði

Typeface: Aisha.
Typeface Designer: Titus Nemeth, Paris. Foundry: www.tntypography.com. Members of Typeface Family/System: Regular. Language: Arabic

Designer's Concept Aisha was created as part of my research within the post-diploma program at L'Ecole Supérieure d'Art et de Design (ESAD) in Amiens, France. Originating from an inquiry into the history of an Arabic metal font cut in the nineteenth century, part of this typeface qualifies as an historical revival. Its reinterpretation provided insights into its creation and the practice of a colleague from the past. Moreover, a redefinition of the historical model within contemporary practice—through the extension of language support and the design of a Latin companion—added value and interest. Based on the calligraphy practiced in the Maghreb, this typeface aspires to be a usable and relevant contribution to the Arabic typography of today.

Penso che un sogno così non ritorni mai più

نَبْغِيهَا عَائِشَةَ وَنَمُوتُ عَلِيهَا

Gianna non cercava il suo pigmalione, Aisha difendeva il suo salario, dall'inflazione

denn ich hab nur von dir geträumt

You are all I long for

Qu'elle est plus belle qu'avant l'été

أَنْتِ عُمْرِي وَأَنْتِ حَيَاتِي تَمَنَّيْتُ

forget about your house of cards

e quando il pane sforno, lo tengo caldo per te

in other words, I love you

Typeface DecoType Nastaliq

Typeface Designer: Mirjam Somers, Amsterdam. Foundry: DecoType. Client: Winsoft, France. URL: http:///www.winsoft-international.com/en/store/tasmeem-fonts-nastaliq.html

Designer's Concept DecoType Nastaliq is the latest fruit of 25 years of analyzing Arabic scripts in their pre-typographic form. Like its close relative Ruq'ah, Nastaliq retains the two-dimensional aspect of Arabic script. To capture this in a Latin-based technical environment is a great challenge. The final glyph set is a minimal set of functional shapes; using this set, any combinations with a diacritic attachment can be generated for all Arabic-script languages. This is possible with the use of ACE, the Arabic Calligraphic Engine, a radical departure from movable-type thinking. ACE was developed by the DecoType team—Thomas Milo, Peter Somers and Mirjam Somers—initially for the Ruq'ah script and later expanded to an analysis of the Naskh script. The Latin parts of the DecoType Nastaliq specimen are set in Grotext Ultra Light, designed by Karsten Luecke.

المخالب الذهبية
Le Crabe aux Pinces d'Or
المخالب الذهبية
خرچنگ پنجه طلائی
رَوى ٱلْحَسَنُ عَنِ ٱلْحَسَنِ عَنْ أَبِي ٱلْحَسَنِ عَنْ جَدِّ ٱلْحَسَنِ أَنَّ أَحْسَنَ ٱلْحُسْنِ ٱلْخُلُقُ ٱلْحَسَنُ
Just has it from Just who has it from Just's father that Just's grandfather passed on the justification that the justest justness is just people

TDC Intro 010

Chairman's Statement

I have always cherished type. It seems almost magical how type can encode stories and information into graphic shapes. But it's not only a very efficient way to store information. By choosing a particular typeface, we interject an emotional tone into those encoded messages. If we choose carefully, we can imply an intonation for the message so that when the reader deciphers the information, it will once again become a voice.

Possessing the highest appreciation and admiration for the printed medium, I initially found motion graphics loud. It almost seemed vulgar compared to the elegant arch of a Caslon, the alignment of a Jan Tschichold book cover, or the rhythm of a Josef Müller-Brockmann poster. But soon I discovered how amazing the marriage of type and motion could be. As I began designing titles for feature films, it struck me how little attention the field was given. It has been clearly one of the most vital and vibrant fields of design, and yet other designers have often approached it with suspicion—as if it were an inferior child that has to be accepted but never validated. My infatuation with motion graphics hasn't faded over the years. I always encourage people to study the craft and philosophy of motion graphics and enjoy the visual poetry that can string words together into a message and turn messages into stories.

It is strange that as ubiquitous as motion graphics have become for everyday communication, there is still scant recognition of the excellence in the field. I started to imagine an annual showcase of title work many years ago, but it wasn't until I joined the board of directors at the Type Directors Club that it all finally clicked. Where could an annual competition for type in motion find a better home?

The history of motion graphics is short, and we all have the opportunity to shape its future by finding new and unexpected paths to excitement and beauty. We hope that TDC Intro will set a high bar for everybody who strives for excellence and will serve as a source of inspiration for those who have decided to enter this truly moving field. My utmost respect and heartfelt thanks to the eminent judges who were generous with their time and enthusiasm. Many hard decisions had to be made to sort out the absolute best from the extraordinary amount of submitted work. I want to take this opportunity to salute the effort of everyone who submitted work to the competition. The overall quality was so impressive. We are very excited to see your new work next year!

—Jakob Trollbäck

Jakob Trollbäck

Justin Cone

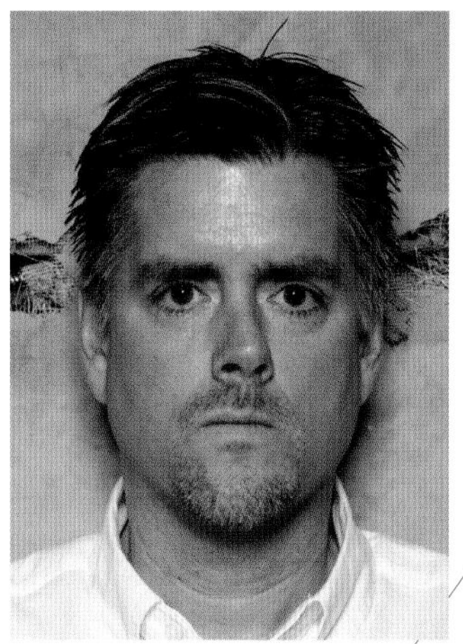
Kyle Cooper

David Peters

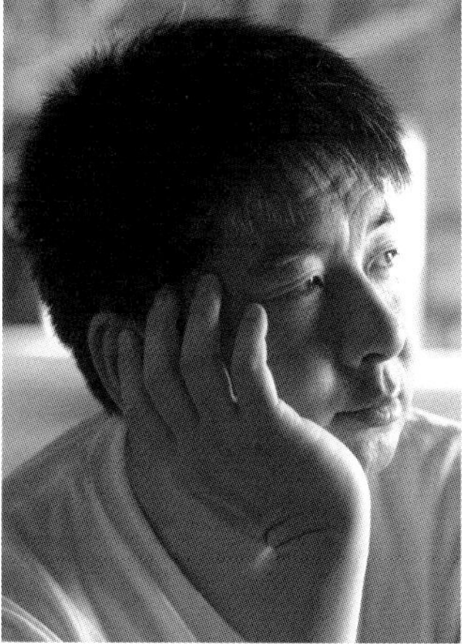
Garson Yu

Jonathon Wells

Jakob Trollbäck, TDC Intro 010, Chairman

A self-taught designer from Sweden, Jakob Trollbäck leads an innovative and highly successful company as president and creative director. Trollbäck + Company in New York City creates seminal and award-winning designs and is an acknowledged industry leader in branding and immersive motion graphic design.

Trollbäck + Company (http://www.trollback.com) was born when the former DJ transferred his aural pursuits to the visual medium, aiming to create emotive pieces that take their audiences to purely sensorial planes. Trollbäck quickly moved his company to the forefront of motion design with an approach that relies on both unorthodox thinking and immersive storytelling, and the belief that an emotional and focused message is essential for any communication to be truly successful. Currently in its eleventh year, Trollbäck + Company, has successfully expanded its creative output to film titles, TV commercials, publication design, music videos, environmental design, and short films.

In addition to serving on the board of the Type Directors Club, he is on the board of directors of the Art Directors Club and the Board of Trustees of the Brooklyn Academy of Music. Trollbäck is an active and sought-after speaker, lecturer, and guest curator. He has presented at the TED Conference, at American Institute of Graphic Arts (AIGA) events across the nation, the Film Society of Lincoln Center, the Broadcast Designers Association conference, the *HOW* Design Conference, and many other events in the U.S. and Europe. He has also lectured and taught at a variety of East and West Coast universities, including the Rhode Island School of Design, Parsons The New School for Design, the School of Visual Arts in New York, and Yale University.

Trollbäck + Company has received dozens of creative-industry awards, including those from the Primetime Emmy Awards, the Association of Independent Commercial Producers (AICP) Show, the Art Directors Club, the Broadcast Designers Association, D&AD, the *Communication Arts Design Annual,* the One Show, and the Type Directors Club. Trollbäck + Company was also included in the Cooper-Hewitt, National Design Museum Triennial for 2006–2007.

Justin Cone, Judge

As the founder and editor of Motionographer.com, Justin Cone has built the leading online source for the best in motion design, animation, experimental filmmaking, and visual effects. Garnering more than 1.4 million page views a month from visitors around the world, Motionographer seeks to be a curatorial voice and a useful archive for creative professionals, students, and enthusiasts. Cone earned his Master of Fine Arts in Motion Graphics from the Savannah College of Art and Design (SCAD) in Savannah, Georgia, and has worked for such companies as NBC-Universal, Apple, and Adobe as a writer, designer, and strategist. He is currently a professor of motion media design at SCAD and co-owner of Poyo Studios, a multidisciplinary design and events studio.

Kyle Cooper, Judge

Kyle Cooper, director and producer of more than 150 main title sequences, has received numerous accolades. *Details* credits him with "almost single-handedly revitalizing the main title sequence as an art form." *Fast Company* named Cooper one of the "100 most creative people in business." *Creativity* magazine named him one of the "Top 50 biggest and best thinkers and doers from the last 20 years of advertising and consumer culture." *The New York Times Magazine* called the title sequence he created for SE7EN "one of the most important design innovations of the 1990s."

He was creative director of R/Greenberg Associates in New York City and Los Angeles before founding two film design and production companies: Prologue Films, a finalist in the 2008 National Design Awards, launched in 2003; and Imaginary Forces, named and cofounded by Cooper in 1996.

Cooper has directed and produced numerous visual effects (VFX) sequences for films, including *Tropic Thunder, Across the Universe,* and *Iron Man*; and he is the visual effects supervisor on Julie Taymor's feature film adaptation of William Shakespeare's *The Tempest.*

He holds the honorary title of Royal Designer for Industry from the Royal Society of Arts, in London, and is a member of the Alliance Graphique Internationale. He earned a Master of Fine Arts in Graphic Design from the Yale School of Art, where he studied independently with Paul Rand.

David Peters, Judge

David Peters is a graphic designer, educator, and curator based in San Francisco. As principal at EXBROOK, he leads progressive organizations in the strategic use of design to communicate ideas and contribute to positive social change.

Among recent projects, Peters was commissioned to produce a two-part program on the works of Saul Bass for the twelfth Future Film Festival in Bologna, Italy. As founder of the research project DESIGN FILMS, he has curated many programs about the relationship between design and film, which have been featured at museums and film festivals throughout the United States, Europe, and Asia. In 1993, the U.S. National Endowment for the Arts recognized him with a design grant for his pioneering work in media history.

David has studied at the European Graduate School, in Switzerland, and at the Nova Scotia College of Art and Design, in Halifax, where he teaches in the Master of Design program each summer.

Garson Yu, Judge

Garson Yu is president and creative director of yU+co., a digital media design and production agency with offices in Hollywood, Hong Kong, and Shanghai. In 1998, Yu founded his business in Hollywood and eight years later established an office in Hong Kong, which led to creation of yuco[lab], a new media, interactive, and experiential design division.

Acknowledged as one of the leading film title designers in the business, Yu has worked on more than 150 feature film titles over the years and has collaborated with A-list directors such as Ang Lee, Sydney Pollack, Oliver Stone, John Woo, Ridley Scott, and Spike Lee. yU+co.'s diverse client list in films, gaming, television, and advertising includes Dreamworks Studios, Paramount Pictures, Sony Pictures, Disney, Warner Brothers, Fox, Universal Pictures, Ubisoft, THQ, Capcom, HBO, Showtime, Nickelodeon, Turner Classic Movies, Draft FCB, Ogilvy & Mather, Chiat Day, and Deutsch. Yu's work has been featured in major design publications worldwide and has won leading industry awards.

A native of Hong Kong, Yu holds a Master of Fine Art degree in graphic design from the Yale School of Art. He lectures frequently at design conferences and universities in Europe, Asia, and the United States. He is a member of the Alliance Graphique Internationale, in Switzerland.

Jonathon Wells, Judge

Jonathan Wells is the founder and for ten years served as festival director of the acclaimed global touring digital film festival RESFEST. Wells also cofounded and served as the original editor of *RES* magazine, a bimonthly (which includes a *RES* DVD in every issue) showcasing film, music, art, design, and culture.

Wells, based in Los Angeles, now runs Flux, a global creative community celebrating film, art, music, design, and culture. His initiative produces experiential events; curates and commissions film, video, and art programming; and hosts physical and virtual events around the world.

Feature Film: Typography—Gold; *Sherlock Holmes*. Creative Direction: Danny Yount, Venice, California. Design Direction: Lisa Bolan, Simon Clowes, and Henry Hobson. Calligraphy: Bonnie Ebbs. Illustration: Jorge Almeida and Chris Sanchez. Editor: Gabriel Diaz. VFX: Jose Ortiz and Todd Sheridan Perry. Animation: Joey Park and Alasdair Wilson. Compositors: Brett Reyenger and Miles Lauridsen. Coordinator: David Kennedy. Producer: Unjoo Byars. Executive Producer: Kyle Cooper. Design Company: Prologue Films. Studio/Client: Warner Bros. and Silver Pictures. Director: Guy Ritchie. Producers: Susan Downey, Lauren Meeks, Joel Silver, and Lionel Wigram. Principal Type: hand-drawn. Production Method/Principal Tools: After Effects, Final Cut Pro, and Photoshop

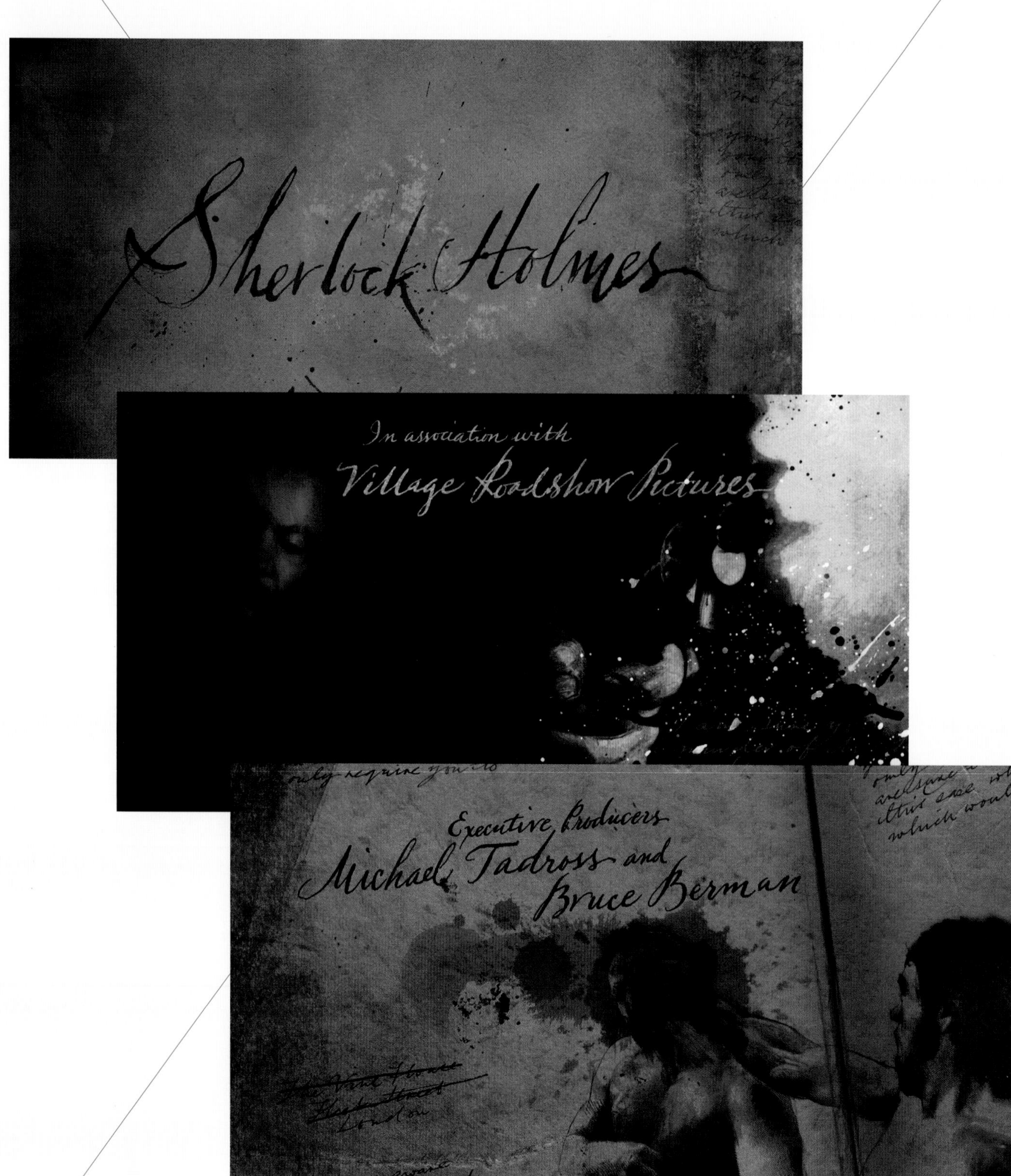

Feature Film: Animation—Gold; *Cirque du Freak: The Vampire's Assistant.* Creative Direction: Garson Yu, Hollywood, California. Art Direction: Etsuko Uji. Design: Edwin Baker and Etsuko Uji. Design Studio: yU+Co. Client: Universal Pictures. Principal Type: custom. Production Method/Principal Tools: After Effects, Avid, Maya, and Photoshop

Feature Film: Visual Design—Gold; *Push.* Creative Direction: Stephan Burle, Pamela Green, and Jarik Van Sluijs, Hollywood, California. Art Direction: Stephan Burle, Pamela Green, and Jarik Van Sluijs. Design: Stephan Burle, Pamela Green, and Jarik Van Sluijs. Design Studio: PIC Agency. Lettering: Jarik Van Sluijs. Client: Summit Entertainment. Production Method/ Principal Tools: Adobe After Effects, digital still photography, HD video, photography, traditional 2-D drawing, and digital graphic design

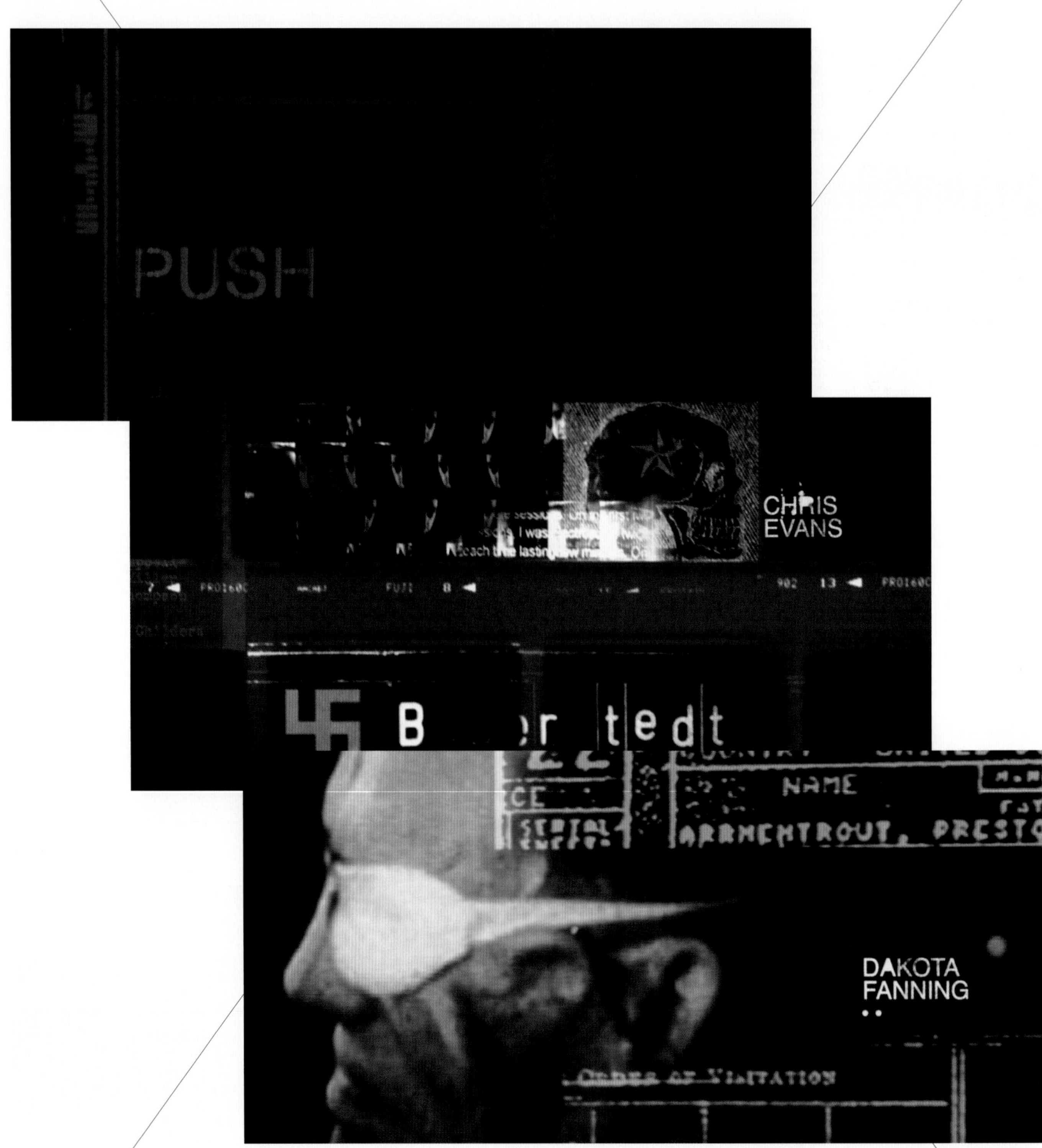

Feature Film: Typography—Honorable Mention; *This is Love*. Creative Direction: Saskia Rüeter, Berlin. Art Direction: Saskia Rüeter. Design: Saskia Rüeter. Design Studio: Untitled Design. Client: Badlands Film. Principal Type: Trade Gothic. Production Method/Principal Tools: Adobe After Effects and InDesign

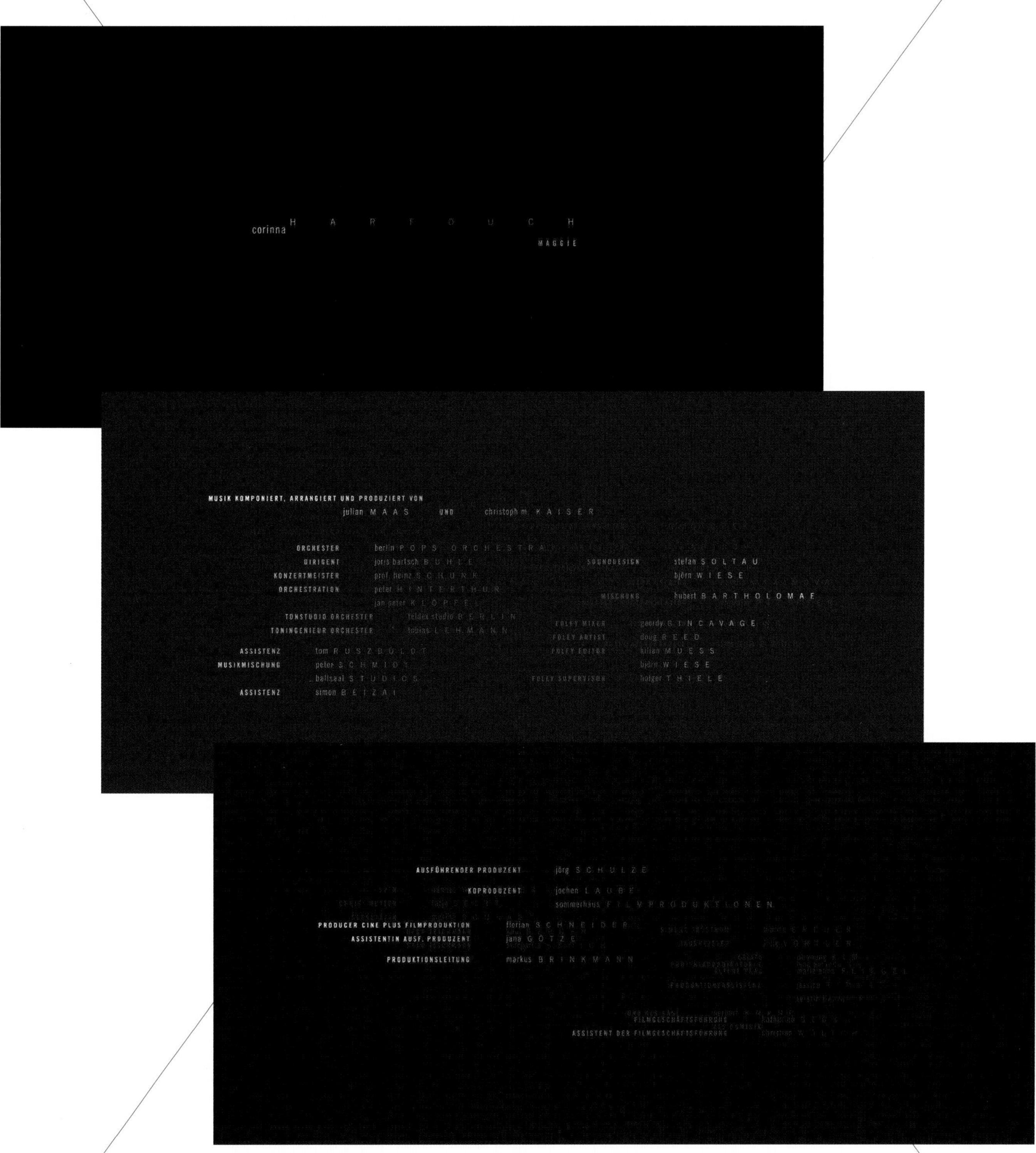

Feature Film: Animation—Honorable Mention; *An Education*. Creative Direction: Nic Benns, London. Art Direction: Nic Benns. Design: Nic Benns. Design Studio: MOMOCO. Client: BBC Films. Principal Type: Gill Sans. Production Method/Principal Tools: Adobe After Effects, drawing, Illustrator

Feature Film: Visual Design—Honorable Mention; *Ninja Assassin.* Creative Direction: Kyle Cooper and Heebok Lee, Venice, California. Editor: Nathaniel Park. Type Designer: José Luis Coyotl Mixcoatl. Producer: Ryan Robertson. Production Team: Reed Casey, Roy Cullen, Jesse Jones, Lee Nelson, Chris Sanchez, and Adam Swaab Design Company, Prologue Films. Client: Silver Pictures. Principal Type: ATCrillee (modified). Production Method/Principal Tools: After Effects, Maya, and Realflow

Feature Film: Visual Design—Honorable Mention; *Superman/Batman: Public Enemies*. Creative Direction: Erin Sarofsky, Chicago. Art Direction: Erin Sarofsky. Design: Nik Braatz, Matt Crnich, Carlos Foxworthy, and Jake Mathew. Lettering: Nik Braatz, Matt Crnich, Carlos Foxworthy, and Jake Mathew. Production Company: Sarofsky Corp. Client: Warner Bros. Animation. Principal Type: Railbox. Production Method/Principal Tools: Cinema 4D and Adobe After Effects

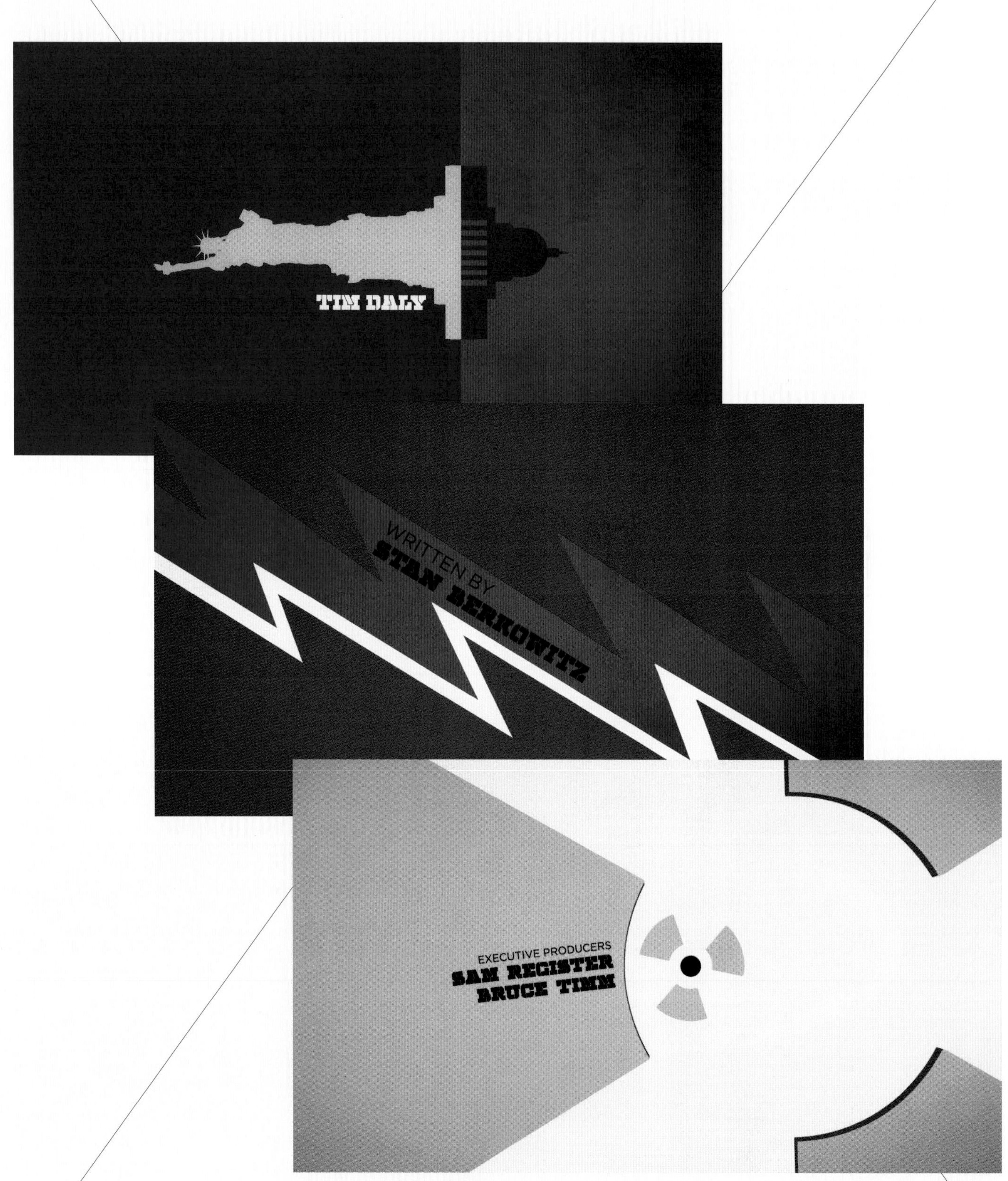

Television: Animation—Honorable Mention; *Community*. Creative Direction: Erin Sarofsky, Chicago. Art Direction: Erin Sarofsky. Design: Gene Park. Calligraphy: Erin Sarofsky, lead, with Halley Bonoma and David Michael Friend. Compositor: Matt Crnich. Animation: Roman Kobryn and Mike Wilson. Technical Director: Eric Thivierge. Producers: Louise Krakower and Rachel Steele. Assistant Producer: Halley Bonoma. VFX Director: Scott Stewart. VFX Supervisor: Andy Zazzera. Production Company: Sarofsky Corp. and Speakeasy. FX Client: Dan Harmon, Anthony and Joe Russo. Principal Type: handlettering. Production Method/ Principal Tools: Adobe After Effects, Photoshop, Softimage XSI, blue BIC Cristal ballpoint pen, and white mulitpurpose paper

Televison: Honorable Mention; *Storymakers*. Creative Direction: James Spindler, @radical media, Los Angeles. Art Direction: Ahmet Ahmet and Grant Lau, Imaginary Forces. Design: Ahmet Ahmet, Grant Lau, and Mike Wasilewski. Calligraphy: Mike Wasilewski. Animation: Orlando Costa, Chris Pickenpaughy, and Arya Senboutaraj. Illustration: Wayne Coe. Design Studio and Production Company: @radical media and Imaginary Forces. Client: AMC Network. Principle Typeface: custom. Production Method/Principal Tools: Adobe After Effects, Photoshop, and hand-drawn

Event: Typography—Gold; AICP Minnesota Show Sponsor Reel. Creative Direction: Scott Wenner, Minneapolis, Minnesota. Art Direction: Amy Schmitt. Design: Scott Wenner and Amy Schmitt. Design Studio: motion504. Client: AICP Minnesota (Association of Independent Commercial Producers). Principal Type: DIN Robo Engschriften, DIN Robo Mittelschrift, DIN Robo Neuzeit Grotesk, and Trajan Pro. Production Method/Principal Tools: Adobe After Effects, Cinema 4D, and REO Camera

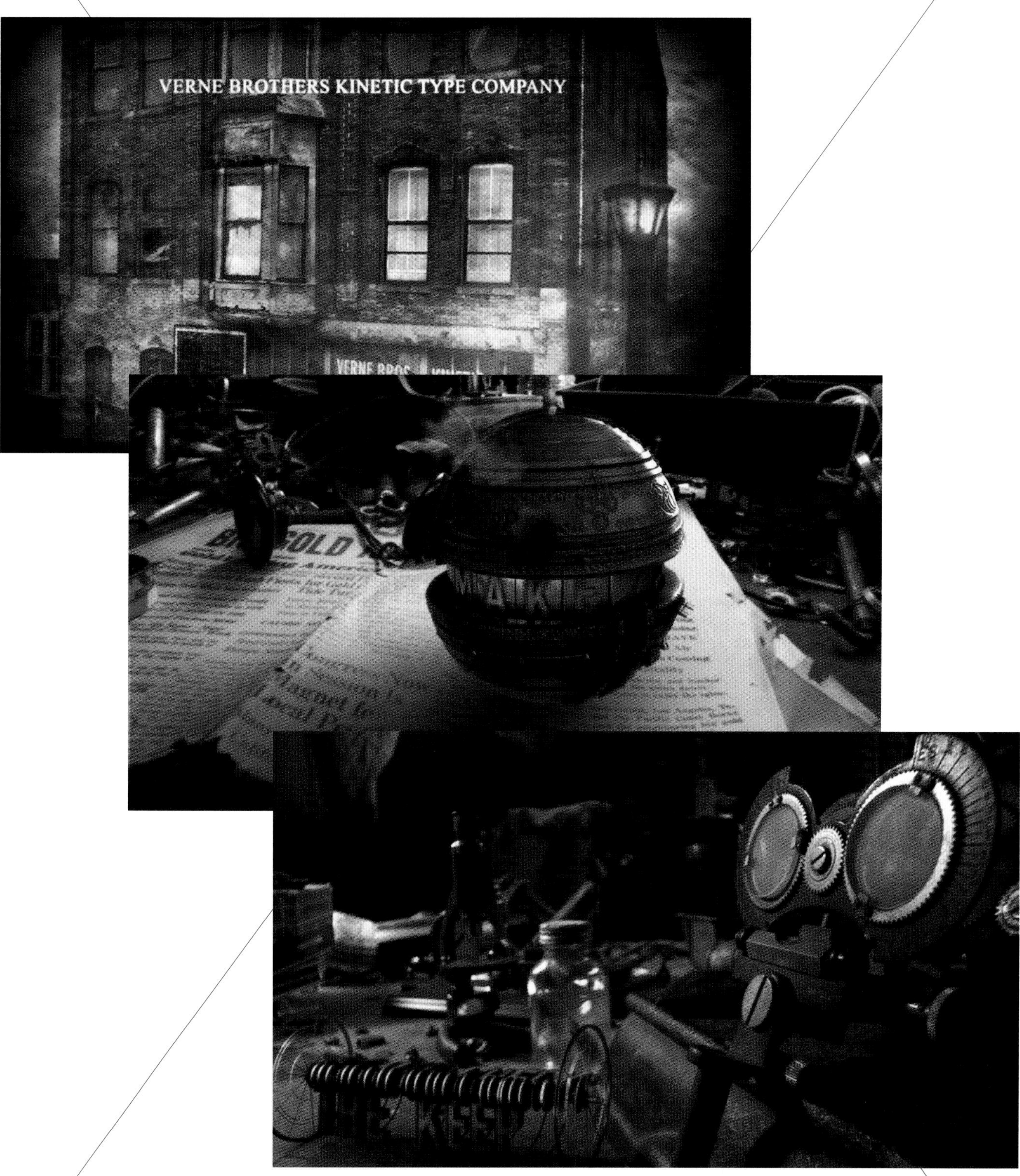

Event: Animation—Gold; OFFF 2009. Design and Direction: Ilya Abulhanov, Venice, California. Executive Producer: Kyle Cooper. Producer: Elizabeth Newman. Sound Design and Music: Hecq Design Company, Prologue Films. Principal Type: Knockout. Production Method/Principal Tools: After Effects, C4C, Illustrator, and Photoshop

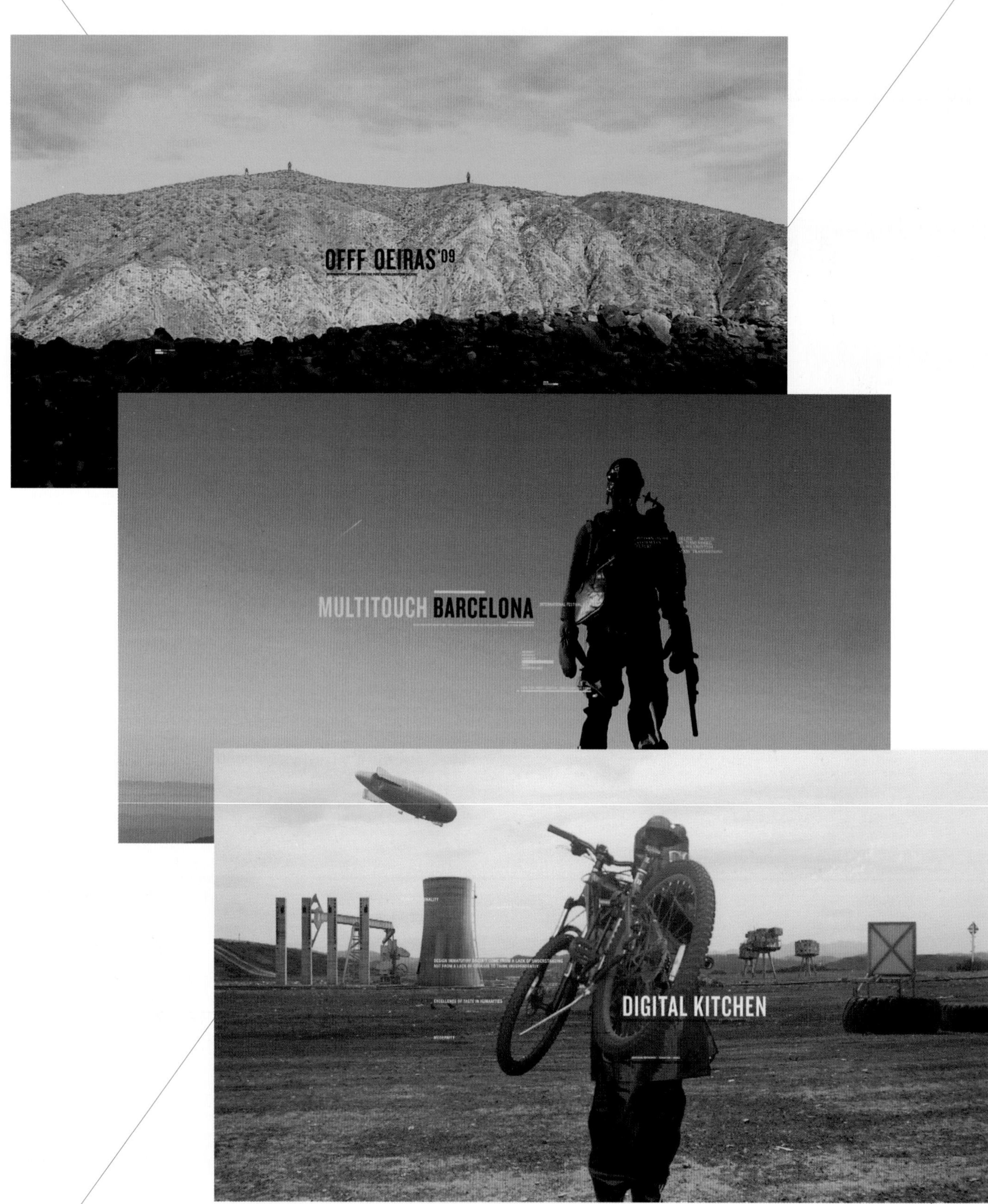

Event: Sound Design—Gold; TED2009 Conference Opener. Creative Direction: Jakob Trollbäck and Joe Wright, New York. Design: Peter Alfano and Paul Schlacter. Producer: Whitney Green. Design Studio: Trollbäck + Co. Client: TED. Principal Type: Helvetica Neue Bold. Production Method/Principal Tools: Adobe After Effects and Maya

Curated: Motion Blur; *A Bout de Mots*. Design: Emanuel Cohen, Montréal. School: Université du Québec à Montréal. Instructor: Denis Dulude. Principal Type: Akzidenz Grotesk and wood prints. Production Method/Principal Tools: Adobe After Effects and negative scans

Curated: Forward Motion Title; *Bored to Death.* Creative Direction: Thomas Barham, New York. Art Direction: Thomas Barham. Design: Thomas Barham. Production Company: Curious Pictures. Client: HBO and Dakota Productions. Principal Type: Garamond. Production Method/Principal Tools: Adobe After Effects and hand-animation

Curated: Future Classic; *Capitu*. Creative Direction: Carlos Bêla and Mateus de Paula Santos, São Paulo, Brazil. Design: Carlos Bêla. Design Studio: Lobo. Client: Globo Network. Principal Type: various. Production Method/Principal Tools: Paper and Stopmotion

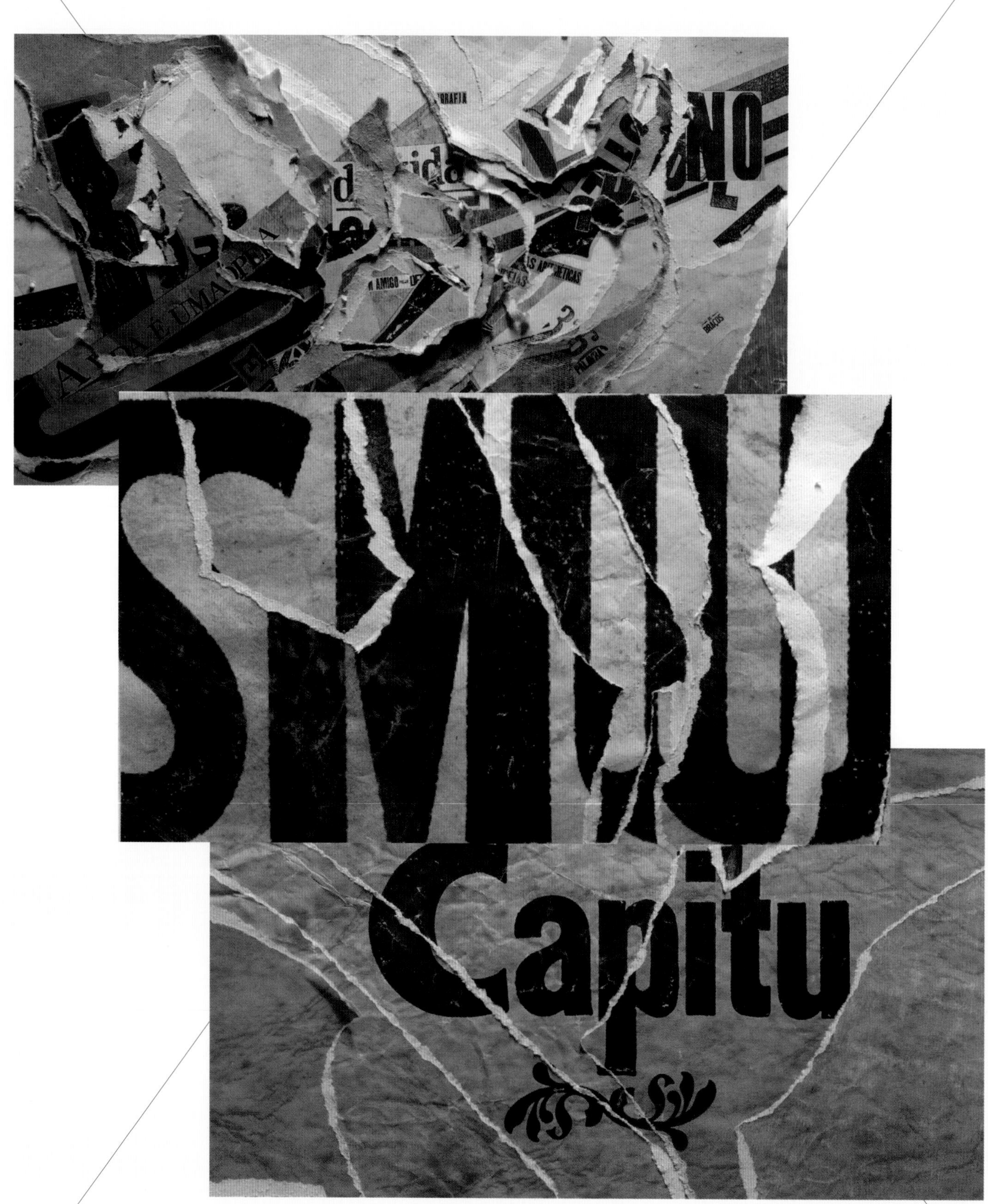

typography '61

The Seventh Annual
Awards Exhibit
of Typographic Excellence
sponsored by
the Type Directors Club
held at
"The Mead Library of Ideas"
New York City, May, 1961

Objectives of the Type Directors Club:

To raise the standards of typography and related fields of the graphic arts.

To provide the means for inspiration, stimulation, and research in typography and related graphic arts fields.

To aid in the compilation and dissemination of knowledge concerning the use of type and related materials.

To cooperate with other organizations having similar aims and purposes.

This exhibition of 187 pieces was chosen from over 2700 entries submitted from all over the United States and Canada.

The Jury:

ROBERT SUTTER:
Graphics Designer, Chairman

GEORGE SALTER:
Book Designer

GEORGE LOIS:
Art Director, Paperta, Koenig & Lois

FREEMAN CRAW:
Vice President & Art Director, Tri-Arts Press

JAMES FOGELMAN:
Art Director, Ciba

ALLAN FLEMING:
Art Director, Cooper & Beatty, Inc.
Toronto, Ontario, Canada

MEMO

From: Jury Chairman

To: Viewers of 1961 T.D.C. Selections

Relax! You have no need to stand on your head, flex your knees, view with alarm or tilt eyebrows at this display. Please remember, I had a hand in selection, thus it is obvious that I must approve of what was chosen.

I don't believe you will find any startling innovations to be considered, nor will you find more than a very few clichés. The pieces we have chosen are all crisp, thoughtful and all the elements are handled expertly, else that opus would not be included. My feeling about our selections indicates that 1960 might be a year of cerebration in our profession. Graphic design shows have been loaded with pyrotechnics for a few years now. We have all seen cherished rules shattered and clichés bent and twisted by the imaginations on display on walls and in printed records of our most widely touted public design exhibits. If you are alive, then you must feel the impact such change makes on your own work. First experiments in a new direction are bound to look strange and awesome, but they are eventually distilled to yield their essence for daily use in solving our own graphics problems. I don't think that there is any piece in this selection which doesn't communicate in a clear concise typographic manner. I keep repeating "typographic" because I see nothing here which is not truly typographic in essence. Finesse in the use of typography and letter forms is apparent everywhere here. So much for what is; however, I should like to take a potshot at what might have been.

The observer of shows only gets to see what was accepted by the jury. He must assume the jury picks what is best and freshest from the piles of work submitted. The pieces selected are old when they are chosen for display. They are completed and their creators have jumped on to the next bright idea. I am surprised, therefore, by the amount of blatant swipes the jury throws away and I must draw the conclusion that many observers don't realize that what they see here as this season's best is bound to be cliché material when used derivatively. And so I would like to invite you, footsore viewer, to come and look around. Be amused, inspired, bemused, outraged, or what you will, but carry away an opinion only. Enough said!

1

designer:	Norman Gollin
art director:	Norman Gollin/ The Design Group
client/agency:	Los Angeles County Museum
typographer:	Advertisers Composition Company

2

designer:	Tony Zamora
art director:	Bob Garguile
client/agency:	Aluminum Extrusions design consultants; George Nelson & Co.
typographer:	Rapid Typographers

3

designer:	Fred Hausman
art director:	Fred Hausman
client/agency:	N. J. Boys' Club/ Wm. F. O'Connor Co.
typographer:	Rapid Typographers

4

designer:	Herb Lubalin
art director:	Herb Lubalin
client/agency:	Jens Risom Design Inc. Sudler & Hennessey
typographer:	Composing Room

5

designer:	Bradbury Thompson
art director:	Bradbury Thompson
client/agency:	West Virginia Pulp and Paper Company
typographer:	Typographic Service Company

6

designer:	Arthur Paul
art director:	Arthur Paul
client/agency:	HMH Publishing Co., PLAYBOY
typographer:	magazine layout—editorial art

7

designer:	Robert P. Smith
art director:	Albert Greenberg
client/agency:	Gentlemen's Quarterly Magazine
typographer:	Haber Typographers

8

designer:	Virginia and Cristos Gianakos
art director:	Virginia and Cristos Gianakos
client/agency:	Virginia and Cristos Gianakos
typographer:	Royal Typographers

9

designer:	Steven Richter
art director:	Arnold Shaw
client/agency:	Time International
typographer:	Huxley House

1

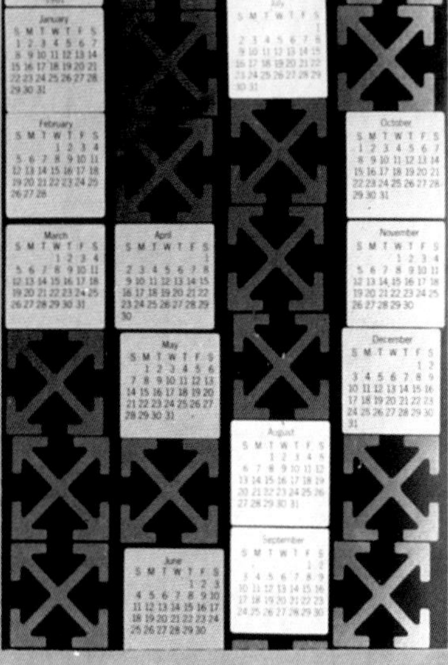

2

3

4

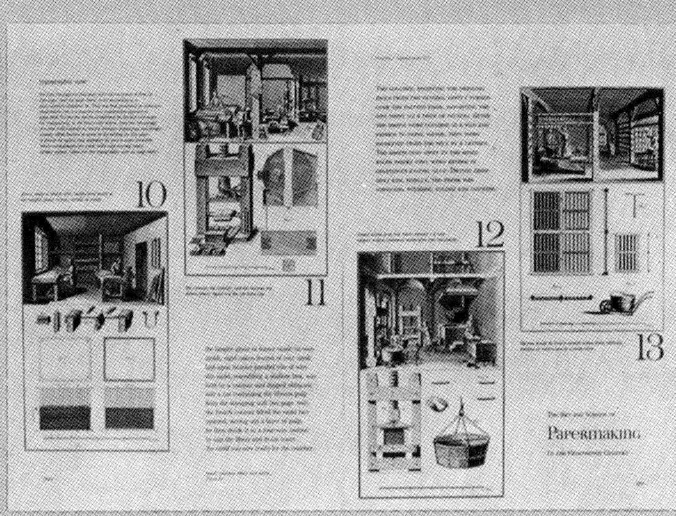
10
11
12
13
Papermaking

5

Ι Χ
Θ Υ
Σ

8

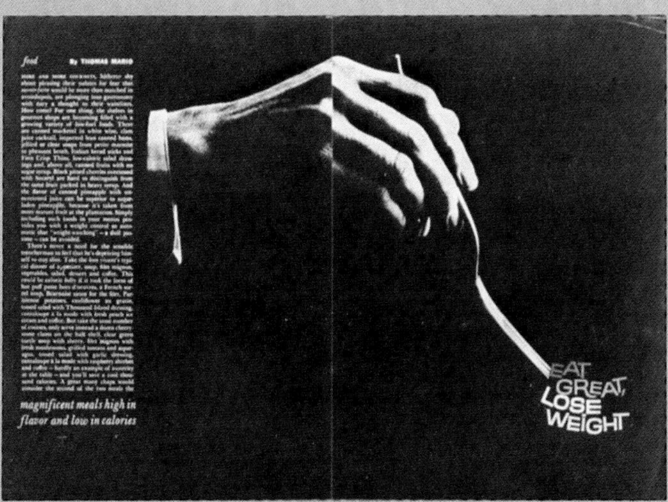
food By THOMAS MARIO
EAT GREAT, LOSE WEIGHT
magnificent meals high in flavor and low in calories

6

Ideas, products and services from companies the world over create a significant display each week in the International Editions of TIME. The quality, the diversity of advertisers make TIME a distinctive guide to "what's new" as well as to "what's news." Why does a manufacturer of earth-movers choose to share the same pages with a producer of computers or a creator of fine jewelry? To share the stage is to have, in common, the same receptive audience. There, the parallel between TIME advertisers ends—the distinction begins.

9

7

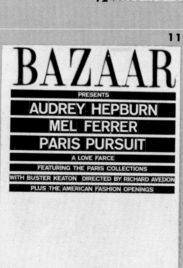

10

designer: Robertson-Montgomery
art director:
client/agency: Robertson-Montgomery
typographer: Spartan Typographers

11

designer: Henry Wolf/Audrey Rosenson
art director: Henry Wolf
client/agency: Harper's Bazaar
typographer: Haber

12

designer: Acey Silliman
art director: Acey Silliman
client/agency: Ramo-Wooldridge Tues. Nite Cinema
typographer: Acey Silliman

13

designer: Saul Bass
art director: Saul Bass
client/agency: John Sturges
typographer: Hand lettered

14

designer: Walter Lefman
art director: Walter Lefman/Leo Kaye
client/agency: Fairchild Pub. Co./ Associated Design
typographer: Associated Design

15

designer: Theo Dimson
art director: Leo Rampen
client/agency: Toronto AD Club
typographer: Cooper & Beatty

16

designer: Ed Blaus-Dick Kline
art director: Dick Kline
client/agency: Dreyfus & Co./Doyle Dane Bernbach
typographer: Provident

17

designer: James H. McWilliams
art director: James H. McWilliams
client/agency:
typographer:

18

designer: Jacqueline S. Casey
art director: none
client/agency: President's office, M.I.T.
typographer: Machine Composition Company

10

12

13

11

When in the Course of human events, it becomes necessary for one people to dissolve the political bands which have connected them with another, & to assume among the Powers of the earth, the separate and equal station to which the Laws of Nature and of Nature's God entitle them, a decent respect to the opinions of mankind requires that they should declare the causes which impel them to the separation.

We hold these truths to be self-evident, that all men are created equal, that they are endowed by their Creator with certain unalienable Rights, that among these are Life, Liberty and the pursuit of Happiness. That to secure these rights, Governments are instituted among Men, deriving their just powers from the consent of the

17

NEWS BRIEFS

16

DOUBLE
POWER
PUNCH!
EN'S 1-2 PUNCH
FOR MAY 2ND

14

We believe that the most truly practical education, even in an industrial point of view, is one founded on The President's Report 1960 *a thorough knowledge of scientific Laws and principles, and which unites with habits of close observation and exact reasoning a large general cultivation.* MASSACHUSETTS INSTITUTE OF TECHNOLOGY

18

I will be ( ) I will not be ( ) present at the opening of the Art Directors Club, Toronto, 12th Annual Exhibition

I will be accompanied by guest(s)

Name

Address

Art Directors Club, Toronto, 12th Annual Exhibition	Art Directors Club, Toronto, 12th Annual Exhibition	Art Directors Club, Toronto, 12th Annual Exhibition	
1	2	3	a D CT 12
classification number	classification number	classification number	
entered by	entered by	entered by	
address	address	address	
art directed by	art directed by	art directed by	
designer	designer	designer	
artist	artist	artist	
advertiser or publication	advertiser or publication	advertiser or publication	
agency or publisher	agency or publisher	agency or publisher	
your entry number	your entry number	your entry number	

15

NEW YORK
UNIVERSITY
REPORT OF
THE PRESIDENT
1959-1960

20

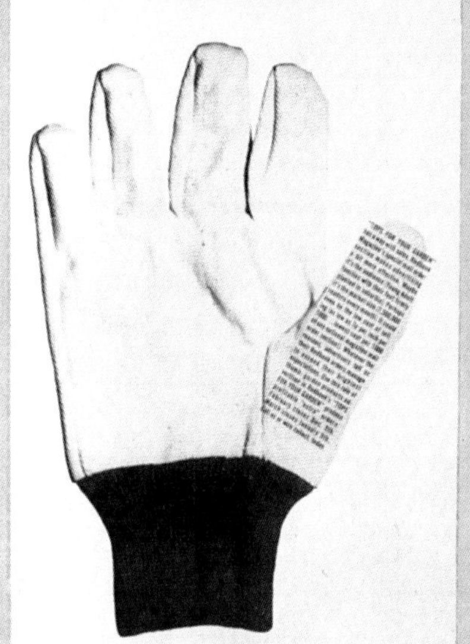

19

FOCUS

HOW MUCH IS A WIFE WORTH

21

22

19
designer: Mike Pennette
art director: Mike Pennette
client/agency: Redbook Magazine
typographer: Provident Typographers

20
designer: Elmer Loemker
art director: Kelvin Arden
client/agency: New York University
typographer: George Grady Press, Inc.

21
designer: William Wondriska
art director: William Wondriska
client/agency: Connecticut General Life Insurance Co.
typographer: CG Printing Dept.

22
designer: Peter Hirsch
art director: Peter Hirsch
client/agency: Harper Brothers Inc.
typographer: Composing Room

23
designer: Theo Dimson
art director: Allan Fleming & Hiroshi Ohchi
client/agency: Idea Magazine
typographer: Cooper & Beatty

24
designer: Sylvia Winter
art director:
client/agency: Kalamazoo Art Center
typographer: Sequoia Press

25
designer: Herb Lubalin
art director: Herb Lubalin
client/agency: CBS Radio
Sudler & Hennessey
typographer: Composing Room

26
designer: Peter Hirsch
art director: Peter Hirsch
client/agency: Deering-Milliken Inc.
typographer: Composing Room

デザイン
宣伝 販売
アイデア
41
6月号

IDEA

23

OUR APOLOGIES TO

FOR TAKING SO MUCH OF YOUR TIME...BUT FIRST THINGS FIRST

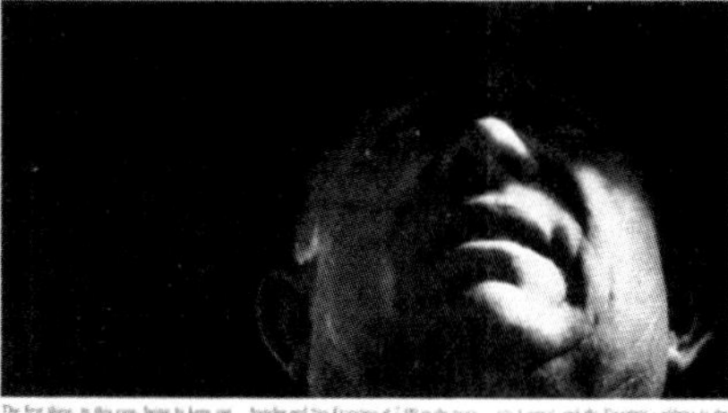

CBS OWNED RADIO STATIONS

25

26

24

27
designer: Henry Wolf
art director: Henry Wolf
client/agency: Harper's Bazaar
typographer: Haber

28
designer: Peter Bradford
art director: Peter Bradford
cleint/agency: Whitney Publications Inc.
typographer: Barnes Printing

29
designer: Randall R. Roth
art director: Randall R. Roth
client/agency: Miyazaki & Associates
typographer: Hayes-Lochner, Inc.

30
designer: Sylvia Winter
art director: William Stone
client/agency: Lee Paper Company
typographer: Sequoia Press

31
designer: Herb Lubalin
art director: Herb Lubalin
client/agency: CBS Radio
Sudler & Hennessey
typographer: Composing Room

32
designer: Virginia Gianakos
art director: Gianokos & Weiner
client/agency: Modern Bride Magazine
typographer: Royal Typographers

33
designer: Kurt Weihs
art director: Kurt Weihs
client/agency: Papert, Koenig, Lois, Inc.
typographer: Composing Room

34
designer: Michael Tesch
art director: Michael Pennette
client/agency: Redbook Magazine
typographer: Provident Typographers

35
designer:
art director: Kurt Weihs
client/agency: CBS Television Network
typographer:

27

SELLING: There was certainly more packaging design in 1960 than ever before, and some of it was better than ever. Since package design is sold as a form of advertisement, it is not surprising that such advertising techniques as the "lifelike" halftone should increasingly find their way onto packages, too.

Cigarette packaging in the U. S. has been characterized more by caution than imagination, but the new Benson & Hedges pack (page 117) is that rare thing — a cigarette case that a grown man can carry on his person with satisfaction. Of course it has always been easier to turn out acceptable designs for luxury goods than for soap flakes, but this year's work included the unusually tasteful treatment of such inexpensive items as stationery and chalk (page 118).

If 1960's pharmaceutical packaging appears unexciting, it is at least partly because almost everyone in the field has now reached the same high level of design, since drug companies think (or at least know that doctors think) that doctors are unusually sophisticated. This curious situation is one of the few cases in which fierce competition is the reason for good design, rather than the excuse for bad.

For the inclusion of many of the packages on the following pages, we are indebted to the American Institute of Graphic Arts, which first presented them in its Packaging, 1960 exhibition.

28

29

THOMAS BEWICK
AND THE ART OF
WOOD-ENGRAVING
LEE
DIMENSIONS
VOLUME IV NUMBER 2
SUMMER 1960

30

EXPANSI(The CBS Radio Network announces for the '60s: an expanded program structure, new audience appeal and selling opportunities seven days a week—all starting November 28th.)ON

NEWS REP(New CBS Radio becomes the first network to present ten minutes of news on the hour. This means more complete coverage by the top news team in broadcasting. In addition: Edward R. Murrow, Lowell Thomas, Allan Jackson, Howard K. Smith, Robert Trout, "World News Roundup," "World Tonight" on a regular schedule, plus the unrivaled coverage of special events by CBS News.)ORTS

INF(Brand new: Lively, five-minute features every day, 43 programs a week. These combine intriguing ideas and people, like "Your Man in Paris" with David Schoenbrun, "A Woman's Washington" with Nancy Hanschman. Others present Charles Collingwood, Douglas Edwards, Zachary Scott, Myrna Loy, Alan King and many more. Long-time CBS Radio information and cultural programs continue, of course, including "Capitol Cloakroom," "Invitation to Learning," "New York Philharmonic," "Face the Nation.")ORMATION

SPORTS SH(Ten more weekend sports programs are scheduled as ex-Yankee Jerry Coleman joins Phil Rizzuto and Pat Summerall in providing knowledgeable sports reporting all week long, 52 weeks a year. And important events—big Bowl games, the full New York Giants football season, horse racing's Triple Crown, the Masters Golf Tournament—are all on the CBS Radio Network.)OWS

PERS(More good company than anywhere else in radio. There's just one place to find a regularly scheduled all-star lineup that includes Arthur Godfrey, Art Linkletter, Garry Moore, Bing Crosby, Rosemary Clooney, Mitch Miller, the colorful new "In Person" program nightly featuring Ron Cochran and people in the news. They're all on the CBS Radio Network.)ONALITIES

31

MODERN BRIDE'S STERLING PATTERN SELECTOR

32

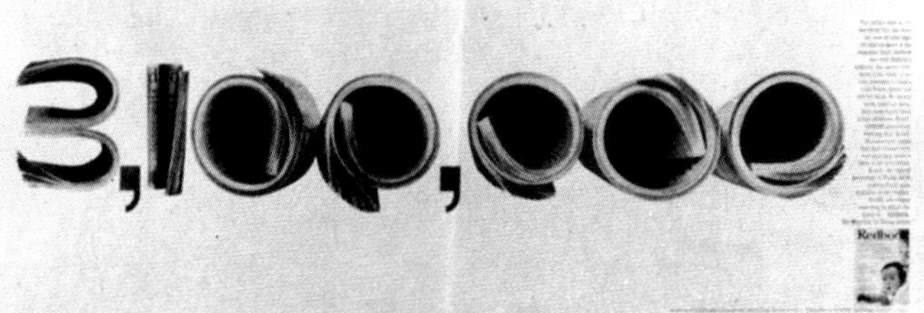

34

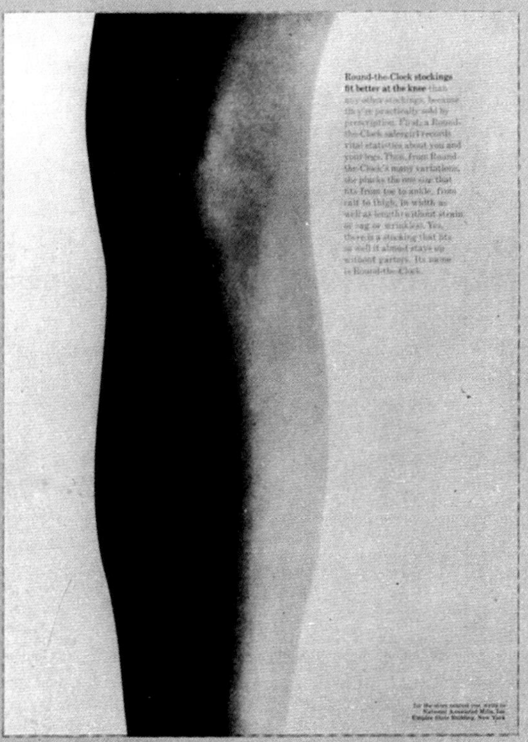

Round-the-Clock stockings fit better at the knee than any other stockings, because they're practically sold by prescription. First, a Round-the-Clock salesgirl records vital statistics about you and your legs. Then, from Round-the-Clock's many variations, she plucks the one size that fits from toe to ankle, from calf to thigh, in width as well as length without strain or sag or wrinkles. Yes, there is a stocking that fits so well it almost stays up without garters. Its name is Round-the-Clock.
National Associated Mills, Inc.
Empire State Building, New York

33

SEE

If you plan to be convening at the Sheraton Park Hotel in Washington this June, you are cordially invited to take a short break from your arduous Convention activities and view some pretty exciting films of CBS Television Network programs in our exhibition booth right near the coffee lounge.

The shows have been selected with an eye toward demonstrating the vast range and diversity of our public affairs programs. For example, you will be able to see the absorbing half-hour film "Mother Love," which was presented on the *Conquest* series this season and which, as you may recall, demonstrates how scientists learned to measure the love of an infant for its mother by means of some remarkable experiments with baby monkeys.

We shall also show the notable *CBS Reports* program "Biography of A Cancer," which followed the progress of cancer patient Dr. Thomas Dooley from his arrival at the hospital to his discharge. Critics throughout the country acclaimed it as one of the best documentary films of the season.

Our public affairs series, *The Twentieth Century*, will be represented by "The Changing Face of Japan," a fascinating two-part examination of today's Japanese youth, and by "Turn of the Century," a nostalgic review of an era, a mood, and a way of life that will never return. Morton Gould wrote the musical score for this reminiscent half-hour which brings back on film such celebrated figures as Emperor Franz Josef of Austria, Edward VII and Alexandra of England, British suffragette Emmeline Pankhurst, Anna Pavlova, Claude Monet, Sarah Bernhardt, James Barrie, George Bernard Shaw and Leo Tolstoi.

Finally, you will be able to see a program of special interest to everyone attending the General Federation of Women's Clubs Convention—Mr. Murrow's memorable visit to the home of Miss Chloe Gifford, the Federation's President, which was broadcast on *Person to Person* last year.

Speaking of Conventions, the Democratic and Republican Parties will be holding theirs in July and the CBS Television Network will again be on hand to bring you all of the significant and colorful events that take place when the delegates meet to draft a platform and choose their Presidential and Vice-Presidential candidates.

CBS News has assembled a staff of more than 250 newsmen, editors, engineers and technicians to cover the pre-Convention activities, the Platform and Seating Committee meetings, the keynote and nominating speeches, the state caucuses, the frenzied demonstrations and the climactic balloting. Among the 25 CBS News correspondents on the scene will be such regulars as Walter Cronkite, Howard K. Smith, Edward R. Murrow, Douglas Edwards and Charles Collingwood, and one newcomer, Nancy Hanschman, our first woman correspondent.

As it demonstrated so clearly in 1952 and 1956, CBS News will bring you a better view of the Conventions than you could get if you were watching the proceedings from a delegate's seat in the hall. So be sure you're at home in front of a television set tuned in to your local station of the CBS Television Network starting Monday, July 11.

CBS

35

36
designer: Amil Gargano
art director: Amil Gargano
client/agency: Swissair/Campbell-Ewald
typographer: Kurt H. Volk, Inc.

37
designer: Frank Kirk
art director: Frank Kirk
client/agency: WNAC-TV/DDB
typographer: Typo Craftsmen

38
designer: Bert Steinhauser
art director: Bert Steinhauser
cleint/agency: Hartmann/Doyle Dane /Birnbach
typographer: Atlas

39
designer: John J. Reiss
art director: John J. Reiss
client/agency: Milwaukee Art Center
typographer: Monsen, Chicago
Zahn Klicka Hill, Milwaukee

40
designer: John Massey
art director: Ralph Eckerstrom & John Massey
client/agency: N. W. Ayer & Son, Inc.
typographer: Frederic Ryder Company

41
designer: Robertson-Montgomery
art director:
client/agency: New Sound Record Dist.
typographer: Spartan Typographers

42
designer: Jon Aron
art director: Jon Aron
client/agency: Pratt & Whitney Aircraft
typographer: So. New England Typographers

43
designer: Ivan Chermayeff
art director: Tony Palladino
client/agency: Chermayeff & Geismar Associates
typographer: Metro & CGA Archives

44
designer: Louis Klein
art director: Louis Klein
client/agency: TIME International
typographer: Typographic Service Co.

There's no business like snow business...right now! Swissair's big new line-up of ski tours starts as low as $499.60, all-inclusive. Your ski-happy clients fly jets right to the Alps and ski the day they depart. No stops. No changing planes. Snow foolin'. SWISSAIR

36

5
6
7
stop!

Now stop at Channel 7 for "American Football League Championship Game" 3:30, "Walt Disney Presents" 6:30-7:30, "Maverick" 7:30-8:30, "Lawman" 8:30-9:00, "The Rebel" 9:00-9:30, "Winston Churchill—Special" 9:30-10:30, "Music for a New Year's Night" 10:30-11:00, and other great ABC-TV programs. The mammoth move to Channel 7 starts today. See the "Tournament of Roses Parade" tomorrow 11:30-1:45.

WNAC-TV CHANNEL 7

37

This is the only folding luggage with a "bustle" to keep clothes from crushing, shifting and falling off hangers: Hartmann 707.
And this is what does it:

38

46 TH
annual
exhibition
of wisconsin
art

39

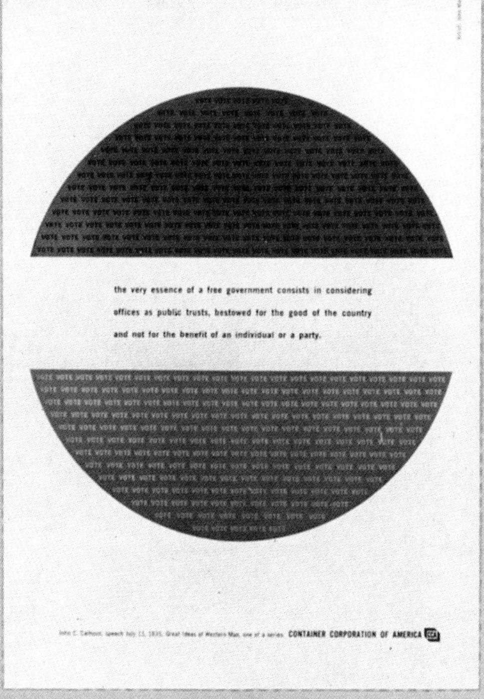

VOTE VOTE VOTE
the very essence of a free government consists in considering
offices as public trusts, bestowed for the good of the country
and not for the benefit of an individual or a party.
CONTAINER CORPORATION OF AMERICA

40

THOUSANDS OF CANADIAN STUDENTS SPEND THEIR SUMMERS OUT OF THE COUNTRY. EACH YEAR THE NUMBER SWELLS.
TIME has always been edited to the college-trained mind. Today it is dedicated to supporting its conviction that the young people of the world, by meeting and exchanging ideas, are the ultimate hope for international understanding. Hence the following review of opportunities open to campus travelers in 1960. **TOURS**—The would-be student traveler can take the plunge as a tour member, exploring a number of countries in the company of other students. Tours come in all sizes and kinds, go almost anywhere and are sponsored by hundreds of commercial and non-commercial organizations, with wide diversification ranging from teen-age groups to special trips for graduate students—from Hobo Tours (motor coach) to Drive-it-Yourself automobile jaunts. Activities are always charted in advance. The most popular type of tour is a group of about 30 (usually coeducational) who travel to and from Europe by ship. If it is a student ship, orientation courses are offered: lively seminars, refresher courses in language, and valuable briefings on the countries to be visited. Depending upon length and scope of the trip, costs run from $800 to $1700. SPECIAL ADVANTAGES: Being part of a tour assures guidance, companionship, planned diversity of interesting activities, a chance to sample a number of countries, an opportunity to meet people of like age in each—and to make lasting friendships. **LIFE WITH AN OVERSEAS FAMILY**—Many collegiates have spent a summer abroad living with a family, taking time to get the feel of one country, getting to know its people almost as well as their own. Last year some 1200 students went to 28 countries. France, Switzerland and Italy are most popular; but the program includes many other adventure spots. Students bound for the same country usually travel in conducted coed groups of ten, on student ships which offer orientation seminars. They are about the same age (for non-European countries, 19 is minimum). Once at destination each student moves in with a different family to live its life, share its activities and problems. The family (which will have been chosen on the premise that it offers most to the student and vice versa) may well contain some members close in age to the student guest. Advance correspondence initiates friendship; and, in most cases, hospitality is just that—with no fees involved. After a month's "homestay" the original group of ten reassembles, augmented by student members of the families stayed with. Then the guests turn hosts on a three-week cycling or camping trip to other parts of the country. The final week may be spent with one's overseas family again or on a group trip to a large city. Fees vary with the locale (as low as $350 for Mexico, as high as $1500 for Japan). In some instances scholarships are available. SPECIAL ADVANTAGES: Living the customs of the country, sharing its traditions, getting to know the people well. In the words of one girl, "I may not speak like a Frenchwoman yet, but I think I could think like one now." **FORMAL STUDY PROGRAMS**—Some students may prefer to use their summer for study. There are courses offered by scores of foreign universities, as well as a number of overseas programs sponsored by Canadian colleges and universities. If the student wishes, a local family will be found for him to live with while he is at school. Some courses are brief enough to leave time for travel as well; others include travel in their plan. Yet however prestigious the university selected, it should not be assumed that the home college will credit points for the overseas course. The student should check with his own dean if this is of importance. Costs depend upon locality and mode of living. Typical estimates range from $750 to $1200 including tuition; chances for summer scholarships are few. SPECIAL ADVANTAGES: Classmates come from all over the world. The student tastes foreign education, travels without being a tourist, and possibly earns credit points, too. **INDEPENDENT TRAVEL**—Those who are in their 20's or who have traveled abroad before might prefer to go on their own. There are many excellent agencies to help plan a trip, choose lodgings and eating places, budget time and funds. Within Europe well-managed, economical student charter flights are available. Moreover, Europe is studded with excellent low-cost hostels, run by Student Unions and patronized by travelers from all over the world. Variables in cost are too manifold to hazard a guess. But however else he economizes, the student must not think he can save money by working his way abroad on a ship or by getting temporary jobs overseas. All experienced hands agree that both these ideas (once practical) are now illusory. Also, accommodations, hard to secure during the summer, should be reserved ahead. SPECIAL ADVANTAGES: The traveler is a free spirit. He can switch countries in mid-stream, explore any fresh ideas discovered. **WORK CAMPS**—Finally, if he wants to give as much as he'll get out of his summer abroad, the student might elect a work camp. For this less cash is needed, but brawn and a no-fooling wish to contribute to the welfare of the community he chooses are musts. Hundreds of work camps are operated in all parts of the world, many under religious auspices. Applicants must be in excellent health, since the work is rugged; they should be able to pay for their own transportation and insurance (about $550). Typically, room and board are furnished but no wages are paid. Frequently it is possible to combine enrollment in a work camp with a bicycle tour of student hostels. Many camps require an enrollment period of three months and a minimum age level of 20. SPECIAL ADVANTAGES: This plan probably offers the most complete divorce from home. Co-workers will be drawn from many countries, with a genuine wish to be of service the one characteristic common to all. **SPECIAL NOTE TO STUDENTS**—For detailed information on any of the student travel programs listed above, write to: National Federation of Canadian University Students, Le Droit Building, 375 Rideau Street, Ottawa. And if those of you who are TIME subscribers will send your itineraries, six weeks before your departure, to TIME International of Canada Ltd., 25 Adelaide West, Toronto, we will be glad to see that your weekly copies of TIME reach you wherever you may be. Remember that when you go abroad you are the authority on Canada. With TIME on hand you can keep up on Canadian affairs and represent your country with intelligence as well as with warmth.

44

The School of Visual Arts announces a course in design to be given simultaneously by Ivan Chermayeff and Tony Palladino on Thursday evenings from 7 to 10, commencing February 9. For further information inquire: The School of Visual Arts, 209 East 23 Street, New York City 10. MUrray Hill 3-8397.

CPHAELRLMAADYIENFOF

43

41

NEW SOUND
50 JULIAN
SAN FRAN
CISCO 3 CAL
UN 1-1900

42

jet power is
coming down to

earth

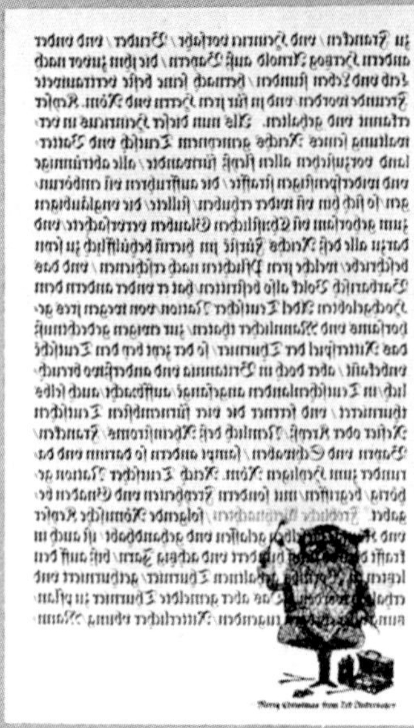

45

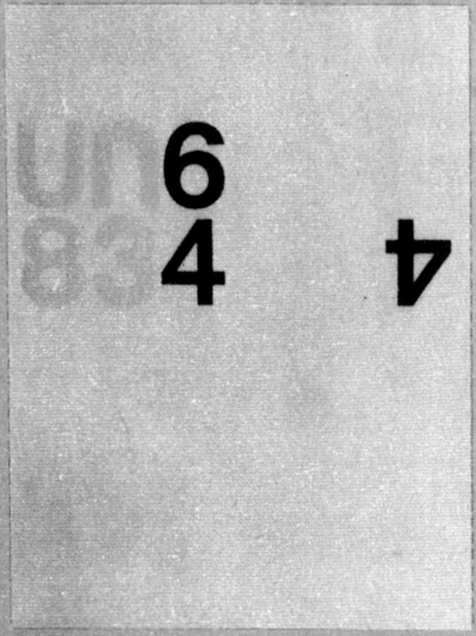

designer: Arnaud Maggs
art director: Gaston Parent
client/agency: Commercial Art Center, Montreal
typographer: Cooper & Beatty, Ltd.

46

designer: Ted Andresakes
art director: Ted Andresakes
client/agency: Ted Andresakes
typographer: Ted Andresakes

47

designer: Don Ervin
art director: Don Ervin
client/agency: United Artists
typographer: Rapid Typographers

48

designer: Eli Tulman
art director: Eli Tulman
client/agency: Sandura Co./Hicks & Golist
typographer: Hand Set

49

designer: Stephen Korbet
art director: Mort Rubenstein
client/agency: CBS-Owned Stations
typographer: Typography Place Inc.

50

designer: Robert P. Smith
art director: Albert Greenberg
client/agency: Gentlemen's Quarterly Magazine
typographer: Haber Typographers

51

designer: Bill Weinstein
art director: John Graham/Rick Levine
client/agency: National Broadcasting Co., Inc.
typographer: Empire

52

designer: Theo Dimson
art director: Leo Rampen
client/agency: Toronto Art Directors Club
typographer: Cooper & Beatty

53

designer: Kurt Weihs
art director: Kurt Weihs
client/agency: Papert, Koenig, Lois, Inc.
typographer: Composing Room

46

45

47

48

CHANNEL 2 ELECTION GUIDE
CHANNEL 2 ELECTION GUIDE
CHANNEL 2 ELECTION GUIDE
CHANNEL 2 ELECTION GUIDE
CHANNEL 2 ELECTION GUIDE
CHANNEL 2 ELECTION GUIDE
CHANNEL 2 ELECTION GUIDE
CHANNEL 2 ELECTION GUIDE
CHANNEL 2 ELECTION GUIDE
CHANNEL 2 ELECTION GUIDE
CHANNEL 2 ELECTION GUIDE
CHANNEL 2 ELECTION GUIDE
CHANNEL 2 ELECTION GUIDE

49

Award for Distinctive Merit presented by The Art Directors Club, Toronto, at The Twelfth Annual Exhibition of Advertising & Editorial Art & Design, 1960

Chairman of The Exhibition Committee   President of The Art Directors Club

52

51

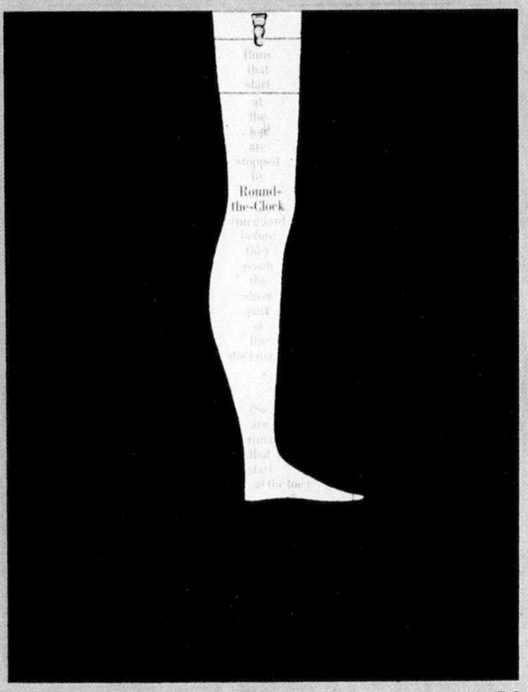

53

50

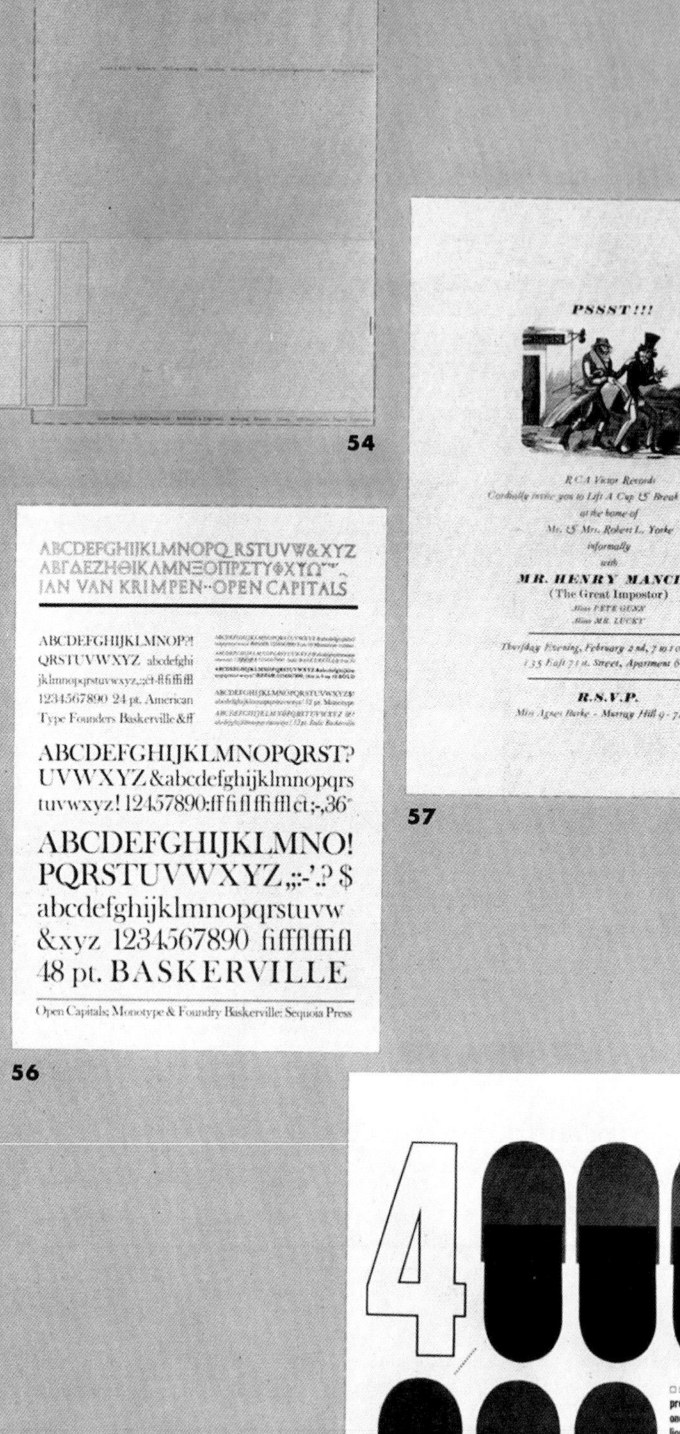

54
designer: Theo Dimson
art director: Theo Dimson
client/agency: GBR Associates
typographer: Cooper & Beatty

55
designer: Roger Cook
art director: Roger Cook
client/agency: Peoples Drug Stores
N. W. Ayer & Son, Inc.
typographer: N. W. Ayer & Son Type Dept.

56
designer: Sylvia Winter
art director: William Stone
client/agency: Sequoia Press
typographer: Sequoia Press

57
designer: Robert M. Jones
art director: Robert M. Jones
client/agency: RCA Victor Records
typographer: Glad Hand Press

58
designer: Joseph Gering
art director: Joseph Gering
client/agency:
typographer: Walter T. Armstrong, Inc.

59
designer: Peter Hirsch
art director: Peter Hirsch
client/agency: Peter Hirsch
typographer: Advertising Agency Service Inc.

60
designer: Eckstein-Stone
art director: S. Seidler
client/agency: Remington Rand Univac
typographer: Master Typo

61
designer. Rick Levine
art director: John Graham/Rick Levine
client/agency: National Broadcasting Co.
typographer: Empire

62
designer: George Lois
art director: George Lois
client/agency: Papert, Koenig, Lois
typographer: Composing Room

61

The Art Directors Club of Philadelphia
and
The Art Directors Club of New York
present
The National Society of Art Director's

ART DIRECTOR OF THE YEAR AWARD
to
WILLIAM GOLDEN
(posthumously)

Poor Richard Club, Philadelphia May 18, 1960

58

Cracklessssssssssssssssssssssssssssssssssssss
ssssssssssssssssssssssssssssssssssssssssssss
ssssssssssssssHummmmmmmmmmmmmmmmmmmm.

HEAR THAT CRACKLE! WHISKERS ARE COMING OFF. THEN HEAR THAT HUM! THOSE WHISKERS ARE GONE. RONSON INTRODUCES THE CFL MARK II–THE "TALKING" SHAVER THAT GIVES THE CLEANEST, QUICKEST SHAVES ON EARTH.
• So good it replaces the shaver rated best • New multi-blade miracle cutter • CFL Mark II was born for Demonstration, Display, Promotion and Sales. • Only Ronson has Super-Trim, Power Clean. Snap-in cutting edges replaceable at home in 10 seconds. (See reverse side) • Massive (and unusual) magazine, newspaper support. Look, TV Guide, Time, True, This Week and the N. Y. Times. • $23.50 suggested retail • Code: 3134 (1 or 2) 3034 (3 or more) No. 84701 gold & scarlet nuclear symbol on charcoal gray
RONSON CFL MARK II with miracle blades: first honest advance in shavers in 6 years

62

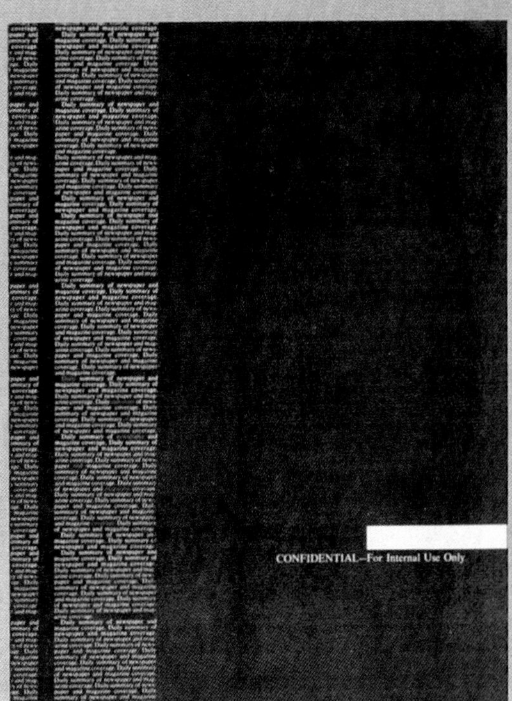

60

1959 1960
the coming year
best wishes for
Florence and Peter Hirsch

59

63
designer: Acey Silliman
art director: Acey Silliman
client/agency: Ramo-Wooldridge Tuesday Nite Cinema
typographer: Acey Silliman

64
designer: George Lois
art director: George Lois
client/agency: Papert, Koenig, Lois, Inc.
typographer: Composing Room

65
designer: Murray Jacobs
art director: Murray Jacobs
client/agency: Volkswagen/DDB
typographer: Typo Craftsmen

66
designer: Jim Donoahue
art director: Allan R. Fleming
client/agency: Cooper & Beatty, Limited
typographer: Cooper & Beatty, Limited

67
designer: Henry Wolf
art director: Henry Wolf
client/agency: Harper's Bazaar
typographer: Haber

68
designer: Norman Gollin
art director: Norman Gollin/The Design Group
client/agency: Ad Compositors
typographer: Ad Compositors

69
designer: Bill Weinstein
art director: John Graham/Rick Levine
client/agency: National Broadcasting Co. Inc.
typographer: Empire

70
designer: Gilbert Lesser
art director: Gilbert Lesser
client/agency: Fortune, Time Inc.
typographer: Composing Room

71
designer: Gilbert Lesser
art director: Gilbert Lesser
client/agency: Robert Saffir
typographer: Hand lettered

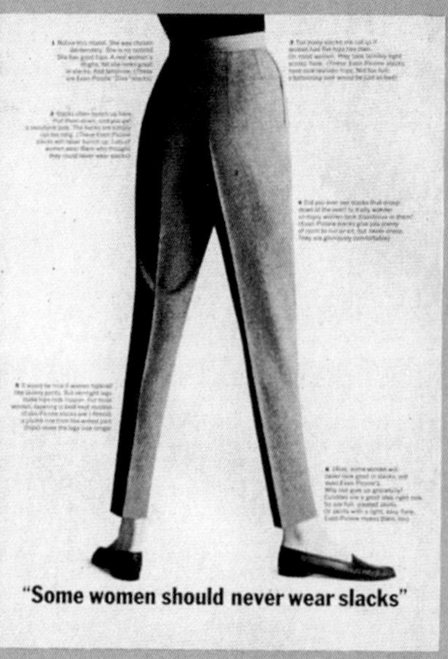

64

63

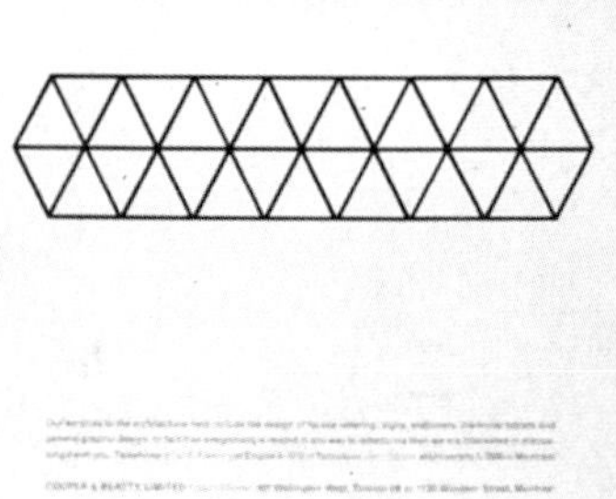
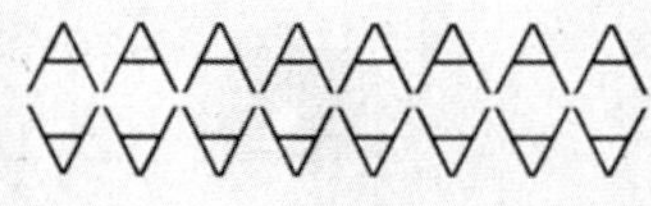

66

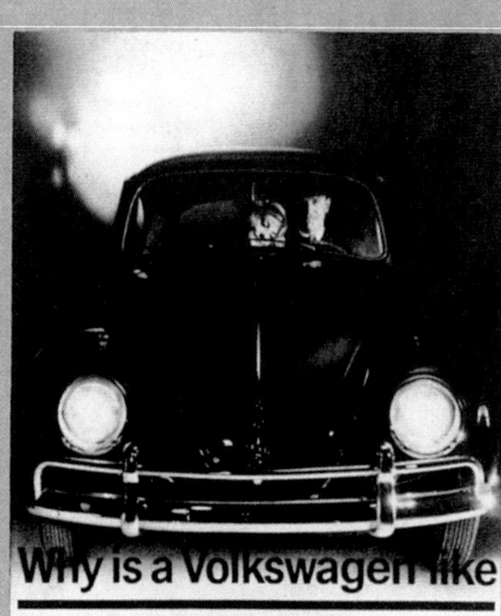

Why is a Volkswagen like
no other car on the road?

65

HARPER'S
BAZAAR
MARCH 1960
60 CENTS
IN AMERICA: THE LILT IN FASHION
FOR BEAUTY: THREE FRESH MAKE-UPS
ON FOOT: SHOES CUT-OUT FOR DAY
FROM PARIS: THE NEW COLLECTIONS

67

CELEBRITY
GOLF

69

71

68

FORTUNE'S 13TH ANNUAL CAR SURVEY 1959

70

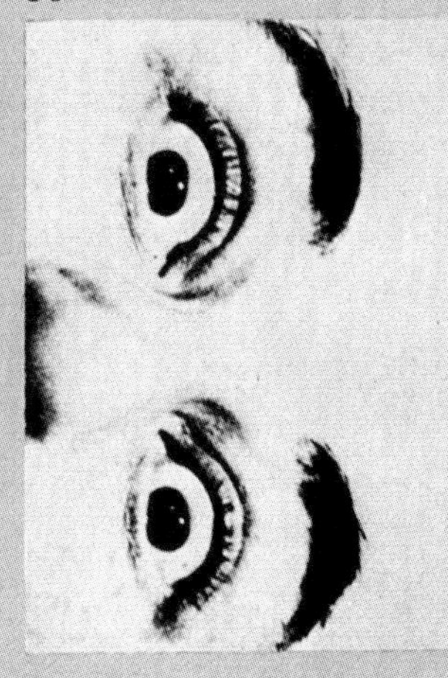
are you tense, nervous, frantic?
do you find it impossible to give
the proper amount of thoughtful
time to working up type "specs"?
relax, AD COMPOSITORS can
provide the answers to your
type problems. we offer personal,
individual service and help to
overloaded art directors
and production managers.
call AD COMPOSITORS at
any time for consultation.
our services include
an excellent type selection,
top repro proofs, cells,
pickup and delivery,
night shift, reprostats.
AD COMPOSITORS
950 Cahuenga Blvd., HO 2-6533
can help you relax and bask in
the warm knowledge that your
typographic problems are
in competent hands.

72
designer: Acey Silliman
art director: Acey Silliman
client/agency: Ramo-Wooldridge Tuesday Nite Cinema
typographer: Acey Silliman

73
designer: Robert M. Jones
art director: Robert M. Jones
client/agency: Robert M. Jones
typographer: Glad Hand Press

74
designer: Lou Theoharides
art director: Ivan Chermayeff
client/agency: Alexandre Georges
typographer: Hand lettering

75
designer: Peter Hirsch
art director: Peter Hirsch
client/agency: L'Aiglon Apparel Inc.
typographer: Composing Room

76
designer: James FitzGerald
art director: Robert M. Runyan
client/agency: Journal of Commercial Art
typographer: Journal of Commercial Art

77
designer: Edward G. De Martin
art director: Edward G. De Martin
client/agency: Du Pont Company Dyes & Chemicals Division
typographer: Delaware Valley Comp. Co.

78
designer: Rene Bittel
art director: Herb Lubalin
client/agency: Rover Motor Corp.
typographer: Sudler & Hennessey

79
designer: Bill Weinstein
art director: John Graham/Rick Levine
client/agency: National Broadcasting Co. Inc.
typographer: Empire

80
designer: George Plataz
art director: George Plataz
client/agency: Herbick & Held Printing Co.
typographer: Herbick & Held Printing Co.

81
designer:
art director: Louis Dorfsman
client/agency: CBS Television Network
typographer:

72

73

74

Lord & Taylor

75

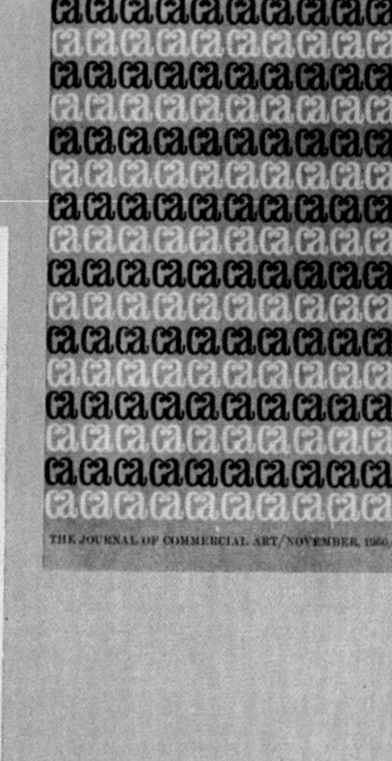

76

We take pleasure in reprinting the accompanying appreciation of the Rover 3-Litre Sedan by the editors of Sports Cars Illustrated. We believe that it will help define, for the interested motorist, the unique qualities that have endeared the Rover to generations of owners.
ROVER
THE ROVER MOTOR COMPANY OF NORTH AMERICA LIMITED

78

77

CONTINENTAL CLASSROOM

79

CBS REPORTS
THE YEAR OF THE POLARIS
8-9 TONIGHT ON
CBS CHANNEL 2

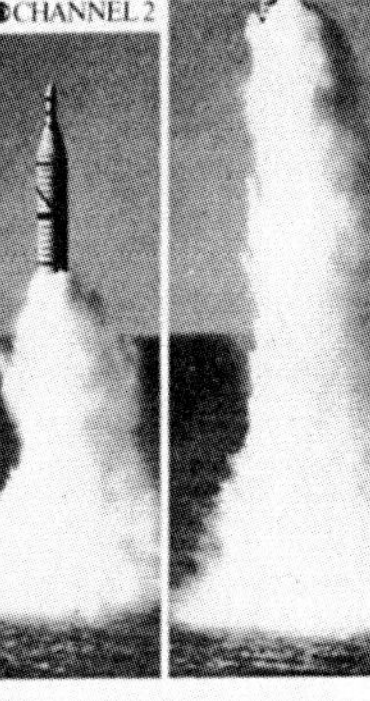

81

FISH

80

82

designer: George Jaccoma
art director: George Jaccoma
client/agency: Lino Craft Typo.
typographer: Lino Craft Typo.

83

designer: Richard Walukanis
art director: Richard Walukanis
client/agency: Fortune
typographer: Franklin, Silverstein

84

designer: Robert M. Jones
art director: Robert M. Jones
client/agency: Glad Hand Press
typographer: Glad Hand Press

85

designer: Robert M. Jones
art director: Robert M. Jones
client/agency: Friends of Bob Leslie
typographer: Glad Hand Press

86

designer: Kurt Weihs
art director: Kurt Weihs
client/agency: Papert, Koenig, Lois, Inc.
typographer: TPI

87

designer: Gerald Cinamon
art director: Gerald Cinamon
client/agency: Esso Education Foundation
typographer: Huxley House

88

designer: Jack Gregory
art director: Jack Gregory
client/agency: Mr. & Mrs. Jack Gregory
typographer: W. T. Armstrong

89

designer: Robertson-Montgomery
art director:
client/agency: SF Museum of Art
typographer: Spartan Typographers

82

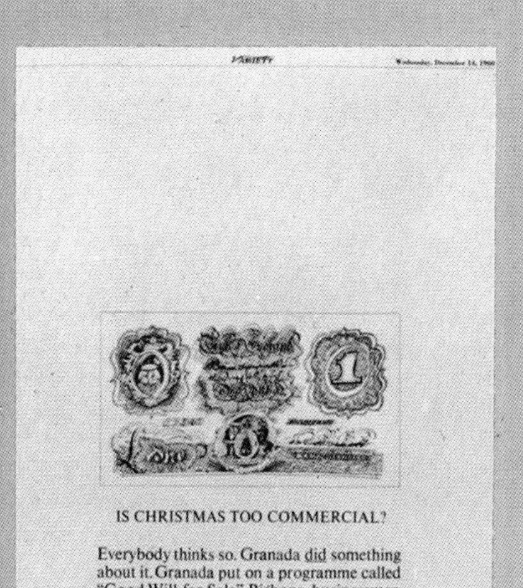
VARIETY
IS CHRISTMAS TOO COMMERCIAL?
Everybody thinks so. Granada did something about it. Granada put on a programme called "Good Will for Sale." Bishops, businessmen, Christmas card printers & toy manufacturers -among others-were asked to give their views. The discussions were lively and enlightening; and-as far as British television audiences are concerned-typical of the kind of programming they expect and get from Granada TV Network.
GRANADA TV NETWORK, ENGLAND

86

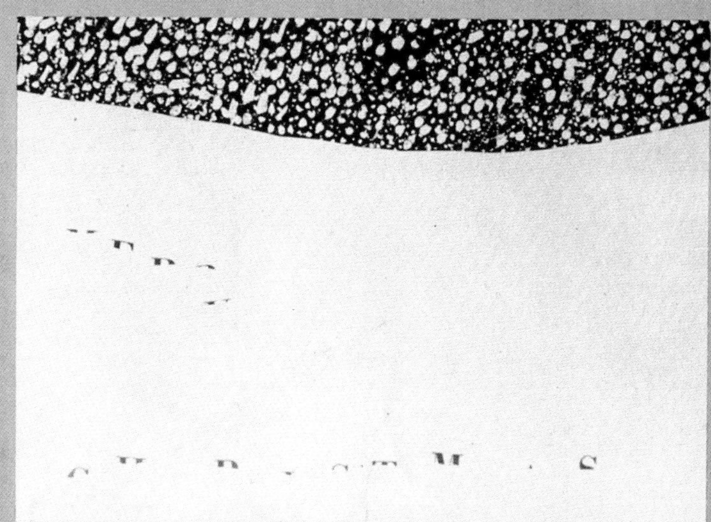

88

89

ESSO EDUCATION FOUNDATION

87

90

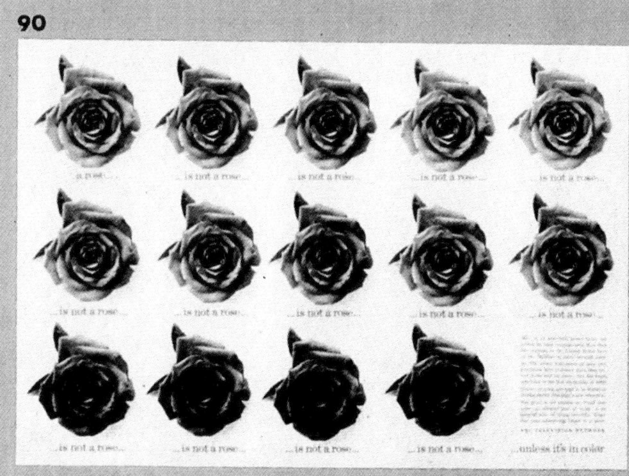
...a rose...
...is not a rose...
...is not a rose...
...is not a rose...
...is not a rose...
...is not a rose...
...is not a rose...
...is not a rose...
...is not a rose...
...is not a rose...
...is not a rose...
...is not a rose...
...is not a rose...
...is not a rose...
...unless it's in color

91

designer:	Walter Bernard
art director:	Aileen Hunt
client/agency:	Ingenue Magazine
typographer:	Haber, W. Bernard, Art Color Inc.

92

designer:	Mort Rubenstein
art director:	Mort Rubenstein
client/agency:	CBS Television Stations
typographer:	Rapid Typographers Inc.

93

designer:	Harry & Marion Zelenko
art director:	Harry & Marion Zelenko
client/agency:	Davis, Delaney, Inc.
typographer:	Composing Room

94

designer:	Amil Gargano
art director:	Amil Gargano
client/agency:	Swissair/Campbell-Ewald
typographer:	Morrell & McDermott

95

designer:	Mort Rubenstein
art director:	Mort Rubenstein
client/agency:	KNXT
typographer:	Typography Place Inc.

96

designer:	Saul Bass
art director:	Saul Bass
client/agency:	The Ranch Club
typographer:	Ad Compositors

97

designer:	James P. Camperos
art director:	Bill Curry
client/agency:	Ramo-Wooldridge
typographer:	Monsen Typographers

98

designer:	Ivan Chermayeff
art director:	Ivan Chermayeff
client/agency:	National Committee for a Sane Nuclear Policy
typographer:	Clark & Way/CGA Archives

If you think apple-polishing is a chore, then this article by a team of high school teachers is specially for you! Here are tried and-tested ways for winning teachers and influencing marks . . . for making school a ball not a bore . . . and for developing that sensitive skill with people which will help you in all situations—in school or out!

91

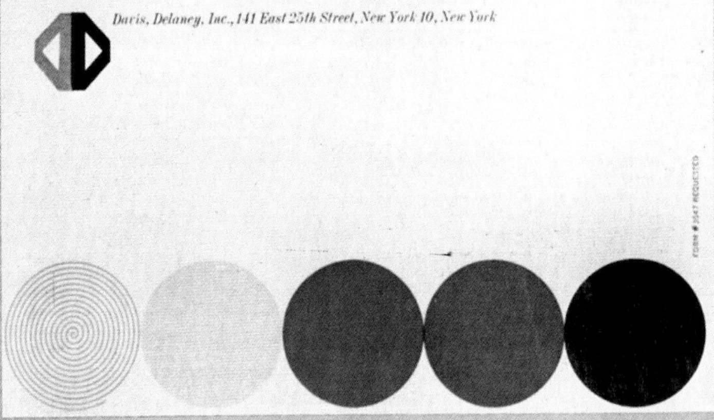

Davis, Delaney, Inc., 141 East 25th Street, New York 10, New York
FORM # 3547 REQUESTED

93

92

$13,757,241 AND 72 CTS

A matter of principle

In 1960 the five CBS Owned television stations devoted nearly 14 million dollars worth of station time and facilities to non-network public affairs programs and announcements. The amount in itself is not of primary importance. But the principle behind it is. For the sum (an all-time high!) is a measure of the emphasis the five CBS Owned stations place on community service programming patterned to the highest production standards. The result is a wide variety of exceptional programs which won better than 40 awards and citations during the year. Information programs ranging from hour-long documentary "specials" broadcast during prime-time evening hours, to station editorials, to on-the-spot reports from the Congo and from many other top-interest locations around the world.

In a real sense, the stations' commercial success makes possible this wealth of public affairs programming. And thus guarantees the program balance which has always been a guiding principle of . . .

CBS TELEVISION STATIONS

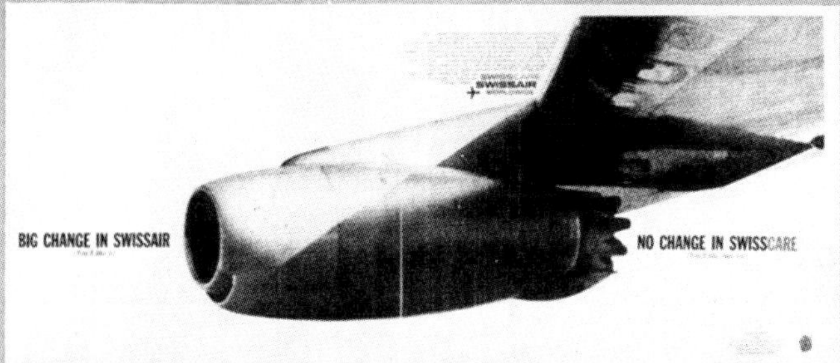

94

97

95

TOWARD
A
SANE
NUCLEAR
POLICY

98

96

99

designer: Gilbert Lesser
art director: Gilbert Lesser
client/agency: Gilbert Lesser
typographer: Hand lettered

100

designer: Randall R. Roth
art director: Randall R. Roth
client/agency: George Sawa
typographer: Hayes-Lochner, Inc.

101

designer: Robert Fabian
art director: Robert Fabian
client/agency: I. Miller Salons
typographer: The Composing Room

102

designer: Arnold Varga
art director: Arnold Varga
Gateway Studios
client/agency: Pittsburgh Presbytery
typographer:

103

designer: Fred Hausman
art director: Frank Droesch
client/agency: N. Y. Herald Tribune
typographer: Donahue & Coe, Inc.
Photolettering

104

designer: Gene Federico
art director: Gene Federico
client/agency: Ad Club of N.Y.
typographer: Composing Room

105

designer: Frank Kirk
art director: Frank Kirk
client/agency: Chemstrand/DDB
typographer: Typo Craftsmen

106

designer: Richard Bergeron
art director: Ken Lavey
client/agency: Parke-Davis
typographer: Empire

107

designer: Charles Piccirillo
art director: Charles Piccirillo
client/agency: Doyle Dane Bernbach (et al.)
typographer: Provident

108

designer: Jim Donoahue
art director: Allan R. Fleming
client/agency: Cooper & Beatty, Limited
typographer: Cooper & Beatty, Limited

an
noun
cing

99

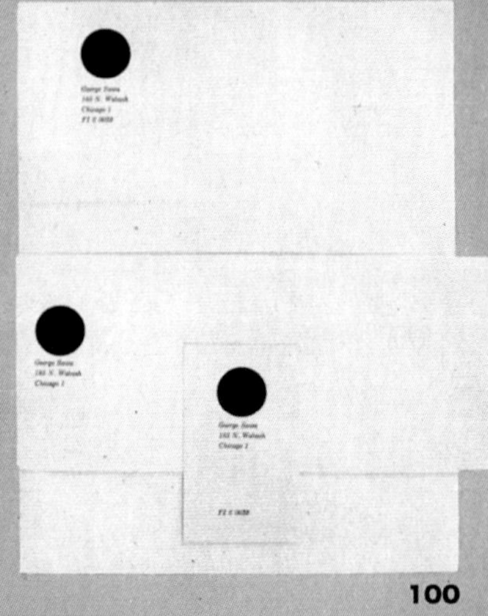

100

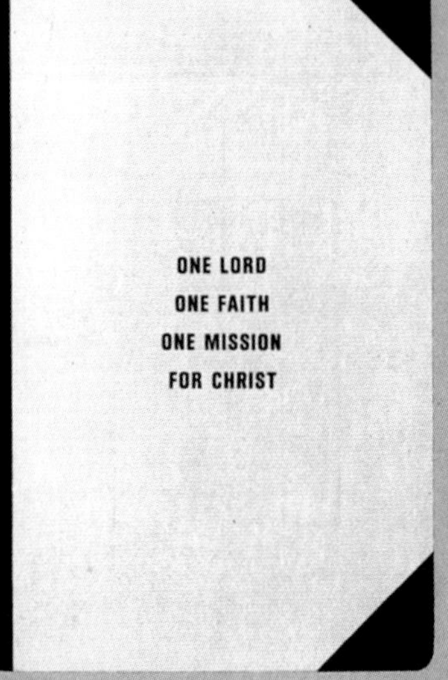

ONE LORD
ONE FAITH
ONE MISSION
FOR CHRIST

102

Here's what's sending Chicago into a spin! The debut of Ingenue... the shoe that catches the young beat of fashion... for you who like to feel excitement right down to your toes! Come see the whole dazzling collection! Ours exclusively. From 19.95
I. Miller

101

don't
miss Walter Kerr, the critic Brendan Behan, author of The Hostage, calls "the conscience of the American Theater." Every Sunday in the Lively Arts magazine of the Herald Tribune

103

39th Annual
National Exhibition
of the New York
Art Directors Club
1960
Astor Gallery

104

MUNICH LONDON
AMSTERDAM ROME
VIENNA ATHENS
JOHANNESBURG
ZURICH TEL AVIV
BRUSSELS PARIS
TEHRAN ISTANBUL

For information, call or write El Al Israel Airlines, Air Cargo Service, N.Y. International Airport, Cargo Building 83, OL 6-5290.

EL AL AIR CARGO

107

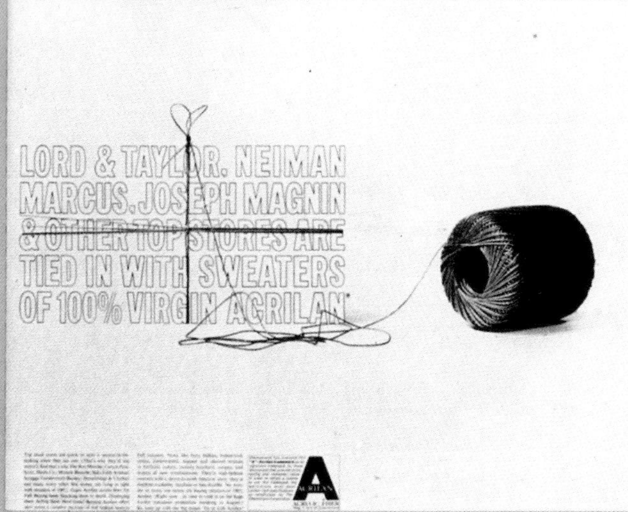
LORD & TAYLOR, NEIMAN MARCUS, JOSEPH MAGNIN & OTHER TOP STORES ARE TIED IN WITH SWEATERS OF 100% VIRGIN ACRILAN

105

TORINO

108

GYNECOLOGIC PROBLEMS OF ADOLESCENCE

106

109

designer: Acey Silliman
art director: Acey Silliman
client/agency: Ramo-Wooldridge
Tuesday Nite Cinema
typographer: Acey Silliman

110

designer: Brownjohn, Chermayeff, Geismar
Herb Lubalin
Lester Beall
Gene Federico
client/agency: The Composing Room, Inc.
typographer: The Composing Room, Inc.

111

designer: Bob Gill
art director: Reba Sochis
client/agency: William Hayett Inc.
typographer: Metro Typographers

112

designer: Samuel N. Antupit
art director: Samuel N. Antupit
client/agency: Morgan Press
typographer: Morgan Press

113

designer: Herb Lubalin
art director: Herb Lubalin
client/agency: CBS Radio
Sudler & Hennessey
typographer: Morgan Press

114

designer: Tom Hollingsworth
art director: Herb Meyers
client/agency: Mead Packaging
typographer: Typography Shop.

115

designer: Rick Levine
art director: John Graham/Rick Levine
client/agency: National Broadcasting Co. Inc.
typographer: Empire

116

designer: Acey Silliman
art director: Bill Curry
client/agency: Ramo-Wooldridge
typographer: Monsen Typographers

117

designer: Acey Silliman
art director: Acey Silliman
client/agency: Ramo-Wooldridge
Tuesday Nite Cinema
typographer: Acey Silliman

109

110

111

112

113

An Introduction to Ramo-Wooldridge

116

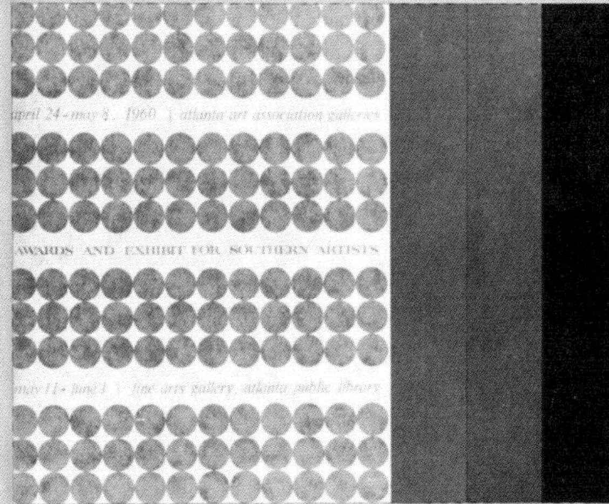

114

117

115

118

designer: Herb Lubalin
art director: Herb Lubalin
client/agency: Bohn Duplicating Co.
Sudler & Hennessey
typographer: Composing Room

119

designer: Morton Goldshall
art director: Morton Goldshall
client/agency: International Mineral & Chemical Corp.
typographer: Monsen Typographers

120

designer: Gordon Martin
art director: Gordon Martin
client/agency: Devorah Sherman Gallery
typographer: Gordon Martin

121

designer: Gilbert Lesser
art director: Gilbert Lesser
client/agency: The Clothes Horse
typographer: Composing Room

122

designer: John Massey
art director: John Massey
client/agency: Container Corp. of America
typographer: Frederic Ryder Company

123

designer: Students, Carnegie Tech.
art director:
client/agency: College of Fine Arts
typographer: Chanter Press

124

designer: K C & S Studios, Inc.
art director: K C & S Studios, Inc.
client/agency: Muller, Jordan & Herrick
typographer: Rapid Typographers

125

designer: George Jacoma
art director: Richard Loew
client/agency: WNBQ—NBC Spot Sales—Grey
typographer: Progressive

126

designer: Allan R. Fleming
art director: Paul Arthur
client/agency: National Gallery of Canada
typographer: Cooper & Beatty, Ltd.

127

designer: Reba Sochis
art director: Reba Sochis
client/agency: William Hayette, Inc.
typographer: Metro Typographers

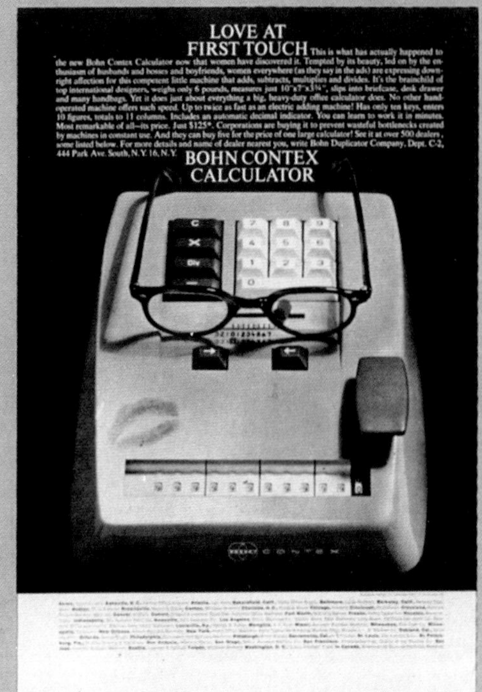

118

119

120

121

GUIDE LINES FOR MARKETING POLICY
CONTAINER CORPORATION OF AMERICA

122

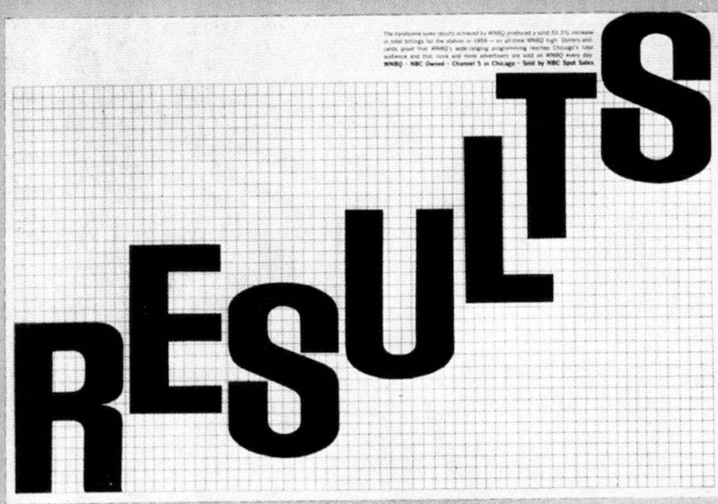

125

124

127

126

19
61

The National Gallery of Canada Engagement Calendar

with reproductions of
engravings, etchings, woodcuts and lithographs
from its collection

To read means to obtain
meaning from written
or printed symbols and
ABCDEFGHIJKLMN
OPQRSTUVWXYZ
abcdefghijklmnopqrstuv
wxyz 1234567890

30 point Janson Antiqua

30 point Janson Italic

*To read means to obtain
meaning from written or
printed symbols and*

123

128
designer: Sheldon Cotler
art director: Sheldon Cotler
client/agency: TIME, The Weekly Newsmagazine
typographer: Typographic Service

129
designer: Hans Kleefeld
art director: Kenneth Zealley
client/agency: Associated Illustrators
typographer: Cooper & Beatty Ltd.

130
designer: Jerome Kohl/J. Marmaras
art director: Jack Marmaras
client/agency: CIBA, Summit, N. J.
typographer: Haber

131
designer: Gilbert Lesser
art director: Gilbert Lesser
client/agency: Fortune, Time Inc.
typographer: Composing Room

132
designer: Roy Kuhlmer
art director: Roy Kuhlmer
client/agency: Franklin Typographers
typographer: Franklin Typographers

133
designer: Tom Hollingsworth
art director: Herb Meyers
client/agency: Mead Packaging
typographer: Typography Shop.

134
designer: Rick Levine
art director: John Graham/Rick Levine
client/agency: National Broadcasting Co. Inc.
typographer: Empire

135
designer: Arnold Varga
art director: Arnold Varga
client/agency: Pleasant Hills Church
typographer:

136
designer: George Lois
art director: George Lois
client/agency: Papert, Koenig, Lois, Inc.
typographer: T.P.I.

CONCENTRATION
&

128

associated ... 10 adelaide st. east, toronto

129

38 FROM FISH TO PHILOSOPHER

an unsegmented body cavity known as the coelom (*koiloma* = a hollow).

In the embryos of all vertebrates the viscera, on the one hand, and the segmented muscles and backbone, on the other, develop from different germinal layers—the viscera from the inner germinal layer or endoderm; the muscles and backbone from the middle germinal layer or mesoderm. The kidney develops not as one might expect from the endoderm with the viscera, but from the mesoderm (as also do the gonads and adrenal cortex), and, like the muscles and backbone, it starts out as a segmented structure. From this fact, and from the structure of the adult kidney in the primitive fishes, it is inferred that the kidney of the protovertebrate was also segmented, and that each segment of the body throughout the length of the coelom carried a bilateral pair of nephric (*nephros* = kidney) tubules. There is some evidence that the membrane lining the coelomic cavity primitively played a role in excretion, and it appears that the nephric tubules were first formed by multiplication of cells belonging to the coelomic membrane. On the interior of the body each of these nephric tubules communicated freely with the coelom by means of an open mouth or 'coelomostome' (*coelom* + *stoma* = mouth, also frequently called 'nephrostomes'); on the exterior they drained either through separate vents in the body wall like the scuppers of a ship, or into a common longitudinal groove in the skin. (See Figure 4a.)

These primitive nephric tubules probably also served to carry off the eggs and sperm, which were shed freely by the gonads into the coelomic cavity; embryonically, the gonads are derived from the coelomic membrane adjacent to the tissue which forms the nephric tubules, and this suggests that reproduction and excretion have had, from far back in vertebrate history, a close affiliation.

This segmented 'kidney'—if we may so designate a dozen or more pairs of primitive nephric tubules—is such as one might expect to find in a segmented animal

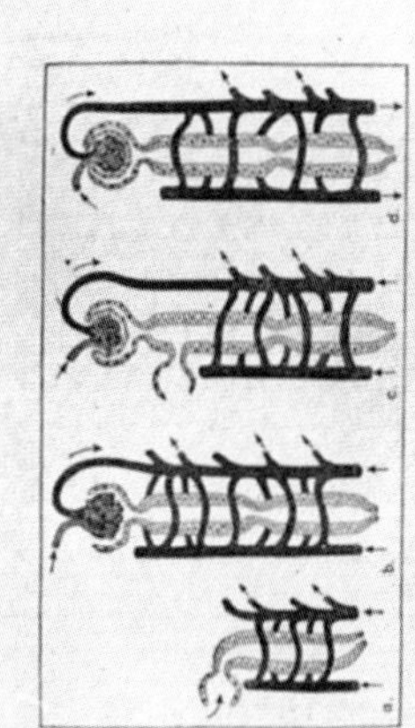

Figure 4. Four Stages in the Evolution of the Vertebrate Nephron—(a) In the protovertebrate the renal tubule drained the coelom or body cavity by means of an open mouth or

130

131

132

mead packaging p.o. box 4417/950 west marietta st. n.w. atlanta 2, ga.

mead packaging p.o. box 4417/950 west marietta st. n.w. atlanta 2, ga.

133

134

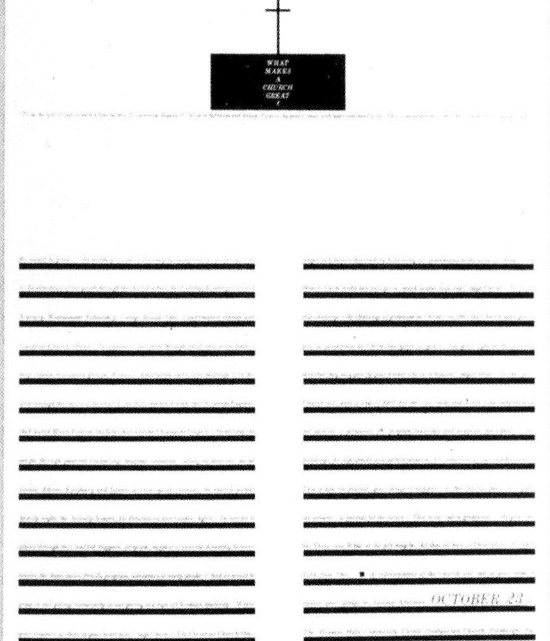

135

What
this country
needs is a chair
you can see
through.
A chair that takes
its place in
crowded rooms, yet
seems to take
no space.
The Invisible Chair
by Laverne.

136

137
designer: Denis Postle
art director: Denis Postle
client/agency: Summer Session Office
typographer: Machine Composition Co. and the Composing Room Inc.

138
designer: James P. Macadam
art director: James P. Macadam
client/agency: School of Printing Management
typographer:

139
designer: Louis Musachio
art director: George Lois
client/agency: Papert, Koening, Lois
typographer: Composing Room

140
designer: Erwin Raith
art director: Erwin Raith
client/agency:
typographer: Tinhorn Press

141
designer: Tom Woodward
art director: Tom Woodward
client/agency: Stat House
typographer: Ad Compositors

142
designer: Ed & Jane Bedno
art director: Ed Bedno
client/agency: American Medical Ass.
typographer: Monsen, Inc.

143
designer: Audrey Rosenson
art director: Henry Wolf
client/agency: Harper's Bazaar
typographer: Haber

144
designer: Art Glazer
art director: Michael Pennette
client/agency: Redbook Magazine
typographer: Provident Typographers

145
designer:
art director: Kurt Weihs
client/agency: CBS Television Network
typographer:

146
designer: Bradbury Thompson
art director: Bradbury Thompson
client/agency: West Virginia Pulp and Paper Company
typographer: Typographic Service Company

masstts. of institute technology
special
1 9 6 1
summer programs
preliminary announcement

137

–The only valid thing in art is that which can not be explained–I wrote once.

I still feel this very strongly. To explain away the mystery of a great painting—if such a feat were possible—would do irreparable harm, for whenever you explain or define something, you substitute the explanation or the definition for the real thing. The same is true of science. Each time a new problem is solved I feel that something of value has been lost. Instead of having matters made clearer, I should like to have them made even more obscure. *Il faut toujours augmenter le trouble.*

What about criticism, then? I am afraid I don't give a damn. Critics should help people to see for themselves, they should never try to define things or impose their own explanations, though I admit that if—as nearly always happens—a critic's explanations serve to increase the general obscurity that's all to the good. French poets are particularly helpful in this respect. Few of them have understood the first thing about modern painting, yet they are always trying to write about it. Apollinaire, for instance: a great poet and a man to whom I was deeply attached, but let's face it, he couldn't tell the difference between a Raphael and a Rubens. The only value of his book on Cubism is that, far from enlightening people, it succeeds in bamboozling them. The same is true of Eluard and the rest of them. Almost the only exception I can think of is Reverdy.

There are certain mysteries, certain secrets in my own work which even I don't understand, nor do I try to do so. Why bother? The more one probes the more one deepens the mystery: it's always out of reach. Mysteries have to be respected if they are to retain their power. *L'art est fait pour troubler; la science rassure.* Art disturbs, science reassures.

If there is no mystery, then there is no "poetry," the quality I value above all else in art. What do I mean by "poetry"? It is to a painting what life is to man. But don't ask me to define it; it is something that each artist has to struggle to discover for himself through his own intuition. For me it is a matter of harmony, of *rapports*, of rhythm, and—most important for my own work—of "metamorphosis."

I will try to explain what I mean by metamorphosis. For me no object can be tied down to any one sort of reality. A stone may be part of a wall, a piece of sculpture, a lethal weapon, a pebble on a beach, or anything else you like, just as this file in my hand can be metamorphosed into a shoe-horn or a spoon, according to the way in which I use it. The first time the importance of this phenomenon struck me was in the trenches during the First World War when my batman turned a bucket into a brazier by poking a few holes in it with his bayonet and filling it with coke. For me this commonplace incident had a poetic significance, I began to see things in a new way.

138

FREE ROUND TRIP ON THE FRENCH LINE TO EUROPE & A RENAULT DAUPHINE FOR $1645

FREE ROUND TRIP ON THE FRENCH LINE TO EUROPE & A RENAULT DAUPHINE FOR $1645

139

140

PRIMUS INTER PARES

Richard N. McArthur

AUGUST MCMLX

MCARTHUR MEMORIAL LIBRARY

PRIVATELY PRINTED FOR THE TYPOCRAFTERS MEETING IN ATLANTA

THE TINHORN PRESS

141

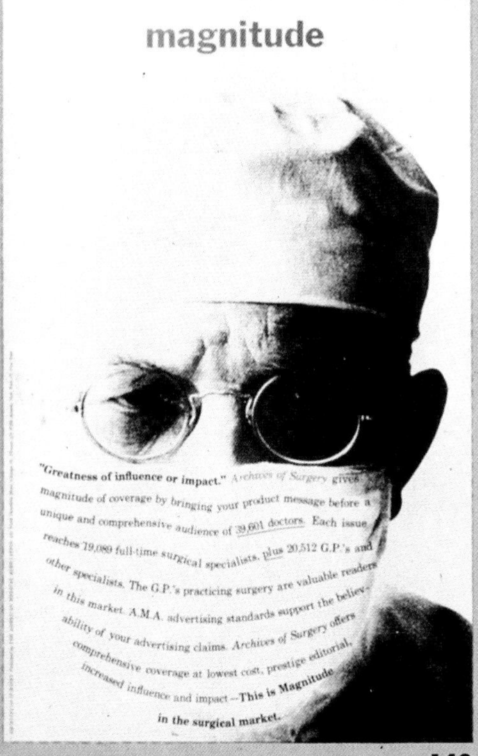

magnitude
"Greatness of influence or impact." Archives of Surgery gives magnitude of coverage by bringing your product message before a unique and comprehensive audience of 39,601 doctors. Each issue reaches 19,089 full-time surgical specialists, plus 20,512 G.P.'s and other specialists. The G.P.'s practicing surgery are valuable readers in this market. A.M.A. advertising standards support the believability of your advertising claims. Archives of Surgery offers comprehensive coverage at lowest cost, prestige editorial, increased influence and impact—This is Magnitude
in the surgical market.

142

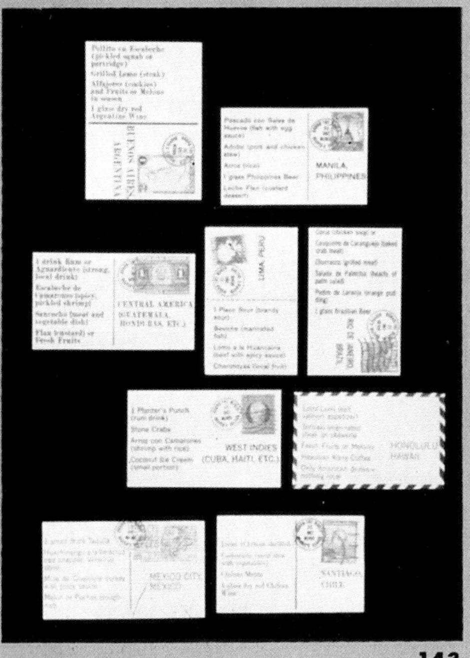

143

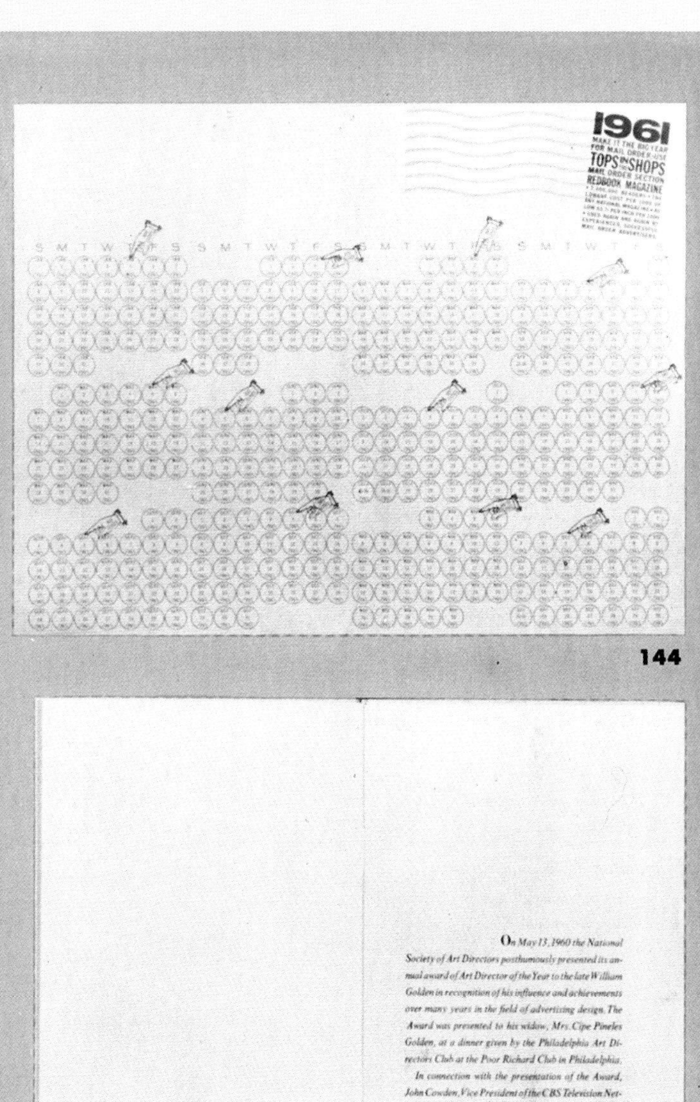

1961
MAKE IT THE BIG YEAR
FOR MAIL ORDER USE
TOPS
SHOPS
MAIL ORDER SECTION
REDBOOK MAGAZINE
On May 13, 1960 the National Society of Art Directors posthumously presented its annual award of Art Director of the Year to the late William Golden in recognition of his influence and achievements over many years in the field of advertising design. The Award was presented to his widow, Mrs. Cipe Pineles Golden, at a dinner given by the Philadelphia Art Directors Club at the Poor Richard Club in Philadelphia.
In connection with the presentation of the Award, John Cowden, Vice President of the CBS Television Network, recalled his long friendship and association with Mr. Golden throughout his career with the Columbia Broadcasting System and paid tribute to his outstanding contributions to the company. The text of his remarks is reprinted in the following pages.

144

145

146

147
designer: James P. Camperos
art director: James P. Camperos
client/agency: Ramio-Wooldridge Tuesday Nite Cinema
typographer: Toyo Printing

148
designer: Eileen Broser
art director: Eileen Broser
client/agency: Felton Chemical Co.
typographer: Composing Room

149
designer: Allan R. Fleming
art director: Allan R. Fleming
client/agency: Canadian National Railways
typographer: Cooper & Beatty, Limited

150
designer: Gilbert Lesser
art director: Gilbert Lesser
client/agency: Sam Mann Contemporary Crafts
typographer: Composing Room

151
designer: Kern Devin
art director: Kern Devin
client/agency: Mercy Hospital/Barton Gillet Co.
typographer: Duvall Co.

152
designer: O. Paccione
art director: O. Paccione
client/agency: O. Paccione
typographer: Artintype

153
designer: Frank Kirk
art director: Frank Kirk
client/agency: Chemstrand/DDB
typographer: Typo Craftsmen

154
designer: Gilbert Lesser
art director: Gilbert Lesser
client/agency: Fortune, Time Inc. Hand Lettering
typographer: Composing Room

155
designer: Tom Woodward
art director: James Cross
client/agency: Northrop Corporation
typographer: Monsen

presents with pride
at the Cafeteria-Auditorium
the Japanese Award-Winning Film
羅生門
RASHO-MON
カンペロス
The story of a merchant and his wife
who were waylaid by a bandit.
The wife was attacked and the merchant killed.
The crime is enacted four times, resulting
in four different stories----
the bandit's, the wife's,
the dead merchant's (as told through a medium),
and the version as told by a witness.

147

An Invitation to Consult with Top Management

Members of the tobacco industry know that the palate is fickle. A cigarette that once tasted just right may one day meet with only tepid response. When this happens, it is time to call in a flavor consultant. Felton is such a consultant. Felton's long experience in flavor research—especially for the tobacco companies—enables us to custom-create specific flavors for specific purposes. Our top people meet with your top people. And naturally, every detail is worked out in the strictest confidence. We will welcome an opportunity to serve you. Felton Chemical Co. Inc., 599 Johnson Avenue, Brooklyn 37, New York.

felton

148

149

150

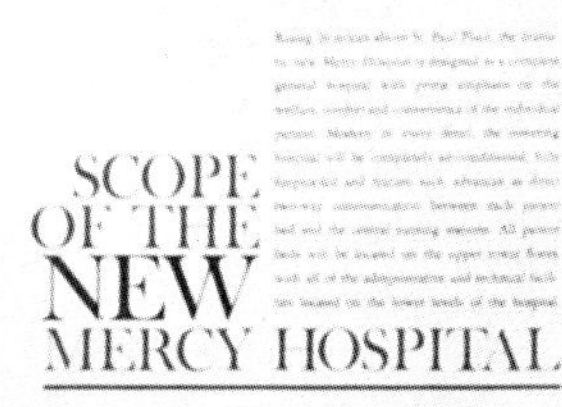
SCOPE
OF THE
NEW
MERCY HOSPITAL

Section Looking East

151

FORTUNE'S
TRUCK SUR
VEY 1959

154

mentholated meristem meristematic message

152

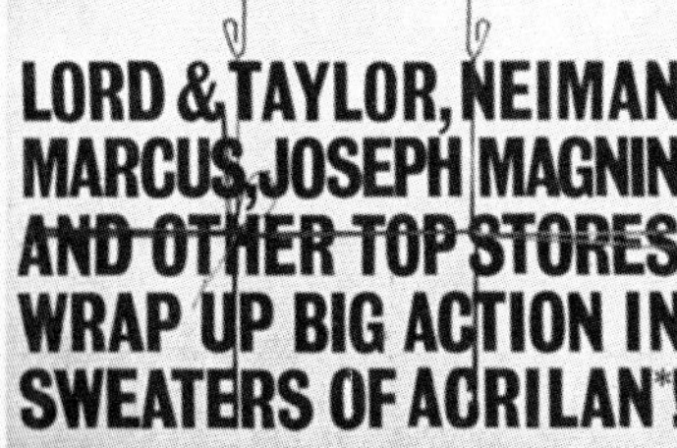
LORD & TAYLOR, NEIMAN
MARCUS, JOSEPH MAGNIN
AND OTHER TOP STORES
WRAP UP BIG ACTION IN
SWEATERS OF ACRILAN*!

153

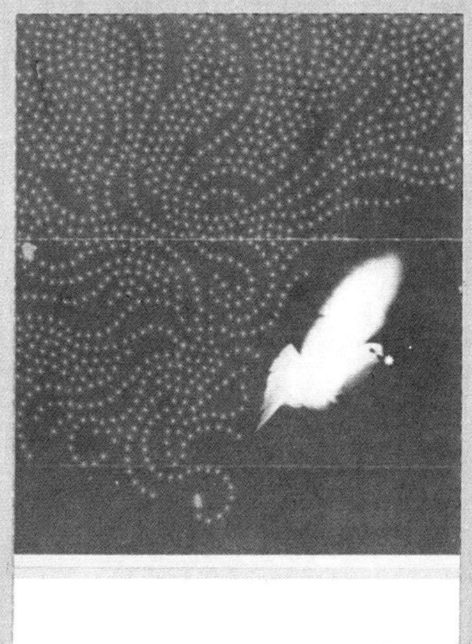

155

156

157

156

designer: James P. Camperos
art director: Bill Curry
client/agency: Ramo-Wooldridge
typographer: Monsen Typographers

157

designer: Design Comm.: Hap Smith
art director:
client/agency: National Merit Scholarship Corporation
typographer: Photo-Lettering

158

designer: Robert Goff & Elliot Epstein
art director: Robert Goff
client/agency: John Wiley & Sons
typographer: Rand McNally

159

designer: Louis Klein
art director: Louis Klein
client/agency: TIME International
typographer: Typo, Haber, Morgan Press, Master

160

designer: Richard Bergeron
art director: Ken Lavey
client/agency: Parke-Davis
typographer: Empire

161

designer:
art director: Kurt Weihs
client/agency: CBS Television Network
typographer:

162

designer: Reba Sochis
art director: Reba Sochis
client/agency: Sochis Advertising & Promotion
typographer: Graphic Arts

163

designer: Herb Lubalin
art director: Herb Lubalin
client/agency: CBS Radio
Sudler & Hennessey
typographer: Composing Room

164

designer: Herb Lubalin
art director: Herb Lubalin
client/agency: Jens Risom Design, Inc.
Sudler & Hennessey
typographer: Composing Room

158

159

160

Trujillo:
PORTRAIT OF A DICTATOR
10-11 TONIGHT CBS CHANNEL 2

161

SOCHIS30E60NYC22

SOCHIS30E60NYC22PL51490

SOCHIS 30E60 NYC22

SOCHIS 30E60 NYC22

SOCHIS 30E60 NYC22

SOCHIS30E60NYC22

162

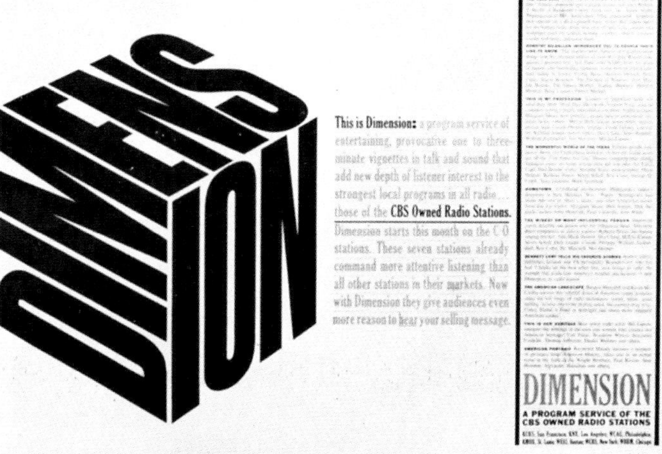

163

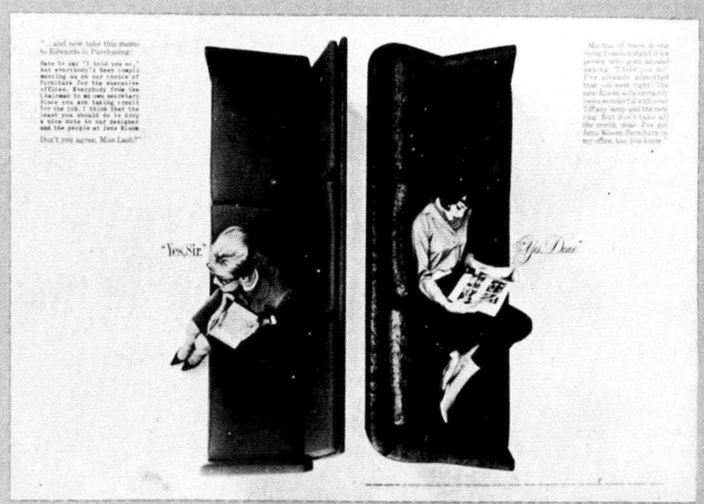

164

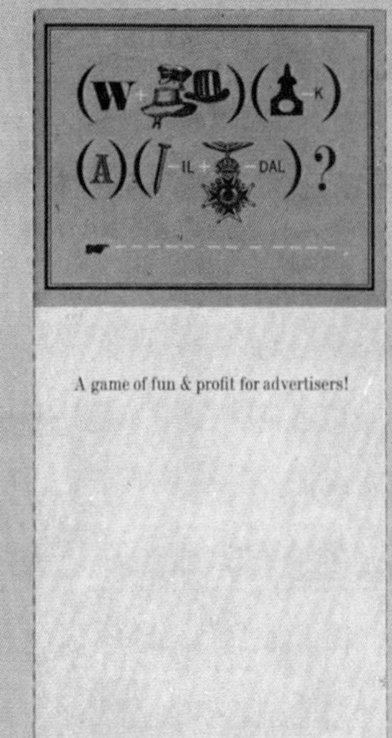

165

166

167

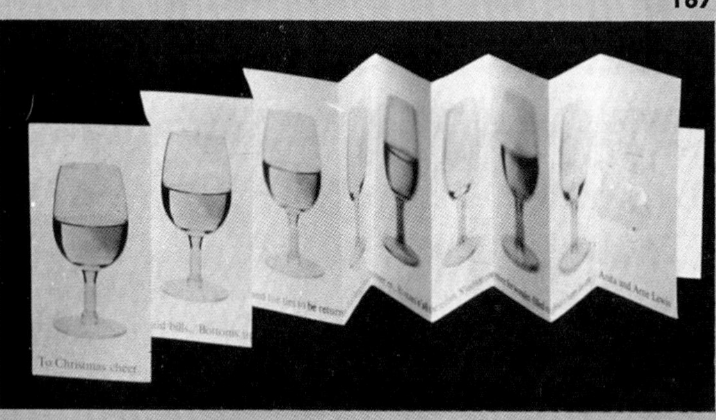

168

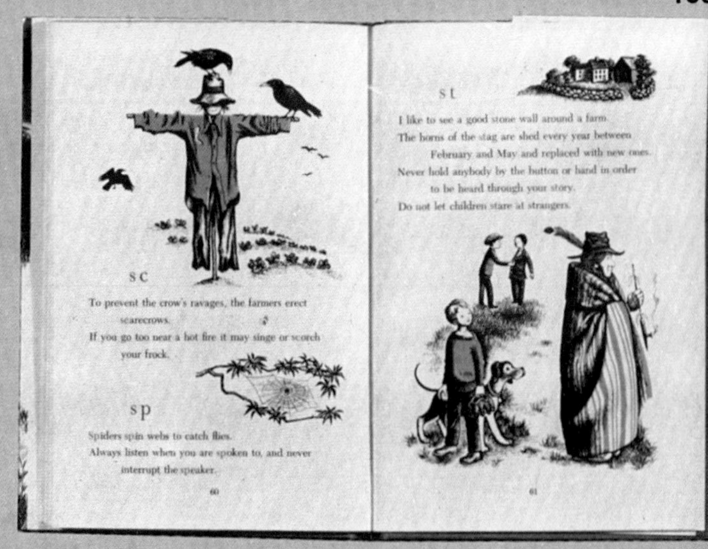

165

designer:	Joe Schindelman, Phil Gips
art director:	Joe Schindelman
client/agency:	CBS Radio Network
typographer:	Composing Room

166

designer:	Al Cascino
art director:	Al Cascino
client/agency:	Cargill, Wilson & Acree
typographer:	Progressive Composition Co.

167

designer:	Arne Lewis
art director:	Anita Lewis
client/agency:	Lewis Family
typographer:	TPI

168

designer:	Terry Pace
art director:	Doris Barrett
client/agency:	Thomas Y. Crowell Co.
typographer:	Howard O. Bullard, Inc.

169

designer:	Herb Lubalin/Rene Bittel
art director:	Herb Lubalin
client/agency:	Rover Motor Corp. Sudler & Hennessey
typographer:	Composing Room

170

designer:	Kern Devin
art director:	Kern Devin
client/agency:	Linotype Composition Co.
typographer:	Linotype Composition Co.

171

designer:	George Lois
art director:	George Loïs
client/agency:	Papert, Koenig, Lois
typographer:	Composing Room

172

designer:	
art director:	Louis Dorfsman
client/agency:	CBS Television Network
typographer:	

reprinted from the December 1959 issue of Road & Track
A ROAD-TEST OF THE
ROVER
3-LITRE
Stately, refined and elegant, an altogether superb automobile.
THE ROVER MOTOR COMPANY
OF NORTH AMERICA LIMITED

169

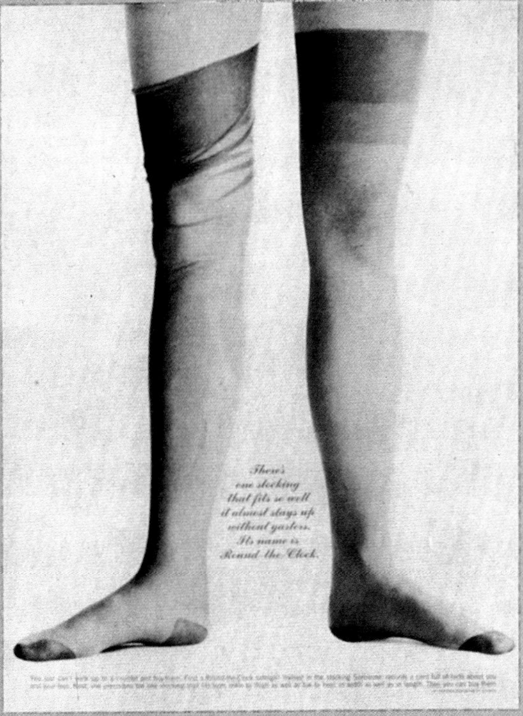
There's
one stocking
that fits so well
it almost stays up
without garters.
Its name is
Round-the-Clock.

171

Torino . . . a new type face
especially imported from Italy
by Bruno . . . is now available in
the Baltimore area for the first time in both
Foundry for repros and Photo Lettering. The
ABCDEFGHIJKLMNOPQRSTUVWXYZ
"TOR
INO"
Photo Lettering by Bruno at
407 East Saratoga Street
Linotype Composition Co.

170

CBS News takes you to Squaw Valley, California to begin its exclusive coverage of the world's greatest sports spectacle – The 1960 Olympic Games. In a vivid demonstration of international good will, 1,000 athletes from 34 countries will participate in today's colorful opening ceremonies. For the next 10 consecutive days, the CBS Television Network will present the thrilling highlights of the men's and women's skiing, skating and ice hockey competitions. From vantage points on the ski slopes and in the skating arenas, sports reporters Chris Schenkel and Bud Palmer, and former Olympic stars Dick Button and Art Devlin will describe the events as they take place. And from his familiar anchor position, Walter Cronkite will bring you up-to-date on the individual results and national standings. CBS News will complete its exclusive Olympic coverage next August with a special series on the Summer Games in Rome.
WINTER
OLYMPICS
STARTING TONIGHT AT 7:30 ON CHANNEL 2

172

173

designers: Student Staff:
Nicholas Fasciari
Helen Linz
Arlene Malitz
Boris Putterman
Jerome Witkin
art directors: George Salter, Leo Manso
client/agency: The Cooper Union School of Art & Architecture
typographer: Clarke & Way, Inc.

174

designer: Arnold Varga
art director: Arnold Varga
client/agency: Cox's, Inc.
typographer:

175

designer: Bradbury Thompson
art director: Bradbury Thompson
client/agency: West Virginia Pulp and Paper Company
typographer: Typographic Service Company

176

designer:
art director: Louis Dorfsman
client/agency: CBS Television Network
typographer:

177

designer: Arne Lewis
art director: Arne Lewis
client/agency: Ampersand
typographer: Rapid Typographers

178

designer: Abe Seltzer
art director: Abe Seltzer
client/agency: Pharmaceutical Advertising Club
typographer: Empire Typographers, Inc.

179

designer: Peter Hirsch, Seymour Chwast
art director: Peter Hirsch
client/agency: L'Aiglon Apparel Inc.
typographer: Composing Room

180

designer: Kurt Weihs
art director: Kurt Weihs
client/agency: Papert, Koenig, Lois
typographer: Composing Room

173

174

175

carrying the torch

176

177

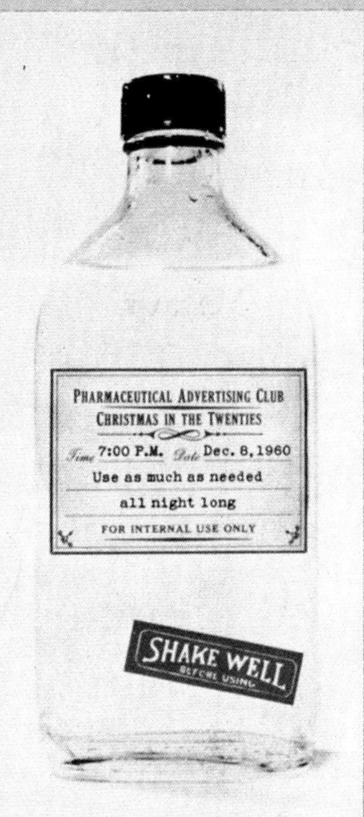

PHARMACEUTICAL ADVERTISING CLUB
CHRISTMAS IN THE TWENTIES
Time 7:00 P.M. Date Dec. 8, 1960
Use as much as needed
all night long
FOR INTERNAL USE ONLY
SHAKE WELL
BEFORE USING

178

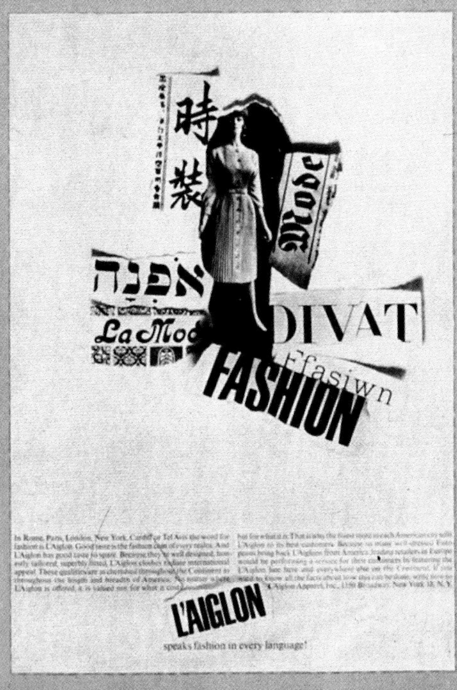

179

These are the 7 best made cars in the world.
One of them costs only $2250 complete.
Its name is Peugeot

180

181

designer: J. J. Suplina
art director: J. J. Suplina
client/agency: Obrig Laboratories, Inc./ Krukowski & Symington, Inc.
typographer: Linocraft

182

designer: Audrey Rosenson
art director: Henry Wolf/Audrey Rosenson
client/agency: Harper's Bazaar
typographer: Haber

183

designer: David Chasman
art director: David Chasman
client/agency: Monitor Records
typographer: Metro Typographers

184

designer: Hector Robledo
art director: Hector Robledo
client/agency: McCall's/Grey
typographer:

185

designer: George Lois
art director: George Lois
client/agency: Papert, Koenig, Lois, Inc.
typographer: Composing Room

186

designer: Herb Lubalin
art director: Herb Lubalin
client/agency: CBS Radio
Sudler & Hennessey
typographer: Composing Room

187

designer: Dick Aldcroftt
art director: Dick Aldcroftt
client/agency: Ketchum, MacLeod & Grove, Inc.
typographer:

THE STORY OF CONTACT LENSES
BY PHILIP L. SALVATORI

181

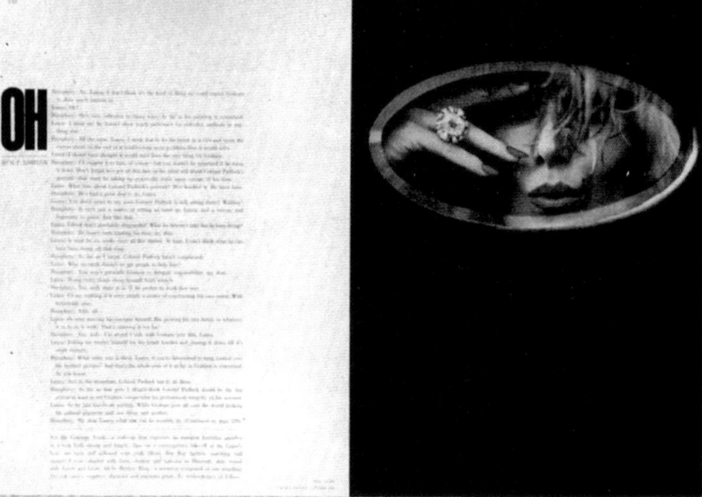

182

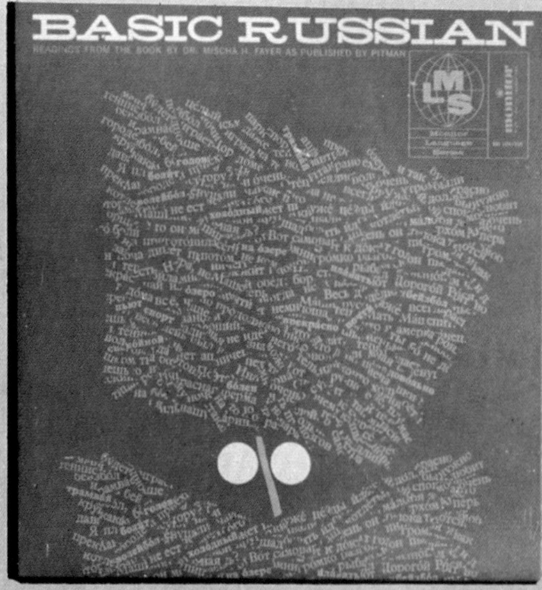

183

THE McCALL CORPORATION PRINTS MORE THAN ONE BILLION MAGAZINES IN A YEAR

1,000,000,000

184

(rā′dĭ·ō)

REDEFINED BY THE CBS RADIO NETWORK

STARTING TODAY, CBS Radio brings new meaning to radio.

Today's world is changing as the clock ticks. Events in the earth's remotest regions affect our lives. New sciences, new nations, new personalities open up new horizons and create new challenges. We need, as never before, to be better informed.

Only radio has the speed and global flexibility to keep pace with these changes. And only CBS Radio has the purpose, the people, the programming to make them meaningful for you so quickly... and to bring you a world of entertainment as well.

Starting today, CBS Radio doubles its news coverage to bring you a full ten minutes of news on the hour, morning through evening. This expanded schedule not only means more on-the-spot news and analysis from all over the world, but more of the caliber of reporting that has made the CBS News team of Edward R. Murrow, Eric Sevareid, Howard K. Smith, Douglas Edwards, Robert Trout, Lowell Thomas and their colleagues an organization without peer in news broadcasting.

Starting today, too, a brand-new schedule of bright, varied and informative CBS Radio Features will be presented right through the week. These five-minute programs include The Moscow Scene, with Marvin Kalb; The Week in Space, with George Herman; Man and Wife, with Zachary Scott; A Woman's Washington, with Nancy Hanschman; The Headliner, with Charles Collingwood—and fourteen others!

In keeping with our redefinition of radio's role, you will find even greater emphasis in the coming year on the public affairs and special events coverage that are a hallmark of the CBS Radio Network.

Increased sports reporting is scheduled also. Ten more weekend programs will be heard as ex-Yankee Jerry Coleman joins Phil Rizzuto and Pat Summerall in providing up-to-the-minute sports information all week long, fifty-two weeks a year. And important events—the Orange Bowl, the Cotton Bowl, horse racing's Triple Crown, the Masters Golf Tournament—are all on CBS Radio.

Star entertainment continues. Unchanged will be outstanding favorites like Arthur Godfrey Time, Art Linkletter's House Party, The Garry Moore Radio Show, Bing Crosby-Rosemary Clooney, and the colorful new In Person program, all Monday through Friday; The Mitch Miller Show, Johnny Dollar, Gunsmoke and The New York Philharmonic on weekends.

Our redefinition of radio's heightened responsibility to keep listeners informed as well as entertained has new meaning for advertisers, too.

CBS Radio's new programming structure commands increased audience attention, creating an ideal sales setting plus an association with the most attractive, most respected names in broadcasting. And the new CBS Radio schedule provides a range of selling opportunities morning to night, seven days a week—from a single segment of Arthur Godfrey Time to a saturation campaign.

As you redefine your advertising objectives for 1961, we invite you to examine the advantages offered by network radio. We know you will find that there are now more reasons than ever before to use the tremendous selling power of **THE CBS RADIO NETWORK.**

186

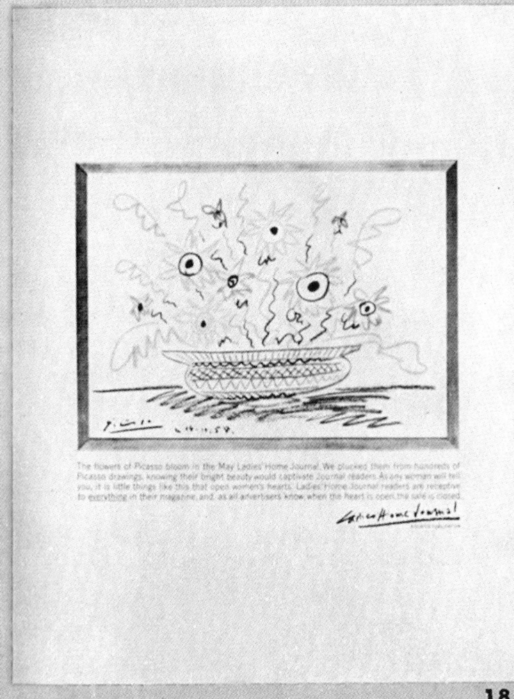

The flowers of Picasso bloom in the May Ladies' Home Journal. We plucked them from hundreds of Picasso drawings, knowing their bright beauty would captivate Journal readers. As any woman will tell you, it is little things like this that open women's hearts. Ladies' Home Journal readers are receptive to everything in their magazine, and, as all advertisers know, when the heart is open the sale is closed.

185

10 9 8 7 6 5 4 3 2 1

WHERE DOES BEYOND BEGIN? Today, the answer changes so fast there is no answer. At Martin-Denver, scientists, physicists, mathematicians in a great many fields are among those pushing beyond in the concepts and vehicles of space. They work in a climate that fosters advancement in the state of the art and professional status. If you would like to join them, write: N. M. Pagan, Director of Technical and Scientific Staffing, Martin-Denver, P.O. Box 1795, Denver, Colorado.

MARTIN
DENVER DIVISION

187

the Type Directors Club:

Sustaining Members:

ADVERTISING AGENCIES SERVICE COMPANY, INC.
AMERICAN TYPE FOUNDERS
AMSTERDAM-CONTINENTAL TYPES & GRAPHIC EQUIPMENT, INC.
COOPER & BEATTY LTD.
CRAFTSMAN TYPE INC.
A. T. EDWARDS TYPOGRAPHY, INC.
ELECTROGRAPHIC CORPORATION
EMPIRE TYPOGRAPHERS
THE HIGHTON COMPANY
HUXLEY HOUSE
KING TYPOGRAPHIC SERVICE CORP.
LANSTON MONOTYPE MACHINE CO.
OSCAR LEVENTHAL, INC.
LINOCRAFT TYPOGRAPHERS
LUDLOW TYPOGRAPH COMPANY
WILLIAM PATRICK COMPANY, INC.
PHILMAC TYPOGRAPHERS, INC.
PROGRESSIVE COMPOSITION COMPANY
RAPID TYPOGRAPHERS, INC.
FREDERICK W. SCHMIDT, INC.
SKILSET TYPOGRAPHERS
SUPERIOR TYPOGRAPHERS, INC.
THE COMPOSING ROOM, INC.
THE TYPOGRAPHIC HOUSE, INC.
TYPO-PHILADELPHIA
TYPOGRAPHY PLACE, INC.
TUDOR TYPOGRAPHERS
KURT H. VOLK, INC.
WESTCOTT & THOMSON, INC.

Active Members:

ARDEN, KELVIN JR.
ARMELLINO, JOSEPH S.
BANK, ARNOLD
BENNETT, PAUL
BERGMAN, TED
BETHKE, AMOS G.
BRUSSEL-SMITH, BERNARD
BURNS, AARON
BURTIN, WILL
CHERRY, BURTON
CLIETT, TRAVIS
CLINE, MAHLON A.
CONNELL, MARTIN
CRAW, FREEMAN
DI LEO, PETER
DE LOPATECKI, EUGENE
DICKMAN, O. ALFRED
DORFSMAN, LOUIS
DUNN, GENE
ETTENBERG, EUGENE M.
FARBER, ROBERT
FEINBERG, SIDNEY
FELTEN, CHARLES J.
FITZGERALD, BRUCE
FOSS, GLENN
GIANNONE, VINCENT
GLASSHEIM, LOUIS L.
GLEASON, WILLIAM P.
GOTTSCHALL, EDWARD M.
HALPIN, JAMES
HINTERMAN, KURT
JONES, ROBERT M.
KARCH, R. RANDOLPH
KISS, ZOLTAN N.
KOLSBY, EDWIN B.
KOMAI, RAY
KONRAD, RAY
KROLL, RICHARD A.
LEE, ARTHUR B.
LEHMAN, ACY R.
LINE, CLIFTON
LITTMAN, WALLY
LONG, GILLIS L.
LOOS, MELVIN
LORD, JOHN H.
LUBALIN, HERB
MALECKI, EDGAR J.
McMASTER, PALMER J.
MERKER, EGON
MERRIMAN, FRANK
MEYERS, HERBERT M.
MONACO, FRANCIS
MOSS, TOBIAS
MUSTO, LOUIS A.
NESBITT, ALEXANDER
O'CONNER, MARTIN S.
OGG, OSCAR
O'NEILL, GERARD J.
OVINK, DR. G. W.
PATTBERG, EUGENE P.
PLOEG, JAN VAN DER
PODORSON, GEORGE A.
POWERS, FRANK E.
REICHL, ERNST
ROAN, HERBERT
ROBERTS, ANDREW
ROCHE, ROBERT
RONDTHALER, EDWARD
ROSSI, FRANK
SAELENS, GUSTAVE L.
SCHMIDT, KLAUS F.
SECREST, JAMES
SEKULER, WILLIAM L.
SHAAR, EDWIN W.
STANTON, WALTER
STOLZ, HERBERT
STORCH, OTTO
STREEVER, WILLIAM A.
SUTTER, ROBERT
TASLER, DAVID B.
TAUBIN, WILLIAM
THOMPSON, BRADBURY
TRAUTWEIN, JOSEPH
VERSH, ABRAHAM A.
WAGMAN, MEYER
WARDE, BEATRICE
WARTIK, HERSCHEL
WATTS, STEVENS L.
WEILER, JOSEPH F.
WERBIN, IRV.
ZAMBONI, HAL
ZAPF, HERMANN
ZINER, ZEKE
ZUDECK, MILTON K.

Committee for Typography '61

Eugene P. Pattberg: *Chairman*
Zoltan N. Kiss: *Design of Catalogue*
Joseph F. Weiler: *Production of Catalogue*
Glenn Foss: *Supervisor of Photography*

K. J. Arden
Peter DiLeo
Frank Orser
William Gleason
Edgar J. Malecki
Arthur B. Lee
Travis Cliett
Joseph S. Armellino
Robert Sutter
James Halpin
O. Alfred Dickman

Printed by: Publication Press
Composition: The Typographic Service Co.
Text paper: Mead Black & White Offset Enamel, Dull
Cover paper: Mead Wheelwright Potomac, White
Photography: F. A. Russo, Inc.
(Abe Fried)

Grateful acknowledgments are made to the following people for their contributions to the success of this exhibition:

Edward Rondthaler and his staff at Photolettering, Inc.

Robert M. Jones and the RCA-Victor Records Division.

Dwight Rockwell and the staff of the Mead Library of Ideas, Mead Corporation.

Board of Directors, 2009–2010

Officers
President: Charles Nix, Scott & Nix, Inc. Vice President: Diego Vainesman, 40n47 Design, Inc. Secretary/Treasurer: Graham Clifford, Graham Clifford Design.
Directors-at-Large
Marc Blaustein, New York Public Library; Scott Citron, Scott Citron Design; Sean King, Landor Associates; Brian Miller, Brian Miller Design; Ina Saltz, Saltz Design; Jakob Trollbäck, Trollbäck + Company; and Anne Twomey, Grand Central Publishing. Chairman of the Board: Alex W. White, Alexander W. White Consultancy. Executive Director: Carol Wahler

Board of Directors 2010–2011

Officers
President: Diego Vainesman, 40N47 Design, Inc. Vice President: Graham Clifford, Graham Clifford Design. Secretary/Treasurer: Matteo Bologna, Mucca Design.
Directors-at-Large
Scott Citron, Scott Citron Design; Roberto de Vicq de Cumptich, deVicq design; Sean King, Landor Associates; Brian Miller, Brian Miller Design; Ina Saltz, Saltz Design; Jakob Trollbäck, Trollbäck + Company; and Scott Valins, Valins + Co. Chairman of the Board: Charles Nix, Scott & Nix, Inc. Executive Director: Carol Wahler

Committee for TDC 56

Chairwoman: Anne Twomey. Call Poster Design: Office of Paul Sahre. Coordinator: Carol Wahler. Assistants to Judges: Matteo Bologna, Graham Clifford, Roberto de Vicq de Cumptich, Deborah Gonet, Nana Kobayashi, Ted Mauseth, Brian Miller, Alexa Nosal, Rosa Odenwalder, Diego Vainesman, Nina Vo, Allan R. Wahler, and Alex W. White

Committee for TDC^2 2010

Chairman: Dave Farey. Call Card Designer: Richard Dawson, HouseStyle Graphics. Assistants to the Judges: Chris Andreola, James Montalbano, Charles Nix, and Maxim Zhukov

Non-Latin Advisory Board (NLAB)

NLAB is an informal group of experts that provides guidance and advice to the judges of the TDC type design competitions in assessing typeface designs developed for non-Latin scripts (Arabic, Cyrillic, Greek, Indic, and many others).

TDC Non-Latin Advisory Board: Gayaneh Bagdasaryan, Akira Kobayashi, Gerry Leonidas, Klimis Mastoridis, Rathna Ramanathan, Mamoun Sakkal, Graham Shaw, Marvel Shmavonyan, Huda Smitshuijzen AbiFarés, and Vladimir Yefimov

2010 TDC Scholarship Recipents

Hyun Jeong Kim, EWHA Womans University, Seoul
Adly M. Elewa, School of Visual Arts, New York
Dasha Marcial, Pratt Institute, New York
Taylor C. Pemberton, Savannah College of Art and Design
Amit Werber, The Cooper Union School of Art

2010 Student Award Winners

First Place ($500): John Curry (California State University, Long Beach)
Second Place ($300): Eunjung Yoo (School of Visual Arts, New York)
Third Place ($200): Wesley Gott (School of Visual Arts, New York, MFA Program)

Type Directors Club Presidents

Frank Powers, 1946, 1947
Milton Zudeck, 1948
Alfred Dickman, 1949
Joseph Weiler, 1950
James Secrest, 1951, 1952, 1953
Gustave Saelens, 1954, 1955
Arthur Lee, 1956, 1957
Martin Connell, 1958
James Secrest, 1959, 1960
Frank Powers, 1961, 1962
Milton Zudeck, 1963, 1964
Gene Ettenberg, 1965, 1966
Edward Gottschall, 1967, 1968
Saadyah Maximon, 1969
Louis Lepis, 1970, 1971
Gerard O'Neill, 1972, 1973
Zoltan Kiss, 1974, 1975
Roy Zucca, 1976, 1977
William Streever, 1978, 1979
Bonnie Hazelton, 1980, 1981
Jack George Tauss, 1982, 1983
Klaus F. Schmidt, 1984, 1985
John Luke, 1986, 1987
Jack Odette, 1988, 1989
Ed Benguiat, 1990, 1991
Allan Haley, 1992, 1993
B. Martin Pedersen, 1994, 1995
Mara Kurtz, 1996, 1997
Mark Solsburg, 1998, 1999
Daniel Pelavin, 2000, 2001
James Montalbano, 2002, 2003
Gary Munch, 2004, 2005
Alex W. White, 2006, 2007
Charles Nix, 2008, 2009
Diego Vainesman, 2010

TDC Medal Recipients

Hermann Zapf, 1967
R. Hunter Middleton, 1968
Frank Powers, 1971
Dr. Robert Leslie, 1972
Edward Rondthaler, 1975
Arnold Bank, 1979
Georg Trump, 1982
Paul Standard, 1983
Herb Lubalin, 1984 (posthumously)
Paul Rand, 1984
Aaron Burns, 1985
Bradbury Thompson, 1986
Adrian Frutiger, 1987
Freeman Craw, 1988
Ed Benguiat, 1989
Gene Federico, 1991
Lou Dorfsman, 1995
Matthew Carter, 1997
Rolling Stone magazine, 1997
Colin Brignall, 2000
Günter Gerhard Lange, 2000
Martin Solomon, 2003
Paula Scher, 2006

Special Citations to TDC Members

Edward Gottschall, 1955
Freeman Craw, 1968
James Secrest, 1974
Olaf Leu, 1984, 1990
William Streever, 1984
Klaus F. Schmidt, 1985
John Luke, 1987
Jack Odette, 1989

International Liaison Chairpersons

England: John Bateson, Bateson Studio, 5 Astrop Mews, London W6 7HR

France: Bastien Hermand, ECV - Ecole de Communication Visuelle, 1, rue du Dahomey 75011 Paris

Germany: Bertram Schmidt-Friderichs, Verlag Hermann Schmidt, Mainz GmbH & Co., Robert Koch Strasse 8, Postfach 42 07 28 55129 Mainz Hechtsheim

Japan: Zempaku Suzuki, Japan Typography Association Sanukin Bldg., 5th Floor 1-7-10 Nihonbashi-honcho, Chuo-ku, Toyko 104-0041

Mexico: Prof. Felix Beltran, Apartado de Correos M 10733, Mexico 06000

South America: Diego Vainesman, 181 East 93 Street, Apt. 4E, New York 10128

Spain: Christian Giribets, Bau, Escola Superior de Disseny, Pujades 118, 08005 Barcelona

Vietnam: Richard Moore 21 Bond Street, New York, 10012

Type Directors Club

347 West 36 Street Suite 603
New York 10018
Phone: 212-633-8943
Fax: 212-633-8944
E-mail: director@tdc.org
www.tdc.org

Carol Wahler, Executive Director
For membership information, please contact the TDC office.

TDC Members

Huda Smitshuijzen Abifarés 2010
Christopher Abrams 2009s
Marcella Accardi-Sanders 1998s
Ana Aguilar-Hauke 2007s
Anastasia Aizman 2010s
Seth Akkerman 2008s
Zahra Al-Harazi 2009
Rafael Almonte 2009s
Tyler Alterman 2010s
Chris Anderson 2008
Greta Anderson 2009s
Jack Anderson 1996
Luck Andreas 2006
Christopher Andreola 2003
Patrick Andresen 2010
J.R. Arebalo, Jr. 2003
Carlos Arriaga 2010
Robyn Attaway 1993
Bob Aufuldish 2006
Gayaneh Bagdasaryan 2007
Peter Bain 1986
Sanjit Fernandes Bakshi 2008
Andreu Balius 2009
Joshua Bankes 2006
Giorgio Baravalle 2007
Neil Barnett 2001
Mark Batty 2003
Dawn Beard 2010
Katja Becker 2008
Misha Beletsky 2007
Paul Belford 2005
Felix Beltran 1988
Ed Benguiat 1964***
Jerome Berard 2010
Marije Berghuis 2010s
Kai Bergmann 2006
Anna Berkenbusch 1989
Sam Berlow 2009
John D. Berry 1996
Peter Bertolami 1969***
William Bevington 2010
Michael Bierut 2010
Klaus Bietz 1993
Richard Bigus 2009
Henrik Birkvig 1996
Heribert Birnbach 2007
Debra Bishop 2008
R. P. Bissland 2004
Roger Black 1980
Marc Blaustein 2001
Anthony Bloch 2010
Anders Bodebeck 2004
Matteo Bologna 2003
Joao Borges 2010
Erica Borkowski 2009s
Maury Botton 2008
Matthew Bouloutian 2008
Kevin Brainard 2008
John Breakey 2006
Ed Brodsky 1980***
Craig Brown 2004
Ryn Bruce 2009
Angelika Brunner 2008
Paul Buckley 2007
Michael Bundscherr 2007
Bill Bundzak 1964***
Christina Burton 2010s
Volker Busse 2010
Steve Byers 2010
Mike Campbell 2004
Ronn Campisi 1988
Christopher Cannon 2006
Francesco Canovaro 2009
Amid Capeci 2009
Wilson Capellan 2007
Tomaso Capuno 2008

Aaron Carambula 2005
Paul Carlos 2008
Scott Carslake 2001
Michael Carsten 2008s
Matthew Carter 1988***
James Castanzo 2008
Marie Castiglioe 2009s
Marta Castrosin 2010
Ken Cato 1988
Jackson Cavanaugh 2010
Laura Cedar 2009
Eduard Cehovin 2003
Nathan Chambers 2009
Caitlin Chandler 2010
Yai-Jung Chang 2008
Len Cheeseman 1993
Jackie Chen 2009s
Joshua Chen 2008
Pingbo Chen 2010
Tao Chen 2009
David Cheung, Jr. 1998
Li-Chuan Chiang 2010s
Alexandra Ching 2009
Chiu-Ping Chiu 2009s
Jessica Cho 2010s
Jueun Cho 2009s
Erica Yujin Choi 2009s
Yeju Choi 2009s
Alan Chong 2009
Siu Chong 2010
Sam Chun 2009s
Jack Chung 2007
Stanley Church 1997
Nicholas Cintron 2003s
Scott Citron 2007
Graham Clifford 1998
Doug Clouse 2009
Angelo Colella 1990
Sarah J. Coleman 2009
Ed Colker 1983***
Nancy Sharon Collins 2006
Cherise Conrick 2009
Nick Cooke 2001
Ricardo Cordoba 2009
Rodrigo Corral 2002
Madeleine Corson 1996
Susan Cotler-Block 1989
James Craig 2004
Freeman Craw* 1947
Kathleen Creighton 2008
Benjamin Crittom 2008s
Andreas Croonenbroeck 2006
Bart Crosby 1995
Carl Crossgrove 2009
Ray Cruz 1999
Noble Cumming 2010s
Brian Cunningham 1996
John Curry 2009s
Rick Cusick 1989
Joseph D'Armiento 2010s
Scott Dadich 2008
Si Daniels 2009
Susan Darbyshire 1987
Joshua Darden 2007
Kathryn Davenel 2009s
Jo Davison 2007
Bill Dawson 2009
Filip de Baudringhien 2008
Josanne De Natale 1986
Roberto de Vicq de Cumptich 2005
Ken DeLago 2008
Laura Deleot 2000
Olivier Delhaye 2006
Liz DeLuna 2005
Richard R. Dendy 2000
Jenna DeNoyelles 2010s

Mark Denton 2001
Stewart Devlin 2010
James DeVries 2005
Cara Di Edwardo 2009
Chank Diesel 2005
Claude A. Dieterich 1984
Kirsten Dietz 2000
Joseph DiGioia 1999
Elisabetta DiStefano 2007s
Peter Disler 2010
Dino Dos Santos 2004
Christian Drury 2007
Christopher Dubber 1985***
Joseph P. Duffy III 2003
Susanna Dulknys 2009
Denis Dulude 2004
Christoph Dunst 2007
Arem Duplessis 2006
Andrea Duquette 2009s
Simon Dwelly 1998
Lasko Dzurovski 2000
Nicholas Eldridge 2009
Colleen Ellis 2010
Garry Emery 1993
Marc Engenhart 2006
Jan Eramus 2008
Joseph Michael Essex 1978
Manuel Estrada 2005
Knut Ettling 2007
Warren Everhard 2007s
Florence Everett 1989
Ted Eyes 2009
John Fairley 2010
David Farey 1993
Matt Ferranto 2004
Gemma Field 2007s
Vicente Gil Filho 2002
Louise Fili 2004
Kevin Finn 2007
Kristine Fitzgerald 1990
Bernadette Fitzpatrick 2008
Julie Flahiff 2004
Linda Florio 2009
Colin Ford 2009s
Carol Forsythe 2009
Louise Fortin 2007
Leigh Foster 2009s
Dirk Fowler 2003
Alessandro Franchini 1996
Carol Freed 1987
Dinah Fried 2009s
Ryan Pescatore Frisk 2004
Adrian Frutiger ** 1967
Kenny Funk 2005
David Fusilier 2009s
Dirk Fütterer 2008
Evan Gaffney 2009
Louis Gagnon 2002
Christina Galbiati 2010s
Gunnar Gamer 2009s
Peter Garceau 2008
Jeffrey Garofalo 2006s
Christof Gassner 1990
David Gatti 1981***
Alex George 2010
Pepe Gimeno 2001
Lou Glassheim * 1947
Howard Glener 1977***
Mario Godbout 2002
Grant Gold 2009
Anton Silveira Gomes 2009
Janine Gomez 2009s
Juan Pablo Gomez 2010s
Giuliano Cesar Gonçalves 2001
Deborah Gonet 2005
Robert Gonzalez 2009s

Hope Miller Goodell 2008
Eber Gordon 2010
Wesley Gott 2010s
Edward Gottschall 1952
Jonathan Gouthier 2009
Mark Gowing 2006
Norman Graber 1969***
Friedrich-Wilhelm Graf 2008
Diana Graham 1985
Marion Grant 2004s
Whitney Grant 2008
Tino Grass 2007
Katheryne Gray 2004
Pamela Green 2010
Joan Greenfield 2006
Fiona Greenwood 2009s
Tim Greenzweig 2009
James Grieshaber 1996
Robson Grieve 2010
Catherine Griffiths 2006
Amelia Grohman 2009s
Katarzna Gruda 2009
Tom Grunwald 2009s
Rosanne Guararra 1992
Nora Gummert-Hauser 2006
Jens Gutermann 2009s
Peter Gyllan 1997
Hoyt Haffelder 2009s
Brock Haldeman 2002
Allan Haley 1978
Debra Hall 1996
Dawn Hancock 2003
Sascha Hanke 2008
Egil Haraldsen 2000
Chantal Harding 2010
Rob Harrigan 2009
Knut Hartmann 1985
Lukas Hartmann 2003
Steve Haslip 2008s
Lynn Hasday 2010s
Katie Hatz 2010s
Luke Hayman 2006
Oliver Haynold 2009
Bonnie Hazelton 1975***
Amy Hecht 2001
Eric Heiman 2002
Anja Patricia Helm 2008
Hayes Henderson 2003
Cristobal Henestrosa 2010
Oliver Henn 2009
Berto Herrera 2009
Earl M. Herrick 1996
Ralf Hermannn 2002s
Klaus Hesse 1995
Paul Heys 2010
Fons M. Hickmann 1996
Jay Higgins 1988
Clemens Hilger 2008
Eric Hillerns 2009
Bill Hilson 2007
Kit Hinrichs 2004
Rakel Hinriksdottir 2009s
Norihiko Hirata 1996
Laura Hirschman 2010s
Amiee Hoban 2008
Michael Hochleitner 2010
Michael Hodgson 1989
Rebekah Hodgson 2008
Julia Hoffmann 2010
Fritz Hofrichter 1980***
Michael Hoinkes 2006
Susanne Horner 2007
Karen Horton 2007
Kevin Horvath 1987
Kiyomi Hoshikawa 2009s

Kathryn Hotler 2009s
Fabian Hotz 2001
Paul Howell 2010
Nazmul Howlander 2009s
Christian Hruschka 2005
Anton Huber 2001
John Hudson 2004
Keith C. Humphrey 2008
Christine Hunt 2010s
Skip Hursh 2009s
Hyun-Jung Hwang 2010
Senad Ibrahimbegovic 2009s
Anthony Inciong 2009
Luca Ionescu 2010
David Isaksson 2007s
Yuko Ishizaki 2009
Christopher Jackson 2008
Donald Jackson ** 1978
Cecilia Jacobsen 2009s
Peter Jacobson 2010s
Torsten Jahnke 2002
Mark Jamra 1999
Etienne Jardel 2006
Darshan Jasani 2010s
Sang Hee Jin 2009s
Thomas Jockin 2010
Robert Johnson 2009
Christa Jonathan 2009s
Matt Jones 2007
Giovanni Jubert 2004
Jin Yeoul Jung 2008s
William Jurewicz 2004
Jeannette Kaczorowski 2009s
Edward Kahler 2010
John Kallio 1996
Alexandra Kalouta 2010s
I-Ching Kao 2002
Milt Kass 2009
Diti Katona 2006
Shigeru Katsumoto 2008
Richard Kegler 2002
Steve Kennedy 2008
Russell Kerr 2005
Claire Kho 2009s
Samira Khoshnood 2009s
Ben Kiel 2006
Shuji Kikuchi 2008
Satohiro Kikutake 2002
Beom Seok Kim 2009
Florence Kim 2010
Hoekeun Kim 2008s
Hoon Kim 2010
June Hyung Kim 2006
Monica Kim 2009s
Yeon Jung Kim 2005
Yuna Kim 2010
Rick King 1993
Sean King 2007
Katsuhiro Kinoshita 2002
Ian Kirk 2010s
Nathalie Kirsheh 2004
M. Cem Kizlikaya 2010s
Arne Alexander Klett 2005
Brandie Knox 2008
Akira Kobayashi 1999
Nana Kobayashi 1994
Claus Koch 1996
Boris Kochan 2002
Masayoshi Kodaira 2002
Alice Koh 2009
Dina Kolada 2009s
Jessica Koman 2007

Yoshimi Kono 2008
Linda Kosarin 2009
Lauren Kosteski 2009s
Rosemary Kracke 2209
Dmitry Krasny 2009
Marcus Kraus 1997
Stephanie Kreber 2001
Bernhard J. Kress 1963***
Gregor Krisztian 2005
Jan Kruse 2006
Hao In Kuan 2010s
Johannes Kuester 2009
Christian Kunnert 1997
Dominik Kyeck 2002
Katsumoto Kyoto 2008
Gerry L'Orange 1991
Raymond F. Laccetti 1987
Bernard Lagace 2010
Caspar Lam 2010s
Melchior Lamy 2001
Mindy Lang 2008
Bernd Langanke 2010
John Langdon 1993
Sebastian Lange 2008
Cory Lasser 2009s
Amanda Lawrence 2006
Grace Lee 2009s
Jun Lee 2007
Kwangyong Lee 2010s
Kyisun Lee 2008s
Lillian Lee 2006
Luis Lee 2010s
Pum Lefebure 2006
Leftloft 2008
David Lemon 1995
Gerry Leonidas 2007
John Lepak 2008
Ludovic Leroy 2009
Matt Letellier 2010
Olaf Leu 1965***
Sherry Leung 2009s
Sonia Levanthan 2009
Stephanie Levy 2009s
Aura Lewis 2010s
Kevin Ley 2009
Gilbert Li 2010
Armin Lindauer 2007
Laura Lindgren 2005
Michael Lindsay 2009
Domenic Lippa 2004
Caren Litherland 2009
Jason Little 2009
Wally Littman 1960***
Alicia Lo 2010s
Sascha Lobe 2007
Ralf Lobeck 2007
Uwe Loesch 1996
Oliver Lohrengel 2004
John Howland Lord ** 1947
Chercy Lott 2008
Mohamed Louanjli 2010s
Arline Lowe 2009
Christopher Lozos 2005
Ken Lubin 2008
Alexander Luckow 1994
Gregg Lukasiewicz 1990
Kendrick Lyons 2009
Liz Macfarlane 2009
Callum McGregor 2009
Danusch Mahmoudi 2001
Rebecca Malley 2008s
Donna Meadow Manier 1999

Klaudia Mann 2008
Andrew Mapes 2010
Gab Marcelli 2009
Marilyn Marcus 1979***
Joe Marianek 2009
Peter Markatos 2003
Nicolas Markwald 2002
Zoa Martinez 2009
Laurel Marx 2010
Shigeru Masaki 2006
Jakob Maser 2006
Klimis Mastoridis 2010
Vijay Mathews 2009
David Matt 2010
Steve Matteson 2006
Michael Matyus 2009s
Ted Mauseth 2001
Andreas Maxbauer 1995
Loie Maxwell 2004
Brian May 2009
Cheryl McBride 2009
Sian McBride 2009s
Rod McDonald 1995
Mark McGarry 2002
Marc A. Meadows 1996
Roland Mehler 1992
Niyati Mehta 2009s
Uwe Melichar 2000
Oswaldo Mendes 2010
Frederic Metz 1985***
Kimou Meyer 2009
Jeremy Mickel 2009
Abbott Miller 2010
Brian Miller 2006
John Milligan 1978***
Dexter Miranda 2009s
Michael Miranda 1984
Mario Mirelez 2008
Ralf Mischnick 1998
Can Misirlioglu 2007
Susan L. Mitchell 1996
Ekta Mody 2009s
Bernd Moellenstaedt 2001
Amanda Molnar 2010s
Sakol Mongkolkasetarin 1995
James Montalbano 1993
Mark Montgomery 2009s
Richard Earl Moore 1982
Minoru Morita 1975***
Keith Morris 2009
Jimmy Moss 2004
Lars Müller 1997
Joachim Müller-Lancé 1995
Gary Munch 1997
Kara Murphy 2006s
Jerry King Musser 1988
Louis A. Musto 1965***
Steven Mykolyn 2003
Ed Nacional 2009s
Miki Nagao 2009s
Norikzu Nakamura 2009
Andrea Nalerio 2008s
Titus Nemeth 2010s
Cristiana Neri-Downey 1997
Helmut Ness 1999
Nina Neusitzer 2003s
Ulli Neutzling 2009
Robert Newman 1996
Joe Newton 2009
Vincent Ng 2004
Maria Nguyen 2009
Young-chen Nieh 2008

Stefan Nitzsche 2009
Charles Nix 2000
Michelle Nix 2008
Conor Nolan 2009
Gertrud Nolte 2001s
Amy Norskog 2009s
Alexa Nosal 1987
Niall O'Kelly 2010
Francesa O'Malley 2008
Tim Oakley 2006
Emily Oberman 2007
Graeme Offord 2008
Gaku Ohsugi 2003
Akari Oka 2010s
Ezidinma Okeke 2005
Akio Okumara 1996
Jeffrey Oley 2010
Robson Oliveira 2002
Kristin Olson 2009s
Toshihiro Onimaru 2009
Alfred Orla 2010
Petra Cerne Oven 2010
Robert Overholtzer 1994
Michael Pacey 2001
Michael Padgett 2009s
Lauren Panepinto 2010
Amy Papaelias 2008
Brian Papp 2007s
Oliver Paradis 2009
Enrique Pardo 1999
Christine Park 2010s
Dohun Park 2009s
Philip Park 2010
Jonathan Parker 2009
Jim Parkinson 1994
Karen Parry 2008
Donald Partyka 2009
Guy Pask 1997
John Passfiume 2010
Dennis Pasternak 2006
Mauro Pastore 2006
Gudrun Pawelke 1996
Harry Pearce 2004
Alan Peckolick 2007
Daniel Pelavin 1992
Andre Pennycooke 2008
Michelle Perham 2009
Regan Perri 2009s
Giorgio Pesce 2005
Steve Peter 2004
Chris Petty 2009
Kyle Phillips 2008s
Max Phillips 2000
David Philpott 2004
Stefano Picco 2010
Clive Piercy 1996
Ian Pilbeam 1999
Melissa Pilon 2010s
Ebru Pinar 2010
J.H.M. Pohlen 2006
Niberca Polo 2009s
Albert-Jan Pool 2000
Aleksandar Popovic 2009s
Mehran Poursmaelli 2009s
Patrick Powell 2009s
Alenka Prah 2008s
Vittorio Prina 1988
James Propp 1997
Lars Pryds 2006
James Puckett 2010
Richard Puder 2009
Martin James Pyper 2007

TDC Members

Ali Qadeer 2009
Mirna Raduka 2009s
Jochen Raedeker 2000
Jesse Ragan 2009
Erwin Raith 1967
Stephanie Rajalingam 2010s
Rathna Ramanathan 2009
Sal Randazzo 1997
Bob Rauchman 1997
Heather L. Reitze 2001
James Reyman 2005
Jeeyon Rhee 2010
Douglas Riccardi 2010
Matthew Richmond 2009
Fabian Richter 2001
Andre Rieberger 2008
Claudia Riedel 2004
Helge Dirk Rieder 2003
Emile Rigaud 2009s
Tamye Riggs 2008
Tobias Rink 2002
Phillip Ritzenberg 1997
Chad Roberts 2001
Phoebe Robinson 2009s
Thomas Rockwell 2007
Claudia Roeschmann 2007
Christine Rogers 2009s
Stuart Rogers 2010
Salvador Romero 1993
Kurt Roscoe 1993
Zvika Rosenberg 2009
Cynthia Roth 2009
Nancy Harris Rouemy 2007
Giovanni Carrier Russo 2003
Sho Rust 2009s
John Rutner 2010a
Erkki Ruuhinen 1986
Timothy J. Ryan 1996
Carol-Anne Ryce-Paul 2001s
Michael Rylander 1993
Jonathan Sainsbury 2005
Mamoun Sakkal 2004
Ilja Sallacz 1999
Ina Saltz 1996
Rodigo Sanchez 1996
Moutaz Sarakhosk 2009
Michihito Sasaki 2003
Nathan Savage 2001
Khaled Sawaf 2008s
Nina Scerbo 2006
Hartmut Schaarschmidt 2001
Hanno Schabacker 2008s
H.D. Schellnack 2009
Robert Schenk 2009
Paula Scher 2010
Laura Scherling 2008s
Zachary Scheuren 2009
Elizabeth Schindo 2009s
Peter Schlief 2000
Hermann J. Schlieper 1987***
Holger Schmidhuber 1999
Hermann Schmidt 1983***
Klaus Schmidt 1959***
Bertram Schmidt-Friderichs 1989
Thomas Schmitz 2009
Guido Schneider 2003
Werner Schneider 1987
Markus Schroeppel 2003
Holger Schubert 2006
Clemens Schulenburg 2006
Eileen Hedy Schultz 1985
Eckehart Schumacher-Gebler 1985***
Robert Schumann 2007
Annie Schussler 2009s
Peter Scott 2002
Leslie Segal 2003
Mariana Serra 2009
Thomas Serres 2004
Patrick Seymour 2006
Li Shaobo 2004
Graham Shaw 2010
Paul Shaw 1987
Lisa Sheirer 2009
Nick Sherman 2009
David Shields 2007
Emily Shields 2010s
Hyewon Shim 2009s
Sangmin Shim 2010s
Jeewon Shin 2009
Inessa Shkolnikov 2008
Manvel Shmavonyan 2007
Philip Shore, Jr. 1992
Bonnie Siegler 2007
Robert Siegmund 2001
Nigel Sielegar 2008s
Diana Simakhov 2009s
Jessica Simmons 2009
Scott Simmons 1994
Danni Sinisi 2010s
Kendra Skaggs 2009s
Pat Sloan 2005
Kevin Smith 2008
Laura Smith 2009
Mark Anderson Smith 2009s
Sarah Smith 2005
Steven Smith 2008s
Steve Snider 2004
Mark Snyder 2009
Bart A. Solenthaler 2008
Jan Solpera 1985***
Mark Solsburg 2004
Jane Song 2009
Jiyeong Song 2009
Brian Sooy 1998
Erik Spiekermann 1988
Brooke Sprickman 2010s
Derek Springston 2009s
Frank Stahlberg 2000
Adrianne Stark 2009s
Rolf Staudt 1984
Matthew Steedman 2009s
Matt Steel 2010
Olaf Stein 1996
Ashley Stevens 2009s
Charles Stewart 1992
Roland Stieger 2009s
Michael Stinson 2005
Clifford Stoltze 2003
Peter Storch 2003
DJ Stout 2010
Charlotte Strick 2010
Ilene Strizver 1988
Hansjorg Stulle 1987
Mine Suda 2008
Yun Gui Sung 2010s
Derek Sussner 2005
Zempaku Suzuki 1992
Don Swanson 2007
Paul Sych 2009
Yukichi Takada 1995
Yoshimaru Takahashi 1996
Katsumi Tamura 2003
Ai Lin Eida Tan 2010s
Chiharu Tanaka 2010s
Jack Tauss 1975***
Pat Taylor 1985
Anthony J. Teano 1962***
Marcel Teine 2003
Nicole Tenbieg 2010s
Mitzie Testani 2007
Paul Tew 2009
Anne Thomas 2007
Charles Thomas 2009
Eric Tilley 1995
Colin Tillyer 1997
James Timmins 2010
Siung Tjia 2003
Christian Toensmann 2009
Laura Tolkow 1996
Alessandro Tramontana 2009s
Jakob Trollbäck 2004
Niklaus Troxler 2000
Minao Tsukada 2000
Tracy Tsutsumoto 2009s
Korissa Tsuyuki 2009
Manfred Tuerk 2000
Marc Tulke 2000
Natascha Tumpel 2002
François Turcotte 1999
Anne Twomey 2005
Andreas Uebele 2002
Katsuhiro Ueno 2008s
Yagmur Uslu 2008s
Diana Uvaydova 2009s
Diego Vainesman 1991
Robert Valentine 2010
Elizabeth Ackerman Valins 2008
Scott Valins 2009
Patrick Vallée 1999
Jeffrey Vanlerberghe 2005
Panos Vassiliou 2007
Meryl Vedros 2010s
Emerson Velazquez 2009s
Brady Vest 2005
Adriana Viaduca 2009
Sarah Vinas 2010
Patricia Vining 2009
Frank Viva 2010
Marc Vleugels 2008
Nina Vo 2010s
Will Voelker 2009s
Nici von Alvensleben 2010
Oscar Von Hauske 2009s
Mark Von Ulrich 2009
Angela Voulangas 2009
Frank Wagner 1994
Oliver Wagner 2001
Allan R. Wahler 1998
Jurek Wajdowicz 1980
Sergio Waksman 1996
Garth Walker 1992
Payton Wallace 2010s
Garret Walter 2010
Katsunori Watanabe 2001
Calvin Waterman 2009s
Cardon Webb 2009
Harald Weber 1999
Kurt Weidemann 1966***
Claus F. Weidmueller 1997
Sylvia Weimer 2001
Craig Welsh 2010
Sharon Werner 2004
Alex W. White 1993
Bambang Widodo 2009
Christopher Wiehl 2001
Richard Wilde 1993
James Williams 1988
Marian Williams 2010
Steve Williams 2005
Grant Windridge 2000
Conny J. Winter 1985
Soung Wiser 2009
Delve Withrington 1997
Burkhard Wittemeier 2003
Peter Wong 1996
Fred Woodward 1995
Heather Wyville 2008
Ping Xu 2008
Sarem Yadegari 2003
Oscar Yanéz 2006
James Yang 2008s
Carmen Yazejian 2010
Henry Sene Yee 2006
Maxim Zhukov 1996
Roy Zucca 1969***

Corporate Members
Diwan Software Limited 2003
Grand Central Publishing 2005
Saatchi & Saatchi 2010
School of Visual Arts, New York 2007

*Charter member
**Honorary member
*** Life member
s Student member
a Associate member
Membership as of May 7, 2010

Type Index

A

Adhesive Black Fulguro 26
Akkurat Laurenz Brunner 69, 84, 121, 182, 206, 213
Akkurat Mono Laurenz Brunner 84
Akkurat Regular Laurenz Brunner 182
Akzidenz Grotesk Bold H. Berthold AG 22
Akzidenz Grotesk Bold Condensed H. Berthold AG 116
Akzidenz Grotesk H. Berthold AG 22, 112, 157, 221, 226, 292
Akzidenz Grotesk Light H. Berthold AG 22
Akzidenz Grotesk Super H. Berthold AG 80
Alpha Headline Cornel Windlin 195
Amanda URW ++ 256
ITC American Typewriter Joel Kaden and Tony Stan 163, 247
Amplitude Christian Schwartz, Amplitude 145
Apex New Medium Chester Jenkins 132
Arnhem Fred Smejiers 58, 66, 111, 149
ITC Avant Garde Herb Lubalin and Tom Carnase 17, 106
Avenir Adrian Frutiger 83, 108

B

Baskerville John Baskerville 106
Baskerville MT John Baskerville 23
Ogilvy Baskerville after John Baskerville 33
Baukloetze Nicole Jacek 86
A2 Beckett Scott Williams and Henrik Kubel 43
Bell Gothic Chauncey H. Griffith 128
Bespoke Zöe Bather and Joe Sharpe 138
Bickham Script Richard Lipton 129
Blender Nik Thoenen 111
Bauer Bodoni after Giambattista Bodoni 156
Berthold Bodoni after Giambattista Bodoni 23
Bodoni after Giambattista Bodoni 124
Bodoni Light after Giambattista Bodoni 27
Bodoni Poster after Giambattista Bodoni 225
Braggadocio W.A. Woolley 46
Braggadocio Regular W.A. Woolley 210
Braille DIN unknown 146

C

Cambria Jelle Bosma 205
Capibara Classic Pieter van Rosmalen 70
Adobe Caslon Carol Twombly after William Caslon 63, 87
Adobe Caslon Pro Carol Twombly after William Caslon 52
Champion Jonathan Hoefler 59
Cholla Sans Sibylle Hagmann 87
Clarendon Hermann Eidenbenz and Edouard Hoffmann 124
Clarendon Condensed Hermann Eidenbenz and Edouard Hoffmann 224
Cloister Black Morris Fuller Benton and Joseph W. Phinney 176
ITC Conduit Mark van Bronkhurst 187
Corporate S Kurt Weidemann 75, 190
Courier Howard Kettler 26, 192
Courier New Howard Kettler 60, 250
ATCrillee (modified) Jose Luis Coyotl Mixcoatl 285

D

Deck Fabian Monod 109
Didot Firmin Didot 108, 124, 221, 268
FF DIN Albert-Jan Pool 167
FF DIN Pro Light Albert-Jan Pool 11
DIN German Institute for Industrial Standards 146
DIN Robo Engschriften German Institute for Industrial Standards 289
DIN Robo Mittelschrift German Institute for Industrial Standards 289
DIN Robo Neuzeit Grotesk German Institute for Industrial Standards 289
DIN Schrift German Institute for Industrial Standards 128
DTL Documenta Frank E. Blokland 5, 55
Dolly Bas Jacobs, Akiem Helmling, and Sami Kortemäki 24

E

Eclat Doyald Young 24, 31, 255

F

Fedra Serif Peter Bilak 184
Filosofia Zuzana Licko 85, 107, 147, 174
Folio Konrad F. Bauer and Walter Baum 124
Franklin Gothic Morris Fuller Benton 93
Franklin Gothic Extra Condensed Morris Fuller Benton 31, 201
Frutiger Light Std Adrian Frutiger 131
Futura after Paul Renner 44, 51, 67, 137, 150, 158, 176, 227
Futura Maxi Victor Caruso 227

G

Galaxy Polaris Chester Jenkins 73
Adobe Garamond Robert Slimbach after Claude Garamond 140, 194, 293
FB Garamond Jill Pichotta after Douglas Crawford McMurtrie, Robert Hunter Middleton, and Claude Garamond 81, 130, 220
ITC Garamond Light Tony Stan 211
Garamont Amsterdam Elsner & Flake Design Studios after Morris Fulle Benton, Thomas Maitland Cleland 90
Gill Sans Eric Gill 284
Glypha (modified) Adrian Frutger 180
Gotham Tobias Frere-Jones with Jesse Ragan 141, 121, 241, 246
Gotham Bold Tobias Frere-Jones with Jesse Ragan 52
Gotham Black Tobias Frere-Jones with Jesse Ragan 139
Gotham Extra Light Tobias Frere-Jones with Jesse Ragan 139
Gotham Rounded Tobias Frere-Jones with Jesse Regan 90
Gotham Ultra Tobias Frere-Jones with Jesse Ragan 225
Gothic MB101 B unknown 210
Foundry Gridnik Light David Quay after Wim Crouwel 243
Monotype Grotesque Monotype Design Studio 64

H

HeiHK W5 DynaComware Design Studio 60
Helvetica Max Miedinger 68, 130, 165, 173, 180, 203, 229, 247
Helvetica Neue D. Stempel AG after Max Miedinger 48, 92, 168
Helvetica Neue Bold D. Stempel AG after Max Miedinger 291
Helvetica Neue Bold Condensed D. Stempel AG after Max Miedinger 193
Helvetica Neue Heavy Condensed D. Stempel AG after Max Miedinger 193
Helvetica Rounded Bold Max Miedinger 15
Hoefler Text Jonathan Hoefler 7, 49

Type Index

Hero Bold Kai Salmela 143
Honmincyo unknown 221
Hornet Thomas Neeser and Thomas Müller 32, 232
Housecut Nicole Michaels 252

I

Impact Geoffrey Lee 185, 191
FF Info Office Erik Spiekermann and Ole Schäfer 172
Insignia Neville Brody 124
Interstate Tobias Frere-Jones 37, 62, 186, 198

J

Jigsaw Stencil Johanna Bilak 69

K

P22 Kilkenny Paul Hunt after Herrmann Ihlenberg 50
Knockout Jonathan Hoefler 26, 56, 78, 135, 151, 219, 290
Koburina Gothic JIYU KOBO Ltd. 226

L

Lake Antiquity Hyun Auh, Brandon Downing and Emanuela Frigerio 56
Letter Gothic Roger Roberson 182
ITC Lubalin Herb Lubalin 17
Lutz Cornel Windlin 27

M

MB31 MORISAWA Fonts 165
Mantinia Matthew Carter 40
Mercury Display Jonathan Hoefler and Tobias Frere-Jones with Jesse Ragan 115
Mercury Text Jonathan Hoefler and Tobias Frere-Jones with Jesse Ragan 115
Merriam Michael Cina 43
FF Meta Erik Spiekermann 169
FF Meta Plus Caps Erik Spiekermann 102
FF Meta Serif Erik Spiekermann 169
Minion Pro Robert Slimbach 32
Moiré Eike Dingler 223
MoMA Gothic Matthew Carter 98, 142, 248
Mona Regular Shingo Noma 170
Mona Regular Stressed Shingo Noma 170
Monospace 821 BT Max Miedinger 55
FTF Morgan Avec Mário Feliciano 85, 96
Mrs Eaves Zuzana Licko 42, 174
Myriad Pro Fred Brady, Robert Slimbach, Christopher Slye, and Carol Twombly 163

N

NAMI Chiharu Tanaka 117
Nemek Regular Tom Grunwald 179
Neutraface Christian Schwartz after Richard Neutra 127, 149
Neutraface Slab Kai Bernau and Susana Carvalho with Christian Schwartz and Ken Barber 153
Nevermind Max Kisman 53
New Aster Francesco Simoncini 48
News Gothic Morris Fuller Benton 28, 227
Nobel Tobias Frere-Jones after Sjoerd Hendrik de Roos 201
CA Normal Stefan Claudius 54
Nyte Dino dos Santos 135

O

OCR-A American Type Foundry 220
FF OCR-F Albert Jan-Pool 238
ITC Officina Sans Erik Spiekermann 174
AG Old Face Günter Gerhard Lange 64

P

Patience C2F: Cybu Richli and Fabienne Burri 220
Playbill Robert Harling 224
Plum BDL unknown 57
Poplar Barbara Lind 220
FF Profile Martin Wenzel 62

Q

FF Quadraat Fred Smeijers 61

R

Railbox unknown 286
Rauschen volcano-type.de 25
Red October Neogrey Creative 184
Rockwell Light Monotype Imaging after Morris Fuller Benton 138
Rotis Serif Std Otl Aicher 122
Rotis Sans Serif Std Otl Aicher 122

S

Sailor Gothic Pablo A. Medina 74
FF Scala Martin Majoor 144
FF Schulbuch Nord Just van Rossum 71
Serifa Black Adrian Frutiger 244
Shelley Script Matthew Carter 124
Shinseikaiyotai MORISAWA 220
Simple (modified) Dimitri Bruni and Manuel Krebs 76
Simple Bold Dimitri Bruni and Manuel Krebs 234
FS Sophie Dieter Zembsch 86
Stella Mário Feliciano 181
ITC Stone Sans Sumner Stone 33
Swift Gerard Unger 94
Swiss 721 BT Max Miedinger 91

T

Times New Roman Stanley Morison and Victor Lardent 31, 41, 249
Times Ten after Stanley Morison and Victor Lardent 126
Titling Gothic FB David Berlow 101
Trade Gothic Jackson Burke 88, 107, 159, 189, 283
Trade Gothic No. 20 Jackson Burke 147
Trajan Pro Carol Twombly 289
T-STAR Mone Round Michael Mischler 71
EF TVNord Vernokia Elsner and Günther Flake 66
TripleMassive Thomas Müller and Thomas Neeser 232

Type Index

U

untitled Nancy Harris Rouemy and Patrick Griffin (Canada Type) 100
United Tal Leming 94
Univers Adrian Frutiger 81, 102, 126, 164, 195
Utopia Std Robert Slimbach 77

V

Vectora LT Bold Adrian Frutiger 29
Vectora LT Std Adrian Frutiger 29
Vista Sans Xavier Dupré 53
Vista Slab Xavier Dupré 53

W

We R.1. Ihu Sun Kim 171

General Index

A

@radical media 288
"Design Life Now" 278
2XGoldstein 157
601bisang 82, 152
702 Design Works 228
A2/SW/HK 43
Abulhanov, Ilya 290
Academy of Art University 117
Adam Swaab Design Company 285
Addison 83
Adobe Systems, Inc. 259
Agren, Theo 205
A-Ha—R.O. Blechman 99
Ahmet, Ahmet 288
AICP Minnesota Show Sponsor Reel 289
air conditioned 34
Alexa McNae 34
Alfano, Peter 291
Allen, Terry 237
Alliance Graphique Internationale 278, 279
Almeida, Jorge 280
Alt Group 67, 150, 212
American Institute of Graphic Arts (AIGA) 2, 3, 30, 255, 278
An Education 284
Anderson, Gail 237, 245, 250, 252, 253, 255, 256
Anonymous 74
Anoroso, Lisa 50
Aparacio, Ernesto 126
Apeloig, Philippe 109, 213
Applied Works 138
Argentato, Alessandro 75
Ariane Spanier Design 35, 205
Armour, Tony 88
Arnholm, Ronald 262, 263
Arsenault, Maude 134
Arsizio, Brusino 221, 226
Art Center College of Design 2, 3, 66, 121, 241, 255
Art Directors Club 2, 3, 278
ARTIUM (Centro-Museo Vasco de Arte Contemporàneo) 44
Association des Bibliothécaires de France 213
Association of Mukojima Studies, Tokyo Metropolitan Foundation for History and Culture 198
Atelier Bundi AG 234
Atelier für Gestaltung Felix Stumpf 25
Atelier Martino & Jaña 94
Atelier Poisson 48, 208
Auh, Hyun 56
Australian Graphic Design Association (AGDA) 115, 160, 192, 193
Aznar, Juanma 81

B

Badger, Lucas 22
Baker, Edwin 281
Barbara Says... 74
Barcelona, Katie 51, 151
Bardesono, Pia 95
Bartlett, Brad 121
Basic Books 52
Bather, Zöe 138
Becker, Jörg 77
Becker, Sam 13
Becky, Sucha 91
Beirut, Michael 45, 51, 141, 143, 151
Belford, Paul 203
Benns, Nic 284
Bergesen, Anders 87
Bergische Universität Wuppertal, Campus Wuppertal 167
Berthelet, Jimmy 28
Biblioteca Universale Rizzoli (BUR) 40, 65
Bibliothèque et Archives Nationales du Québec 164
Bichler, Gail 99, 100, 135, 137
Biegert & Funk 11
Biegert, Marco 11
Binder, Eve 136
Birnbach, Professor Heribert 167
Bisson, Sébastien 93
Blacknell, Ben 86
Bloomberg Creative Services Department 112
Blue Pencil Editions 64
Blume, Julia 5
Boesch, Nina 246
Bolan, Lisa 280
Bologna, Matteo 18, 30, 40, 65
Bonoma, Halley 287
Bonomelli, Rex 41, 42
Boros 68
Bosco, Rosina 243
Bose, Günter Karl 5
Boucher, Melanie 164
Bourcellier, Laurent 265
Braatz, Nik 286
Brainard, Kevin 201
Brand Union, The 12, 13
Brawidjaya, Howard 66
Broadcast Designers Association 278
Brown, Bill 201
Bruce, Tim 88
Brugger, Peter 120
Brynes, Sam 244
Buckholz, Taylor 116
Bundi-Bonjour, Stephan 234
Bungard, Brigitta 78
Bünnagel, Peter 187, 225
Burle, Stephan 282
Büro Grotesk 195
Burri, Fabienne 236
Burton, Tim 248
Bush, Anne 122, 131
Byars, Unjoo 280
Byrom, Andrew 118

C

C&G Partners 56, 197
C2F 236
CakeLab 70
California State University, Long Beach 118, 344
Cañizares, Ricardo 81
Cao, Ke 242
Caparrós Comunicación 81
Caputo, Nicole 52
Cardinal, Chelsea 101, 133, 136
Carson, Carol Devine 38
Carvalho, Rita 69
Cascades Communication Department 93
Casey, Reed 285
Cavalli, Francesco 2, 4
Cavazos, Rod 117
Cehovin, Eduard 154
Cergueira, Filipe 94
Chan, Eva 163
Chen, Hanna 72
Cheong, Ha Tin 214
Cheong, Kuokwai 60
Chèvre, Florence 48
Chiao, Marian 241
Cho, Ok-hee 82
Choi, Erica Yujin 227
Chou, Ingrid 73
Chouinard School of Art 255
Christel, Martin 84, 169
Christie, Janice 72
Christie, Scott 72
Cirque du Freak: The Vampire's Assistant 280
Clarke, Georgina 251
Classen, Ramon 32, 232
ClearType 255
Clément, René 23, 92, 93, 110, 186
Clouse, Doug 105
Clowes, Simon 280
Clunkers—Takashi Okada 99
Cluss, Professor Uli 95
Codeluxe/CDLX 84, 169
CODEX Foundation, The 63
Coe, Wayne 288
Colbourne, Richard 83
Collins, Brian 2, 14
Communication Arts Design Annual 278
Community 287
Condak, Henrietta 176
Cone, Justin 278
Connolly, Tamara Gildengers 240
Cooper, Kyle 278, 280, 285, 290
Cooper-Hewitt, National Design Museum 255, 278
Corban, Ben 150
Corral, Rodrigo 36
Cortis & Sonderegger 27
Costa, Orlando 288
Cota, Inva 73
Cox, Darren 201
Creature 199
Crnich, Matt 286, 287
Cromotex 79
Cullen, Roy 285
Cullen, Steve 199
Cultural Affairs Bureau of the Macao S. A. R. Government 60
Curnow, Toby 67
Curry, Jack 118

D

D&AD 278
D & L Screenprinting 199
Darren Pascoe, &coe 86
Dawson, Richard ii, 255, 344
de Bartolo, Carolina 117
de Cumptich, Roberto de Vicq 18, 50
de la Nuez, Ena Cardenal 44, 79
De Leo, Anthony 168
de Vicq design 50
de Wilde, Barbara 45
DecoType 275
Delve Fonts 270
Design Army 22, 91, 116
Design Center 154
Design Dept. 31
DESIGN FILMS 278
Desmaras, Mariano 197
Devetak, Tanja 154
Diaz, Gabriel 280
Dietz, Kirsten 147
DiMatteo, Kristina 2, 10
Dingler, Eike 223
DNP Art Communications Co. 221
Doret, Michael 264
Downey, Susan 280
Downing, Brandon 56
Doyle, Stephen 45, 177
Drozdowski, Martin 95
Duffy, Joe 2, 8
DuMont Buchverlag 68
Duplessis, Arem 99, 100, 135, 137
Dyakova, Sonya 108

E

Ebbs, Bonnie 280
Editions Cheneau-de-Bourg 48
Edwards, Aaron 150, 212
Egert, Lars 55
Ellerton, Wendy 114, 115
Elliot 164
emerystudio 89
enzed 229
Erler, Johannes 24
Espinoza, Ramiro 267
Estudio Ibán Ramón 19
European Graduate School 278
EWHA Women's University 130
EXBROOK 278
Expolab advanced communication and design 106

F

Factor Design 24, 140, 194
Fahrmaier, Anna 103
Faith 134
Fakultät fur Gestaltung, Hochschule Pforzheim 189
Farey, Dave 253, 255, 344
Fashion Institute of Technology ii, 158
Faubert, Pierre-Luc 164
Fence Books 56
Fengel, Martin 49, 104
Field, Ann 34
Fili, Louise 3, 149
Fischer, Anne 24
Fischer, Katy 196
FLAME 159
Flux 279
Flynn, Joey 173
Folkwang Hochschule 125
Folkwang Universität 167
Fong, Karin 242
Fons Hickmann M23 47
Fontana Publishers 62
fonts.com 272
Ford, Randal 202
Forss, Sarah Nelson 17
Fox Ash 63
Foxworthy, Carlos 286
Fraefel, Stefan 55
Fragmental Museum 180
Frankfurter Akademie 148
Friend, David Michael 287
Frigerio, Emanuela 56
Frisk, Ryan Pescatore 21
Fuchs, Julia 90
Fujitsuka, Mitsumasa 221
Fukuda, Hideyuki 217
Fukutake Foundation for the Promotion of Regional Culture 159
Fukutake, Soichiro 159
Funk, Andreas 11
Fussenegger, Iri 225

G

Gaberthüel, Martin 146
Gabriel, Thomas 103
Gaffney, Evan 52
Gagnon, Louis 23, 28, 46, 92, 93, 110, 124, 186
Galeria Municipal de Matosinhos 69
Galerie Reussbad 233
Gall, John 45
Gallery 5610 226
Garbett, Paul 160
Garwood, Steve 72
Gautier, Monica 145
Geissbuhler, Steff 197
Genemix 163
Gill, Eric 255
Gimeno, Pepe 81
Ginza Graphic Gallery 221
Goeldner, Hugo 84, 169
Goldberg, Carin 36, 171
Goldstein, Abby 64
Gomes, António Silveira 74
Gondor, Darius 182
Goodman, Timothy 201
Gott, Wesley 252, 344
Gould, Annabelle 173, 184
Gowing, Mark 191
Graf, Friedrich-Wilhelm 27
Graphic Atelier Imboden 233
Graphic Design for Love (+$) 224
Graphic Design Museum 21
Green, Pamela 282
Green, Whitney 291
Greenbaum, Hilary 99, 135
Greter, Wolfgang 26
Grotrian-Steinweg, Gesine 47
Grotrian-Steinweg, Uma 47
Grunwald, Tom 179
GT 238, 239
Guarnieri, David 46
Günter, Alina 27
Guthrie, Alistair 67

H

Hacker, Helen 195
häfelinger + wagner design 71, 182
Häfelinger, Annette 71, 182
Hamlett, Phil 117
Harrington, Brian 185, 247
Hart, Mike 193
Hass, Sascha 72
Hauert, Helen 120
Haven, Jim 199
He, Jianping 57
Hecq Design Company 290
Hedesign 57
Hefele, Jürgen 166
Heffner, August 78, 98
Heiligensetzer, Ramona 120
Heine Warnecke Design 85
Heine, Dirk 85
Helle, Raphaél 92
Heller, Steven 255
Henestrosa, Cristobal 266
Henke, Simone 139
Herbster, Udo 148
Herburg Weiland 49, 104
Herrmann, Johannes 75
Hesse, Klaus 190
Hester, Joshua 240
Heuer, Jed 111
Hickmann, Fons 47
Hill, Nadine 102
Hinrichs, Elizabeth 4, 5
Hische, Jessica 149
Hobson, Henry 280
Hoch, Kevin 72
Hochleitner, Michael 103, 257
Hochmann, Jana Aylin 54
Hochschule Augsburg 166
Hochschule für Angewandte Wissenschaft und Kunst (HAWK) 225
Hochschule für Bildende Künste (HFBK) 54
Hochschule für Grafik und Buchkunst (Academy of Visual Arts) 5
Hoffmann, Julia 73, 78, 98, 248
Hofstede Design 114, 115
Hofstede, Dominic 114, 115
Hojo, Motoyasu 198
Hong Kong Designers Association 163
Houbart, Catherine 31
HouseStyle Graphics ii, 255, 344
Howard, Andrew 69
Hubert Jocham Type 269
Hubert, Philipp 59
Hughes, John 34
Hülsbömer, Frank 75

I

i_d buero + cluss 95
Imaginary Forces 3, 278, 288
Imboden, Melchior 233
Institut pour la Ville en mouvement 31
International Typeface Corporation 255, 263
Ioukhnovets, Anton 136
Ip, Hong Chong 214
Ising, Stephanie 49, 104
Ising, Tom 49, 104
Ittner, Aileen 4, 5

J

Jacek, Nicole 86
Jaedicke, Nils 71
Jaña, Alejandro 94
Janssen, Petra 53, 181
Japan Graphic Designers Association 217
Jennifer Sterling Design 9
Jocham, Hubert 269
Jockisch, Steven 65
Johnston, Edward 255
Johnston, Simon 241
Johnstone, Liam 72
Jones, Jesse 285
Jung, Jong-in 82, 152, 161
JUNO 26
Jury, David 63

K

K2 Impressions Inc. 219
Kalt, Pat 106
Katamura, Fumihito 159
Kaul, Dave 199
Kaye, Michael Ian 127, 129
Kennedy, David 280
Kerbel, Serge 134
Kessler, Michaela 148
Kidd, Chip 45
Kiepenheuer & Witsch Verlag 49
Kim, Hoon 227
Kim, Ihn Sun 171
Kim, Insohngii 130
Kim, Jiwon 172
Kim, Julianne 121
Kim, Namoo 238, 239
Kim, Soo-hwan 82
Kim, Young Bum 249
Kinczli, Veronika 71
Kitagawa, Takeshi 226
Kitschenberg, Lisa 142, 172
Kivikoski, Benjamin 120
Klein, Nicole 26
Kleiner, Ori 249
Klimiuk, Emilia 88
Knopf, Alfred A. 38
Knopf, Thomas 33
Kobryn, Roman 287
Koch, Anne-Katrin 119
Kodaira, Masayoshi 159
Koll, Markus 140, 194
Korea Design Foundation 238

Kotte, Barbara 187, 225
Krakower, Louise 287
Krantz, Wally 13
Krimmel, Oliver A. 95
Kuan, Hao In 131
Kubel, Henrik 43
Kurata, Miyuki 211
Kureshi, Hanif 155
Kuroki, Tatsunori 156
KW43 BRANDDESIGN 139

L

L2M3 Kommunikationsdesign 76
Lack, Chris 66
Lamontagne, Gabrielle 174
Landor Associates 192
Lau, Grant 288
Lauridsen, Miles 280
Lee, Heebok 285
Lee, Sharon 244
Lefebure, Jake 22, 91, 116
Lefebure, Pum 22, 91, 116
Lefebvre Financial Communications 92
Lefebvre, Marcel 93
Leida, Edward 97
Leifer, Tom 75
Lenk, Krzysztof 227
Les Allusifs 46
Leung, James Wai Mo 163
Levy, Joshua Marc 113
Library of Congress 255
LINDA GRAPHICA & LIBIDO 165, 220
Linotype 221, 255, 263
Lintl, Carolin 119
Little, Jason 192, 193
Lobe, Sascha 76
Lodigiani, Giona 40, 65
Los Angeles City College 255
Los Angeles Trade-Technical College 255
Losinski, Thomas 176
Louise Fili Ltd. 149
LOWERCASE 88
Lozach, Max 67, 150, 212
Lucerne University of Applied Sciences and Arts, Illustration Department 55
Ludwig, Yve 141
Lunwerg Editóres 44
Lux, Björn 26

M

Mackinnon and Saunders 248
Magraw-Mickelson, Jacob 137
Maia, Oscar 94
Marchand, Brian 72
Marianek, Joe 143
Mark Gowing Design 191
Markowski, Kamil 66
Marquette, Jamus 201
Marreiros, Victor Hugo 214
Martino, Alvaro 94
Martino, Joao 94
Martinovic, Ivana 193
Marty, Samuel 29
Maruyama, Arata 221, 226
Mashiba, Yusuke 216
Masunaga Design Team 216
Masunaga, Akiko 215, 216
Mathew, Jake 286
Mayer, Birgit 261
McFetridge, Geoff 135
Meeks, Lauren 280
Melhuish, Julian 244
Mendelsund, Peter 38, 39, 45
Meredith, David 7
Meyer, Helmut 33
Michaelov, Aviva 137
Migration 231
Miki, Sentaro 198
Miller, Abbott 3, 4
Miller, Jason 83
Milo, Thomas 275
Milton Glaser Design Study Center and Archives 255
Mir, Diego 19
Miura, Yoshihiro 165
Mixcoatl, José Luis Coyotl 285
Mizusaki, Naomi 201
Modern Dog Design 204
Moench, Andrea 106
MOMOCO 284
Monotype 272
Montreal Museum of Fine Arts, The 58, 186
Moore, R. Stevie 74
Morigaki, Ken 198
Morimoto, Kaoru 231
Morissette, Martin 93
motion504 289
Mucca Design 18, 30, 40, 65
Müggler, Jonas 55
Müller, Thomas 32, 232
Munch, Gary 253, 255, 258, 344
Murase, Takaaki 183
Musée Historique Lausanne 208
Museum of Art Lucerne 236
Museum of Modern Art (MoMA) Department of Advertising and Graphic Design, The 73, 78, 98
Museum of Modern Art, The (MoMA) 142, 248

N

Nadine Hill Design 102
Nakamura, Kazuto 211
Nakamura, Tomiko 211
Nakamura, Yumi 129
Nam, Seung-youn 152
Namaizawa, Tetsuya 228
nanilani co. 183
Naughtyfish Design 160
Neal, Chris Silas 200
Neeser & Müller 32
Neeser, Thomas 32, 232
Nelson, Lee 285
Nemeth, Titus 274
Netthoevel, Andreas 146
New Ornamental Type 255
Newman, Elizabeth 290
Nicholas, Robin 272
Nicole Jacek™ 86
Niemann, Christoph 37
Nikitas, Kali 224
Niklaus Troxler Design 206, 207, 209
Ninja Assassin 285
Nishizawa, Tomokazu 215, 216
Nishizuka, Ryoko 259
Noma, Shingo 170
Nova Scotia College of Art and Design 278
Novamondo Design 90

O

O'Callaghan, Kevin 178
Oakfield Press 67, 150
Ochsenhirt, Julia 147
OFFF 2009 290
Ogilvy Frankfurt 33
Ohsugi, Gaku 228
One Show 2 278
orangetango 58, 219
Organizing Committee of the International Festival for Arts and Media Yokohama 2009, The 183
Ortiz, Jose 280
Ota, Takumi 198
Otis College of Art and Design, Communication Arts Department 224

P

Padamada, Geminesse 66
Pantheon Books 3, 39
Paprika 23, 28, 46, 92, 93, 110, 186
Paradise, Megan 251
Park, Gene 287
Park, Hae-rang 152
Park, Jiwon 130
Park, Joey 280
Park, Kum-jun 82, 152, 161
Park, Nathaniel 285
Parsons The New School for Design 278
PastPresentFuture 180
Paul Shaw Letter Design 64
Paul, Jamie 107
Payson, Colin 72
Pearce, Harry 80
Pelavin, Daniel 253, 255, 260, 344
Pemberton, Sam 193
Penguin Graphics 211
Penguin Press 50
Pentagram 3
Pentagram Design Austin 202
Pentagram Design New York 51, 141, 142, 143, 151, 246
Pentagram London 80
Pepe Gimeno—Proyecto Gráfico 81
Perry, Tamaye 37
Perry, Todd Sheridan 280
Pesce, Giorgio 48, 208
Peter Behrens School of Architecture 223
Peter Mendelsund Design 39
Peters, David 278
Peters, Kate 66
Peterson, Matt 199
Phaidon Press 108
Pham, Peter 9
Phantonym—Lowman 99
PIC Agency 282
Pickenpaughy, Chris 288
Piercy, Clive 34
Pina, Pedro 69
ping-pong Design 230
Piscatello Design Centre 158
Piscatello, Rocco 158
Pleasure 201
Pohlen, Joep 62
Poirier, Judith 61, 174
Polka Design 62
Poole, Dean 67, 150, 212
Porchez, Jean François 268
Positype 271
Poyo Studios 278
Princeton Architectural Press 105
Products of Poetry 77
Proff, Anne-Lene 187, 225
Proffit, Tony 67
Prologue Films 278, 280, 285, 290
Push 282
Pylon 72

Q

Quadflieg, Sven 125

R

R/Greenberg Associates 3, 278
R2 Design 153, 235
Rädeker, Jochen 147
Rake, Marshall 66
Ramalho, Lizá 153, 235
Random House 3, 37, 51
Rask, Trine 273
Rebelo, Artur 152, 235
Reeves, Howard 123
Rempen, Thomas 125
Requeni, Daniel 19
RESFEST 279
ReType 267
Reüter, Saskia 283
Reyenger, Brett 280
Rhéault, Sylvie-Diane 93
Rhee, Jeeyoon 180
Rhode Island School of Design 3, 126, 227, 278
Rhodes, Anthony P. 237
Richard, Monic 23, 92, 93
Richli, Cybu 236
Rienermann, Lisa 187
Riley, Michael 3, 12
RISD Alumni Association in Korea 239
Ritchie, Guy 280
Ritoh, Linda 165, 220
Robertson, Ryan 285
Rockel, Miriam Magdalena 166
Rodrigo Corral Design 36
Rodríguez, Ibán Ramón 19
Rong, Liang 20
Rose, Robert 166
Rota, Daniela 32, 232
Rother, Daniel 4, 5
Rouemy, Nancy Harris 100
Roussel, Kathrin 54
Royal Society of Arts 278
Rüther, Christian 182

S

Saatchi Design 244
SAGA 156
Sagae, Kota 156
Sagmeister, Stefan 243
Sainte-Marie, Sophie Audet 124, 128
Saint-Georges, François-Xavier 28, 186
Samara, Timothy 171
Sanchez, Chris 280, 285
Sandberg, Douglas 63
Santos, M. A. 74
Sarofsky Corp. 286, 287
Sarofsky, Erin 286, 287
Sautter Repro + Druck 102
Savannah College of Art and Design 278, 344
Savarsky, Julie 202
Savoie, Alice 272
Scher, Paula 142, 172, 344
Schiff, Robbin 37
Schlacter, Paul 291
Schmid + Widmaier Design 15
Schmid, Sabine 15
Schmitt, Amy 289
Schneider, Arne 87
Schneider, Sebastian 26
Schoenhaar, Sabine 139
Scholz, Jessica 167
School of Visual Arts, New York 2, 3, 123, 127, 129, 171, 172, 175, 176, 177, 178, 179, 237, 243, 245, 249, 250, 252, 255, 278, 344
School of Visual Arts MFA Program 123, 177, 178, 243, 245, 250, 252
Schrod, Dirk 148
Schrott, Thomas 47
Schutz, Dave 107
Schwartz, Christian 117
Schwarz, Stefanie 189
Schwefer, Björn 68
Schwitzke, Barbara 26
Scribner 41, 42
Scrollan 187, 225
secondfloorsouth 146
Senboutaraj, Arya 288
SenseTeam 20
Shannon, Susanna 31
Sharpe, Joe 138
Shaw, Paul 64
Sherlock Holmes 280
Sherman, Samuel 78
Shim, Sangmin 126
Shimbo, Keita 183
Shimbo, Misako 183
Shirahama, Fumiko 228
Shown, Benjamin K. 184
Silver, Joel 280
Simoneau, Guillaume 93
Skaggs, Steven 270
Smith, Rodney 6, 7
Smyth, Robin 72
Snor Publishers 53
Society of Illustrators 2, 3, 255
Society of Publication Designers 2, 255
Society of Typographic Aficionados (SOTA) 255
Solomon, Carrie 112
Somers, Mirjam 275
Somers, Peter 275
Sorvino, Skip 175
Soukup, Karin 245
Spanier, Ariane 35, 205
Speakeasy 287
Spiekermann, Erik 117
Spindler, James 288
SpotCo 255
St. John, Todd 242
Staatliche Akademie der Bildenden Künste Stuttgart 119, 120
Staton, Sarah 86
Steele, Rachel 287
Stein, Olaf 140, 194
Sterling, Jennifer 9
Stern, Aaron 98
Stewart, Scott 287
Stoklossa, Uwe 125
Storymakers 288
Stout, DJ 202
Strange Attractors Design 21
Strassburger, Michael 204
Strausfeld, Lisa 246
Strichpunkt 147
Strohl, Christine Celic 30
Studio 1 a.m. 77
Studio Andrew Howard 69
Studio Apeloig 109, 213
Studio Bergesen 87
studio Boot 53, 181
Studio Fuku-De 217
Studio8 Design 138
Stumpf, Felix 25
Stuttgart State Academy of Art and Design, Department of Industrial Design 87
Sugimoto, Kazumi 216
Summerour, Neil 271
Sungkar, Jefton 193
Sunil, V. 155
Sunwoo, Ann Im 127
Superman/Batman: Public Enemies 286
Sussner Design 107
Sussner, Derek 107
Sych, Paul 134

T

Taiyo Printing Co. 226
Takematsu, Yukiharu, E.P.A. 159
Takimoto, Mikiya 159
Tamaye Perry Design 37
Tan, Andrew 241
Tanaka, Chiharu 117
Taoda, Mitsunori 210, 218
Tardy, Jules 250
TED 2009 Conference Opener 291
Temporale, Todd 144
Tenbieg, Nicole 148
Thinkprint 140, 194
This is Love 283
This is Real Art 203
Thivierge, Eric 287
Thoelke, Eric 196
Thomas, Anne 145
Thomas, Dennis 13
Tichborne, Chris 248
Tjia, Siung 96, 132
tntypography 274
TOKY Branding + Design 196
Tom Leifer Design 75
Tom Leifier Photography 75
Toma Objects 145
Transcontinental Litho Acme 58, 110
Trochut, Alex 222
Trollbäck + Company 278, 291, 344
Trollbäck, Jakob 276, 278, 291, 344
Troxler, Niklaus 119, 120, 206, 207, 209
Twomey, Anne iv, 2, 344, 347
Type Directors Club ii, iv, 2, 3, 255, 276, 278, 344
TypeCon 255
Typejockeys 103, 257
Types United 273
typographies.fr 265

U

Udo, Koji 170
Uhlig, Yvonne 146
Uji, Etsuko 281
unfolded 27
Université du Québec à Montréal (UQAM) 124, 128, 174, 219, 292
University of Bridgeport 255
University of Hawai'i at Mānoa, Graphic Design Program 122, 131
University of Washington 173, 184
Untitled Design 283

V

van Dijk, Hans 126
van Middelkoop, Catelijne 21
van Rosmalen, Pieter 70
Van Sluijs, Jarik 282
Vega, Lou 132
Verlag Niggli 55
Vintage Books 45
Visiotypen 59
Viva & Co. 144, 162
Viva, Frank 144, 162
Voettiner, Christian 139
Voice 168
Vollebergh, Edwin 53, 181
von Hellberg, Katharina 106
von Lehsten, Bastian 90
Voulangas, Angela 105